Gramsci and Languages

Historical Materialism Book Series

The Historical Materialism Book Series is a major publishing initiative of the radical left. The capitalist crisis of the twenty-first century has been met by a resurgence of interest in critical Marxist theory. At the same time, the publishing institutions committed to Marxism have contracted markedly since the high point of the 1970s. The Historical Materialism Book Series is dedicated to addressing this situation by making available important works of Marxist theory. The aim of the series is to publish important theoretical contributions as the basis for vigorous intellectual debate and exchange on the left.

The peer-reviewed series publishes original monographs, translated texts, and reprints of classics across the bounds of academic disciplinary agendas and across the divisions of the left. The series is particularly concerned to encourage the internationalization of Marxist debate and aims to translate significant studies from beyond the English-speaking world.

For a full list of titles in the Historical Materialism Book Series available in paperback from Haymarket Books, visit:
www.haymarketbooks.org/category/hm-series

Gramsci and Languages

Unification, Diversity, Hegemony

Alessandro Carlucci

Haymarket Books
Chicago, IL

First published in 2013 by Brill Academic Publishers, The Netherlands
© 2013 Koninklijke Brill NV, Leiden, The Netherlands

Published in paperback in 2014 by
Haymarket Books
P.O. Box 180165
Chicago, IL 60618
773-583-7884
www.haymarketbooks.org

ISBN: 978-1-60846-413-5

Trade distribution:
In the US, Consortium Book Sales, www.cbsd.com
In Canada, Publishers Group Canada, www.pgcbooks.ca
In the UK, Turnaround Publisher Services, www.turnaround-psl.com
In all other countries, Publishers Group Worldwide, www.pgw.com

Cover design by Ragina Johnson.

This book was published with the generous support of
Lannan Foundation and the Wallace Global Fund.

Printed in Canada by union labor.

10 9 8 7 6 5 4 3 2 1

Library of Congress Cataloging-in-Publication data is available.

Alla mia famiglia: operai e contadini.

Contents

Preface

Antonio Gramsci was born in 1891 in a remote corner of Sardinia, and he spent his childhood in this backward, poverty-stricken periphery of the Western world. Through years of political and personal hardship, he went on to become a leading figure among Italian communists, who were organised at the time in a small party called the *Partito Comunista d'Italia* [Communist Party of Italy], but he did not become widely known. He died in 1937, after spending the last part of his life first in prison (until November 1933) and then in a clinic under police custody. The Italian Fascist régime, which had imprisoned Gramsci (in November 1926) and crushed the Italian labour movement, was to remain in power for a further six years, and did not show any signs of imminent collapse. Popular consent for Mussolini's régime was at its peak at the time of Gramsci's death. What was to happen only a few decades later would have seemed almost inconceivable in the historical context of the time.

After the Second World War, Gramsci's thought became increasingly influential in Italy and abroad, and remained relevant throughout the second half of the century. In the 1970s, the historian Eric Hobsbawm was already speaking about *The Great Gramsci*,[1] and in the 1980s he pointed out that the list of the most frequently cited authors in international literature on the humanities and arts, though including few Italians, only five of whom were born after the sixteenth century, did include Gramsci.[2] In the mid-1990s, the *Bibliografia gramsciana* ['Gramscian Bibliography'], edited by John Cammett, already consisted of more than ten thousand titles in various languages (including Afrikaans, Albanian, Arabic, Bengali, Korean, Macedonian, Norwegian, Swedish, and Turkish).[3] At the time, moreover, academic circles, political movements and cultural institutions in various countries were in the process of organising a vast number of events to mark the sixtieth anniversary of Gramsci's death.

A decade later, especially during the 2007 seventieth anniversary, it had become clearer still that his intellectual legacy was enjoying extensive and

---

1. Hobsbawm 1974.
2. See Santucci 1995, p. xi (cf. Hobsbawm 2011, pp. 339–40).
3. See Santucci 2005, p. 159.

enduring influence worldwide. Even more events took place this time, including several official commemorations and international conferences. The 2007 anniversary marked a further expansion of Gramscian studies, and saw the emergence of new developments, especially in Italy. In particular, it had become evident that Gramsci stood out as one of the very few Marxists whose influence had not declined since 1989. According to the on-line, updated version of the *Bibliografia gramsciana*, 6,480 publications on Gramsci appeared worldwide between 1989 and 2007 (including new editions and translations of his writings). This figure corresponds to approximately one third of all the works published on Gramsci since 1922, the total number now nearing twenty thousand. The number of studies of his life and work, and of original applications of his ideas to different fields of research, has continued to rise since 2007. His influence ranges from literary criticism to the social sciences, from international relations to language studies, not to mention disciplines where his legacy has traditionally played a central role, such as political theory, history and philosophy. A world classic on a par with Dante, Machiavelli and Vico, Gramsci has become one of the most translated Italian authors of all time, as well as being the most widely studied Italian political thinker of the twentieth century.

Today, it is generally agreed that his political thought has highly original and personal features, as confirmed by the exceptionally long-lasting relevance of his legacy. As Hobsbawm reasserted in 2011:

> Such typically Gramscian terms as 'hegemony' occur in Marxist, and even in non-Marxist discussions of politics and history as casually, and sometimes as loosely, as Freudian terms did between the wars. Gramsci has become part of our intellectual universe. His stature as an original Marxist thinker – in my view the most original thinker produced in the West since 1917 – is pretty generally admitted.[4]

In this book, I offer an explanation of this originality by looking at his lifelong interest in language, especially in questions of linguistic diversity and unification. Gramsci's life was characterised by a wide range of significant experiences involving linguistic and cultural diversity – for example, his Sardinian-Italian bilingualism and his contacts with his Russian wife's multilingual émigré family.[5] In addition, he studied linguistics at university and maintained a keen interest in this discipline for the rest of his life. Familiarity with debates on language, and first-hand experience involving dialects and national languages (including his

---

4. Hobsbawm 2011, p. 316.
5. In my discussion, 'bilingualism' and 'multilingualism' refer to the presence of two or more languages at the individual and/or social level. I use 'linguistic diversity', instead, in a less specific manner to refer to the presence of more than one language, or simply of variation within the same language – from clearly defined regional varieties to slight, marginal differences of personal style.

work as a journalist and translator), made Gramsci particularly sensitive to the relationship between historically changing practices and theory-based prescriptive abstractions. In particular, from nineteenth- and early-twentieth-century linguistics, he learned to understand language as a collective activity always characterised by geographical, social and stylistic diversity, into which attempts at imposing unity are introduced, often with little or no success. Reflections on language therefore fostered his awareness of the importance of working towards unification through carefully considering diversity – not through ignoring diversity, disparaging it, or eliminating it by force. Such awareness affected Gramsci's political views during various phases of his militancy in the Italian and international labour movement, above all in his *Prison Notebooks* (1929–35), helping him to keep away from theoretical simplifications and ideological dogmatism.

Gramsci reconsidered problems concerning languages which had already been addressed by the 'bourgeois' and Marxist traditions, giving special attention to the question of national and international linguistic unification. This book adds to the theoretical discussion and critical assessment of Gramsci's linguistically relevant writings – which has been the subject of a number of other contributions – a special focus on three elements which have, up till now, been insufficiently examined in the Italian secondary literature, and almost completely ignored outside of Italy. The first is *Gramsci's life*, with specific reference to his use of the Sardianian language; second, a number of his *lesser-known writings*, especially texts that he and his associates wrote in the late 1910s and early 1920s; and third, Gramsci's multiple *sources*, both in language studies (including non-Italian sources), and in other fields linked to the political handling of languages and language-based conflicts.

It is my hope that the significance of my interpretation should not be confined to the study of Gramsci as an autonomous, isolated subject; but I am well aware that this hope exceeds, at least in part, the scope of this book. Some aspects of his life, and the highly stimulating insights that can be found in his writings, are, I believe, relevant to current debates about language and society. These aspects are especially relevant to the study of issues with political overtones, such as those regarding minority languages (or dialects), language standardisation, linguistic rights, language policies, and language and education, to mention only a few. Therefore, Gramsci's approach to language in society might be of particular relevance to those interested in developing a critical, interdisciplinary outlook for the study of the 'politics of language'.[6] On the other hand, however, I do not mean to encourage an indiscriminate or facile use of Gramsci's legacy. Though

---

6. This definition has already been used, with reference to Gramsci, by Peter Ives (2004b) in one of the very few existing books on Gramsci's linguistic interests. I use 'politics of language' to refer to the more general theoretical implications of language policies. I will try to limit my use of this definition accordingly, employing it only when

I do not address this point in detail (since doing so would take me too far from my main objectives), my discussion shows that Gramsci's relevance should not be overextended to include subjects, within linguistic disciplines, to which his legacy does not seem to have much to offer.

In the Introduction, I will present the main orienting perspectives of the work, as well as the key theses that will be explored further in the various chapters. Then, in Chapter One, I will describe Gramsci's relationship with Sardinian culture and the Sardinian language(s). Although special attention will be given to the linguistic aspects of this relationship, it will become clearly apparent that Gramsci maintained emotional, intellectual, and political ties with Sardinian culture throughout his life. My description is based on: a) an analysis of Gramsci's writings, aimed at gathering useful elements with which to determine the role of Sardinian in Gramsci's bilingual linguistic repertoire; and b) a historical, biographical reconstruction of significant episodes in which Gramsci used Sardinian for oral communication. Finally, I will move from a descriptive to an interpretative examination, and use experiences in Gramsci's life to contextualise and better illustrate his views on national linguistic and cultural unification – including his opinions on (what we today call) multilingualism, the emergence and standardisation of a national language in Italy, and the use of non-standard varieties.

Chapter Two analyses the formation of Gramsci's ideas on language, language planning, and language policy. Even though the definitions of *language policy* and *language planning* have been used for a relatively short period of time to identify well-established academic disciplines, the subjects that these disciplines study have been present in many societies for centuries. Language policies, whether *de jure* or simply *de facto*, have existed ever since the emergence of multiethnic, literate and culturally advanced states in the ancient world. In this sense, therefore, it is not anachronistic to speak of Gramsci's views on language policy and planning. In Chapter Two, I focus on the sources for these views. Dedicating relatively less attention to the more obvious (and already studied) influence of Italian authors, such as the linguist Graziadio Isaia Ascoli (1829–1907) and the novelist Alessandro Manzoni (1785–1873),[7] I especially examine the influence that Soviet authors and debates had on Gramsci. I show that this influence may well account for the similarities between Gramsci's ideas on language and the ideas that Ferdinand de Saussure (1857–1913), the father of linguistic Structuralism, expressed in his *Cours de linguistique générale* ['Course in General Linguistics']. No documentary evidence exists confirming that Gramsci read the *Cours*; however, specific elements in Gramsci's life, especially from the years he spent in Russia, and in his writings,

---

my argument deals with general themes which are significant to both (socio)linguistic and political debates.

7. On Gramsci's early work on Manzoni, and on the latter's views, see Appendix, section 4.2.4.

make it possible to argue that Saussure's ideas were part of the cultural milieu that influenced the development of Gramsci's thought.

Finally, in Chapter Three, I focus on the political implications of Gramsci's lifelong journey through languages, language issues, and linguistic disciplines. In particular, I further clarify how his practical experiences involving languages, and also contacts with specialised research on language, contributed to shaping his views on diversity and unification through the various stages of his work. Gramsci's political reflections and practice are discussed in the light of new documents which have only recently been discovered and published. Similarities are highlighted between those of Gramsci's writings which most overtly condemn the imposition of abstract forms of political unification, and some of his earlier (and also contemporaneous) writings on language. In this respect, the 'question of language and languages'[8] emerges as a significant source for Gramsci's philosophy of praxis, or, in other words, for the distinctiveness of his version of Marxism. I will not, however, present Gramsci as some sort of forerunner of post-Marxism, let alone a representative of 'non-Marxism';[9] nor will I present him as a Structuralist, or post-Structuralist, theorist of language and culture. Unlike other authors who have looked at Gramsci's interest in language, and the impact of linguistic matters on the development of his political views, I will maintain that the author of the *Prison Notebooks* was still a Marxist, though there were, in his Marxism, outstandingly personal and original features.

Before beginning my discussion, I need to explain briefly my use of texts and translations. Throughout the book, references to Gramsci's *Prison Notebooks* follow the internationally established standard of notebook number, followed by number of note. Thus, Q11, §12 indicates Notebook 11, note 12. These are also accompanied by the page number(s) of Valentino Gerratana's critical edition of the *Quaderni del carcere*, first published in 1975.[10]

Texts are quoted directly in English. In the case of long or particularly significant quotations, I have provided references to the specific volume of Joseph Buttigieg's translation of the *Prison Notebooks*,[11] or to the anthology of Gramsci's writings, from which the passage is taken (also indicating cases in which I have modified the published English text). Textual quotations from the *Letters from Prison* are taken from the English translation published by Columbia University Press in 1994. As far as quotations from the pre-prison letters are concerned, I am indebted to Derek Boothman for his generous advice and for letting me take

---

8. Gramsci 1975, Q10II, §44, p. 1330.
9. Lo Piparo 2010b.
10. Cf. Appendix: 4.3.
11. Gramsci 1992b, 1996b and 2007b.

several passages directly from his own translation, which will soon be published by Lawrence and Wishart.

Finally, I would like to thank those who helped me with this research project and the writing of the present book. I am grateful to Derek Boothman (again), Jane Everson, Mirko Francioni, Joanna Impey, Giulio Lepschy, Renzo Martinelli, Nicole Masri, Jeni Nicholson, Peter Thomas, Arturo Tosi, and Ann Wesson Garau; while a special acknowledgement is due to Fabio Frosini for his comments on earlier drafts, and for his most valuable suggestions and encouragement. My access to Sardinian and Turinese sources was facilitated, at various stages, by the hospitality and competent help of the Biblioteca Gramsciana (Gonnosnò, Oristano) and the Fondazione Istituto piemontese Antonio Gramsci (Turin). I also profited greatly from correspondence and conversations with Caterina Balistreri, Mimmo Boninelli, Alessandro Chidichimo, Tullio De Mauro, Kerim Friedman, Salvatore Garau, Nicola Gardini, Luciano Giannelli, Peter Ives, Stefano Jossa, Carl Levy, Franco Lo Piparo, Malinka Pila, Guy Puzey, and with Maria Luisa Righi and Giancarlo Schirru of the Fondazione Istituto Gramsci (Rome). All weaknesses are mine, not theirs.

Oxford, November 2012

Introduction

*The selfsame professional study that I've made of
the technical forms of language obsesses me...*[1]

Linguistic reflections as an integral part of Gramsci's legacy

Gramsci's ideas on language were the ideas of a political leader, a man of action – one could even say 'a fighter', as he calls himself in a letter of August 1931.[2] It would be reductive and essentially wrong to turn to his writings in search of a pure, systematic theory of language. Of his most important work, it has been said: 'The *Prison Notebooks* are not a book, they were not written as such, they only became a book after the death of their author'.[3] This statement could easily be extended to all of Gramsci's writings, whether from his time in prison or from the pre-prison years.[4] Gramsci himself explained that, at various stages of his career, he chose not to publish sizeable works in

---

1. Letter to Giulia Schucht of 9 February 1929: Gramsci 1994a, I, p. 247.
2. Gramsci 1996a, p. 448.
3. Gerratana 1997.
4. The Appendix to this book deals with the reception that Gramsci's writings have enjoyed so far. It provides a detailed bibliographical introduction to the Italian and Anglo-American editions of Gramsci's writings. Reviewing the editions and translations is – for the reasons stated above – no mere erudite curiosity when studying an author like Gramsci. In addition, the size, complexity, and heterogeneity of the secondary literature on Gramsci make a bibliographical survey all the more necessary. Therefore, in the Appendix I also review contributions from secondary literature in Italian and English which seem especially relevant to the topics examined in this book, and I discuss the strengths and weaknesses of recent language-oriented 'uses' (cf. Portantiero 1977; Baratta 2003; Davidson 2008) of Gramsci's legacy.

which his ideas could appear to have assumed a systematic form; and that his articles 'were written for the day...and were supposed to die with the day'.[5] In this context, the second occurrence of the word 'day' (*dopo la giornata*) would seem to retain the military meaning of joining battle, of serving in the army on a day of battle, which can be found, most notably, in Machiavelli's works.[6] Gramsci's writings – certainly the *Prison Notebooks*, but also many of his *Letters from Prison* – are contributions to political and ideological debates, and especially his newspaper articles were strongly polemical interventions, part of an ongoing 'fight'. Gramsci's linguistic reflections form an integral part of this political and intellectual work, and they need to be studied as such.

In particular, if one loses sight of this indivisibility of Gramsci's legacy, and of the politico-practical nature of his work, one is much more likely to misinterpret the one element that is pivotal to my discussion of Gramsci's ideas on language – namely, his outlook on diversity, and on cultural and linguistic unification. By focusing on this and other related elements, I shall provide a language-oriented interpretation which aims at casting light on Gramsci's work *in toto*, and not just on his ideas on language inappropriately separated from his politics. These ideas can only be isolated from the rest of his thought, and from his political practice, for the purposes of historical reconstruction, in order to understand better their formation and the role they came to play. As I shall argue in Chapter Three, a language-oriented study should not compromise the fecund peculiarity of Gramsci's approach by presenting him as a professional linguist who happened, as it were, to be a politician as well. Such an infelicitous outcome would be as irrelevant to current debates on language and society, as to the general interpretation of Gramsci. In other words, very little would be obtained by considering in isolation pages, passages, or even lines written by Gramsci that seemingly present him as a sociologist of education and languages, a sociolinguist, a philologist, or a philosopher of language.

The study of language has greatly changed during the last four or five decades, and especially the study of language in society has assumed a new, discrete disciplinary profile, the like of which was unknown to Gramsci and to the linguists of his period. But apart from these questions of historical and epistemological contextualisation, one cannot skate over the self-evident truth that Gramsci was not concerned with language studies as an isolated, specialist area – except during

---

5. Gramsci 1994a, II, p. 66 (cf. Gramsci 1996a, p. 457).
6. Mainly as a consequence of the French Revolution, new and more intimate connections emerged between military and political meanings: the French *journées* (and in part also the Italian *giornate*) became a symbol of insurrection, and has been used since to identify those historically momentous days on which one side abandoned conventional procedures and cautious long-term strategies, and risked everything to prevail over the other side (cf. Richet 1988, p. 113; Battaglia 1970, p. 819; Migliorini 2000, pp. 379–80).

his university studies (and even then, only to a certain degree).[7] Leaving his politics aside, to present him as a specialist in cultural, social, and linguistic studies, could probably be equated to betraying the core of Gramsci's ideas; namely, his conviction that issues regarding the elaboration, mediation and spread of ideology and intellectual culture are fundamentally interconnected, and that they connect, in turn, to other issues pertaining to economics and politics.[8] At the end of his writing life, in Notebook 29, Gramsci sketched out an analysis of the links between grammar and politics, and stated that discussions about language should not be dismissed as futile or politically irrelevant:

> It is not correct to say that these discussions were useless... Every time the question of language surfaces, in one way or another, it means that a series of other problems are coming to the fore: the formation and enlargement of the governing class, the need to establish more intimate and secure relationships between the governing groups and the national-popular mass, in other words to reorganise cultural hegemony.[9]

Evidently, Gramsci 'does not shy away from the links between language and politics. Noam Chomsky explicitly separates the two, several Marxist positions neglect the former, and some poststructuralists tend to obscure the latter'.[10] Gramsci, in contrast, constantly uses 'the relationship between language and politics to benefit our understandings of both'.[11] Indeed, few other thinkers from the past are now regarded – to the extent that Gramsci is – as still topical, and not just as outdated forerunners, to the critical study of the social and cultural aspects of language. His reflections have appealed, and continue to appeal, to intellectuals regardless of whether or not they endorse a Marxist approach. But even within non-Marxist trends, no serious interpretation has overlooked Gramsci's political perspective, which was radically critical of capitalism in general, and of the Italian society of his time in particular. In their efforts to highlight Gramsci's ideas on culture and language, and grant them wide circulation, interpreters that were significantly influenced by the idealist philosophy of Benedetto Croce (1866–1952) have themselves acknowledged that Gramsci's interest in linguistics

---

7. In 1918, he wrote: 'I am preparing my degree thesis on the history of language, *trying to apply the critical methods of historical materialism to this research as well*' (Gramsci 1982, p. 612 – my emphasis).
8. See the note 'Nesso di problemi' ['Connection of Problems'] in Gramsci 1975, Q21, §1, pp. 2107–10.
9. Gramsci 1975, Q29, §3, p. 2346 (English translation from Gramsci 1985, pp. 183–4, with slight modifications).
10. Ives 2004b, p. 172.
11. Ives 2004b, p. 173.

entails fundamental questions regarding his political philosophy.[12] This is confirmed by Steven Mansfield's introduction to Gramsci's *Notes on Language* (published in the journal *Telos* in 1984):

> After his imprisonment in late 1926 Gramsci began to devise a plan of study to help him combat his monotony and isolation. Since linguistic and literary issues were important to Gramsci earlier in his life, it is not surprising that they constitute a large part of that plan.... [M]any significant comments on language are interspersed throughout the notes and ... Gramsci's last notebook deals entirely with language and grammar ... Throughout, the problem of language figures in the discussion of hegemonic relations between classes, the formation and role of intellectuals, the development of the national state, and the relations between state and civil society.[13]

Virtually all of those who have turned to Gramsci's ideas on culture and language would seem to have intuitively grasped, and, in some cases, fully realised, that those ideas are inseparable from the rest of his thought and activities. Moreover, interpreters such as Tullio De Mauro, Franco Lo Piparo and Peter Ives, have persuasively shown that Gramsci's attention to language not only helped to shape his interpretation of cultural and political power, but also operates within this interpretation.[14] Nonetheless, it is still quite common to play down the significance of language-related themes when discussing Gramsci's life and thought.[15] The reason for this can be found in a polemical comment by De Mauro: 'either one deals with language and linguistics, and therefore not with Gramsci, or one deals with Gramsci the politician and, again, not with Gramsci the linguist'.[16] Ives proposes an explanation that is more articulate, yet similar in its fundamental argument, when he speaks of 'a problem of disciplinary languages': while past research, especially by Italian linguists, 'has corrected the record concerning the role of linguistics in Gramsci's intellectual trajectory, it has not been used

---

12. Here, I am especially referring to the works of Luigi Russo, Tullio De Mauro, and Paul Piccone (and their collaborators). One of Croce's favourite disciples, Russo (1947) was among the first to draw attention to Gramsci's unpublished writings (at the time, only his *Letters from Prison* were available to the public) and to his interest in linguistic subjects. For discussion of the approach shared by these non-Marxist commentators, including its evolution and internal differences, see Kaye 1981, Eley 1984, De Mauro 1998, Buttigieg 1995b, Boothman 2005.

13. Mansfield 1984, p. 120.

14. See also the articles that were published in the journal *Rethinking Marxism* in 2008: issue 21, 3, pp. 335–74.

15. For illustrious examples of the underestimation of Gramsci's thoughts on language, see the introduction to Ives and Lacorte 2010.

16. De Mauro 2010b, p. 258.

to rethink, clarify, or alter interpretations of Gramsci's political and cultural analyses'.[17]

My work aims to show the potential that a reinterpretation of Gramsci enlightened by a thorough consideration of linguistic themes has, especially in regard to Gramsci's intellectual biography, assimilation of Leninism, and his stance on diversity and unification. In other words, I hope that the following chapters may help to reduce further the barriers to which De Mauro and Ives point.

Modern linguistics and the philosophy of praxis

In the course of my discussion, I shall reiterate that one should not make the mistake of portraying Gramsci as a professional linguist, philosopher of language, or language-policy expert. However, political and cultural issues involving language attracted Gramsci's attention throughout his life. His personal and educational background made him particularly receptive to the findings of nineteenth- and early-twentieth-century linguists.

Among these findings were various data and notions that showed how normative abstractions – usually plans for linguistic unification – had limited impact on the actual development of languages. Linguistic change cannot be planned and imposed on speakers simply in the name of rationality, logic, or science; new standards and norms will only be widely accepted if they are ultimately tied to linguistic models that are already being adopted (even if unreflectively, or embryonically) by particularly important social groups. This point, which had had long-standing contacts with historicist philosophy,[18] became clearer and theoretically farther-reaching with modern language studies, especially in works that tended to see language as a 'collective activity'[19] based on a shared set of mainly implicit models.

As far as language is concerned, rules are immanent in practical activity. The rules that linguists – these representatives of the 'science of language' – describe are the ones unconsciously followed by communities of speakers (who say, for instance, 'I like you' or 'I like bread', and not 'I like to you', hence the rule that the English verb 'to like' takes a direct object).[20] Moreover, norms of 'correct'

---

17. Ives 2004b, p. 175.
18. See, for instance, the passages from the *New Science* (1744) in which Giambattista Vico recalls the failure of spelling reforms, such as those devised by the Roman emperor Claudius and the Italian humanist Giovan Giorgio Trissino, and ridicules those authors who believed that peoples, in order to develop languages, 'must first have gone to school to Aristotle' (Vico 2008, pp. 310 and 323–4).
19. Terracini 1925, p. 23.
20. For Gramsci's discussion of 'the grammar "immanent" in language itself', see Gramsci 1975, p. 2342ff.

usage – expounded by linguists in their currently marginal, but long-established, role as grammarians – do not become accepted by a whole language community unless they concur, to some extent, with the particular rules and sub-rules employed by some prestigious group of speakers in that language's oral, and especially written, use. Incidentally, the language in question may be Japanese, French, Catalan, or any other language for which such norms are being introduced as the norm in English that recommends the phrase 'my friend and I' as a subject, instead of 'me and my friend'.

Today, these points are almost obvious to historians and sociologists of language, but their general philosophical – and indeed political – implications were quite 'instructive' to an early-twentieth-century revolutionary socialist. In fact, it is essentially in this respect that Gramsci's concern with language-related issues, and his attention to cultural and linguistic diversity, became significant factors in the approach he took to revolutionary politics and cultural unification programmes. As we shall see, reflections on language were one of the major sources for Gramsci's insistence on the ties between what ordinary people (or speakers) 'feel' and what professional philosophers (or linguists) 'know'.[21] In particular, within his philosophy of praxis, such ties were necessary, in the form of an unfailing relationship of mutual exchange and renovation, between the subaltern groups and their intellectual and political leaders.

In the following chapters, I will provide specific information to illustrate how languages and reflections on language had an impact on Gramsci's political activities, and on his intellectual trajectory, through various phases of his life. The level of interconnection and cross-fertilisation between language and politics, which we can detect in his writings, changes as we move from his early years in Turin to his prison years. Giancarlo Schirru has recently confirmed and further clarified that an especially high level is reached in the *Prison Notebooks*.[22] Another aspect that changed during Gramsci's life – also as a result of the shifting background in which he operated – was his wariness of state and party interventions and planning in the field of language (and in related cultural and educational fields), the level of this wariness being higher in his pre- and early-prison writings, as opposed, in particular, to Notebook 29. However, what did not change was, in short, the belief that planning and interventions are *ultimately* impotent in the face of usage, of collective linguistic practices – that is to say, in the face of what the members of a language community are already 'spontaneously deciding' will be the course of their language.

---

21. See Gramsci 1975, Q4, §33, pp. 451–2. Cf. Saussure 1959, pp. 183–90; Iordan and Orr 1937, p. 288.
22. See Schirru 2008a.

On the whole, this cross-fertilisation between language and politics had a more significant impact on Gramsci's politics than his linguistics,[23] in that the renovation of political philosophy and action was – from the years 1918–19 onwards – at the centre of Gramsci's reflections, while he conceded that linguistics is, to an extent, a discipline that needs to follow established scientific methods which he did not call into question. For instance, his critical remarks on the cultural and political implications of applying 'the positivist-naturalist method to the study of the history of languages'[24] did not lead him to recast mainstream notions used in internal linguistics to analyse the most highly technical aspects of language.[25]

Towards a better understanding of Gramsci's views

I would now like to specify which particular aspects of Gramsci's life and writings I do not think have been explored in a fully satisfactory way. This is necessary in order to provide both a context to the substance of my analysis and argumentation, as developed in the following chapters, and an introduction to the claims to novelty of my own study. I would like to start by noting that i) secondary literature rarely refers to a sufficient number of Gramsci's writings when summarising his linguistic ideas. Moreover, language-oriented research has often neglected or misinterpreted: ii) Gramsci's life (especially the least known parts of it) and the role of Sardinian in his biography; iii) the socio-political context, cultural background and scholarly sources of Gramsci's reflections on language; and iv) the role of linguistic themes in defining Gramsci's stance on cultural diversity, as well as on political diversity and unification.[26] Each of these points requires further discussion and clarification, which I shall provide here.

1. *The limited number of writings usually considered*

There are striking disparities in the degree of attention that different writings by Gramsci have received. Especially in the secondary literature written in English, these disparities have also resulted in a limited number of writings normally being used by those authors who are not Gramsci specialists. English translations only exist of some writings, the coverage being still quite incomplete with regard to Gramsci's pre-prison production. Moreover, certain parts of his works are studied, quoted, and paraphrased a great deal more than others. This can be

---

23. Cf. Lepschy 1985, p. 214.
24. Gramsci 1975, Q29, §5, p. 2347. See also Appendix, section 4.5.5.
25. See Chapter 3, section 3.1.
26. For a detailed discussion of secondary literature, on which the points made here are largely based, see the Appendix.

found not only in applicative studies (where Gramsci's concepts are developed towards original uses) but, to a certain extent, also in interpretative works.

It is, of course, perfectly natural that not all of the notes from the *Prison Notebooks* gave rise to the same amount of discussion. Likewise, it would have been strange if every prison letter had produced an equally intense debate (expecting that to happen would be rather absurd). But in the field of language studies, the situation is not simply that of a different success rate for some texts, or passages, as opposed to others. The number of texts normally referred to is surprisingly small, and this is true of both interpretative and applicative works in this field. Applicative works, especially, often give the impression of a very selective knowledge of Gramsci's concepts (that of *hegemony* prevailing over all others), which would seem to be based far more on secondary sources than on a direct, extensive reading of his writings.[27]

In my interpretation, I shall depart from this overly selective approach by using a wider range of texts. In some cases, especially in Chapter One, I will also use texts that were not written by Gramsci himself, such as posters and leaflets, as well as articles that appeared in the socialist periodicals *Il Grido del Popolo* ['The Cry of the People'], *Avanti!* ['Forward!'] and *L'Ordine Nuovo* ['The New Order'] (the latter was later a Communist Party newspaper). These articles are significant, in that they testify to Gramsci's knowledge of specific topics and sources. Moreover, especially in the case of *L'Ordine Nuovo*, they indirectly document his views, insofar as these articles express views that were shared by the editorial board, of which Gramsci was a key member and which he very much influenced.

2. *The risks involved in neglecting Gramsci's biography*

It was Gramsci himself who, in some latently autobiographical comments, pointed to the study of political thinkers' lives as key elements for understanding their thought.[28] This approach is especially relevant to the study of authors who never 'systematically expounded' their 'conception of the world',[29] and of 'personalities in whom theoretical and practical activity are indissolubly intertwined'.[30] Indeed, this approach can be fruitfully applied to the intellectual biography of a 'young Sardinian'[31] who lived at the beginning of the twentieth century.

---

27. This impression is confirmed by the incompleteness of the collections that have so far been published with the aim of making Gramsci's language-related writings readily available: see Appendix, section 4.4.
28. See Garin 1997.
29. Gramsci 1975, Q4, §1, p. 419.
30. Ibid.
31. Gramsci 1975, Q15, §19, p. 1776.

The close interconnection between Gramsci's life and thought was also stressed by Palmiro Togliatti, Gramsci's associate and successor to the Italian Communist leadership, who claimed that his work can only be understood if the 'theme running through this work' is sought in his 'concrete activities'.[32] Other, less personally involved scholars have confirmed that 'never has there been a clearer example of the importance of biography for understanding a political theorist's teaching'.[33] The necessity of a biography-sensitive approach has been advocated with reference to Gramsci's ideas on language, also. An eminent scholar such as Tullio De Mauro, with decades of experience in this field, has argued that biographical data should not be neglected when studying 'Gramsci the linguist'.[34] As with Lev S. Vygotsky (1896–1934), who could not have discovered 'the social roots of the processes of thought and verbalisation without the great experience of educational reorganisation'[35] in the Soviet Union, and as with Ludwig Wittgenstein (1889–1951), whose views would not have formed without his 'contacts with the social-democratic reform of education in Austria, and without his direct, lived experience as a school master',[36] with Gramsci, too, practical experiences as an 'activist, organiser, and leader of the working class'[37] played a considerable role in the formation of his ideas on language.

Indeed, Gramsci had direct experience of diverse (and sometimes conflicting) linguistic realities, from his own Sardinian-Italian bilingualism to the complex linguistic situation of Turin's working class;[38] from the multilingualism of his wife's family, who used a number of different languages (especially Russian, French, and Italian), to the 'Babel' existing within the structures of the Third International. In this respect, his was 'really and literally the non-erudite philosophy of a varied and direct praxis. His readings in linguistics – Ascoli, Bréal, Bartoli and, do not forget, Croce – catalyzed this non-erudite philosophy, but his raw materials were constituted by his life and his activities as an intellectual'.[39]

In the following chapters, I shall consider Gramsci's interest in linguistics between 1915, when he sat his last university exam,[40] and 1926, when he was

---

32. Togliatti 1979, p. 162.

33. Germino 1986, p. 22. In the same period, Lo Piparo regretfully stated that 'biographical information is waiting to become part of the reconstructions and theoretical treatises on Gramsci' (Lo Piparo 2010b, p. 23). This comment derives from the centrality this scholar ascribes to Gramsci's lifelong interest in language studies (cf. Lo Piparo 1979, 2010a). On the importance of biographical data for understanding Gramsci's political thought, see also Vacca 1999a, 2005, 2012.

34. Cf. De Mauro 2010a, 2010b.

35. De Mauro 1979b, p. xiii.

36. De Mauro 1979b, p. xiv.

37. Ibid.

38. See Boothman 2008b, pp. 43–5, Nicholson 2000.

39. De Mauro 2010a, pp. 53–4.

40. See D'Orsi 2002, p. 154.

arrested. This part of his life, which includes the periods he spent in Russia and in Vienna between 1922 and 1925, needs to be carefully weighed up when studying Gramsci's views on language and education, and on language and culture. There are very few contributions on this matter. In terms of biographical reconstruction, this is due to a scarcity of evidence on where Gramsci went, what activities he was involved in, what he read and whom he met while outside of Italy. This lack of evidence was especially limiting when Russia was still under Soviet rule. Up until the end of the 1980s, historians and other commentators had to recognise that this potentially relevant information was simply not accessible. The Soviet régime persisted in refusing 'to permit access to the Comintern's files concerning Gramsci, despite sixty years having elapsed since the time when the great Sardinian, huddled in his gigantic Russian overcoat, trudged through the snow to the meetings of the Italian Commission and the Executive of the Third Communist International'.[41]

Recent research has made new information available. Although wider access to archives has been partial and intermittent in post-Soviet years, it is now possible to compare Gramsci's writings with those of Russian and European educationists, psychologists, linguists, and cultural theorists. Alongside turbulent political developments, an extremely lively cultural atmosphere existed in Russia and Vienna, in the years when Gramsci lived there. Particularly in the fields of education and language planning, these years posed extraordinary challenges, for the solution of which huge resources were deployed, including the fervent work of leading intellectuals and scientists. In Chapter Two, I shall compare some of Gramsci's observations on language to those of other intellectuals and politicians (including Lenin) who lived in this cultural atmosphere, whether or not positive evidence exists to prove that Gramsci was directly acquainted with their writings.

Gramsci's lifelong interest in languages and linguistics, and his contact with Soviet language policy, are not the only aspects of his biography that deserve better consideration than that provided by the existing secondary literature. Some studies of his life show a certain degree of unease, perhaps even reluctance, when having to acknowledge a simple fact: Gramsci spoke Sardinian in his childhood and throughout his adult life, in various contexts and for different communicative purposes. I shall explore also this aspect of Gramsci's life. In Chapter One, my main aim will be to counter those interpretations that portray Gramsci as a modern progressive intellectual who, as such, would necessarily have turned his back on his Sardinian identity.

---

41. Germino 1990, p. 146. Cf. Caprioglio 1988 and Somai 1979, pp. 9–10.

Skating over the fact that Gramsci spoke Sardinian is not the only way in which his connection to regional identity was presented as marginal, merely sentimental, and essentially negative. When it was not neglected or marginalised, Gramsci's linguistic 'Sardinianness' was often misinterpreted. Sometimes, his relationship with the Sardinian language has been regarded as a source of his most negative observations on linguistic diversity, and on dialects and minority languages in particular. Gramsci has been assimilated to a philosophical tradition that dates back to the eighteenth and nineteenth centuries and can still be found, for example, in Ferdinand Brunot's *Histoire de la langue française* ['History of the French Language'].[42] This tradition is characterised by a strong emphasis on the benefits of linguistic unification. This had both authoritarian and progressive political implications, and had its most representative actualisation in late eighteenth-century France, when the Jacobins began to introduce language policies that were openly hostile to regional linguistic and cultural identities.[43]

Interpretations portraying Gramsci as intolerant of local languages have achieved international circulation, the accusation of 'linguistic Jacobinism' being thrown at him again in recent years by the French philosopher of language Jean-Jacques Lecercle. Again, Lecercle argues that Gramsci's Sardinian origins encouraged his hostility to dialects: 'Gramsci, who was Sardinian and knew what a dialect was, is hard on them'.[44] My discussion of Gramsci's life will show these interpretations to be largely fallacious. Although Gramsci certainly stressed the negative consequences of an insufficient degree of national linguistic unification, his attitude towards local and minority languages, to Sardinian in particular, was neither hostile nor dismissive.

3. *Identifying sources and cultural links: a productive trend in recent research*

Researchers are still assimilating the great variety of debates which took place in 2007, upon the seventieth anniversary of Gramsci's death. As emerged during the Gramsci events of 2007 and in the following years, one line of study which currently appears particularly productive, and likely to expand further, concerns the analysis of Gramsci's sources.[45] I shall contribute to this research trend by adopting a non-reductive approach. In tracing the origins of Gramsci's reflections and concepts, I will not so much try to produce evidence, based solely on the bibliographical references that can be found in Gramsci's writings, of the direct

---

42. See Savoia 2001, p. 27. Gramsci became familiar with Brunot's monumental *Histoire* while studying linguistics at Turin University: see Lo Piparo 1979, p. 197ff.
43. See De Certeau, Julia and Revel 1975 and Renzi 1981.
44. Lecercle 2004, p. 83 (English translation by G. Elliott).
45. See, for example, Boothman 2008a and 2008b, and many of the contributions in Giasi 2008 and Carlucci 2012.

influence which some particular author exerted on him. Rather, I will try to place Gramsci within some of the cultural networks of his historical period. This does not mean, however, that a phylogenetic relationship can be established based on merely impressionistic, or altogether arbitrary observations. Often, a sufficient number of 'clues' makes it possible to infer that Gramsci's cultural experiences resulted in his being influenced by a particular author, or group of authors. Only when this is the case will such influence be discussed, regardless of how direct or conscious it might have been.

In Chapter Two, I shall combine this trend with my specific focus on language. Language-oriented research is another field of study that is capable of further boosting Gramscian studies. Unfortunately, however, this research has not reached an adequately wide public, even amongst Gramscian scholars, nor does it seem to have fully explored all the aspects that have emerged from the works of Lo Piparo, De Mauro, Leonardo Salamini, Niels Helsloot, and, more recently, from those of Ives, Schirru and Derek Boothman.[46] Nonetheless, these authors have succeeded in establishing two specular research objectives: one aims at giving language-related reflections their proper place in Gramsci's thought, while the other wants 'to give Gramsci his due place in the history of linguistic thought'.[47] I shall pursue both of these objectives – and especially the first one – while reconstructing the scholarly sources, socio-political context, and cultural and biographical background of Gramsci's reflections on language.

4. Linguistic themes and the debates on Gramsci's Leninism

A conceptual relation between multiplicity and unity is revealed in Gramsci's comments on the optimal functioning of the state, and in his views on the organisation of revolutionary parties, where he emphasises the benefits of *democratic centralism*, as opposed to the setbacks caused by the imposition of a superficial political unity (*bureaucratic centralism*). Most of those who have dealt with this topic have found that the study of Gramsci's views on unification requires some degree of consideration of his relationship with Soviet communism. For instance, it is on this relationship (investigated in both theoretical and historical terms) that most of the debates on the 'totalitarian' implications of Gramsci's thought have focused. Consequently, the discussion of Gramsci's drive for unity, homogeneity, and coherence, and the comparison between his Marxism and Lenin's, have often been linked in past interpretations of Gramsci.

---

46. See Appendix, especially sections 4.5.1 and 4.5.2.
47. Helsloot 2005, p. 235. Here, Helsloot also states that the existing 'literature is still limited and demands expansion. Any relevant publication on Gramsci's theory of language would be a welcome addition'.

The comparison between Lenin and Gramsci has been a pivotal subject, and probably one of the most intensely analysed topics, in the history of Gramscian studies. As early as 1958, Togliatti's contribution to the first conference specifically devoted to Gramscian research focused precisely on Gramsci's Leninism.[48] The debate continued during the 1960s, and was greatly influenced by Norberto Bobbio's interpretation of Gramsci's departure from Marx and Lenin on the themes of civil and political society, and of cultural leadership, which Bobbio put forward at the major Gramsci conference that followed in 1967.[49]

In the next decade, there were still further controversies. Gramsci's stance on the plurality of political programmes and initiatives, as guaranteed by liberal-democratic institutions, became the main focus of attention. In the mid-1970s, the Italian Communist Party (PCI) was extending its political influence and electoral support, while gradually breaking its links with the USSR. Political space was shrinking for the Italian Socialist Party (PSI), amid steps towards a convergence between the PCI and the Christian-Democratic Party such as to bring the PCI into the governing parliamentary majority. At this time, some intellectuals close to the PSI (within which fiercely anti-communist tendencies were beginning to prevail) almost completely overturned the interpretation of Gramsci that other socialists had previously put forward.[50] No longer regarded as a democratic socialist moving away from Leninist dogmatism during his prison years – and, therefore, partially betrayed by the Italian Communists, who, long after Gramsci's death, continued to proclaim their orthodoxy to Leninism – Gramsci was now portrayed as totalitarian, and his worldview claimed to be incompatible with democratic politics.[51] His detractors revived accusations which had previously been expressed by both the reformist Right of the Italian labour movement[52] and the anti-authoritarian ultra-Left.[53]

Some contributors to the 1976–7 debate on Gramsci and pluralism vociferously supported the reduction of Gramsci's views to a mere application of Lenin's

---

48. See Togliatti 1979.

49. See Bobbio 1969.

50. For an example of a socialist, anti-Leninist rendering of Gramsci's concept of hegemony, see Tamburrano 1963, pp. 245–97. See also Fiori 1991's (pp. 83–4, 95) and Liguori 1996's (pp. 23–4) discussions of the role that the Socialist (and former Communist) Angelo Tasca had in divulging documents revealing Gramsci's dissent with regard to Stalin.

51. See Coen 1977.

52. '[S]ocial democrats, liberals, and humanists of many varieties, who, despite their obvious differences, are united by their common spatial positioning to the right of the Communist Party on the ideological continuum' (Femia 1987, p. 167). This faction included Rodolfo Mondolfo, one of Gramsci's most prominent Socialist critics (see Mondolfo 1962, 1968).

53. 'Trotskyist, Bordiga revivalists, workers' control enthusiasts and other theoreticians associated with the far (beyond the PCI) Left' (Femia 1987, p. 167).

teachings. To a large extent, this was a clear attempt to discredit the PCI, whose leaders frequently referred to Gramsci as an authoritative foundation for their pursuit of direct participation in the Italian government. However, debates on Gramsci and pluralism should not be dismissed as obviously biased and simply reflecting contingent polemics in Italian political history. Potentially 'totalitarian' implications have been identified in Gramsci's thought by interpreters from different political backgrounds, from countries and historical periods quite distant from 1970s Italy.[54]

The anti-communist attitude that occasioned arbitrary attacks on Gramsci's Leninism is itself a phenomenon that went beyond the contours of Italian, and European, cultural and political life.[55] The most vehement attacks and dismissive judgements were exported to the US, too, through one of the leading public-policy think tanks of that country, the Hoover Institution. In 1981, the Hoover Institution Press published *Gramsci: An Alternative Communism?* by Luciano Pellicani.[56] During the 1976–7 dispute about Gramsci and Italian communism, this author had expressed a view which is quite relevant to my discussion, stating that the PCI should abandon Gramsci's legacy since it was of no use for the development of 'socialist pluralism'. And this, for the simple but decisive reason that Gramsci's strategy operates within a Leninist blueprint and is, as such, quintessentially and irremediably *totalitarian*'.[57]

Similar rejections of Gramsci's thought would periodically resurface in later years. Even Paul Piccone, an author who had previously emphasised Gramsci's

---

54. See Paggi 1984, Femia 1987 and 1995, and Vacca 1999a, pp. 13–70. It may be worth reminding ourselves that the negative use of the adjective *totalitarian* which many commentators have made, especially when this term was 'part of the armoury of Cold War propaganda and invective' (Gentile 2002, p. 142), does not appear in Gramsci's writings, where the same term (together with its derivatives) has a significantly different meaning, with largely positive connotations (see Caputo 2009). Hence my use of inverted commas. I shall return to this historicisation issue in Chapter Three.

55. The Italian case (where the Communist Party represented one third of the electorate) was only partly exceptional. Most of the attacks on Gramsci are better understood if one places them in the historical context of 1970s Europe, where the Communist Parties of various countries were experiencing an increase in their electoral support and, at the same time, their Marxist philosophical roots were being questioned by various philosophers and intellectuals (see Callinicos 1982, for a general discussion; and Bobbio 1976, for a particularly significant critique of Marxist socialism).

56. English translation of Pellicani 1976. According to Joseph Buttigieg (1995a, pp. 88–9), the Hoover Institution was interested in undermining the notion – already proposed, in the US, by the collection of Gramsci's writing edited by Carl Marzani in 1957 (see Appendix, section 4.3) – of 'Open Marxism', and of Gramsci as perhaps the most representative example of such a non-dogmatic Marxism. In the late 1970s, this notion could indeed provide a legitimate intellectual basis for Eurocommunism (see Nairn 1982; Piccone 1991–2). On Pellicani's book, see also Finocchiaro 1984.

57. Pellicani 1977, pp. 101–2.

distance from Lenin,[58] would eventually dismiss Gramsci's outlook on diversity and unification:

> [Gramsci's] culture-centered alternative formulation of Marxism-Leninism also ends up postulating that arbitrary and abstract Enlightenment homogenization which turned out to be the Achilles' heel of 'really existing socialism'. When all is said and done, cultural hegemony presupposes the primacy of mythical entities such as the 'class', in whose interest the new culture is deployed in order to achieve a higher rational form of humanity. No matter how positively this humanity is depicted, it inevitably turns out to be a kind of egalitarian night in which all proletarian or post-proletarian cows are black. In the age of multiculturalism and the resurgence of ethnic identities as irrational spontaneous reactions to bureaucratically-imposed homogenization, this ideal is not likely to find widespread reception.[59]

In sum, despite the scholarly insignificance of the most manipulative pseudo-interpretations, the intertwined topics of Gramsci's Leninism and his attitude to diversity have proved crucial to past debates and interpretations. Indeed, the problematic relation between, on the one hand, unity and homogeneity, and, on the other hand, multiplicity and diversity, permeates most of Gramsci's writings, and, therefore, deserves to be critically clarified in all its aspects. From a perspective which accords cultural and linguistic themes a central role, this relation has been assessed, during the last few decades, by the above-mentioned Niels Helsloot and Peter Ives, and by Martin Jay and Craig Brandist.[60] My discussion of questions of language policy has something to add to the pictures offered by these authors, and, as should become apparent in Chapter Two, also to the general interpretation of Gramsci's Leninism.

Diversity and unification: a few considerations in conclusion

It should be clear, by now, that showing the importance of linguistic themes in Gramsci's writings is useful for many reasons. In the following chapters, I shall examine several of these reasons in detail; but my primary focus will be on creating support for two specific arguments. One is that Gramsci's attitude to the plurality of languages he encountered was remarkably perceptive and open-minded, as can be seen in his original and well-balanced judgements, largely untainted by dogmatism or oversimplification. The other is that this positive relationship

---

58. See Piccone 1974 and 1976.
59. Piccone 1991–2, p. 183.
60. See Jay 1984, Chapter Four, Helsloot 1989, Brandist 1996a and 1996b. See also my Appendix.

with linguistic diversity was crucial for his awareness of the perils inherent in imposing cultural and political unification. Demonstrating the validity of these two arguments is the central aim of my work.

Attention to diversity was never an end in itself for Gramsci; but while the achievement of unification was his ultimate concern, that attention introduced complex and original aspects into his views on unification, especially on how unification is to be achieved. In other words, by looking at Gramsci's lifelong interest in language, especially in questions of linguistic diversity and unification, we can better explain the originality – and trace the origins of some specific features – of his Marxism. This is different, however, from both the marginalisation of Gramsci's Marxist perspective, which is sometimes found in culturalist applications of his concepts, and from the creation of an artificial contrast between his Marxism and his interest in language and linguistic disciplines. Likewise, on a more strictly political level, I find it quite problematic to claim that Gramsci's prison writings show an acceptance of liberal-democratic institutions, as suggested by some of those involved in debates on Gramsci and pluralism, and especially by certain interpretations of *hegemony* as a linguistically inspired notion.[61]

Far from being something created by my own interpretation, the tension between diversity and unification comes from Gramsci's own experience, reasoning and intellectual personality: on the one hand, his views were shaped by the receptiveness to diversity and autonomy that his rural Sardinian background almost inevitably provided, and by the influence of authors such as Sorel, Bergson and Croce, with their insistence on spontaneity, creativity and distinction (countless articles and books have been written on this, especially with reference to the 'young' or 'pre-Leninist' Gramsci);[62] but on the other hand, he was influenced by Machiavelli, Marx and Lenin, that is to say, by their emphasis on the advantages of unification and centralised coordination. From a Gramscian point of view, it was no coincidence that the first of these two positions was ultimately a-political (Bergson, Sorel) or meta-political (Croce), while the second position arose from the need to 'do' politics – from an unambiguous engagement

---

61. See especially my comments on Franco Lo Piparo's works: Chapter Two, section 2.5.3; Chapter Three, section 3.4.1. Whereas Lo Piparo especially emphasises the liberal attitudes of Gramsci's sources, it will emerge from my survey that his attention to linguistic diversity was fostered by Marxist sources and debates as much as by non-Marxist ones.

62. For a recent and particularly thorough discussion, see Rapone 2011, pp. 333–51. It is worth adding that Croce's theorisation of aesthetics culminated in a rejection of 'the search for a model language, or for a method of reducing linguistic usage to unity' – a dismissal, in other words, of both 'the search for a universal language' and 'the question of the unity of language' (Croce 1990, pp. 188–90).

in political action. Gramsci was never dismissive of autonomous struggles and group-specific demands; however, (in contradistinction to what we would now broadly refer to as 'postmodern sensibility') he saw this plurality of independent projects as ultimately insufficient for bringing about a new global society. In other words, an exclusive concern with diversity (difference, plurality, autonomy and so on) would result, *de facto*, in an acceptance of the world as it is, and would essentially have relegated Gramsci within the liberal horizon, while the implementation of unity was needed to conceive and organise the transition beyond this horizon.

Gramsci's concept of hegemony overcomes this impasse by implying that there can – and probably will – be diversity in a culturally and linguistically unified world.[63] The tension between the two poles – unification and diversity – can never be entirely resolved. History does not destroy, it simply rearranges. Unity does not mean uniformity, and there may be a deeper level of autonomy and diversity in a future unified world than there is within the present conflict-ridden and divided humanity.[64] The same happens in language, where a good command of a unitary language does not rule out the possibility of personal styles and usages,[65] or of local variation, and does not necessarily impede the maintenance of local tongues as part of bilingual repertoires; whereas the exclusive knowledge of local tongues often means exclusion, passivity and mutual diffidence. So (as will become evident in Chapters Two and Three) the essential political dichotomy turns out to be – beyond the one between diversity and unification – the one between bureaucratically imposed unification (according to a pre-determined 'rational' model or theory) and open-ended unification, allowed by the existence of adequate and necessary conditions and obtained through the active participation of large and diverse sections of the population. Throughout his prison writings, Gramsci remained convinced that the latter type of unification – which we could call *hegemonically obtained unification* – had begun to be put into practice in Soviet Russia under Lenin, with the introduction, above all, of the New Economic Policy in the early 1920s.

---

63. Cf. Frosini 2010, pp. 22–6, and also Ives 2004b, pp. 84–96, and 2010.
64. 'Each new social stratum that emerges in history, that organizes itself for the good fight, introduces new currents and new uses into the language and explodes the fixed schemes established by the grammarians for the fortuitous convenience of teaching. In history, in social life, nothing is fixed, rigid or definitive. And nothing *ever will be*. New truths increase the inheritance of knowledge. New and ever superior needs are created by new living conditions. New moral and intellectual curiosities goad the spirit and compel it to renew itself, to improve itself, to change the linguistic forms of expression by taking them from foreign languages, by reviving dead forms and by changing meanings and grammatical functions' (Gramsci 1982, pp. 672–3. My emphasis. English translation from Gramsci 1985, p. 31).
65. See also Gramsci 1975, Q29, §2, p. 2343.

What we have again, here, is hegemony as a concept developed by a 'fighter' – that is, by Gramsci as someone whose writings were not, as he himself put it, those of an academic who loves 'studying for study's sake'.[66] They were the writings of a revolutionary, who was firmly convinced that the possibility of moving beyond liberalism and capitalism was both rationally well-founded and morally desirable. I believe that only by keeping this in mind can we accurately understand the role played by linguistic facts and notions in the shaping of Gramsci's concept of hegemony, and in his general political outlook.

---

66. Gramsci 1994a, I, p. 369.

Chapter One
Experiencing Linguistic Diversity and Cultural Unification

1.1. Sardinian in Gramsci's life

I shall begin this chapter by posing a question: *did Gramsci speak Sardinian?* A few words of introduction are required, in order to explain this question. Why ask if Gramsci spoke Sardinian? What is the use of posing a question to which the answer might seem rather obvious? There are, in fact, many reasons. In the first place, the real meaning and significance of Gramsci's use of the linguistic resources of the island where he was born are neither fully assessed, nor explained, by an affirmative answer such as: *yes, he spoke Sardinian.* This simple answer leaves room for further questions about when, how, why, and with whom Gramsci used Sardinian; about whether he did so in years and contexts which were not connected to his Sardinian childhood; and about the way in which Italian and Sardinian positively coexisted within his personality[1] and throughout his experiences as a political militant.

---

1. In October 1931, Gramsci wrote to his sister-in-law: 'my culture is fundamentally Italian and this is my world; I have never for a moment felt that I was torn between two worlds, although something to that effect was written in the *Giornale d'Italia* of March 1920, where a two-column article explained my political activity in Turin by, among other things, my being Sardinian and not Piedmontese or Sicilian etc.' (Gramsci 1994a, II, p. 87). Later, however, in a letter to his wife, he admitted that his Sardinian origins had introduced specific features into his Italianness: 'In Italian literature it has been written that if Sardinia is an island, every Sardinian is an island within the island, and I remember a very amusing article by a writer for the *Giornale d'Italia* who in 1920 tried in this way to explain my intellectual and political tendencies. But perhaps there is a bit of truth, enough to impart an accent (actually imparting an accent is no little matter but I don't want to start analyzing; let me just say "the grammatical accent" and you will be merely amused and admire my cricket-like modesty)' (p. 376). Lina Corigliano,

Furthermore, questions over Gramsci's knowledge and use of a particular variety of Sardinian need to be asked in order to confirm, or eventually reject, certain hypotheses which have been put forward concerning how this tongue became part of Gramsci's individual linguistic repertoire. Some years ago, in a rich and stimulating contribution to the study of Gramsci's linguistic interests, the linguist Eduardo Blasco Ferrer stated that Sardinian was 'most probably "learnt" [by Gramsci] from linguistics books, rather than naturally "acquired" at home orally'.[2]

Blasco Ferrer's hypothesis could be seen as a marginal biographical comment, requiring no specific demonstration or discussion. Yet this aspect of Gramsci's biography takes on considerable importance in view of the diverse and largely conflicting opinions that interpreters have expressed (directly or indirectly) with respect to Gramsci's stance on dialects and minority languages, on Sardinian especially. Gramsci has often been referred to, sometimes even quoted, in debates on the protection of local languages. He has been referred to in scholarly and political discussion on the desirability of promoting the unification and official recognition of the varieties used within a certain region (again, with special reference to Sardinia). Gramsci's authority has been upheld by both those who wanted to overcome the plurality of languages traditionally existing in Italy and those who were, instead, in favour of safeguarding and promoting this plurality.[3]

The 'linguistic views developed by Gramsci in the *Quaderni*' have been equated with 'cultural-historical categories such as reactionary idealism and traditional nationalism',[4] and have been interpreted as containing 'an outright attack on dialects'.[5] In contrast to these interpretations, Gramsci has been presented as an advocate of the teaching of dialects at school.[6] Other interpretations have emphasised the apparent, partial inconsistency of Gramsci's position on dialectophony. His position has been described in terms of its 'incongruity' and 'flaws',[7] as being characterised by 'variable views';[8] in other words, as an 'uncertain evaluation of

---

a patient in the same clinic where Gramsci spent the last two years of his life, also confirmed: 'he didn't speak about politics with me...even though it was obvious that he was hostile towards the régime. One conversation I had with him convinced me that he was a staunch regionalist. "What nationality do you think you are?" he asked me. "I am Italian", I answered, astonished at his question. To which he responded: "Not at all. You are Calabrian before you are Italian, just as I am Sardinian"' (in Palumbo 1977, p. 181. Cf. Germino 1990, p. 10 note 22).

2. Blasco Ferrer 1999, p. 58.

3. See in particular the interventions collected in Murru Corriga 1977. In passionately arguing for the protection and promotion of local languages, Pier Paolo Pasolini offers a particularly significant example of this use of Gramsci (Pasolini 1987, pp. 47–57).

4. Savoia 2001, p. 30.

5. Mengaldo 1994, p. 17.

6. See Broccoli 1972, p. 196, Grassi *et al.* 2004.

7. De Mauro 1979a, 135.

8. De Mauro 1980a, 98.

dialects'.[9] Not surprisingly, caution has been called for, with some interpreters raising doubts about the possibility of finding reflections of immediate relevance to present debates on dialects in the writings of an author who was born at the end of the nineteenth century and was profoundly influenced by glottopolitical views that are no longer accepted today.[10]

In view of so many and such diverse readings, it seems appropriate to ask what role Sardinian played in Gramsci's life and if, and in what way, he used this language. Through a detailed analysis of this topic (which Blasco Ferrer only incidentally considers), I also intend to try and recreate the context in which Gramsci developed his ideas on the fate of geographically restricted linguistic traditions, which tend to be socially and culturally marginalised by the expansion of national languages. Such a reconstruction is particularly necessary with an author like Gramsci. Apart from their heterogeneous nature, his writings were not conceived as purely speculative contributions, nor were they subjected to the accurate revision and systematisation that academic works are normally given. Analysing their historical context and biographical implications seems therefore essential.

Gramsci can be seen as one of those 'personalities in whom theoretical and practical activity are indissolubly intertwined' – to quote the words that he himself used in his *Prison Notebooks*, when writing about Marx.[11] Hence, these words can be usefully combined with those included in another prison note, in which Gramsci discusses the importance of autobiographical writing and provides indicative comments about his own life:

> In many respects, this kind of writing can be...useful...if it refers to life processes which are characterised by a continuous attempt to go beyond backward ways of living and thinking typical of a Sardinian at the beginning of the [twentieth] century, and to appropriate ways of living and thinking no longer regional or 'village-like', but national. In fact, these were national in so far as one tried to become part of European ways of living and thinking, or, at least, in so far as one tried to compare national ways with European ways, Italian cultural necessities with European trends and cultural necessities (obviously, within the possibilities of one's own personal situation; but still, according to strongly felt exigencies and needs). If it is true that one of the most prominent necessities of Italian culture was to become less provincial even in the most advanced and modern urban centres, then those processes should appear all the more evident as experienced by a 'triple or quadruple provincial', as a young Sardinian certainly was at the beginning of the century.[12]

---

9. Cortelazzo 1984, p. 107.
10. See De Mauro 1979a, pp. 135–6, Lo Piparo 2004, pp. 171–95.
11. Gramsci 1975, Q4, §1, p. 419 (cf. p. 1841).
12. Gramsci 1975, Q15, §19, p. 1776.

In the following sections of this chapter, I shall apply these indications first to Gramsci's letters, and then to various sources and materials concerning his practical activity.

1.2. Gramsci's correspondence

Although my primary concern is with Gramsci's oral use of Sardinian, I do not intend to establish a marked separation between his life and his writings. Accordingly, this chapter will include frequent references to Gramsci's writings and to those of his associates, even in sections where Gramsci's life constitutes the focus of my attention. The elements that emerge from Gramsci's correspondence will be expanded upon and further clarified through a detailed discussion of some pertinent episodes from his life.

Another caveat is necessary. So far, I have been using a term, 'Sardinian', which is largely misleading from a strictly linguistic point of view. Evidence can be obtained, both from his letters and from testimonies by those who met Gramsci, as to the variety of which he was a native speaker. However, this aspect of the question is not particularly relevant to my discussion. As we shall see, a generic definition of *sardo* [Sardinian] is acceptable from a Gramscian point of view. Moreover, this definition indentifies a pertinent element in the biographical background and historical context against which Gramsci's views need to be assessed.

During Gramsci's life, Sardinian was a group of language varieties which had come to be socially and culturally subordinated to the unified national language. This subordination essentially applied to Sardinian as a whole. On the one hand, as we shall see, the question of the status that should nominally be accorded to this group of varieties was not regarded as a prominent issue by Gramsci: he referred to Sardinian in his writings both as a *lingua* [language] and a *dialetto* [dialect], and was aware that any choice between the two terms would be somewhat debatable. On the other hand, he saw the formation of a cohesive national language as politically progressive.[13] It is, therefore, interesting to look at Gramsci's relationship with Sardinian as a local or regional language which potentially conflicted with this progressive process of linguistic unification, rather than focusing only on the exclusively individual relationship with his own native variety.

Let us now turn to the teaching that Gramsci received from the linguist Matteo Bartoli (1873–1946) at Turin University:

---

13. See Gramsci 1975, Q10II, §44, p. 1331, and Q29, §2, p. 2344.

How many neo-Latin languages are there, and what are they? By convention, we say that there are as many as there are *literary or written languages*; this is the most solid and by now generally accepted classification. Certainly, it does not include all of them, but what other criterion could be used in its place? Since there are no clear boundaries between one language and another, we cannot say where one language finishes and the next one begins, while with literary languages this can be done, since they are generally written within the confines of a nation. Starting from the literary criterion, we may number the following neo-Latin languages, beginning from the East: Romanian, Italian, Ladin, French, Provençal, Catalan, Spanish, Portuguese. To these Meyer-Lübke adds Sardinian and Dalmatian, detaching himself from the literary criterion, since even if Sardinian had a small amount of literature, Dalmatian had none at all. So what was his reasoning? It was as follows: these two languages are important for the history of Romance languages because they preserve a phase of spoken Latin that in the other regions had already been surpassed long before; this factor is easily explained if one thinks of their history and their geographic position.[14]

As a result of this and other inputs, Gramsci became aware of the inherent difficulty of making a final, absolute decision as to whether Sardinian should be defined as a dialect or a language. Here lies the origin of his later, virtually interchangeable use of these two terms with respect to the language of his island. Although the issue of what status Sardinian should be assigned captured the attention of many nineteenth-century linguists,[15] Bartoli's lessons clarified that only by arbitrarily privileging one criterion over other possible ones could any choice be made. Only in this way could the group of Sardinian varieties – including the most prestigious ones, endowed with a literary tradition – be defined as a language or as a dialect. Some factors were, certainly, important in trying to establish the correct criteria according to which languages and dialects could be distinguished – most notably, the grammatical and lexical characteristics produced by the historical development of a certain group of varieties, and the prestige acquired through written uses. However, Gramsci's university training made him aware of the caution that discussion on the status of Sardinian required, and, in general, of the need to avoid rigid classifications when determining the status of Romance varieties.

We also need to consider other elements that contributed to the formation of Gramsci's ideas on languages as expressed in his writings, his letters in particular. These other elements should help interpreters not to overemphasise some

---

14. Bartoli 1912–13, p. 74.
15. See Devoto and Giacomelli 2002, p. 154.

of Gramsci's terminological choices and to avoid overstating the literal meaning of some passages. Amongst these elements are the practical conditions in which Gramsci's writings were produced. Since he never wrote as a professional linguist, he was not in the position of a specialist obliged to adopt a univocal terminology, to use it consistently, and to define it explicitly. Gramsci introduced comments on languages and dialects in texts of a rather heterogeneous nature – from essentially private writings (some of his letters), and public non-technical texts (for example, theatrical reviews and other articles for daily and weekly papers), to provisional notes that were meant to be further elaborated, and certainly not to be published as they were in his notebooks. In addition, one should not forget Gramsci's well-known tendency to put his vocabulary through a constant process of semantic rearrangement, using the same terms in different ways in writings belonging to different periods.[16]

---

16. Similarly to the opposition between *lingua* and *dialetto*, also the one between *lingua* and *linguaggio* is best understood in context, according to the particular way in which Gramsci uses the two terms in the article, letter or other piece of writing under scrutiny. Depending on the context, Gramsci uses *dialetto*, *gergo* [jargon], *lingua* and *linguaggio* to refer to national languages, local or sub-standard or special varieties, artificial languages (usually Esperanto), and natural languages conserved mostly in written texts but no longer widely used or developed through mass social intercourse (namely, 'dead' languages such as Latin). Given the shifting context and the political – and often polemical – nature of Gramsci's work, we do not find a perfectly consistent use of *lingua* and *linguaggio* in his writings (see Rosiello 1976 and 2010; and the entries *lingua* and *linguaggio* in Liguori and Voza 2009). For instance, it is not always clear which one is used as the hyperonym and which as the hyponym, and we should, therefore, avoid static or mechanical equations between Gramsci's use of these two terms and the way in which *langue* and *langage* have been used in linguistics and language philosophy following Saussure's influential distinctions. In Gramsci's Italian, *lingua* usually refers to a historically-determined system of verbal signs: such as English, Romanian, Japanese, 'Medieval Latin' (Gramsci 1994a, I, p. 360), but also 'the language [*lingua*] of workers' organisations' (Gramsci 1975, Q6, §184, p. 830). In some passages, *linguaggio* would seem to include *lingua*, referring to a more general semiotic faculty; while elsewhere it seems to refer to a group's (stylistically marked and sometimes innovative) actualisation of the system(s) available, through particular instances of spoken or written communication (cf. Saussure's *parole*). *Linguaggio* also refers to the typical and cohesive terminology of a philosophical movement, or – we could say – to the terminological surface of a certain epistemological paradigm (such as 'the language [*linguaggio*] of liberal economics': Q10II, §20, p. 1258); and, more broadly, to the mode of expression (including non-verbal expression) of particular cultural, artistic, or political trends (such as the language of jazz music: Gramsci 1994a, I, pp. 179–80).

For useful remarks on how Italian linguists defined *lingua* and *linguaggio* within their theories of language during the first half of the twentieth century (with reference, in particular, to Giulio Bertoni), and on how these two terms related to *langage*, *langue* and *parole*, see also Devoto 1951, pp. 3–11.

Further complications arise when trying to find the most appropriate English translation of *lingua* and *linguaggio*, as commentators and translators of Gramsci's writings have come to realise (see Nowell Smith, in Gramsci 1971c, p. 348 note 32; Mansfield 1984; Boothman 2005; Ives and Lacorte 2010, p. 12). On the whole, there is no reason to refrain from translating both terms with the English 'language'; however, in some of

Excessive concern with terminological issues, which in itself tends to favour a static approach, could impede a full appreciation of the dynamic development of Gramsci's thought – a development which was the result not only of contingent factors, but also of his intellectual inclinations. This is quite evident, if one considers the simple and yet revealing fact that Gramsci, at various stages of his career, chose not to publish sizeable works in which his ideas could appear to have assumed a systematic form.[17] At a deeper level, moreover, a static approach to Gramsci's writings could also impede a correct interpretation of the contents of his thought. The meaning of the words that he used in his writings changed considerably over time, and, at the same time, Gramsci saw institutions and power relations – and, therefore, also words, concepts, social and linguistic habits – as being subject to processes of redefinition. These processes may occur through history (that is, diachronically); or they may occur according to changes in the situations considered and in the agents, individual as well as collective, operating in each of these situations (that is, synchronically). Reading Gramsci's writings with the aim of finding within them a rigorous terminological grid, consisting of fixed oppositions unaffected by fluidity, would lead to shaky interpretative results. Such an interpretation would largely compromise fundamental aspects of Gramsci's thought, which concern the historical mutability of distinctions, and, therefore, the non-absolute value of definitions.

It thus seems advisable to avoid mechanical readings of the terms and arguments that Gramsci used. Likewise, it would be mistaken to overemphasise a particular statement from one of his prison letters, in fact of limited value, even though it may at first seem straight forward and clear-cut: I shall quote and discuss again this statement, according to which 'Sardinian is not a dialect, but a language in itself'.[18]

After these preliminary points, we can now look at the useful clues that Gramsci's correspondence provides for understanding the role that Sardinian played in his life. First of all, it is worth mentioning the fact that Gramsci used some Sardinian words, phrases, and traditional popular expressions, sometimes even short sentences, in the letters that he wrote (in Italian) to his correspondents, especially in those he wrote from prison to his mother. In addition, some letters contain recollections of his own childhood – 'my somewhat savage and

---

the quotations in this and the following chapters, I shall add the Italian term in square brackets, in those cases when 'language' may prove ambiguous.

17. See, for instance, Gramsci's own account of this choice in Gramsci 1976, pp. 260–71, and Gramsci 1996a, pp. 457–8. For discussion, see also Paladini Musitelli 1996, pp. 99–100; and especially the third chapter of Thomas 2009.

18. Gramsci 1994a, I, p. 89.

primitive childhood',[19] as Gramsci defines it – which include detailed analyses of the island's lexicon and folklore.[20]

I would now like to focus on samples, from Gramsci's correspondence, that deserve particular attention. These include a group of letters from his university years, and a letter from prison. The former consists of letters dating back to the period from January 1912 to March 1913, in which the young Gramsci asks his sister Teresina and his father for detailed information on specific aspects of the Sardianian dialects (mostly phonology and vocabulary). These requests were aimed at providing Gramsci's glottology professor, Matteo Bartoli, with the information he needed for his research.[21] This group of letters gives a somewhat ambiguous impression. Here, Gramsci's Italian is characterised by some typical regional features. It has some traits of Sardinian Italian, and is perhaps also influenced by Sardinian (as a language, or dialect, different from Italian): *mi ho fatto prender la misura* [non-standard for 'I was measured'] for an overcoat by a tailor;[22] *non so neppure come scolparmi* ['I don't even know how to justify myself'];[23] *Mario ... sta facendo da bravo* [non-standard for 'Mario is being a good boy'].[24] At the same time, though, it would seem that Gramsci's own linguistic competence was inadequate to satisfy Bartoli's scientific curiosity; or perhaps he felt the need to turn to others, also outside his family, because of

---

19. Gramsci 1992a, p. 289.

20. See also note 152 in this chapter.

21. See Gramsci 2010, pp. 90–125. Schirru has recently suggested that some of Gramsci's inquiries may have been part of the informal research network revolving around the publication of Meyer-Lübke 1935 (see Schirru 2011, pp. 953–963). On Bartoli and 'glottology' (better known, in the English-speaking world, as 'comparative philology') see Appendix, section 4.2.1.

22. Gramsci 1992a, p. 63. This use of *avere* [to have] instead of *essere* [to be], as an auxiliary verb in phrases where *essere* would normally be required, existed for a long time in Italian (see Migliorini 2000). It is widely used in the dialects of Italy, especially the southern ones (see Rohlfs 1966–9, III, pp. 124–5). However, it can be viewed as a Sardinian linguistic feature (see Iorio 1997, p. 39, Abbruzzese 1987, pp. 77–8).

23. Gramsci 2010, p. 98. Whereas standard Italian has two options, *scolpare* and *discolpare*, the Italian spoken in Sardinia tends to have *scolpare* only. This is due to 'the influence that dialects have on occurrences in Sardinian regional Italian, since in Sardinian dialects negative forms are also often formed by attaching the prefix *s-* to verbs and nouns' (Loi Corvetto 1993, pp. 169–70. See also Iorio 1987, p. 51).

24. Gramsci 2010, p. 98. This is one of the typical expressions which Sardinians have created using the verb *fare*, and which they often use (see Abbruzzese 1987, pp. 118–19). Tuscan-based standard Italian would have 'fare *il* bravo'. In Gramsci's writing, as in that of his brother Gennaro, another Sardinian feature often appears: the imprecise use of double and single consonants (see Rossi and Vacca 2007, pp. 209–13; Leonetti's comments in Melis 1975, p. 6; and Gramsci 2007a, pp. 892–4). Once he wrote to his mother: 'The memory really reappeared very clearly of the time when I was in the first or second elementary grade and you would correct my homework: I can recall perfectly that I was never able to remember that *uccello* [bird] is written with two *c's* and you corrected this error at least ten times' (Gramsci 1994a, II, p. 40).

the unusualness of Bartoli's queries. Indeed, most of the requests that Gramsci passed on to his sister and father concerned infrequently-used words, often archaic in form, and belonging to a variety different from the one which Gramsci regularly used and in which he felt comfortable.

The prison letter that I have decided to single out for discussion is often referred to by scholars aiming at demonstrating that Gramsci favoured the preservation of linguistic plurality and the acquisition of several languages by children. This letter was written by Gramsci to his sister, Teresina, on 26 March 1927. Here, Gramsci advises his sister to let her son, Franco, speak Sardinian. Franco was only two at the time. I shall now quote extensively from this letter, using italics to highlight a passage that describes the linguistic environment around Franco's family. This linguistic background must have been fairly similar to the one in which Gramsci himself had grown up.

> It was a mistake, in my opinion, not to allow Edmea to speak freely in Sardinian as a little girl. It harmed her intellectual development and put her imagination in a straitjacket. You mustn't make this mistake with your children. For one thing, Sardinian is not a dialect, but a language [*lingua*] in itself, even though it does not have a great literature, and it is a good thing for children to learn several languages, if it is possible. Besides, *the Italian that you will teach them will be a poor, mutilated language made up of only the few sentences and words of your conversations with him*, purely childish; he will not have any contact with a general environment and will end up learning two jargons and no language: an Italian jargon for official conversation with you and a Sardinian jargon learned piecemeal to speak with the other children and the people he meets in the street or piazza.... Take Delio, he began by speaking his mother's tongue [Russian], as was natural and necessary, but he also quickly learned Italian and besides he used to sing little French songs without becoming confused or mixing up the words of the different languages. I wanted to teach him to sing also: *Lassa sa figu, puzone*, but his aunts in particular strenuously objected.[25]

On the one hand, this letter indicates that Gramsci, in the period immediately preceding his arrest, continued to be fairly attached to the Sardinian language, as he wished to teach his son a traditional song from Sardinia. On the other hand, one should not exaggerate the importance of this letter. When he states that the Sardinian language is not a dialect, Gramsci seems to be simultaneously referring

---

25. Gramsci 1994a, I, p. 89. Edmea was Gramsci's niece (Gennaro's daughter). Delio, one of Gramsci's two sons, was about two years old when the episode which Gramsci recounts in this letter took place. *Lassa sa figu, puzone* ['Hey bird, leave the fig tree alone'] is a Sardinian folk song.

to the genetic autonomy of Sardinian tongues from the Italian language, and to the fact that these tongues were, at times, used by intellectuals (*intellettuali*, in the broad Gramscian meaning of the word).[26] Only a few, relatively marginal examples exist of this use in Sardinian history. Nonetheless, it is true that as a consequence of this use by culturally active and socially prominent groups, some varieties of Sardinian spread widely and acquired a certain socio-cultural prestige, developing vast semantic, functional, stylistic and textual potentialities. However, in the non-specialist context of a letter to his sister, Gramsci did not feel the need to further clarify the distinction he had introduced.[27] Any interpretation wishing to treat the definition of Sardinian as a *lingua* in terms of a theoretically aware, well thought-out judgement would somehow have to ignore the context in which this definition was expressed. In any case, such interpretations would be contradicted by Gramsci's own use of the word *dialetto* – or, even more accurately, the phrase 'various dialects of Sardinia'[28] – with which he indicates Sardinian in various texts before and after this letter.[29]

Gramsci's use of *lingua*, in this context, can be regarded as aimed at nothing more than overcoming his sister's anti-dialect bias and convincing her that she should not 'prevent his nephew from acquiring Sardinian'.[30] This interpretation avoids the risk of making an assumption that Gramsci himself intuitively avoided making. Indeed, he did not make the mistake of assuming that the technical sense of his own terms would be completely clear to his non-specialist addressee. It is well known that 'dialect' still today has – and certainly had eighty years ago, in a small Sardinian town – a misleading evaluative meaning. Most people usually

---

26. By 'intellectuals', one must understand 'not only those strata commonly described by this term, but generally the entire social stratum which exercises an organisational function in the wide sense – whether in the field of production, or in that of culture, or in that of political administration' (Gramsci 1975, Q19, §26, p. 2041). See also Gramsci 1996a, p. 458.

27. See Matt 2008. According to Rosiello, in this letter Gramsci speaks as an expert who is 'used to thinking of Sardinian dialects as an autonomous variety of Romance languages, without any sociolinguistic consideration of their communicative function. On the other hand, he shows that he is aware that the free formation of a complete linguistic proficiency cannot but favour languages' learning' (Rosiello 2010, p. 31). This opinion is also shared by Blasco Ferrer 1999 (pp. 57–8). Lilliu 1999 suggests a different interpretation, according to which Gramsci sees Sardinian as a *lingua* not only on the basis of its independent origins, but also as a socio-communicative tool with fully developed characteristics (though lacking the requisite of having a rich literary tradition).

28. Gramsci 1984, p. 360.

29. Those who examined this letter very rarely reached similar conclusions. Some interpreters went as far as to argue that Gramsci was in favour of teaching dialects (see Broccoli 1972, p. 196, Grassi *et al.* 2004, p. 91). Others simply believed this letter to contain a defence of bilingualism. Lo Piparo 1979, p. 221, specified that Gramsci was in favour of bilingualism not in terms of a simultaneous acquisition of languages and dialects, but of languages [*lingue*] only. See also Pira 1978, pp. 198–9, and Selenu 2005, pp. 270–2.

30. Sgroi 1982, p. 326.

understand this term as referring to an incorrect way of speaking – that is, an inaccurate or degenerated way of employing what is perceived as good language. Alternatively, 'dialect' is sometimes understood as a local or regional version of the national language (what sociolinguists currently define as a diatopic variety). Neither of these two meanings is appropriate with regard to Sardinian (nor to any of the Italo-Romance varieties, except for the Tuscan and Roman ones). Thus Gramsci resorted to his sister's common-sense terminology to prevent her from rejecting Sardinian.

Finally, a few more details need to be added to what I have said so far on the language used by Gramsci in his writings, especially in his letters. The linguist Tullio Telmon has noticed that Gramsci's letters contain a regional lexical item, *tolaio* – a noun meaning 'plumber'. This is a Piedmontese form, but it also exists in some Sardinian varieties,[31] and is used twice in Gramsci's letters:

> Gramsci was born in Sardinia and had evidently acquired this term, which nowadays is not part of Sardinian regional Italian, from the Campidanese dialect. It is well known that he then moved to Turin to undertake his university studies. Finding the same term in Piedmontese regional Italian probably led him to believe that he was using a more standard Italian term.[32]

This is an interesting clue, as were the ones discussed in the previous pages. However, I have not yet accumulated enough elements to answer the question – did Gramsci speak Sardinian? – with which I opened this chapter. So far, only some features of a Sardinian variety of Italian have emerged from Gramsci's letters. This regional variety of Italian is probably close to the Italian which Gramsci would normally have used in oral communication. Yet one cannot equate regional uses with mental translations from a local language (such as Sardinian) into the national language. A person who normally uses a regional variety of Italian 'is using an autonomous language variety, so much so that there are people who speak the Sardinian regional variety of Italian without knowing Sardinian (and the same can be said for any other region in Italy)'.[33]

In conclusion, my question can only be answered by turning to Gramsci's life. Before doing so, however, it is worth recalling the conclusions of other authors, besides Telmon and Matt, who have looked at Gramsci's writings in their entirety (that is, not only at his letters). Michelangelo Pira asserts that there are many 'aspects of Gramsci's personality that can be explained by his Sardinian mentality', and observes that Gramsci's reasoning often reflects, 'even at the

---

31. See Pittau 2000, p. 925, who confirms the Piedmontese origin of the word. See also Poddu 2000, p. 1635, Espa 1999, p. 1226.
32. Telmon 2001, p. 89.
33. Matt 2008, p. 56.

syntactic and lexical level, typically Sardinian ways of feeling and thinking'.[34] Leonardo Sole has emphasised the influence of Sardinian language varieties and folk poems on certain aspects of Gramsci's style, especially with regard to metric, syntactic, and pragmatic patterns.[35] Finally, Lucia Borghese has identified uncommon lexical forms, which closely resemble Sardinian forms, in Gramsci's Italian translation of some of the Grimm brothers' tales.[36]

1.3. The Sardinian years

In order to understand Gramsci's writings, we need to reconstruct his biography. This reconstruction will bring to the fore the role of multilingualism in the formation of Gramsci's identity as an intellectual and a politician. To date, Gramsci's frequent use of his native Sardinian tongue has often been neglected. Apart from a few earlier exceptions, it was only with Giuseppe Fiori's *Vita di Antonio Gramsci* ['Life of Antonio Gramsci'], first published in 1966, that things changed substantially. Fiori's book marked a turning point in studies of Gramsci's life and initiated an innovative line of research, based on using the memories of people who had met Gramsci and his family, shared the same experiences or had been involved in the same political activities. In most cases, these people were interviewed, the interviews normally being tape-recorded[37] and then transcribed and published in written form. Unlike earlier biographical research on Gramsci, there was no longer an almost exclusive focus on politics. Moreover, these memories were no longer filtered through political-ideological schemata privileging glorification and 'hagiography', which had, however, influenced earlier collections of memories on Gramsci.[38]

Some of the publications that appeared during the 1970s and 1980s provided new relevant information. Journalists, activists and politicians who had worked with Gramsci contributed to the clarification of different points in Gramsci's biography, including his attitude towards the use of Sardinian. For instance, Alfonso Leonetti wrote that Gramsci 'loved ... to speak Sardinian'.[39] And Umberto Terracini, conversing on this matter with Pier Paolo Pasolini,[40] confirmed that Gramsci's way of speaking Italian was clearly influenced by his Sardinian background, although this influence was mitigated by several factors: Gramsci's

---

34. Pira 1966.
35. See Sole 1999.
36. See Borghese 1981.
37. See Bermani 1987, p. 7.
38. As in the case of Togliatti *et al.* 1945.
39. From a letter published in Melis 1975, p. 6. Cf. Germino 1990, p. 29, who echoes Leonetti's letter in writing that 'Gramsci loved the Sardinian language'.
40. See Pasolini 1972, pp. 58–9.

education, academic training and rich cultural interests; his contact with other dialects, particularly with Piedmontese ones; and, finally, the fact that his father was not Sardinian and normally spoke Italian with his wife, Gramsci's mother.

Let us start, then, by looking at Gramsci's childhood. The socio-cultural environment in which Gramsci grew up, in small villages and towns in south-central Sardinia, was dominated by the local language varieties.[41] According to Tullio De Mauro, this was a 'dense'[42] dialect-speaking environment, as is confirmed by Gramsci himself, who, in the above-quoted letter of March 1927, says that about thirty years later, his nephew Franco would still need Sardinian to speak with other children and with the local population in general.

Francesco Gramsci, Antonio's father, was born in Campania.[43] He went to university (albeit for only a short period of time, and without completing his studies), and then began to work in the public administration. He most certainly used Italian with his children. His Sardinian wife, Peppina Marcias, a passionate reader of Italian poems and novels (albeit having received very little schooling), was probably quite comfortable using Italian. These impressions are confirmed by the letters that Gramsci and his parents wrote to each other while he was at Turin University. His mother's letters reveal some Sardinian linguistic features (especially in the use of single and double consonants in spelling); but on the whole, in their letters to Antonio, his parents show a fairly good command of the Italian language and only a marginal use of Sardinian in separate, incidental passages about local cultural life and traditions.[44]

Not only did Peppina like reading, she also loved singing. Indeed, she would often sing in Sardinian.[45] And she would use this language when talking to her children: 'Although she could speak Italian very well and had a "continental" husband, Peppina Marcias had always spoken to her children in Sardinian. They too spoke to her and to each other in Sardinian'.[46] Unsurprisingly, Gramsci and

41. Paulesu Quercioli writes that in 1880, 'Ghilarza was already a large town with 2,200 inhabitants, of whom only 10 percent knew how to read and write'. On Sunday mornings, 'the first mass was celebrated in Sardinian' (Paulesu Quercioli 2003, pp. 52 and 73).

42. De Mauro 2010a, p. 52 (*una realtà compattamente dialettofona*, in the original).

43. It is likely that Gramsci's father never achieved real fluency in the local variety of Sardinian spoken in Ghilarza, where he spent most of his life. A person from this town, who knew Francesco Gramsci, told Fiori that '*[t]owards the end*, he even spoke our dialect *in his own fashion*' (Fiori 1970, p. 9. My emphasis).

44. See the following passage, from one of the letters written to Gramsci by his mother: 'You remember our proverb *chie fae su gustu suu ura chent'annos de prusu cando no es de menu*... ["he who does as he likes lasts more than a hundred years, if not less..."]' (in Gramsci 2010, p. 120).

45. See Paulesu Quercioli 1977, pp. 13–15. According to Alastair Davidson, Peppina Marcias came from a family who spoke 'the Campidanese dialect as well as Italian' (Davidson 1977, p. 20).

46. Paulesu Quercioli 1991, p. 117. Mimma Paulesu Quercioli is the daughter of Gramsci's sister, Teresina. A phrase – *Nde cheria chentu domus e prus* ['I would like a

his younger brother Carlo used the Sardinian language while they were playing together. It probably began to be used even more frequently, within Gramsci's family, after 1898 – the year Francesco was arrested. Antonio was seven. As his father remained in prison until 1904, Antonio lost

> the paternal figure in a significant phase of his psychological development, while the maternal model inevitably became an increasingly important point of reference, and an example to him... But another strong bond – the bond of 'Sardinianness' – had existed between Gramsci and his mother since childhood. Peppina had always spoken to her children in Sardinian... For this reason, his relationship with his mother was also a relationship with Sardinia and became a fundamental part of his personality.[47]

In the town of Ghilarza, where Antonio went to school, knowing Italian gave him a great advantage over his classmates, as he later narrated in a letter from prison:

> almost all of my schoolmates spoke Italian very badly and with great difficulty and this put me in a position of superiority, because the teacher was expected to take into account the average pupil, and knowing how to speak Italian fluently was already a circumstance that made many things easier (the school was in a rural village and the great majority of the pupils were of peasant origin).[48]

The Sardinian dialect was also used for socialising outside school; as one of Gramsci's childhood friends was later to recall in an interview, 'small groups of us would gather under his window and call up at him from the street: *O Antò, o Antò su gobeddu* ["Hey Antonio, hey Antonio the little hunchback"] *andamus a papanzolu*: and so we would head for the graveyard where fresh and tasty grass grew, which we would eat raw'.[49]

Therefore, Gramsci and his siblings must have grown up in an environment which can be considered bilingual. This interpretation allows for a reconciliation of the positions that have been expressed by two of Gramsci's biographers: Scalambrino, who believes that Gramsci regularly spoke 'the Italian

---

hundred houses of that, even more'] – which was often used by Gramsci's brother, Carlo, to express how much he had liked a meal, became part of the 'Gramsci family's lexicon' (Paulesu Quercioli 2003, p. 71; cf. Gramsci 1996a, p. 48). Note the preservation of [k] (spelt *ch*) in *chentu*, typical of Logudorese (cf. note 138 in this chapter).

47. Paulesu Quercioli 1999, p. 273.
48. Gramsci 1994a, II, p. 356.
49. Quoted in Cutrì 1949. See Longiave 1910, p. 27, for ethnographic and linguistic information on Sardinian children eating *papanzolu* ('tarassacum officinale', according to this contemporary lexicographer).

language, and not dialect',[50] at least with his family; and Davidson, who instead claims that, during his years in Ghilarza, Antonio, 'like the rest of the village,... spoke dialect', and that he continued to do so with Sardinians in Turin.[51] As further confirmation of this situation of (broadly defined) bilingualism, we can cite an episode that Peppino Mameli, from Ghilarza, narrated to Giuseppe Fiori. In the summer of 1912, Gramsci was short of money and agreed to give Mameli private lessons in Greek and Latin. The local dialect appeared to Gramsci, at least in practical terms, to be a communicative tool of sufficient quality for teaching Mameli classical languages: Gramsci 'would put the questions to me – always in dialect – and then comment on my answers',[52] said Mameli to Fiori.

Finally, between 1908 and 1911, Gramsci studied at an upper secondary school, a *liceo*, in Cagliari. One of his teachers was Raffa Garzia, whom I shall mention again in this and the following chapters. According to various scholars, the young Gramsci's command of the Italian language was somewhat unsound.[53] During the years in Cagliari, however, his cultural and political outlook broadened, and the first instances of a politically motivated use of both the national and the local language began to appear:

> Raffa Garzia had realised that the young man from Ghilarza was knowledgeable and talented, despite the fact that his Italian was still poor (letters from that period confirm this). Through studying, he would be able to overcome 'village-like mentality', and to escape the dialect linguistic background that, incidentally, Garzia himself was familiar with. He would be able to broaden his outlook and open himself up to new ideas. A letter of recommendation from his teacher secured him the role as correspondent from Aidomaggiore for *L'Unione Sarda* ['The Sardinian Union']... though in fact he only wrote one article for this newspaper.
>
> Antonio preferred to continue his training as a political journalist in a club promoting 'free thought', of which he had been one of the founders and which was named after Giordano Bruno. He would meet up with dock workers, fishermen, local artisans, with *is piccioccus de crobi*, and with the 'sorrowful and angry Cagliari' described every day by the radical (republican and socialist)

---

50. Scalambrino 1998, p. 16.
51. Davidson 1977, pp. 33, 49. Other commentators have more radical and incompatible views. According to Sberlati, since Gramsci 'was Sardinian, his mother tongue and native language had, of course, to be foreign to Italian' (Sberlati 1998, p. 348). As noted at the beginning of this chapter, Blasco Ferrer 1999 takes a completely different position.
52. Fiori 1970, p. 80.
53. On this point, see the comments by the linguist Luigi Matt (Matt 2008), and by the biographers Giuseppe Fiori (in Gramsci 1994b, pp. 3–4) and Francesco Scalambrino (Scalambrino 1998, p. 20).

newspaper *Il Paese* ['The Country']. His main task consisted of reading this newspaper to illiterate workers, spurring them on to discussions in dialect, since, unfortunately, they did not know the national language.[54]

1.4. Turin

Gramsci moved to Turin in 1911. As we have seen, since his birth he had lived in a cultural context where Sardinian language varieties coexisted with the literary language, the latter being in the process of slowly becoming a fully-fledged national language. Once in Turin, his experience of language plurality grew in intensity. The slowness of the process by which the national language was being formed was particularly evident in a modern, industrial city like Turin. It is easy to imagine the communicative difficulties and sense of cultural displacement which Gramsci experienced when he first arrived in Turin, terrified as he must have been 'not just by traffic and trams and noise, but by the realisation that he did not understand a single word the natives were saying'.[55] The Piedmontese dialects, so different from both the Sardinian dialects and the national Italian language, with which Gramsci was already familiar, would now become part of his everyday linguistic experiences – at least in terms of passive exposure to them. New elements were entering Gramsci's life, which would gradually contribute to shaping his intellectual profile and his views on diversity and multiplicity.

Practical experiences concerning linguistic multiplicity went hand-in-hand with a dedicated analysis and theoretical study of this form of multiplicity at Turin University. And, on the verge of the First World War, he also began to write theatre reviews as well as his first political articles. He soon realised that 'a dialect is always the most typical language for the majority' of the population,[56] and that declamation 'becomes considerably less rhetorical if delivered in dialect'.[57] On the contrary, 'the literary language needs an internal translation that dampens the spontaneity of imaginative reactions and the freshness of understanding'.[58] In an article written in 1917, entitled 'Analfabetismo' ['Illiteracy'], Gramsci explained that, for a community whose cultural exchanges are geographically limited and whose worldview is backward and parochial, local

---

54. Podda 1977, p. 107. This description of Gramsci's activity is based on testimonies by Renato Figari, one of Gramsci's schoolmates in Cagliari (cf. Podda 1999). The *piccioccus de crobi* were children from poor families who helped ladies from higher social backgrounds by carrying their food and shopping. Finally, the Italian *paese* can also mean 'town'.

55. Nicholson 2000, p. 65.

56. Gramsci 1980, p. 805.

57. Gramsci 1980, p. 820.

58. Gramsci 1980, p. 805.

dialects are a perfectly adequate means of communication – this communication being almost entirely oral. The spread of literacy, and of a language of wider circulation, was a desirable goal, which socialist cultural activities and political communication were helping to achieve. On the one hand, however, this goal could only be achieved if there was a general cultural and economic growth of the entire nation, while political militancy and specific cultural interventions could only facilitate and speed up the accomplishment.[59] On the other hand, as suggested by a passage from an article of August 1918, the limits of dialectophony should not be viewed as absolute constraints, as if there existed a mechanical and inescapable link between languages and worldviews: to those who polemically suggested that Turin, a modern city with 'European-level production', should not have a proletariat 'that thinks in dialect',[60] Gramsci replied that, 'in Turin, heroism and beauty' consist of 'persistent, unremitting work', independent 'thinking, even when thinking in dialect, and strong will'.[61]

In another article of 1917, 'Il socialismo e l'Italia' ['Socialism and Italy'], Gramsci discussed a topic which appears in most of his reflections on Italian history. The political movements that unified Italy during the nineteenth century created a national state without involving the population at large, and without gaining its consent and active support. No collective social or cultural progress was promoted. As a result, the rural masses, especially those of southern Italy, perceived the unified state as an extraneous, authoritarian imposition.

> Fifty years ago there was no such thing as an 'Italian people' – it was just a rhetorical expression. There was no social unity in Italy then; there was only geographical unity. There were just millions of individuals scattered throughout Italian territory, each leading his own life, each rooted in his own soil, knowing nothing of Italy, speaking only his own dialect, and believing the whole world to be circumscribed by his parish boundary. He knew the tax collector, he knew the policeman, he knew the magistrate, the Court of Assizes; and that, for him, was Italy. Yet this individual, many of these millions of individuals, have progressed beyond this parochial stage in their development. They have formed a social unity. They have discovered themselves to be citizens, sharing a life which goes beyond their local horizon and stretches across ever vaster tracts of the world, across the entire world. They have come to feel

---

59. See Gramsci 1982, pp. 17–18.
60. Gramsci 1984, p. 255.
61. Gramsci 1984, pp. 256–8. In this article, Gramsci disputes the views of Paolo Orano, as expressed by the latter in 'Le nostre città e la Guerra' ['Our Cities and the War'], published in *Il Resto del Carlino* on 13 August 1918. Orano was a Socialist politician until 1906. Later, he joined the Sardinian Action Party, and then became a Fascist in 1922. He was strongly influenced by positivist sociology. As a Fascist, he was an eager supporter of anti-Semitism.

solidarity with other men; they have learned how to judge other men; they have learned to speak Italian, as well as their own dialect [*oltre il dialetto*]. All because a new social organism has come into being in Italy; an organism created by these men themselves, which they feel themselves to be part of, and which has given them access to the life of the world, to the history of the world.[62]

I shall mention the Italian word *oltre* [literally 'beyond'] again towards the end of this chapter. This word points to the shortcomings of knowing only a dialect; yet, unlike words meaning 'in substitution for' or 'instead of', *oltre* leaves the door open to the idea that the spread of a national language will not necessarily imply the disappearance of other linguistic codes and sub-standard varieties – that is, that a national language can be added to the already existing knowledge and use of dialects.

Not long after writing 'Il socialismo e l'Italia', Gramsci gave up his university studies. Through these studies, he had become acquainted with the debates on the 'language question' that had taken place in the second half of the nineteenth century, when Graziadio Isaia Ascoli had opposed the followers of Alessandro Manzoni. Therefore, both personal and academic inputs led Gramsci to pay careful attention to the complex issue of linguistic unification. Indeed, especially in 1919, the political vicissitudes of Turin's subaltern classes also led him to experience the dramatic level of tension that cultural and linguistic differences can reach in situations of exasperated socio-political conflict.

An insurrection had broken out in Turin in August 1917. In the working-class areas of the city, the struggle against the War, and the working conditions that the militarisation of factories had brought about, lasted for five days.[63] Ultimately, the armed forces crushed this insurrection, taking advantage of two main weaknesses displayed by the insurgents: their lack of political leadership, with spontaneous protests remaining unguided and the insurrection continuing to be disorganised and ineffective; and the insurgents' inability to win the support of the soldiers who had been sent in to put down the revolt. In March 1921, Gramsci described the revolt of 1917 as follows:

---

62. Gramsci 1982, p. 350 (English translation in Gramsci 1994c, p. 28). The 'organism' that Gramsci mentions in this article is the Italian Socialist Party; but, as in other writings, he is also referring to working-class political and trade-union organisations in general. Elsewhere in this article, he clearly states that thanks to these organisations, 'a peasant farmer from Puglia and a worker from Biella have come to speak the same language' and express similar views on the same issues and events, despite their cultural and geographical distance.

63. The days in question were 22–25 August 1917. In the issue of 25 August 1925 (which the authorities confiscated), *Il Grido del Popolo* referred to them as *Le cinque giornate del proletariato torinese* ['The Five Days of the Turin Proletariat'] (see Carcano 1977, p. xi). Cf. Introduction: note 6.

For five days the workers fought in the streets of the city. With rifles, grenades and machine-guns at their disposal, the insurgents even managed to occupy several quarters of the city and to make three or four attempts to gain control of the centre, where the government institutions and military command posts were situated. . . . In vain they counted on support from the soldiers – but these latter had allowed themselves to be taken in by insinuations that the revolt had been staged by the Germans.[64]

Some of those who witnessed these events would later mention a few, partial exceptions to the general lack of solidarity between the troops and the rebellious population.[65] The *Alpini* would seem to have been the only troops who sided with the insurgents, or at least refused to open fire on them. This attitude, which may, in some cases, even have resulted in the soldiers handing their rifles over to the population, has been explained on the basis of the common language background (Piedmontese or, more broadly, Gallo-Italian) that the *Alpini* and the working-class population shared. Normally, most of these alpine troops would be 'recruited from the local area, and therefore would speak the local dialects'.[66]

Others have also mentioned the presence of the Sardinian Sassari Brigade amongst the military forces who were sent in to crush the insurrection, and who were totally indifferent to the insurgents' call for solidarity.[67] The reliability of these recollections might be debatable. For instance, although Gramsci himself would later recall that the Sassari Brigade took part in the repression of the uprising of August 1917,[68] Fiori believes that 'this was not so'.[69] Historians have verified the presence of 'alpine troops, alongside *carabinieri* and police guards',[70] and, given the difficult circumstances, also 'engineering officer cadets stationed in Turin'.[71] Documents of the time, however, would seem to confirm the presence of the Sassari Brigade.[72] In any case, during the uprising of 1917

---

64. Gramsci 1987, p. 604 (English translation in Gramsci 1977, pp. 310–20).
65. See Noce 1975, p. 26, and the testimonies published in Bermani 2007, p. 287. A detailed reconstruction of the events, and an interpretation of what happened, have been provided by the historian Paolo Spriano (see Spriano 1960).
66. Nicholson 2000, p. 66. Cf. Monticone 1958, p. 85. On the geographical provenance of the *Alpini*, see Scolè 2007.
67. See Carsano 1952, and the testimony of Gino Castagno, in Bermani 2007, p. 284. The American political historian John Cammett used these testimonies in his study of the origins of Italian communism (Cammett 1967, pp. 79–81).
68. See Gramsci 1971a, p. 143.
69. Fiori 1970, p. 110 note 2.
70. Monticone 1958, p. 79.
71. Ibid.
72. See the letter that the editor of the Turinese newspaper *La Stampa*, Alfredo Frassati, wrote to Giovanni Giolitti on 26 August 1917: 'the worst has been avoided thanks to a brigade of Sardinians (the Sassari Brigade)' (in Frassati 1979, I, p. 219).

Gramsci neither had an important position, nor immediate responsibilities. He was perhaps involved (unless we interpret some of his references to these events inaccurately) in implementing, or observing the effects of, the fraternisation tactics between rebels and armed troops, which had proved to be very successful during the February Revolution in Russia. Undoubtedly, groups of politically advanced workers, and large strata of workers and ordinary people, considered that revolution as a model to be replicated in Turin at the time.[73]

However, Gramsci played a much more significant and active role in 1919. In doing so, as we shall see, he drew on the example of the Russian Revolution as well as on his own experiences and reflections regarding the history, culture, and language of Sardinia.

1.5. The Sassari Brigade in Turin, April–July 1919

1.5.1. The arrival of the Brigade

In April 1919, the Sassari Brigade[74] was 'sent on garrison duty to Turin'. The local authorities feared that the Socialists might be organising demonstrations aimed at disturbing 'the celebrations for the brave Sassari Brigade officers'.[75] In fact, no major protest demonstrations took place. A parade was held along the River Po on the morning of 13 April 1919, during which the *Sassarini* were reviewed by the military authorities. Jubilant members of the higher social classes gathered in the streets of the city centre to welcome the soldiers. Gramsci wrote an article for the Piedmontese edition of the Socialist newspaper *Avanti!* but, the following day, the article that should have appeared in the newspaper had, in fact, been entirely censored, a blank space appearing in its place.[76] Evidently, the activities of the Socialists were, for the moment, easily held in check by the authorities.

Only seventy years later was the text of Gramsci's censored article discovered and published for the first time.[77] Some passages bear great relevance to my discussion. It is evident in these passages that attempts were made from the very beginning to overcome cultural divides, and to familiarise both the soldiers

---

73. Romano 1965, p. 223.
74. The Brigade consisted largely of Sardinian shepherds and peasants, with 'only a small number of mine-workers from the Iglesias field' (Gramsci 1971a, p. 144).
75. The last two quotations are taken from the telegraphed message which the Prefect of Turin sent to the Minister of the Interior on 14 April 1919, now held in the Archivio Centrale dello Stato (Rome) (henceforth, ACS), Ministero dell'Interno, Direzione generale Pubblica Sicurezza (henceforth, DgPS), Divisione affari generali e riservati, 1919, b. 76.
76. See Fiori 1991, especially p. 182.
77. See Caprioglio 1982.

with the demands of the Turinese proletariat and the Turinese proletariat with the harsh conditions of life in much of Sardinia. There was no time to waste, as demonstrations and a great strike were being organised for 20 and 21 July 1919, in support of the newly-born Soviet republics in Russia and Hungary. The strike was also called to demand 'demobilisation and a general amnesty'.[78]

The censored article included references to a popular Sardinian anthem against feudal lords, which celebrates the 1796 uprising led by Giovanni Maria Angioy (1751–1808). These references constitute a politically oriented use of the historical, linguistic and cultural knowledge that Gramsci had acquired at school, when studying with Raffa Garzia.[79] The article also contains an interesting comment, regarding the word *comune*, which links vocabulary to politics:

> Turinese gentlemen, the bourgeoisie of Turin, who have always considered Sardinia a colony of exploitation ... this whole swarm of parasites who sucked the generous blood of Sardinians, together with the descendants of those Piedmontese barons against whose vexations and ferocity the revolutionary songs of Giomaria Angioy are still sung today by shepherds and peasants – all of this riff-raff, elegant and well fed, now celebrate the peasants, shepherds and artisans of the Sassari Brigade. ... We believe, however, that the bourgeois and the aristocrats are greatly mistaken about the feelings of the Sardinian peasants and shepherds. Sardinian proletarians have searing recollections of misgovernment, and of the abuses committed by the state. ... The word *comune* is one of the most widely used in the Sardinan dialect; amongst Sardinian peasants and shepherds a religious aspiration for the *comune* exists, for the fraternal cooperation of all of the men who work and suffer, to get rid of the parasites, the fat cats who steal the bread of the poor man and force his little son to go out to work for a mere crust.[80]

During the next few days, Gramsci writes two other articles on Sardinia for the Piedmontese edition of the newspaper *Avanti!* They did appear in this newspaper, but only in an incomplete form, due to the intervention of the censor. The second of these two articles, published on 22 April 1919, has an ironic title – 'Il sardo lingua nazionale?' ['Sardinian as a National Language?'] – and deals directly with linguistic and cultural issues. It reports that 'General Sanna ... delivered a speech in Sardinian', during the welcoming ceremony for the 'soldiers and officers of

---

78. Fiori 1991, p. 182.
79. The *inno angioyano* (cf. Leydi 1963, pp. 31–55) was the subject of an essay by Raffa Garzia, published in 1897 (see Romagnino 2005, pp. 150–1). For a modern edition of this anti-feudal anthem, see Mannu 2002; and for an early English translation, Tyndale 1849, III, pp. 281–92.
80. Gramsci 1984, pp. 590–4. It is worth noting that in this article, Gramsci indicates the Sardinian language by using the term 'dialect', not 'language'.

the Sassari Brigade and the 22nd Cavalry regiment',[81] which had taken place the day before. General Carlo Sanna was very popular amongst the Sardinian soldiers, and his attitude towards the Turinese proletariat was particularly hostile. Gramsci would recall this hostile attitude years later, in February 1924, in a letter to the newly-founded newspaper *L'Unità* ['Unity']. The letter was published under a pseudonym and was convincingly attributed to Gramsci only sixty years later. The following passage is particularly relevant, here:

> Many soldiers from the Sassari Brigade probably remember the stance General Sanna took in Turin in 1919, and the acts of enraged propaganda that he carried out against the workers. Many will undoubtedly remember one of his speeches in which he said that if a Sardinian soldier had been hurt then the whole city would have been put to fire and sword, and that even five-year-old children would have suffered as a result.[82]

In his article of 22 April 1919, Gramsci did not discuss the contents of the speech that Sanna had delivered the previous day. He simply emphasised the insulting ambiguity of the patronising way in which the troops had been treated. In so doing, Gramsci avoided both ridiculing and exalting the use of Sardinian, and focused on what soldiers from different regions had in common, rather than on what divided them. He refrained from grounding his remarks in the divisive factors, though he could easily have picked many with which to support his polemical attack on the military authorities:

> Was it the General's duty to make himself understood by everyone? It was enough that his soldiers could understand him, so that his speech would not be useless! Everyone speaks as he is able. Besides, it is easier to make oneself understood when using one's own jargon. This is not the reason why the cavalry ought to complain. They should rather feel displeased with the gifts which are given to soldiers on similar occasions. They should feel offended that the gratitude shown to them, by the country for which they have fought, should consist of postcards, cigars and Easter eggs.[83]

Two more articles by Gramsci about the Sassari Brigade appeared on 13 and 16 July. The first is explicitly addressed 'to the Sardinian proletarian comrades'.[84] Here, Gramsci inserts Sardinian words, as well as a number of references to Sardinian regional culture. The article also includes the slogan – which had been proposed by two soldiers, defined in the article as 'two Bolsheviks from

---

81. Gramsci 1984, p. 611.
82. G. Marcias [A. Gramsci], 'I sardi e il blocco proletario' ['Sardinians and the Proletarian Bloc'], *L'Unità*, 26 February 1924. Reproduced in Caprioglio 1987.
83. Gramsci 1984, p. 611.
84. Gramsci 1987, p. 136.

the Sassari Brigade'[85] – of the forthcoming socialist revolution in Sardinia. The slogan is in Sardinian, and contains the word *comune*, which Gramsci had used and discussed in his article of 14 April: 'Viva *sa comune sarda, de sos massaios, de sos minadores, de sos pastores, de sos omines de traballu*' ['Long live the Sardinian commune of peasants, miners, shepherds and working men!'].[86]

1.5.2. *The editorial board of* L'Ordine Nuovo

Obviously, in 1919 Gramsci's journalistic activities did not only consist of articles on the presence of the Sassari Brigade in Turin. His political commitment and theoretical research were extremely intense. The first issue of *L'Ordine Nuovo* was published on 1 May 1919. Remarkably, while his practical activity was mostly devoted to conciliating different collective identities, Gramsci wrote some of his first articles for the new weekly publication on the topic of how cultural diversity would be handled in a communist society. He wrote articles about the Sardinian soldiers and, as we shall see, he also communicated with these soldiers both in person and with the aid of leaflets. At the same time, he recurrently discussed possible ways in which the new communist society would organise the state so as to favour a spontaneous process of national and international unification. He envisaged this process as based neither on coercion, nor on any other authoritarian form of imposed unification, but rather on free cultural development. He repeatedly pointed in the direction of new forms of state power: a future 'councils-state', with local and regional organisations. These organisations would function within the new communist society, where the solution of public problems – Gramsci explained on 7 June 1919 – would be sought 'gradually in factories, villages, urban, regional and national Councils, and within the framework of the International'.[87]

On 14 June, *L'Ordine Nuovo* published 'Il Comunismo e la Valle d'Aosta' ['Communism and the Valle d'Aosta'], an article signed by an anonymous 'Valdostan communist'. The article contains the following, particularly interesting passages (emphasis in the original):

> The communist state will create the greatest local autonomy organised in a unitary system of cooperation and social centralisation. The Valle d'Aosta, which is neither French nor Italian but *above all Valdostan*, has to fight to make Italian nationalists recognise her sacred right to speak and study the language of her ancestors, and to use this language when dealing with public affairs.

---

85. Gramsci 1987, p. 137.
86. Ibid.
87. Gramsci 1987, pp. 55–6.

The people of Valle d'Aosta always have to struggle; they have to search historical accounts to confirm the origin of French in the Valley. They have to present petitions and accept several vague promises in return. All of these practices will automatically become unnecessary within the Council system. The Valle d'Aosta will have a regional Council, will speak her own language, and no one will ever dream of Italianising it.

The editorial staff of *L'Ordine Nuovo* did not introduce the article with a critical note; nor did they publish a comment distancing themselves from some of the arguments of the anonymous author, as was often the case with other texts, published during this period, with which Gramsci and his collaborators partly or totally disagreed. The approach taken by *L'Ordine Nuovo*, with the publication of this article, was one marked by political timeliness and broadmindedness.

The advent of a political revolution seemed almost inevitable in that period. As the Socialist Party was dramatically expanding its influence in Valle d'Aosta, the potential support of peasants and ex-servicemen, as well as the incorporation of regional autonomist demands into the Socialists' agenda, were seen as key factors to ensure the accomplishment of revolutionary outcomes.[88] Endorsing the demands for linguistic rights was a step in the direction of creating organic links between autonomist and Socialist policies. At the same time, however, the publication of 'Il Comunismo e la Valle d'Aosta' showed considerable ideological openness, in that the endorsement of linguistic rights prevailed over other political concerns. In Valle d'Aosta, the defence of the French language had traditionally been advocated by the Catholic Church and by conservative forces. These conservative political connotations did not prevent Gramsci and his group from taking a broadminded position on language policy.

Thus, the seemingly progressive option represented by a tacit imposition of Italian was openly refused in the article. Evidently, the editorial board of *L'Ordine Nuovo* was not content with fatalistic expectations as to the emergence of a revolutionary proletarian consciousness, as if the unity of subaltern groups were the inevitable outcome of socio-economic modernisation. Rather, the cultural and political aggregation of subaltern social groups (especially the workers of Piedmont and Valle d'Aosta, who were potentially in conflict with each other)[89] was expected to come about through a painstaking process based on recognition of differences.[90]

---

88. See Soave 1995, pp. 686–9.
89. See Omezzoli 1995, p. 175ff.
90. The only weakness that today's reader may find in this article, if he or she favours the preservation of minority languages, is that the author of 'Il Comunismo e la Valle d'Aosta' does not mention the Franco-Provençal patois.

The pragmatic and open-minded attitude in this article does not signify, however, an exaltation of the cultural and linguistic identity of Valle d'Aosta; nor does it entail the praise of any regional identity as such. It is interesting to note that, only a few months after the publication of 'Il Comunismo e la Valle d'Aosta', an unsigned article, 'L'unità nazionale' ['National Unity'], attributed to Gramsci,[91] warned the readers of *L'Ordine Nuovo* about the real motives of property-owning groups supporting secessionist efforts. Gramsci wrote, here, that in the socio-political turmoil of post-war Italy, these propertied groups might try to gain economic advantages by avoiding central government taxation. To do so, they would probably also claim that 'the peoples of Sardinia, Sicily, Valle d'Aosta, Friuli etc. are not Italian, and have long aspired to independence';[92] and that their 'forced Italianisation' by the central government, including 'the compulsory teaching of the Italian language, has failed'.[93] Such arguments are mockingly, but still resolutely, rejected in the article.

We shall see that this balance between contrasting demands is often addressed in Gramsci's writings: progress and unification, on the one hand, and cultural diversity as a heritage deserving attentive consideration, on the other. In this respect, both 'L'unità nazionale' and 'Il Comunismo e la Valle d'Aosta' can be held to represent Gramsci's general position. In the following sections and in Chapter Three, I shall again draw links between Gramsci's positions and those expressed in anonymous or other authors' articles. By taking this approach, I do not mean to suggest that these texts express Gramsci's personal ideas, or that they are therefore equivalent to his own writings. Simply, I believe these texts to be useful for an understanding of Gramsci's position on the basis of two widely recognised factors: the collective nature of most of the editorial work at *L'Ordine Nuovo*; and the influence that Gramsci had on the members of the editorial board, on the groups and individuals that gravitated around *L'Ordine Nuovo* and, more generally, on the cultural and political milieu that was expressed by this periodical.

Three different series of issues were published: *L'Ordine Nuovo* was at first a weekly publication, with Gramsci as *segretario di redazione* [secretary of the editorial board], from May 1919 to the end of 1920; then a daily paper, with Gramsci as *direttore* [editor in chief], from the beginning of 1921 until 1922; and finally a fortnightly publication, from March 1924 to April 1925 (with several interruptions during this last period). Within Gramscian studies, special attention has been

---

91. This article has been attributed to Gramsci by the editors of his pre-prison writings, on the basis of the testimonies of Felice Platone, Angelo Tasca and Palmiro Togliatti.
92. Gramsci 1987, p. 232.
93. Ibid.

paid to the weekly *Ordine Nuovo*,[94] which most scholars see as the series with the richest cultural contents and broadest theoretical scope. As we have seen, during the publication of the first series, Gramsci was nominally the secretary of the editorial board; however, 'as unanimously recognised, he was much more', in that he functioned as 'the authentic moving spirit' of an enterprise that granted Turin 'an international outlook, quite similar to the outlook of those debates that groups of young Marxists were holding in various contexts and locations on both sides of the Atlantic'.[95] As for the daily *Ordine Nuovo*, Gramsci's highly influential role is confirmed by various testimonies and accounts.[96] Later, Gramsci again had a central role during the publication of the fortnightly series.[97]

In September 1919, Gramsci himself wrote that the articles published by *L'Ordine Nuovo* were born of the 'spiritual partnership and intimate collaboration of three, four, five comrades, of whom Gramsci is one, Angelo Tasca another, Palmiro Togliatti a third.[98] In 1920, he described the creation of *L'Ordine Nuovo* as a collective enterprise: 'in the month of April 1919, three or four or five of us...decided to begin publishing this review, *L'Ordine Nuovo*'.[99] The same collective approach, based on discussions within the editorial board and outside this board, continued during the months following the first issues of this periodical:

> its articles were not cold, intellectual structures, but sprang from our discussions with the best workers; they elaborated the actual sentiments, goals and passions of the Turin working class, that we ourselves had provoked and tested.... [I]ts articles were virtually a 'taking note' of actual events, seen as moments of a process of inner liberation and self-expression on the part of the working class.[100]

1.5.3. *The successful campaign among Sardinian soldiers*

Early in 1919, the Socialists of Turin, including the *Ordine Nuovo* group, conducted an intense campaign to spread their ideas among the troops. Gramsci participated in this campaign, and was in the frontline especially in the attempts to approach and win over the soldiers of the Sassari Brigade. This year was particularly intense with respect to the efforts made by Socialists and anarchists to propagate their views among soldiers, with the aim of promoting solidarity

---

94. See, in particular, Spriano 1963.
95. D'Orsi 2004, p. 68.
96. See, for example, Leonetti 1970, and Giardina 1965.
97. See Somai 1979, pp. 132–43. On the second series, see also Salvetti 1975, pp. 109–48; on the third, Leonetti 1970, pp. 85–104, and Salvetti 1975, pp. 293–302.
98. Gramsci 1987, p. 196.
99. Gramsci 1987, p. 619.
100. Gramsci 1987, p. 622 (English translation in Gramsci 1977, pp. 291–4).

between the proletariat and the troops. Discontent was growing among these soldiers in this period, as a result of their postponed demobilisation. Yet the attempts which working-class political movements made to raise support among the military were partly defensive in character. They hoped to confute the rumours surreptitiously circulated by the upper ranks of the military, according to which the postponed demobilisation should be blamed on the workers' political unrest, and on their agitations, which continuously posed a threat to law and order. Turin was one of the cities where the working-class movement was most active in trying to improve the relations between the impatient soldiers and the protesting population. Leaflets and small posters were printed and distributed to remind the soldiers of the interests that they had in common with the workers. Most of the slogans printed on the leaflets stressed the common social origins of soldiers and workers, in that they all fundamentally belonged to the same social class.

Useful information on this campaign can be found in archival documents.[101] These documents confirm that the sense of belonging to the same region was also an element used to promote solidarity between the soldiers and the Socialist militants who came from Sardinia but lived in Turin.[102] This use of regional identity was instrumental to the following ends: encouraging as many soldiers as possible to share the revolutionary enthusiasm of the working classes; and propagating modern political views based on the belief that social progress would be the result of class conflict. Regional identity was not presented as a form of identity to be admired or preserved. We shall see that many of those who collaborated with Gramsci later recalled that the Sardinian language was used during this campaign. Yet this use of Sardinian was also functional in the attempt to bring the soldiers onto the side of the popular masses, while it did not entail praise of linguistic otherness as a value in itself.

This campaign consisted of a series of actions, involving both direct oral communication and the distribution of leaflets. According to various testimonies, Gramsci was always 'eager to welcome someone from his same region,

---

101. ACS, Ministero dell'Interno, DgPS, Divisione affari generali e riservati, 1919, b. 78. See also Sechi 1967, and 1969, p. 24ff.

102. On 28 May 1919, the Prefect of Turin wrote: 'within subversive groups, it had been agreed to approach those soldiers of the above-mentioned Brigade who were considered the most reliable, with the aim of persuading them to carry out acts of subversive propaganda amongst their fellow soldiers. This was aimed at bringing the soldiers closer to Socialist circles, and putting them in contact with the Socialists through Sardinian subversives. The latter were expected to turn to regional sentiments in order to overcome the opposition of the soldiers more easily' (ACS, Ministero dell'Interno, DgPS, Divisione affari generali e riservati, 1919, b. 78). See also the testimonies collected by Cutrì 1949.

with whom he would gladly speak in dialect',[103] was passionately engaged in the campaign, and played a crucial role in most of the actions. Since the arrival of the soldiers the situation had been critical. On 16 July, Gramsci wrote that 'the Sardinians mistakenly placed all of Turin's citizens in the same class – "the gentlemen" '.[104] Despite this, he succeeded in using 'the fact that he was Sardinian, and that he could master their dialect, to set about convincing them'.[105] The Socialist militant, and later Communist leader, Mario Montagnana left this description of Gramsci's activity:

> Any excuse was good for a drink with one or two of these soldiers, and we would kindly pay for it in a nearby *osteria*. Likewise, we would walk a few miles with them; we would strike up conversation with them, talking about their region, about Turin, about how they lived and what the demands of the workers were. We would also let some brief, straightforward and persuasive flyers slip into their hands. These had been written especially for them by Antonio Gramsci himself, not in Italian, but in the dialect of their own island.[106]

Another militant provided an account of Gramsci's work, mentioning the use of small posters and adding information on the oral use of Sardinian:

> The Sassari Brigade barracks were constantly flooded with small posters and leaflets...In addition to this large amount of general propaganda material written almost entirely by Gramsci, the work of our ward clubs was even wider and further-reaching (and was, of course, also organised and co-ordinated by Gramsci)...I was lucky enough to be able to take part in many of the meetings that Gramsci held in a whole range of places: in the ward clubs, at the trade-union and newspaper headquarters, at his flat and even in a small café owned by a very kind Sardinian comrade...In these meetings Gramsci, almost always speaking in Sardinian dialect, would explain to the soldiers of the Sassari Brigade that the Turin workers did not look down on them, and did not despise them at all.[107]

---

103. Viglongo 1967, p. 34. Viglongo's direct testimony is consistent with what Mario Berlinguer (a Sardinian lawyer, elected to the national parliament in 1924) would later write about Gramsci's years in Rome: 'Gramsci had remained very typically Sardinian, just as our other antifascists who lived far away [from Sardinia], such as Lussu, Fancello and Schirru. Without taking these origins into account, it is impossible to examine fully their thoughts and actions'. Gramsci would smile 'if he heard even just one word in Sardinian dialect, or if one of his childhood friends called him *Tonino*' (Berlinguer 1967).
104. Gramsci 1987, p. 140.
105. Scalambrino 1998, p. 84.
106. Montagnana 1949, p. 137.
107. Carsano 1952.

As recounted to Scalambrino by Albina Lussu, a young worker in 1919, Gramsci set out to meet up with soldiers from the Sassari Brigade

> every night to try and convince them not to open fire, and to explain to them what was happening in Turin, because, firstly, seventy to eighty percent of them were illiterate and so didn't know how to read, and, secondly, he spoke *sardagnolo* [non-standard form for 'Sardinian'] and they understood him very well.[108]

The Sassari Brigade was finally withdrawn from Turin, just before the strike that took place in support of the Soviet republics of Russia and Hungary. Gramsci announced their departure in an article 'I nostri fratelli sardi' ['Our Sardinian Brothers'],[109] published in the Piedmontese edition of *Avanti!* on 16 July. The efforts of the Turinese Socialists had been successful in spreading their views among the soldiers. With the aid of Gramsci's inter-cultural mediation and political translation, results were achieved which had initially seemed improbable.

The testimonies of Montagnana, Carsano, and Albina Lussu clearly indicate the role that Gramsci's linguistic 'Sardinianness' played in the events of April-July 1919. Indeed, Gramsci knew what the linguistic repertoire of the Sardinian soldiers was, despite the internal variation associated with the different local origins of the soldiers. In most situations, Sardinian was likely to be perceived as the language of solidarity, as well as the language that symbolically evoked the common destiny of all of those who could understand it and use it.

Gramsci did not indulge in an idealisation of Sardinian cultural and linguistic identity. Nor did he snobbishly condemn Sardinian as a language (or a group of language varieties) which an intellectual committed to the cause of social and political revolution should not use. As we have seen, he offered some brief accounts of the life and history of the subaltern classes in a geographically marginal region, as Sardinia was at the time. At the same time, this attention to the past and present culture of the Sardinian poor was accompanied by recognition of the vitality of their language, which Gramsci did not refrain from using. Yet he did not turn to the regional language as a symbol of identity with which boundaries might be erected, leading to the exclusion of those who do not share that particular identity. On the contrary, he emphasised the common demands of peasants in southern Italy and the working-class population of the North; and he used Sardinian words in a manner that was functional to the achievement of this inclusive goal.

In the context of a cultural encounter that risked turning into a cultural (and also physical) conflict, Gramsci performed a work of *translation*, not only in the

---

108. Quoted in Scalambrino 1998, p. 87.
109. Later reproduced in Gramsci 1987, pp. 139–41.

literal sense of the term, but also in the sense of cultural translation. He tried to introduce modern revolutionary concepts into the culture of the soldiers, so as to eradicate their parochialism and make their worldview more receptive to the advanced political aims of the northern working class. At the same time, however, he made sure that the aims of the working class were presented in such a way that they would seem in harmony with the culture of rural Sardinia, from where most of the soldiers came. In this respect, the emphasis he placed on the word *comune* is emblematic of the way in which Gramsci worked, in that he chose a word whose form, though slightly different in each local variety of Sardinian (such as *comunu*, *comuna*, and *cumona*), clearly resembled the form of its counterparts in most European languages.[110] He probably chose to use this word because it could easily fulfil three tasks. Firstly, it could be said to express a spontaneous demand for social renovation, which was widespread among Sardinian peasants and shepherds; that is, among the members of a traditional, rural society. As we have seen above, in April 1919 Gramsci wrote that 'amongst Sardinian peasants and shepherds a religious aspiration for the *comune* exists'.[111] This word, from the Latin *commūnis*, and its cognates in Romance languages have a long history, and, in Sardinia, words deriving from *commūnis* were part of the lexicon of the local pastoral society, and of its ancient customs, for centuries.[112]

Secondly, the word resonated with overtones of modern, urban revolutions, most notably the Paris Commune of 1871 (that is, the second Paris Commune, indeed the most important and most celebrated working-class uprising of the nineteenth century). The French term *commune*

> enshrined the most extreme tradition of the first French Revolution, the organization of the popular districts of Paris into a political body rivalling the authority of the central government. It had been the first Paris Commune that

---

110. On Soviet efforts to establish agricultural *kommuny* in the years of War Communism (1918–21) see Atkinson 1983, pp. 219–21: 'The first *kommuny* sprang up spontaneously. Official support was quick to follow, however, ... as a response to the peasants' own expression of interest in *kommuny*, an interest especially evident among the poor peasants. The very name of the new collectives, "resonant with the ultimate goal of the Bolshevik Party – the building of communism", was said to attract sympathy to them. ... Most of the first collectives for which data are available were formed on peasant allotment land, but it soon became more typical for them to arise on confiscated gentry land'. On the failure of these *kommuny*, and on Lenin's increasing disillusionment with them between April 1919 and March 1921, see Lih 2011, pp. 172–81.

111. Gramsci 1984, p. 592.

112. According to Max Leopold Wagner, the great Romance linguist who studied Sardinian in the first half of the twentieth century, the word *kumòne* (whose form is probably the result of vocalic metathesis) refers to the sharing of something, and especially to the collective ownership of flocks: see Wagner 1996, pp. 217, 242, 332; and also Wagner 1989, pp. 369, 429. Cf. Meyer-Lübke 1935, pp. 197–8; and the entries *comune* and *cumòne* in Spano 2004, pp. 190, 204.

had brought Robespierre to power, had given control of the ruling Committee of Public Safety to the Jacobins, and so had inaugurated the most radical phase of the great French Revolution.[113]

Thirdly, the word *comune* (which could also evoke memories of what the Italian *comuni* had been, and stood for, during the Middle Ages) referred to the ideas of local autonomy and self-government which Gramsci, as we have seen, repeatedly addressed in articles of this period.

These linguistic choices are not only relevant as confirmation of Gramsci's attention and sensitivity to language; they also add significant elements to his intellectual biography, and to our historical understanding of his cultural and political activities. Today, these elements can be better understood in the light of some of the interpretative categories that the study of language and culture has recently generated. This study has shown that acts of linguistic communication are also *acts of identity*.[114] As a result, 'historians are learning from the sociolinguists to study the occasions on which bilingual people switch from one language to another',[115] and are focusing especially on the cultural, symbolic value of code-switching. Gramsci's intention to retain a connection with his Sardinian roots emerges not only from the accounts of those who were with him at the time, but also from his writings. The presence of a few Sardinian words in his articles from 1919 did not have a merely referential value; it also had a symbolic value. As explained by a leading expert, Camilla Bettoni, loyalty and affiliation to a certain cultural-linguistic background can be conveyed by using even just a few words.[116] Inserting words from a minority language into one's own writings, even if these writings are in the language of the majority, still signals the intention to retain a connection with that language (especially if these words are used in texts that portray the culture to which the minority language belongs in largely positive terms).

Therefore, if linguistic variation, 'as a fundamental symbolic resource of communication',[117] is a core element of one's self-fashioning, then the 1919 episode of the Sassari Brigade contradicts those interpretations of Gramsci's life which have been grouped under the definition of *desardizzanti* [de-Sardinianising].[118]

---

113. Edwards 1973, p. 9.
114. See D'Agostino 2007, Kramsch 1998.
115. Burke 2008, p. 98.
116. See Bettoni 2008, p. 28. Cf. Bettoni 2010.
117. D'Agostino 2007, p. 135.
118. I take this definition from Selenu 2005, pp. 261–2. Within Italian Gramscian studies, the most radical exponent of this interpretative trend is probably Lepre 1998 (p. 11), who writes that Gramsci tried to 'erase his Sardinianness' and only retained, once he had left Sardinia, an emotional connection with his homeland, which sporadically gave him nostalgic feelings at times when his rational convictions wavered. Outside specialised research, the most significant example is provided by the American philosopher Michael

The events triggered by the presence of the Sassari Brigade in Turin, as well as Gramsci's reflections around these events, are incompatible with biographical accounts which unconvincingly describe him as a modernist intellectual and an internationalist politician seeking to remove all the traces of his rural Sardinian background.[119] Finally, these events and reflections also lead one to question, or at least to reconsider, the views of those authors who presented Gramsci as being essentially dismissive of traditional, local linguistic and cultural identities, on the basis of literal readings of some of his prison notes.[120]

1.6. From Turin to the prison years

Gramsci was arrested as a result of the strike called to show solidarity with the Soviet republics of Russia and Hungary. This time, he spent only a few days in a cell of the Carceri Nuove prison, in Turin. Montagnana, who was arrested with Gramsci, would later recount that Gramsci, after 'only thirty-six hours in his cell...had managed to conquer and fascinate a number of the warders – Sardinian like himself – by speaking to them in their own dialect, in that characteristic way of his, simple and popular, yet at the same time full of feelings and ideas and facts'.[121]

During the years of L'Ordine Nuovo's publication, it became necessary to establish a group of armed militants to guard the building in which Gramsci and the rest of the editorial staff worked. Fascist attacks became increasingly frequent in Turin, and the headquarters of L'Ordine Nuovo were finally torn down during one of these attacks, shortly after Gramsci had left for Russia. Vincenzo Bianco was one of the guard-militants. One day he heard a conversation between Gramsci and his brother Gennaro:

Walzer, when he writes that Gramsci 'hated Sardinian backwardness' and broke away radically 'with the "Sardinia" of common sense as he had done with the actual Sardinia where he was born and raised' (Walzer 1989, p. 95).

119. Piero Gobetti was the first to speak of Gramsci in these terms. In one of his writings, Gramsci is described as having 'come from the countryside to forget tradition, to get rid of the sick, anachronistic heritage of his island and replace it with a single-minded, inexorable drive towards modernity' (quoted in Fiori 1970, p. 93). In the case of later commentators, this unconvincing interpretation would seem to be based, yet again, on an overly selective, or overly generalising, reading of some of Gramsci's (implicitly or explicitly) autobiographical remarks – especially the one on the 'triple or quadruple provincial' (which I quoted at the beginning of this chapter). In fact, Gramsci's strongly-felt need to overcome cultural provincialism did not entail any outright disposal of Sardinian elements.

120. For example, Lo Piparo 1979, especially the third chapter; Savoia 2001; Lecercle 2004.

121. Quoted in Fiori 1970, pp. 121–2.

One evening, Gramsci and his brother, Gennaro, were standing at the entrance to the newspaper headquarters and were chatting to each other in Sardinian. At one point, the head officer of the local carabinieri went up to them and asked 'Aren't you Mr Gramsci?' and Gramsci replied 'Yes, I am'. 'Aren't you Sardinian?' 'Yes, I'm from Ghilarza'. And so they began to converse. I didn't know what they were saying because they were speaking in Sardinian and I couldn't understand anything.[122]

There were two Sardinians among the group of armed militants. Many years later, one of them, Peppino Frongia, from Teulada, near Cagliari, provided an interesting account of his conversations with Gramsci:

> I met Gramsci at a meeting of the *Ordine Nuovo* defence groups, of which I was a member.... After the meeting, we saw each other again and we spoke in dialect about various Sardinian things, as we would whenever we spent time together. At the *Ordine Nuovo* we would see each other every day, and often [Pietro] Ciuffo [another Sardinian, from Cagliari] and I would go out with Gramsci in the evening.
>
> Back then people would travel by tram, so we would spend a long time together and always had the chance to reminisce about Sardinia, and to have fun. Ciuffo kept us entertained with several jokes, but Gramsci's sense of humour was just as salacious as that of the comrade from Cagliari.[123]

Interviewed by the historian and anthropologist Cesare Bermani, Frongia subsequently specified: 'If we were talking about politics we would speak in Italian, whereas if we were talking about Sardinian things, we would speak in dialect'.[124] Thus, the selection of one or the other of the two available codes does not seem to have been free, but rather dependent on the content of the communication. Bermani also asked Battista Santhià, another member of the *Ordine Nuovo* group, whether or not Gramsci could speak Piedmontese. Santhià answered as follows: 'No, just a few phrases, also because he spoke Sardinian. Sardinians would tell me that he could still speak it well'.[125]

The journalistic and cultural activities that Gramsci organised in this period bear some significance to my discussion. First of all, the newly-founded *Istituto di Cultura Proletaria* [Institute of Proletarian Culture], based in Turin and designated as the Italian section of the Russian Proletkult, inspired by Alexander Bogdanov (1873–1928) and Anatoly Lunacharsky (1875–1933),[126] organised a number

---

122. In Paulesu Quercioli 1977, p. 33.
123. In Paulesu Quercioli 1977, pp. 60–1.
124. In Bermani 1987, p. 126.
125. In Bermani 1987, p. 115.
126. See also Chapter Two (especially section 2.5).

of events in the last months of 1921 and early 1922. As shown by Bermani, Gramsci played a pivotal role in the creation and development of this institute, so much so that the central committee of this Italian Proletkult began to meet far less frequently after May 1922, once Gramsci left for Russia.[127] The events that took place in this period prove that Gramsci continued to have a benevolent attitude towards dialects – an approach which had already been evident in his theatre reviews. Amongst the events organised was a conference on Piedmontese dialectal poetry, which was reported in *L'Ordine Nuovo* on 19 December 1921, and some musical evenings with a programme of 'Italian regional songs and foreign folk songs', which *L'Ordine Nuovo* announced on 11 May 1922.

There is evidence of Gramsci's interest in folk music and protest songs,[128] and so it is likely that the musical events of May 1922 received his approval, even though he left for Moscow in that period and could not participate directly. These events featured the 'singer, guitarist and lutist Maria Rita Brondi', who sang 'songs from Sicily, Abruzzi, Naples, Venice and Sardinia'.[129] Given the large presence of Sardinian immigrants in Turin, the Sardinian songs were received with particular enthusiasm.[130]

In 1925 Gramsci insisted on the need for the Italian Communist Party to spread its slogans among the local masses of each Italian region, using the means of expression which could best be understood by those masses.[131] While the Fifth Congress of the *Partito sardo d'azione* [Sardinian Action Party] was being organised, the Italian Communists set out to establish a political relationship with the left-wing groups of this party.[132] The political document that the Italian Communists addressed to the Sardinian party congress, on behalf of Krestintern (the Moscow-based Peasant International), was influenced by Gramsci, as has been confirmed by Ruggero Grieco, who drafted the document.[133] Hence, it is probable that the Communists' decision to prepare a Sardinian translation of their document also reflected Gramsci's influence.[134]

During the period he spent in Rome (as a member of the national parliament) between 1924 and 1926, Gramsci had fresh opportunities to use Sardinian in oral communication. Agostino Chironi, a Communist from the Sardinian town of Nuoro, was with Gramsci on one of the occasions when the latter spoke in

---

127. See Bermani 2007.
128. Bermani 1995.
129. Bermani 1981, p. 30.
130. See 'Il Concerto di M.R. Brondi per l'Istituto di Cultura Proletaria' ['M.R. Brondi's Concert for the Institute of Proletarian Culture'], signed 'g.c.', in *L'Ordine Nuovo*, 14 May 1922.
131. See Gramsci 1971a, p. 62. See also Chapter Two.
132. See Gramsci 1992a, pp. 442–4, Melis 1975, pp. 25–34, 187.
133. See Melis 1975, p. 192.
134. See also Lilliu 1999.

Sardinian. Chironi was invited by Antonio Dore, 'another Communist, also from Nuoro', to join a Communist meeting in Rome – a semi-clandestine meeting 'that some Sardinian comrades were going to hold, with the aim of setting up an association for poor peasants in their island too, as had been done in Apulia':[135]

> The meeting was held on a Sunday morning, outside Porta San Giovanni.... We sat, rather uncomfortably, on some rocks, in the open countryside. Gramsci was the first to begin to speak. He gave a clear and dramatic account of the political situation. At a certain point, he stopped speaking. It began to pour with rain, and so we were forced to find shelter in a nearby *osteria*.
>
> Gramsci resumed his speech, talking at length about Sardinia, since the meeting had been convened to guide us islanders.... As a precaution, comrade Gramsci spoke in Sardinian dialect. He wanted to avoid any possibility of being surreptitiously reported to the Fascist police; in other words, to avoid the intervention of the police during or after the meeting. But the owner of the *osteria* became suspicious. He came over to our table, and told us curtly that we had to leave.... Being particularly concerned for comrade Gramsci, we finally decided to go away.[136]

During his imprisonment Gramsci sometimes also had the opportunity to speak Sardinian (that is, after 1926). One of the inmates of the Turi di Bari prison, Giovanni Lai, another political prisoner, later recalled his conversations with Gramsci in Sardinian. Lai came from Pirri. Like Teulada, the small town Frongia was from, Pirri is also in the province of Cagliari – that is, near the city where Gramsci had lived when he studied at one of the local secondary schools. It is well known that the language varieties spoken in the north of Sardinia (especially Sassarese) differ considerably from those spoken in the southern and central parts of the island.[137] Therefore, the variety normally used by Gramsci was probably of a southern-central type.[138]

---

135. De Murtas 1982.
136. Chironi 1988, p. 35. Cf. Chironi 1967.
137. See Francescato 1993, pp. 333–4, and Loi Corvetto 1993, pp. 7–8. See also Wagner 1993. Sassarese and Gallurese may be defined as 'dialects of Sardinia' rather than Sardinian dialects.
138. See also Gramsci 1996a, p. 405. I have not been able to determine where Nino Bruno was from. As a young militant, he spoke Sardinian with Gramsci during a regional Communist Party congress in October 1924. However, this congress took place near Cagliari, where Bruno worked (see Fiori 1970, pp. 182–3, Restaino 1963). On the map of Sardinian 'dialects' and 'sub-dialects' (which Loi Corvetto reproduced from Virdis 1988, p. 905), the areas where Gramsci lived, before moving to Turin, belong to the Campidanese variety (Ales and Cagliari) or the Arborense variety (Ghilarza, Sòrgono, and Santu Lussurgiu, where Gramsci studied at the local *ginnasio*). The Arborense variety, which had previously been 'considered as a sub-variety due to the "mixed" features it shares with Campidanese and Logudorese, is now defined as an autonomous system' (Loi Corvetto 1993, pp. 6–8).

Here is Lai's account of his first conversation with Gramsci in prison:

> I told him that I was Sardinian, from Cagliari, and that I had seen him and met
> him during the 1924 regional conference, and he was extremely kind. He spoke
> to me in Sardinian, probably to give me the chance to overcome the embar-
> rassment that I felt, and that he couldn't fail to notice. He asked me an endless
> amount of questions about Sardinian comrades whom he had met, about the
> situation in our Party with regard to Sardinia, about the peasants, shepherds
> and builders. He also asked me about the Sardinian Action Party, about how
> I had made use of my time in prison, about the comrades whom I had got to
> know while I was in prison, and about the ways in which these comrades were
> living and studying.[139]

Not only did Gramsci speak Sardinian with fellow Sardinian prisoners,[140] he
also explained his views on dialects to the other political prisoners. According
to Ercole Piacentini, another inmate at Turi di Bari, Gramsci stressed the necessity of using dialects in education (at least at an early stage) in order to improve
one's linguistic skills and thereby to achieve real cultural improvements:

> One day he talked to us about propaganda, and about how we, as workers,
> could be trained culturally and politically. First of all we dealt with words,
> which can explain events in basic terms, adapting to different ways of think-
> ing and to the different people in the audience, and which can therefore also
> establish a connection with practical matters that are familiar to the audi-
> ence. Gramsci gave us the following example: 'I am Sardinian, and I talk to
> Sardinians. I talk to them in dialect. Knowing their ways of thinking and the
> environment in which they have lived, I effectively succeed in making myself
> understood. And the same should be done with people from Sicily, Calabria,
> or Milan'. Then he mentioned the newspapers, which require a certain level
> of preparation, since reading them is not easy at all. For instance, what is Ger-
> many? 'Germany', or 'England', is a word, but Germany has its financial, agri-
> cultural and industrial potential, as well as a history and a given geographical
> position. Only when we have acquired all that, can we say that we know the
> real value of the word 'Germany'.[141]

---

139. In Paulesu Quercioli 1977, p. 205.
140. In the Turi prison, at least one of the guards was Sardinian, and was from a village near Ghilarza (see Fiori 1977, p. x, Fiori 1991, p. 39). This was perhaps the person with
whom Gramsci spoke in Sardinian, during an episode recalled by Gustavo Trombetti (see
Scalmbrino 1998, p. 192).
141. In Bermani 1987, p. 167. See also the following passage from a letter to Giulia of
19 November 1928: 'Books and magazines only offer general ideas, sketches (more or less
successful) of general currents in the world's life, but they cannot give the immediate,
direct, vivid impression of the lives of Peter, Paul, and John, of single, real individuals,
and unless one understands them one cannot understand what is being universalized

Piacentini's testimony is extremely important, in that it closely resembles a letter that Gramsci had written many years earlier, in 1918. This letter was written to Giuseppe Lombardo Radice (1879–1938), to inform this renowned educationist of the pedagogic methods adopted by the *Club di vita morale* [Club of Moral Life], which Gramsci and other young men had set up in Turin the previous year:

> Through this club we intend to accustom the young people who join the Social-
> ist political and economic movement to the disinterested discussion of ethical
> and social problems. We intend to accustom them to research; to disciplined,
> systematic reading; to setting out their convictions in a clear and objective
> manner.... The young people involved are all workers: Turinese Socialism is
> distinctly working-class in character and the few [university] students we have
> are away on military service. Although the young people we are working with
> are intelligent and willing, we are having to start from the simplest and most
> elementary things: from language itself.[142]

To return to Gramsci's imprisonment, other episodes also need to be considered. In March 1933, his already precarious health began to further deteriorate. He suffered from frequent physical and mental crises. During these crises, his confused thoughts, sometimes hallucinations, were expressed in the language of his native island. On 21 March 1933, he wrote to his sister-in-law Tatiana Schucht:

> As I already said to you, during the first days I experienced certain curious
> pathological signs that I partly remembered and that partly were described
> to me by those present. For example, I spoke at great length in a language
> [*lingua*] that no one understood and that certainly was Sardinian dialect [*dia-
> letto*], because as late as a few days ago I noticed that I was unconsciously
> mixing Sardinian words and sentences with Italian.[143]

He also wrote, on 24 July 1933: 'Now that I feel better, those who were around me when I reached the critical moment of my illness have told me that in my moments of delirium there was a certain lucidity in my rantings (which were interspersed with long tirades in Sardinian dialect)'.[144]

---

and generalized. Many years ago, in 1919 and 1920, I knew a very naive and very pleasant young worker. Every Saturday evening, after work, he would come to my office to be one of the first to read the review I was editing. He often said: "I wasn't able to sleep, oppressed by this thought: what will Japan do?" Japan of all places obsessed him, because the Italian newspapers write about Japan only when the Mikado dies and an earthquake kills at least 10,000 people. Japan escaped his grasp; therefore he was unable to form a systematic picture of the world's forces and so it seemed to him that he understood nothing at all' (Gramsci 1994a, I, p. 233).

142. Gramsci 1992a, pp. 92–3 (English translation in Gramsci 1994c, pp. 51–3).

143. Gramsci 1994a, II, p. 282.

144. Gramsci 1994a, II, p. 314. It should be noted that in these letters Gramsci uses *dialetto* and *lingua* as synonyms, writing, once again, *dialetto sardo*.

These passages from Gramsci's letters, and the episodes recalled earlier concerning Gramsci's use of Sardinian, cast light on the way in which this language became part of his own linguistic repertoire; and so does the evidence, described above, of Gramsci's constant exposure to this language during his childhood. Blasco Ferrer's above-mentioned hypothesis – according to which the Sardinian language was learnt by Gramsci 'from linguistics books', rather than naturally acquired 'at home orally' – must, therefore, be rejected. This is one of the conclusions that can be drawn from what I have said so far.

I would like to draw other conclusions, too. In his writings, Gramsci did not explicitly or systematically theorise about local-national bilingualism. Yet he experienced and used such bilingualism throughout his life. In one of the above-quoted passages from his prison letters, Gramsci highlighted the early educational privileges that he had enjoyed because of the presence of Italian in the linguistic repertoire of his family, which was uncommon in late nineteenth-century Sardinian families. Indeed, at school, 'the teacher was expected to take into account the average pupil, and knowing how to speak Italian fluently was already a circumstance that made many things easier'.[145]

Gramsci, however, also observed that real educational and cultural advantage could only come with bilingualism, and that, above all, rigorous school education was needed, aimed at maximising the potential benefits of the pupils' bilingualism; whereas knowing Italian could even have negative effects:

> In Sardinian village schools it will happen that a girl or boy who is accustomed to speaking Italian at home (even though little and badly) by that simple fact is superior to his classmates, who know only Sardinian and thus learn to read and write, to speak, to compose sentences in a completely new language. The former seem to be more intelligent and quick, whereas sometimes this is not so, and therefore both at home and at school people neglect training them to do methodical and disciplined work, thinking that with their 'intelligence' they will overcome all difficulties, etc.[146]

This passage contains evident affinities with the language-education recommendations that Graziadio Isaia Ascoli had given in his 'Proemio' ['Preface'] to the first issue of the *Archivio Glottologico Italiano* ['Italian Glottological Archive'] in 1873, and in a paper he had written for the Ninth Italian Pedagogical Congress (of 1874). In the 'Proemio', Ascoli briefly describes the 'privileged position ... of *bilingual children*',[147] who continue to speak their mother dialect and also learn the national language. In his 1874 paper, Ascoli stressed that schools should

---

145. Gramsci 1994a, II, p. 356.
146. Gramsci 1994a, I, p. 240.
147. Ascoli 1975, p. 31.

encourage 'reflection upon the phenomena of language and thought',[148] so as to enable children to compare their own dialect with the national language, and therefore progress 'consciously' from what they 'already owned and could use ... to the ownership and use of what was foreign to them':[149]

> some ... might think that those children are privileged whose mother tongue, being more or less similar to the written language, initially allows them to use the latter naturally and therefore more finely, without requiring any help from true reflection. ... But perhaps the truth is that this privilege neither exists now, nor may exist in the future. Because the smaller the friction of relevant difficulties, the more the wheel slides – and the less it turns.[150]

On the whole, Gramsci's 'Ascolian' remarks on language education are part of his generally open-minded attitude to linguistic plurality. This attitude first came to light in the translation work he did in Cagliari, when still a student, whereby political issues were communicated to dock workers, fishermen, artisans and working children in a language that the local population at large could understand. As is also confirmed by his letter to Lombardo Radice quoted above, Gramsci attached great importance to the linguistic aspects of cultural and social differences and inequalities. At the same time, he did not wish to use linguistic differences to set Italian and Sardinian identities off against each other.

On the one hand, we have those written texts and oral-communication events in which the choice of Sardinian was almost obligatory, since Gramsci's interlocutors had a very poor understanding of the national language. On the other hand, the choice of Sardinian was optional on those occasions when he and his interlocutors shared a bilingual (Italian and Sardinian) repertoire. The first group of texts and episodes shows a functional, practically-motivated recourse to the linguistic code that ordinary people tended to understand best.[151] The second group consists, instead, of episodes in which Gramsci's use of both languages was functional to the contents of the communication. In some cases, switching to Sardinian was necessary to introduce a word that could not be replaced by an Italian word.[152] In other cases, the episodes in the second group reveal

---

148. In Raicich 1981, p. 430.
149. In Raicich 1981, p. 427.
150. In Raicich 1981, pp. 430–1.
151. A similar linguistic strategy had already been applied within the political life of pre-unification Italy (see Leydi 1963). The Italian Jacobins had seen the use of local languages, as well as the recourse to simple styles and popular themes, as a transitional, and yet inevitable necessity. The dialects of Italy were, indeed, intensely used in political communication between 1797 and 1799 in Venice and Naples (see Cortelazzo 1984, pp. 548–53, Renzi 1981, pp. 141–4).
152. See, for example, Gramsci 1996a, pp. 48, 93, 60, 336–8, 496. The range of Sardinian words and expressions that Gramsci used in his letters is quite wide, including the

Gramsci's acute awareness of the expressive efficacy, and of the sense of common affiliation, that could be fostered by using a code different from the national language. This efficacy and this sense of solidarity were, indeed, very strong in Gramsci's time, when the national language lacked sufficient unitary vocabulary and phraseology with which to express many aspects of everyday life fluently and naturally. Gramsci pointed out this shortage, especially in his writings on theatre.[153]

On some occasions, a different reason also led Gramsci to choose Sardinian. This reason was the need to make communication cryptic, that is, to make the decoding of a message only possible for the intended receiver. However, the aim of preventing other listeners from understanding what was being said would seem to have been dominant only in the episode during Gramsci's Roman years recalled by Agostino Chironi.

One should not underestimate the significance of the fact that Gramsci continued to use Sardinian when he was no longer in Sardinia and, above all, when he had become an intellectual and a revolutionary operating within a modern, international, and internationalist political movement. Using Sardinian during his childhood and early youth, when he still lived in Sardinia, was perhaps perfectly normal. As a young man, moreover, he was in favour of Sardinian 'national independence'.[154] However, continuing to use Sardinian, later in his life and for purposes which were not directly related to Sardinia, showed specific choices, and thus constitutes a noteworthy aspect of Gramsci's biography.

1.7. Gramsci's views on national linguistic unification

1.7.1. 'Every individual... is a philosopher'

Gramsci's journey through different language backgrounds and his encounter with many languages played a considerable role in his intellectual biography. I shall discuss this role more thoroughly in Chapters Two and Three. Here, I would

---

names of animals and fantastic creatures. See, for instance, '"they will butcher my sons", which in Sardinian is terrifyingly more expressive than in Italian: *faghere a pezza*. *Pezza* is the meat put up for sale, whereas for a human being the term *carre* is commonly used' (Gramsci 1994a, I, p. 87); *scurzone* (pp. 334–7); *musca maghedda* (I, p. 118, II, pp. 101–2); and *donna bisodia* (ibid.). For useful information about these words and expressions, and as an introduction to Gramsci's reflections on Sardinian folklore, see Delitala 1973–4, pp. 306–54. See also Lombardi Satriani 1980, Chapter One; Miselli 1988, p. 7 and pp. 13–15; Tripodi 1989; Grassi *et al.* 2004, pp. 96–7; and Boninelli 2007.

153. See also Davico Bonino 1972, De Mauro 1979a, Sgroi 1982, Borsellino 1983, and Lo Piparo 2004, pp. 181–7.

154. Gramsci 1992a, p. 271.

like to stress some consistencies in Gramsci's approach which have emerged in this chapter. Throughout his life, Gramsci refused to glorify cultural-linguistic identities as exclusive, self-sufficient entities. Instead, he repeatedly mentioned the advantages of being able to use more than one language, as well as the positive role of translation in overcoming linguistic barriers.[155] At the same time, he saw linguistic codes as historical products and rejected immutable hierarchies whereby one language has a higher status and another language a lower status – for instance, the status of *dialetto*. He did not see the higher or lower efficacy obtained through the use of different linguistic codes in absolute terms. Rather, he saw this efficacy as a relative, situation-bound variable.

Gramsci's writings contain stimulating reflections on the existence, in modern societies, of a cultural and ideological *continuum*. The higher section of this *continuum* is occupied by mainstream, highbrow philosophy. Gramsci called these advanced philosophical viewpoints 'philosophers' philosophies'.[156] The lower section is occupied by the interrelated, spontaneous worldviews of *senso comune* [common sense] and *folklore*.[157] Gramsci believed that each man is a philosopher – a statement that needs to be understood in a precise, non-rhetorical

---

155. 'The aims that you [Giulia, Gramsci's wife] could and ought to set for yourself in order to utilize a quite considerable part of your past activity would in my opinion be the following: to become an increasingly qualified translator from Italian. And this is what I mean by qualified translator: not only the elementary and primitive ability to translate the prose of business correspondence or of other literary expressions that on the whole can be described as journalistic prose, but the ability to translate any author, whether literary or political, historical or philosophical, from early times to this day, and therefore to learn specialized and scientific languages and the meanings of technical terms in the various periods. And even that is not enough; a qualified translator should be able not only to translate literally but also to translate the conceptual terms of a specific national culture into the terms of another national culture, that is, such a translator should have a critical knowledge of two civilizations and be able to acquaint one with the other by using the historically determined language of the civilization to which he supplies the informative material. I don't know whether I have explained myself with sufficient clarity. But I do believe that this kind of work deserves to be done, indeed deserves committing all one's efforts to it' (Gramsci 1994a, II, p. 207). Cf. the prison note entitled 'Types of Periodicals: Foreign Contributors' (Gramsci 1975, Q7, §81, pp. 913–14).

156. Gramsci 1975, Q10II, §17, p. 1255.

157. See Liguori 2004. Many authors have noted how difficult it is to find an accurate English translation for the Italian *senso comune*. This phrase – as explained by the editors in Gramsci 1971c, p. 322 – is used 'by Gramsci to mean the uncritical and largely unconscious way of perceiving and understanding the world that has become "common" in any given epoch. (Correspondingly he uses the phrase "good sense" [*buon senso*] to mean the practical, but not necessarily rational or scientific attitude that in English is usually called common sense.) The critique of "common sense" and that of "the philosophy of the philosophers" are therefore complementary aspects of a single ideological struggle'. Recently, Peter Thomas has added that '*senso comune* progressively assumes in the *Prison Notebooks* the status of a central philosophical concept, which Gramsci uses in order to redefine the nature of philosophy itself' (Thomas 2009, p. 16).

sense.[158] Every person has some form of ideology, a non-systematic way of thinking, or at least the basic elements of a worldview. Therefore, the philosophy of philosophers is quantitatively, not qualitatively different from the spontaneous philosophy of the less educated. The latter's worldview is spontaneous in the sense that it has been uncritically absorbed in the social environment in which they have culturally developed, and it has, therefore, been formed in an uncontrolled, and to some extent incoherent, manner. Every human being 'carries on some form of intellectual activity',[159] in that he or she always has a worldview, regardless of how inconsistently and implicitly he or she expresses it. At a very basic level, the expression of this implicit worldview merely consists in using a linguistic code. In this sense, a social group's or even an individual person's language is a set 'of determined notions and concepts and not just of words grammatically devoid of content'.[160]

This *continuum* also operates among languages and varieties of a language. In his list of the sources that either introduce or help to spread linguistic innovations, Gramsci includes: a) 'the relations of "conversation" between the more educated and less educated strata of the population'; and b) the 'local dialects, understood in various senses (from the more localised dialects to those which embrace more or less broad regional complexes [*complessi*]: thus Neapolitan for southern Italy, the dialects of Palermo and Catania for Sicily)'.[161] Elsewhere he observed: 'One might say that every social group has a "language" of its own, yet one should still note that (rare exceptions aside) there is a continuous adhesion and exchange between popular language and the language of the cultured classes'.[162] In fact,

> the language of the people remains the dialect backed by an Italianizing slang which consists, for the most part, in a mechanical translation of the dialect. The various dialects have a strong influence on the written language because even the cultured class speaks the language in certain situations and the dialect in family conversation, namely where speech is most vivid and closest to immediate reality.[163]

These passages confirm the absence of rigid, a-historical hierarchies or separations. There are, instead, multidirectional influences that operate horizontally –

---

158. Cf. Gramsci 1975, Q4, §51, p. 488.
159. Gramsci 1975, Q12, §3, p. 1550.
160. Gramsci 1975, Q11, §12, p. 1375 (see also p. 1342). Cf. Chapter Three, note 4.
161. Gramsci 1975, Q29, §3, p. 2345 (English translation in Gramsci 1985, pp. 183–4).
162. Gramsci 1975, Q6, §62, p. 730.
163. Gramsci 1975, Q1, §73, pp. 81–2 (English translation in Gramsci 1992b).

between languages with a similar status[164] – and vertically – that is, descending from the superposed variety to the local, sub-standard varieties, while also ascending from less prestigious to more prestigious varieties. Gramsci linked his own judgements and aims to these mainly descriptive observations. He firmly believed that, within this *continuum*-like situation, there should be more contact and interaction between professional intellectuals, with their sound mastery of humanist culture and up-to-date scientific acquisitions, and 'the humble',[165] with their often parochial, anachronistic popular culture. He argued that the popular masses should have access to the national culture that professional intellectuals had historically developed and passed down from one generation of intellectuals to the next. Yet he also believed that national culture should become increasingly receptive to the cultural life and needs of the popular masses.[166] Indeed, the most advanced philosophical achievements of restricted intellectual groups would remain weak and politically ineffective if these groups failed to create 'ideological unity between the bottom and the top'.[167]

1.7.2. *The shortcomings of monolingualism*

There is a note in Notebook 11 which may initially appear to contain an outright dismissal of regional languages, local varieties and sub-varieties. In actual fact, this note contains an implicit recognition of the validity of local-national bilingualism. Both tongues, the local and the national one, are *lingue* [languages] from the technical point of view of linguistics, in that they are structurally characterised by the same properties that characterise all natural languages. But, since the national language has historically developed a series of specific socio-cultural characteristics, Gramsci believed that this language could consequently offer possibilities less available in regional languages. He wanted the whole population to be able to take advantage of such possibilities. Yet he did not imply that this widespread ability to use national languages should inevitably lead to the abandonment of local and minority languages. He was against an exclusive knowledge of languages of restricted circulation and low socio-cultural status; he never condemned knowing or using these languages alongside widely circulating

---

164. In particular, 'the national language cannot be imagined outside the frame of other languages that exert an influence on it through innumerable channels which are often difficult to control. (Who can control the linguistic innovations introduced by returning emigrants, travellers, readers of foreign newspapers and languages, translators, etc.?)' (Gramsci 1975, Q29, §2, pp. 2343–4. English translation in Gramsci 1985, pp. 180–2).

165. Gramsci 1975, Q21, §3, p. 2112.

166. See Frosini 1999, Broccoli 1972.

167. Gramsci 1975, Q8, §213, p. 1070.

national languages. Not surprisingly, in the note in Notebook 11, Gramsci used the adverb *solo* [only]:

> If it is true that every language contains the elements of a conception of the world and of a culture, it could also be true that from anyone's language one can assess the greater or lesser complexity of his conception of the world. Someone who only [*solo*] speaks dialect, or understands the standard language incompletely, necessarily shares in an intuition of the world which is more or less limited and provincial, which is fossilised and anachronistic in relation to the major currents of thought that dominate world history. His interests will be limited, more or less corporate or economistic, not universal. While it is not always possible to learn a number of foreign languages in order to put oneself in contact with other cultural lives, it is at the least necessary to learn the national language properly. A great culture can be translated into the language of another great culture; that is, a great national language, with historic richness and complexity, can translate any other great culture and can be a world-wide means of expression. But a dialect cannot do this.[168]

The word *solo* can be seen as the key term in Gramsci's argument. It is not enough to know only a dialect. Forming one's own cultural identity exclusively through contacts with regional cultural life will limit one's chances and choices. Gramsci states this even in letters which contain affectionate recollections of his childhood in Sardinia, as well as positive memories of Sardinian material culture (including traditional recipes). For instance, on 26 February 1927 he writes: 'Since Edmea [his niece] will also have to get ahead on her own, we must make sure that she's strengthened morally and prevent her from growing up surrounded

---

168. Gramsci 1975, Q11, §12, p. 1377. English translation in Gramsci 1971c, pp. 323–43 (I have slightly altered Hoare and Nowell-Smith's translation). In contrast to the approach I have chosen to take, many interpreters looked at this note in isolation from the rest of Gramsci's writings, with little or no reference to his overall biography, and often comparing it quite mechanically with Gramsci's letter to his sister Teresina of 26 March 1927 (quoted above, in section 1.2). Once this restricted comparison has been established, the most plausible interpretations are either the one based on terminological distinctions (with Gramsci suggesting that in language education, Italian-Sardinian bilingualism should be encouraged because 'Sardinian is ... a language in itself', whereas bilingual education should not be pursued if the other language to be acquired, alongside the national language, is 'a dialect'), or else the one that identifies a change in Gramsci's pedagogical views between 1927 and 1932, when the note from Notebook 11 was written (from a phase in which spontaneity had been given a central role, to a phase during which more emphasis was placed on discipline and conformism, and Gramsci viewed in openly negative terms the spontaneous influence of the socio-cultural environment where primary socialisation takes place). The first interpretation was put forward by Lo Piparo 1979, while the second had been advocated by Manacorda 1970. I do not share either of these two interpretations.

only by the aspects [*dai soli elementi*] of fossilized small-town life'.[169] Moreover, monolingualism in general is liable to hamper individual development significantly, in view of the increasingly globalising processes of modern economic and cultural life. Indeed, as early as 1918, Gramsci argued for an 'accurate learning of the Italian language *and* of one or two of the other languages that are most widely spoken and known in the world'.[170]

At the same time, local languages had a force and efficacy which Gramsci used throughout his life and which he repeatedly recognised in his writings. The Italian language was inadequate in many communicative situations, and during his prison years Gramsci found that very little progress had been made, in this respect, since he had begun to write theatre reviews in the late 1910s. Furthermore, during Gramsci's life, even that minority of the Italian population who did frequently use the Italian language had difficulties in mastering this language. This unsound mastery amplified the inadequateness of the national language and confined its use to a narrow range of communicative domains. Gramsci specified in the letter of 26 March 1927 that 'the Italian' that his family was going to teach to his nephew, Franco, 'will be a poor, mutilated language'.[171] The national language, based on the literary language, was 'a partial language'[172] and had not yet acquired 'a mass "historicity" '.[173]

> In reality there are many 'popular' languages in Italy and they are the regional dialects that are usually spoken in private conversation in which the most common and diffused feelings and emotions are expressed. The literary language is still largely a cosmopolitan language, a type of 'Esperanto', limited to the expression of partial notions and feelings.
>
> When the literary language is said to be very rich in expressive means, something equivocal and ambiguous is being asserted. The 'possible' richness of expression recorded in the dictionary or lying inert in 'authors' is being confused with individual richness that can be used on an individual basis. The latter, though, is the only real and concrete richness, and it is through it that one can measure the degree of national linguistic unity that is given by the living spoken language of the people, the degree of nationalisation of the linguistic patrimony.[174]

---

169. Gramsci 1994a, I, p. 77. My emphasis. Cf. Gramsci's letter to his sister of 26 March 1927 (quoted in 1.2): 'it is a good thing for children to learn *several languages*' (my emphasis).
170. Gramsci 1982, p. 593. My emphasis.
171. Gramsci 1994a, I, p. 89.
172. Gramsci 1975, Q3, §73, p. 350.
173. Gramsci 1975, Q23, §39, p. 2235.
174. Ibid. A few years after Gramsci's death, the Italian linguist and philologist Emilio Peruzzi gave a vivid description of the consequences of this situation. In Italy, there was

Only through a process of transformation – of which dialects would be active components, and not its designated passive victims – would the literary-based national language become a common language, which the whole population could effectively use in any communicative situation and to talk about any topic. Again, in Gramsci's writings this prediction is both a description of on-going or foreseeable processes, and a prescriptive judgement on how politically progressive linguistic unification should be achieved.

In Chapters Two and Three, we shall see that his comments on language policy point exactly in the direction of gradual unification. Thus, there is no contradiction between Gramsci's insistence on the aulic and overly formal character of the literary language, which he contrasts with the expressive versatility and richness of dialects, and his insistence on the necessity of moving beyond dialects, towards the use of a common, unified language. Firstly, Gramsci distinguishes between the notion of *literary Italian* and that of a *common language*.[175] Notwithstanding its various connections with the language of literature, the latter is not a given reality – the emergence of a generally shared language is a goal that will only be achieved through complex historical processes. Secondly, Gramsci was well aware of the limits of the Italian language used in his time, which was, indeed, still in the process of becoming the language of the whole nation.

In sum, Gramsci aimed at overcoming the overall backwardness of Italian culture – including the backwardness of educated élites, which revealed itself in the very fact that they were separated from what he called 'the national-popular mass'. He did so by arguing that this mass of people should be given access to the 'learning of the educated language',[176] which was traditionally monopolised by small educated groups from the dominant social classes. In this way, all Italians would be able to go *oltre il dialetto* [beyond dialects];[177] that is, to use the national language alongside their local, native varieties, without necessarily having to abandon these varieties. As far as method was concerned, Gramsci placed great emphasis on the study of the grammar of the national language, viewing this study as especially useful in the case of school-aged children. Excluding

'a national vocabulary to discuss the immortality of the soul, exalt civil valour, describe a sunset, and lyrically express grief about a lost love'; but there was not yet 'a commonly accepted, unequivocal vocabulary to talk about the little things of everyday life' (quoted by De Mauro 1991a, p. 30). See also Teresa Poggi Salani: 'as we can still see nowadays, unification had taken place almost entirely in writing, and had indeed failed to affect day-to-day words used for simple things – that is, for those everyday-life matters that nonetheless concern each one of us. Since the living use of the language (which would have brought greater simplification and economy to the flow of the language) was not widely practiced, too many grammatical and lexical variants continued to exist, which an abstract norm could not effectively organise' (Poggi Salani 1986, p. 119).

175. See Passaponti 1981, pp. 127–8.
176. Gramsci 1975, Q29, §6, p. 2349.
177. See above, section 1.4.

'grammar...from education', Gramsci wrote in Notebook 29, simply means that the 'only thing excluded is the unitarily organised intervention in the process of learning the language'.[178] Once again, he followed Ascoli, who had defended the pedagogic usefulness of grammar against those scholars who had turned to the authority of Jacob Grimm's views in order to support their rejection of grammar teaching.[179]

1.7.3. Final remarks

The three main points that summarise Gramsci's views on language education, as they have emerged from my assessment of his writings and biography, are:

i) the spontaneous acquisition of the language variety spoken in the environment where primary socialisation takes place, regardless of the status enjoyed by this variety (whether *dialetto* or *lingua*), in a process that Gramsci describes as 'natural and necessary';[180]
ii) the study of the grammar of the national language at school, so as to 'increase the organic knowledge of the national language'[181] and give all social classes access to the educated language;
iii) the emphasis placed on the learning of foreign languages.

These views[182] on language education are crucial for an understanding of Gramsci's stance on the relationship between diversity and unification. His position did not imply, as a necessary consequence and fixed outcome of unification, the immediate disappearance of differences and plurality. By understanding the role that Gramsci envisaged for dialects in producing a truly common language, we can begin to appreciate a highly specific aspect of Gramsci's approach to the construction of socialism. Indeed, not only did Gramsci view the mutual

---

178. Gramsci 1975, p. 2349. See also Chapter Two.
179. See Ascoli's 'Relazione al IX Congresso pedagogico italiano' ['Speech to the Ninth Italian Pedagogical Congress'], in Raicich 1981.
180. Gramsci 1994a, I, p. 89.
181. Gramsci 1975, Q29, §4, p. 2346.
182. These views consistently form part of Gramsci's politico-philosophical thought. For instance, in a study of literary criticism in Gramsci's *Prison Notebooks*, Romano Luperini shows that 'in rejecting the distinction between "literature" and "poetry", between institution and creative lyricism, Gramsci emphasises the connections between the work of art and the status of the writer in society, as well as the mutual interdependency between literary and ordinary language, between creativity and the common sense [*senso comune*] of an epoch' (Luperini 1999, p. 52). Similarly, Gramsci's approach to party-organisation – that is, his interpretation of 'democratic centralism' – pays special attention to the necessary interconnection between the masses and the central governing bodies (see Ferri 1987, Paggi 1984, pp. 190–7 and 212, and Femia 1987, p. 151ff.).

influence between local and national languages positively, but he also came to see the reciprocal influence between specialised knowledge and popular culture, and that between a unitary political leadership and the diverse groups following this leadership, in similarly positive terms. Moreover, in a note which I shall quote and discuss in Chapter Three,[183] he recognised that this fruitful influence can be facilitated by democratic liberties such as freedom of expression, freedom of thought, and freedom of association.

When this fruitful exchange occurs, local dialects can take an active part in creating 'a common national language' or 'unified national language',[184] no longer 'fossilised and pompous';[185] folklore and common sense can dialectically participate in the creation of a new common culture; traditional theatrical production, characterised by the use of dialects, can contribute to the renewal of the national theatre and of its language; subaltern groups can *educate* (in the broad sense which Marx assigned to this term in the third of his *Theses on Feuerbach*,[186] and which Gramsci often echoes in his prison notes) the élites who are in charge of education; and, most importantly, citizens can systematically move 'from the led groups to the leading group'.[187] Clearly, a connection between Gramsci's linguistics and his politics begins to emerge, here. But before this connection can be described in more detail, and the links between the two elements correctly analysed, it is necessary to look at Gramsci's intellectual biography, especially at the way in which his ideas on language formed.

---

183. See Gramsci 1975, Q10II, §44, pp. 1330–2.
184. Gramsci 1975, Q29, §2 and §3, pp. 2344–5.
185. Gramsci 1975, Q23, §40, p. 2236.
186. Cf. Marx and Engels 1976, pp. 3–8.
187. Gramsci 1975, Q8, §191, p. 1056.

Chapter Two
Influences and Differences: The Formation of Gramsci's Views

2.1. Gramsci's direct and indirect sources in language studies

Gramsci was born in the village of Ales, in central Sardinia. This was a rural, backward, poverty-stricken, and culturally marginal area. However, local intellectual production was not insignificant in Ghilarza, a small town near Ales where Gramsci spent most of his childhood. Here, he came into contact with a priest, Michele Licheri, who was interested in linguistics and in the study of dialects and folkloric culture.[1] After moving to Turin to study at the local university, Gramsci did not forget Father Licheri, and when needing information about Sardinian dialects, he wrote to his sister Teresina and asked her to consult him as a reliable, qualified source.[2]

In Cagliari, while still a high-school student, Gramsci caught the attention of one of his teachers, Raffa Garzia. Garzia was the editor of the daily newspaper *L'Unione Sarda* (still published today) and also a fine connoisseur of the history and language of Sardinia.[3] It was thanks to this teacher that Gramsci had the

---

1. See Deias 1997, p. 60.
2. See Gramsci 1992a, p. 71.
3. See Podda 1999, p. 183. Also appreciated as a writer and philologist, Raffa Garzia would later teach Sardinian linguistics at the University of Cagliari between 1927 and 1930 (see Angioni 1987, Romagnino 2005, Podda 1977).

opportunity to write his first newspaper report, in 1910.[4] As we have seen in Chapter One, in an article written as part of the successful campaign that the Turinese socialists conducted among Sardinian troops in 1919, Gramsci referred to a popular Sardinian anthem against feudal lords (the *inno angioyano*), on which Garzia had published a study in 1897.

Gramsci's high-school teachers in Cagliari also included Francesco Ribezzo, 'a "specialist" in Aryo-European comparative linguistics'.[5] In this field, however, the main influence on the young Gramsci came from Matteo Bartoli – Gramsci's professor of glottology at the University of Turin. Bartoli asked Gramsci to transcribe and edit the lecture notes for his 1912–13 course, and probably expected his Sardinian student to become an academic linguist. These expectations were to remain unrealised: though continuing to work on what should have been his thesis 'on the history of language'[6] for a few more years, Gramsci eventually abandoned his university studies without graduating.

One of the founders of the *Partito Comunista d'Italia* in 1921, Gramsci soon became a target of Fascist political persecution. He spent the last years of his life in prison. He was arrested in 1926, and died in a clinic, still under police surveillance, in 1937. During this period, he wrote the notes that began to be published more than a decade after his death with the title of *Quaderni del carcere*. Remarks on linguistic subjects are present in many of his prison notebooks, and the last one – Notebook 29, written during the first half of 1935 – consists entirely of theoretical reflections on 'national language and grammar',[7] bearing the title 'Note per una introduzione allo studio della grammatica' ['Notes for an Introduction to the Study of Grammar'].[8]

Gramsci was allowed to write throughout most of his time in prison, but his ability to do so was somewhat limited by the restrictions imposed by his jailers on his access to writing materials, books and other printed matter. These restrictions applied most of all to the type and number of books that he was allowed to consult in his cell. Other difficulties arose, with respect to his access to books on linguistics, as a result of external impediments – as is proved, for instance, by the fact that Gramsci realised it would not be easy to obtain Matteo Bartoli and Giulio Bertoni's *Breviario di neolinguistica* ['Handbook of Neolinguistics'], and simply resigned himself to this.[9]

Today, the bibliographical information that Gramsci included in his prison letters and notes, along with a list of the volumes that he owned (published

---

4. See Bergami 1993, and Fiori 1966, pp. 68–9.
5. Gramsci 1975, Q3, §89, p. 372. Cf. Schirru 2011.
6. Gramsci 1982, p. 613.
7. Gramsci 1975, Q29, §9, p. 2351.
8. Gramsci 1975, p. 2339.
9. See Gramsci 1996a.

in the fourth volume of Valentino Gerratana's critical edition of the *Prison Notebooks*),[10] provide us with fairly detailed knowledge of his sources. Amongst these sources were books by important scholars such as Michel Bréal,[11] Franz Nikolaus Finck,[12] Thérèse Labande-Jeanroy,[13] Vittore Pisani,[14] Ciro Trabalza,[15] and Karl Vossler;[16] and also works in the philosophy of language by those Italian authors that Gramsci often groups under the collective definition of *pragmatisti* [pragmatists]: Vilfredo Pareto,[17] Giuseppe Prezzolini,[18] and Giovanni Vailati.[19] It would be absurd, however, to regard this list as complete in any sense. It is unlikely that all the volumes that Gramsci had during his life were preserved and eventually added to the Fondo Gramsci – the archive collection containing all the books that he owned, held in Rome at the Fondazione Istituto Gramsci (on which Gerratana's list is based). And, obviously, it would be ridiculous to expect Gramsci to have quoted in his prison notes all the books, articles, and other publications about language that he had previously read. This is why the present chapter explores Gramsci's familiarity with other sources in this field. These include both sources where Gramsci's knowledge can be documented, and others for which such knowledge can only be inferred through the study of his writings and of his life.

We can list those linguistic themes on which Gramsci might have been influenced also by other authors and debates, and not just by the ones he explicitly mentions in the *Prison Notebooks*. Each of these four themes will be examined in this chapter:

> Echoes of Ferdinand de Saussure's ideas
> Language and social classes
> The glottopolitical aspects of Lenin's influence on Gramsci
> The search for a universal language

This list does not include those language-policy issues with regard to which Gramsci most evidently drew on debates that had taken place in Italy during the late nineteenth century (when a far-reaching *querelle* saw Graziadio Isaia Ascoli opposing Alessandro Manzoni and his followers). This area has already attracted

---

10. See Gramsci 1975, pp. 3035–160.
11. Bréal 1900 (first published in 1897).
12. Finck 1910, 1923. On this author, see Appendix, section 4.2.2.
13. Labande-Jeanroy 1925a, 1925b.
14. Pisani 1929.
15. Trabalza 1908.
16. Vossler 1908.
17. See Pareto 1935 (originally published in 1916; Gramsci had the second edition, published in 1923).
18. Prezzolini 1904.
19. Vailati 1911.

considerable scholarly attention,[20] so it will only be briefly touched upon in these pages. Moreover, in Chapter One I already pointed out that Gramsci's views on language education were influenced by Ascoli's views.

2.2. Echoes of Saussure's ideas

Ferdinand de Saussure is generally considered to be the key figure of twentieth-century linguistics. In this section of the present chapter, I shall focus on some of the ideas contained in his *Cours de linguistique générale*, and in Gramsci's *Quaderni del carcere*. The first similarity that comes to the fore, when comparing these two books, is that they were both published after the authors' deaths, in a form which had not been worked out for publication by either Saussure or Gramsci (two of Saussure's most talented students – Charles Bally and Albert Sechehaye – collected and edited the notes which formed the text of the first edition of the *Cours*). Furthermore, both books have become extremely influential outside the domains of linguistic and political thought, in which they originated, making their authors two key figures of twentieth-century intellectual history as a whole. Yet, as this section will aim to show, less extrinsic connections exist between these two foundational works. More precisely, notwithstanding the obvious difference between a politician like Gramsci and a professional linguist like Saussure, Gramsci's reflections on language might owe something to the influence of Saussure's *Course in General Linguistics*.

2.2.1. *Grammar*

The first element that needs to be taken into account, when discussing Gramsci's ideas against the background of Saussurean linguistics, is the distinction between the *synchronic* and *diachronic* study of language. According to Bally and Sechehaye's edition of the *Course in General Linguistics*, it is 'the intervention of the factor of time'[21] that forces linguists to choose between these two divergent paths. The difference between static and evolutionary linguistics can be compared to that between 'political history' and 'the science of political institutions',[22] yet a more appropriate equivalence can be found in the clear duality that separates 'political economy and economic history'.[23]

In his *Prison Notebooks*, Gramsci writes at length on *grammatica storica* [historical grammar], understood as the diachronic description of a language; but he also

---

20. For instance, Carrannante 1973, Lo Piparo 1979, Rosiello 2010.
21. Saussure 1959, p. 79.
22. Ibid.
23. Ibid.

points to the possibility of a synchronic description. Especially in Notebook 29, Gramsci makes a clear distinction between the two viewpoints which in the *Course in General Linguistics* are termed 'static and evolutionary linguistics'[24] – the latter being occasionally referred to, by Saussure, too, as *grammaire historique* [historical grammar].[25] Traditionally (as acknowledged also in the *Course in General Linguistics*),[26] synchronic descriptions have been used as 'normative grammars',[27] in which case they differ from historical grammar in the same way that 'politics' differs from 'history'.[28]

Still in the same notebook, Gramsci is certainly thinking of synchronic descriptions when he writes that grammar 'is the "photograph" of a given phase of a national (collective) language that has been formed historically and is continuously developing, or the fundamental traits of a photograph'.[29] Unsurprisingly, Notebook 29 has been singled out by Luigi Rosiello to highlight that Gramsci, 'starting from a sociological and objectivist conception of linguistic facts, intuitively understood language as the systematic organisation of expressive signs'.[30] Rosiello also states that in 'dealing with the function of grammar in general, and with the types of grammar that can exist, Gramsci distinguishes between aspects that place his reflections on what could be termed, once again, Saussurean terrain'.[31]

Gramsci had already used the comparison with photography to indicate the synchronic description of the grammar of a language. This description, which can be used for didactic and normative purposes, presents the means of expression used by a linguistic community at 'a given time and place' (Notebook 6),[32] 'photographed in one abstract moment' (Notebook 12).[33] Rosiello's statements can be further vindicated by noting that the *Course in General Linguistics* contains a similar comparison between grammar and photography;[34] and that, furthermore, the idea of the synchronic description of a *language-state* from which

---

24. Saussure 1959, p. 79ff.
25. This, in spite of the fact that the *Course in General Linguistics* explicitly condemns 'historical grammar' as a contradictory definition: 'the discipline so labeled is really only diachronic linguistics' (Saussure 1959, p. 134). At least in one case, Gramsci seems to have had similar reservations as to the use of 'historical grammar' – when he incidentally notes that 'the history of language' may be a better definition (Gramsci 1975, Q29, §5, p. 2348).
26. Cf. Saussure 1959, pp. 1, 82–3.
27. Gramsci 1975, Q29, §5, p. 2347.
28. Ibid.
29. Gramsci 1975, Q29, §1, p. 2341 (English translation in Gramsci 1985, pp. 179–80).
30. Rosiello 1969, p. 358.
31. Rosiello 1969, p. 359.
32. Gramsci 1975, Q6, §62, p. 730.
33. Gramsci 1975, Q12, §2, p. 1545.
34. See Saussure 1959, p. 212ff.

'the intervention of time is excluded',[35] as an operation of abstraction from the real, constantly changing existence of a language, is a landmark of Saussurean linguistics:

> An absolute state is defined by the absence of changes, and since language changes somewhat in spite of everything, studying a language-state means in practice disregarding changes of little importance, just as mathematicians disregard infinitesimal quantities in certain calculations, such as logarithms.... Besides, delimitation in *time* is not the only difficulty that we encounter in defining a language-state: *space* presents the same problem. In short, a concept of a language-state can be only approximate. In static linguistics, as in most sciences, no course of reasoning is possible without the usual simplification of data.[36]

Finally, Gramsci also explains that, of course, grammarians cannot ignore the history of the language they intend to describe; however, their work needs to be based on the description of an ideally stable phase in the history of the language.[37] Their work is essentially one of synchronic description. This is consistent with Saussure's statements:

> It would be absurd to attempt to sketch a panorama of the Alps by viewing them simultaneously from several peaks of the Jura; a panorama must be made from a single vantage point. The same applies to language; the linguist can neither describe it nor draw up standards of usage except by concentrating on one state. When he follows the evolution of the language, he resembles the moving observer who goes from one peak of the Jura to another in order to record the shifts in perspective.[38]

2.2.2. Metaphors

I shall now move on to Gramsci's views on the role of metaphors in language. Through his remarks on this topic, Gramsci comes essentially to share three of the general principles that are specific to Saussure's views, as expressed in Bally and Sechehaye's edition of the *Course in General Linguistics*: a) linguistic conventions are arbitrary, and thus different from other social institutions that are to some degree based on the 'natural relations of things';[39] b) instead of being fixed once and for all by the completely free decision of an individual or a restricted

---

35. Saussure 1959, p. 80.
36. Saussure 1959, pp. 101–2. My emphasis.
37. See Gramsci 1975, Q29, §2, p. 2343.
38. Saussure 1959, pp. 81–2.
39. Saussure 1959, pp. 75–6, 80.

group,[40] linguistic conventions are the 'product of social forces';[41] and c) linguistic conventions are 'the heritage of the preceding period', since 'social forces are linked with time'.[42]

Famously, the *Course in General Linguistics* deals with both the immutability and the mutability of linguistic signs (or, more precisely, of both the systematic relationships amongst signs, and the internal relationship between the two elements that constitute each sign – the *signifier* and the *signified*). The following remarks are particularly worth quoting:

> the sign is exposed to alteration because it perpetuates itself. What predominates in all change is the persistence of the old substance; disregard for the past is only relative. That is why the principle of change is based on the principle of continuity. Change in time takes many forms... One might think that it deals especially with phonetic changes undergone by the signifier, or perhaps changes in meaning which affect the signified concept. That view would be inadequate. Regardless of what the forces of change are, whether in isolation or in combination, they always result in *a shift in the relationship between the signified and the signifier*.[43]

Finally, the *signifiés* [signified], whose value is defined by the linguistic system, shape and organise extra-linguistic entities; that is, they do not reflect given concepts:

> If words stood for pre-existing concepts, they would all have exact equivalents in meaning from one language to the next; but this is not true. French uses *louer* (*une maison*) 'let (a house)' indifferently to mean both 'pay for' and 'receive payment for', whereas German uses two words, *mieten* and *vermieten*; there is obviously no exact correspondence of values.[44]

Notwithstanding Saussure's unquestionable originality, it can be stated that, to an extent, he and Gramsci were inspired by common sources – particularly by Michel Bréal (1832–1915). During his years in Paris, Saussure had been a student and associate of Bréal, and Gramsci would mention the latter in Notebook 7:

> All language is metaphor, and it is metaphorical in two senses: it is a metaphor of the 'thing' or 'material and sensible object' referred to, and it is a metaphor of the ideological meanings attached to words in the preceding periods

---

40. See Saussure 1959, pp. 71–2, 78.
41. Saussure 1959, p. 74.
42. Ibid.
43. Saussure 1959, pp. 74–5. Emphasis in the original.
44. Saussure 1959, p. 116.

of civilization. (A treatise on semantics – for ex., Michel Bréal's – can provide a catalog of the semantic mutations of different words).[45]

Gramsci develops these general assertions at different times across his prison writings, coming close to the views expressed in the *Course in General Linguistics* on at least two points: a rejection of what Gramsci calls the 'the utopia of fixed and universal languages'[46] – I shall return to this point later – and a qualification of the explanatory value of etymological analyses. For instance, in Bally and Sechehaye's edition of the *Cours*, we read that all definitions made with respect to a single word 'are made in vain';[47] that 'starting from words in defining things is a bad procedure';[48] and that etymology is 'the explaining of words through the historical study of their relations with other words. To explain means to relate to known terms, and in linguistics, to explain a word is to relate it to other words'.[49] In one of his prison letters, Gramsci observes that 'life formulas... expressed in words'[50] can easily lead to misleading overinterpretations.[51] Moreover, in the

---

45. Gramsci 1975, Q7, §36, p. 886 (English translation in Gramsci 2007b). Gramsci is obviously referring to the *Essai de sémantique* ['Essay on Semantics']. See especially the second part of Bréal's book (entitled *Comment s'est fixé le sens des mots*, in the original): Bréal 1900, pp. 97–177.

46. Gramsci 1975, Q7, §36, p. 887; cf. Q11, §24, p. 1427.

47. Saussure 1959, p. 14. Cf. Bréal: 'Sometimes it is a synonym which extends itself, and contracts by just so much the domain of its colleague. At other times it is an historical event which comes to modify and renew the vocabulary' (Bréal 1900, p. 113). In any case, it must be remembered that 'each time, the words are placed in surroundings which predetermine their value' (p. 141); and the 'actual and present value of a word exercises such a power over the mind that it deprives us of all feeling for the etymological signification' (p. 176). I have slightly altered the English translation.

48. Saussure 1959, p. 14. Cf. the following passage from another book that Gramsci repeatedly mentions in his *Prison Notebooks*, Vilfredo Pareto's *Trattato di sociologia generale* ['Treaty on General Sociology']: 'Anyone asking what value is, what capital is, what income is and the like, shows by that mere fact that he is concerned primarily with words and secondarily with things.... In science the course followed is the exact opposite: first one examines the thing and then hunts up a name to give it' (Pareto 1935, p. 63). Needless to say, Pareto's positivist response to this issue was different from the approach taken by Bréal, Saussure, and Gramsci – with the latter referring to Pareto as one of those authors who find themselves 'confronted with the fact that words as they are commonly used – and also as they are used by the educated classes and by learned people working in the same discipline – continue to retain their old meaning. They react: Pareto creates his own "dictionary" that epitomizes the tendency to create a mathematical language, that is, a totally abstract language. The pragmatists make a philosophical issue out of this, and they theorize about language as a source of error. But is it possible to strip language of its metaphorical meaning? It is impossible' (Gramsci 1975, p. 887; English translation in Gramsci 2007b).

49. Saussure 1959, p. 189.

50. Gramsci 1994a, II, p. 33.

51. It is interesting to note the chronological proximity between this letter, written on 18 May 1931, and the previous passage on language and metaphors, which Gramscian scholars have dated to the spring of 1931 (see Francioni 1984, 1992).

first part of his argument, Gramsci intuitively grasps that the value of a word is defined by the synchronic relationships between the possible occurrences of this sign, and of other associated signs, within the language, not by a comparison with the signs of other languages:

> I once had a curious discussion with Clara Zetkin who in fact admired Italians because of their zest for life and thought she could find subtle proof of it in the fact that Italians say: 'a happy night' and not 'a tranquil night' like the Russians or 'good night' like the Germans, etc. It is quite possible that the Germans, Russians, and also the French do not think of 'happy nights', but the Italians also speak of a 'happy journey' and of 'a happily concluded business deal' that diminishes the symptomatic value of 'happy';[52]

whereas the next sentence relapses on a more traditional approach, adding a diachronic (typically Bréalian) explanation: 'on the other hand, the Neapolitans say about a beautiful woman that she is *buona* "good", certainly without malice, because beautiful (*bella*) is in fact a more ancient *bonula*'.[53] Bréal had written:

> Whether from a more or less rational belief in the necessary truth of language, or from respect for ancestral wisdom, it has been the unfailing habit, at every epoch and amongst all nations, to refer to words for information concerning the nature of things.... Yet a little reflection might have shown that it is scarcely reasonable to expect lessons in physics or in metaphysics from language, a work of improvisation, in which the most ignorant man has often the largest share, and on which accidental events have set their mark.... How should language teach us about substance and quality? It can but give us the echo of our own thought: it registers faithfully our prejudices and our mistakes. At times it may astonish us, like a child, by the frankness of its answers or the ingeniousness of its representations; or it may furnish us with valuable pieces of historical information, of which it is the involuntary depositary; but to take it for teacher and for master would be to misjudge its character.[54]

Other instances of Gramsci's elaboration on the notion of metaphor can be found in his prison writings. In Notebook 11, he specifies that 'no new historical situation, however radical the change that has brought it about, completely transforms language, at least in its external formal aspect';[55] and that when a new conception of the world replaces the previous one,

---

52. Gramsci 1994a, II, pp. 33–4.
53. Gramsci 1994a, II, p. 34.
54. Bréal 1900, pp. 173–4.
55. Gramsci 1975, Q11, §16, p. 1407.

the previous language continues to be used but is, precisely, used metaphorically. The whole of language is a continuous process of metaphor, and the history of semantics is an aspect of the history of culture; language is at the same time a living thing and a museum of fossils of life and civilisations.[56]

Hence, Gramsci concludes, when 'I use the word "disaster" no one can accuse me of believing in astrology' and 'when I say "by Jove!" no one can assume that I am a worshipper of pagan divinities'.[57] In the same notebook, he also writes:

Language is transformed with the transformation of the whole of civilisation, through the acquisition of culture by new classes and through the hegemony exercised by one national language over others, etc., and what it does is precisely to absorb in metaphorical form the words of previous civilisations and cultures. Nobody today thinks that the word 'dis-aster' is connected with astrology or can claim to be misled about the opinions of someone who uses the word. Similarly even an atheist can speak of 'dis-grace' without being thought to be a believer in predestination (etc.).[58]

This is the second draft of the prison note in which Gramsci had first mentioned Bréal (see above). At this stage, however, Gramsci seems to have intuitively realised that he was going somewhat beyond Bréal. Hence, though retaining the reference to Bréal's *Essai*, Gramsci is now hesitant about using the terminology he had used in the first draft:

the question of the relationship between language and metaphor is far from simple. Language, moreover, is always metaphorical. If perhaps it cannot quite be said that all discourse is metaphorical in respect of the thing or material and sensible object referred to (or the abstract concept) so as not to widen the concept of metaphor excessively, it can however be said that present language is metaphorical with respect to the meanings and the ideological content which the words used had in preceding periods of civilisation. A treatise of semantics (that of Michel Bréal for example) can provide an historically and critically reconstructed catalogue of the semantic mutations of given groups of

---

56. Gramsci 1975, Q11, §28, p. 1438. English translation in Gramsci 1971c, pp. 449–50. The image of language as a museum can also be found in Bréal: 'The auspices were of such great importance that it is not surprising to discover traces of them in the common language... The word *influence*, of which so much use is made at the present day, takes us back to the superstitions of ancient astrologers.... All languages might in this way make their museum of metaphors.... So many obsolete customs are perpetuated in an expression which has become commonplace: in saying of some great personage that he is *invested* with a title or dignity, no one at the present day thinks of the investiture' (Bréal 1900, pp. 126–8).

57. Gramsci 1975, p. 1438.

58. Gramsci 1975, Q11, §24, p. 1428 (English translation in Gramsci 1971c, pp. 450–2).

words... The new 'metaphorical' meaning spreads with the spread of the new culture, which furthermore also coins brand-new words or absorbs them from other languages as loan-words *giving them a precise meaning* and therefore *depriving them of the extensive halo they possessed in the original language.*[59]

I have italicised parts of the last sentence, where Gramsci's accord with Sausssure seems to have again emerged. The value of signs is defined by their relationships within a certain language, regardless of the value they had in earlier stages of the same language, or in another language from which they were borrowed. 'Like Saussure and Wittgenstein', Gramsci clearly 'rejects the nomenclature model of language':

> Instead, all three see language as a system or process of meaning production. And they all agree that meaning is not produced primarily through the relationship between the individual words and non-linguistic objects or ideas. Instead, all three see that meaning is produced within language through the relationship among words and other elements... such as sounds... phrases, sentences, etc.[60]

Finally, it should be noted that in Notebook 12 Gramsci makes further remarks that are also reminiscent of the principles spelled out in the *Course in General Linguistics*. As I have already noted, the *Cours* presents linguistic signs as forming a system, in that the value of each sign is defined by its relationship with the other signs belonging to the same language. At the same time, Saussure also stresses that linguistic signs are not merely conventional – they are social and historical products. The use that people make of a language through time contributes to redefining the systematic relationships amongst its signs.[61] The *Cours* contains clear statements regarding the duality between 'the system of values per se and the same values as they relate to time'.[62] The above-mentioned duality between *linguistique statique* [static linguistics] and *linguistique évolutive* [evolutionary linguistics] is not only an epistemological device adopted by linguists for the sake of a more accurate understanding of their subject matter; in actual fact, it is inherent in the object of linguistics.[63] Similarly, Gramsci writes about 'the distinction and the identification of words and concepts' in relation to the

---

59. Gramsci 1975, pp. 1427–8.
60. Ives 2004a, p. 85. On Saussure's criticism of the view of language as nomenclature, see Tullio De Mauro's commentary to the French edition of the *Cours* (Saussure 1972, p. 427), including references to manuscript sources; on the importance of this criticism and of its philosophical implications, see Joseph 2004, pp. 62–4.
61. See De Mauro 1991b.
62. Saussure 1959, p. 80.
63. For instance, static phenomena operate in the minds of speakers, and are essentially the only ones that matter to them in their use of language: see Saussure 1959, pp. 81, 90, 100, 183–4.

'historical movement of the entire language, that changes through time, and is developing and not only static'.[64]

2.2.3. *Language planning*

The third and last element that I would like to highlight is the caution about language planning and artificial languages expressed, in similar terms, in both the *Course in General Linguistics* and the *Prison Notebooks*. Gramsci's sceptical evaluation of artificial languages is consistent with Saussure's views on the aspiration to create 'a fixed language that posterity would have to accept for what it is'.[65] In the *Course in General Linguistics*, this scepticism applies to Esperanto, and to any attempt at intervening in the verbal communication patterns of a society. 'A language constitutes a system', and this 'system is a complex mechanism that can be grasped only through reflection; the very ones who use it daily are ignorant of it'.[66] One can legitimately expect to be able to modify a linguistic system through the organised intervention of 'specialists, grammarians, logicians';[67] but experience shows us that such attempts have never produced major results.

> The prescriptions of codes, religious rites, nautical signals, etc., involve only a certain number of individuals simultaneously and then only during a limited period of time; in language, on the contrary, everyone participates at all times, and that is why it is constantly being influenced by all. This capital fact suffices to show the impossibility of revolution. Of all social institutions, language is least amenable to initiative. It blends with the life of society, and the latter, inert by nature, is a prime conservative force.[68]

Gramsci had already come close to these positions in an article of April 1916. He had realised that the more a semiotic system becomes used by the masses, the less possible it is for it to be revolutionised. Its signs and their denotative and connotative meanings, as well as the senses that these meanings have in different contexts and to different speakers, tend to escape the control of our will. Gramsci's reflections on this point were inspired by the history of playing cards. In 'times of upheaval', and of 'bestial hatred' against the past,[69] revolutionaries tried to replace kings and queens with bourgeois icons, such as republican fasces

---

64. Gramsci 1975, Q12, §2, p. 1545.
65. Saussure 1959, p. 76.
66. Saussure 1959, p. 73.
67. Ibid.
68. Saussure 1959, pp. 73–4. Rudolf Engler's edition of the *Cours*, which gives a synopsis of all available notes by Saussure and his students, shows a somewhat less resolute scepticism regarding the potential of interventions by logicians and grammarians (see Saussure 1967–74, p. 163).
69. Gramsci 1980, p. 283.

and the symbolic figures of Freedom and Equality. While this bourgeois revolutionary spirit eventually came to an end, 'the old cards stayed', rooted as they are in the 'mental habits' of their users. Hence Gramsci concludes:

> The old playing cards – which draw on medieval illuminations portraying Longobard kings – have a language of their own, and nothing poses so many obstacles to innovations as language does. So much so, that after many years Esperantists are still in the state of a cocoon from which a butterfly is yet to emerge, despite the number of those who have taken up their cause, from Leibniz to Dr Zamenhof.[70]

Attempts at creating a 'perfect language'[71] must have been familiar to Gramsci ever since his early years at the University of Turin. Certainly, he studied there in the same years as the renowned mathematician and logician Giuseppe Peano (1858–1932) was teaching at this university. Peano wrote about the need for an international auxiliary language, and created a simplified version of Latin to be used as 'a written lingua franca for international scientific communication'.[72] Peano saw this universal language, called *latino sine flexione*, as a remedy to the ambiguity, mutability and formal redundancy of natural, historically developing languages.[73] The historian Angelo d'Orsi, an expert on Gramsci's years in Turin, does not rule out the possibility that Gramsci may have occasionally attended Peano's lectures, and also points to the fact that his prison notes contain a number of references to Peano's work.[74]

In 1918, Gramsci disagreed with other Italian Socialists about the desirability of the Party promoting the study and use of Esperanto. In one of the articles he wrote as part of this controversy, he backs his confutation of the desirability of learning artificial languages by emphasising the complexity of languages, and the unreflective use that speakers make of them. He writes that languages 'are very complex and subtle organisms' and that 'linguistic change is slow and only occurs as a result of the new contacts that the life of complex societies brings about. Changes are spontaneous and cannot be determined in an intellectualistic way'.[75]

---

70. Gramsci 1980, p. 284.
71. See Eco 1995. Proposals for spelling reforms, which had recently led to the foundation of the Italian Spelling Society, continued to be discussed in periodicals during 1911.
72. Eco 1995, p. 323.
73. See De Mauro 1996c, Vercillo 2004.
74. See D'Orsi 1999, pp. 47–8, and 2002, p. 157. Peano had already devised his project for an international auxiliary language when Gramsci arrived in Turin. He continued to promote this project during the years when Gramsci was intensely participating in the cultural and political life of the city (that is, from 1911 until 1922).
75. Gramsci 1982, p. 593. In his altercation with the Esperantists, Gramsci drew explicitly on the 'Proemio' to the first issue of the *Archivio Glottologico Italiano* (in which Graziadio Isaia Ascoli had rejected the adoption of contemporary Florentine as a fixed model for the linguistic unification of Italy): Gramsci 1982, p. 670; cf. Ascoli 1975. It

It is easy to see that these explanations resemble the above-mentioned passages from the *Course in General Linguistics*. Later, in the *Prison Notebooks*, Gramsci confirms his scepticism about international languages, which now receives further support from his views on the role of metaphors in language.[76]

2.2.4. *The penetration of Saussurean concepts into Italian intellectual culture*

The similarities between Gramsci's views and those expressed in the *Course in General Linguistics*, which I pointed out in the previous paragraphs, partly coincide with – and partly need to be added to – other such similarities, as identified by numerous Gramsci scholars,[77] as well as by two experts of structural linguistics, Luigi Rosiello and Tullio De Mauro.[78] Yet, no evidence has been found which proves that Gramsci read the *Cours*. This leads us to ask whether, and to what extent, Gramsci knew Saussure's ideas on language.

There has been virtually no historical discussion on how much Gramsci knew about Saussure's linguistics, and, irrespective of whether or not he knew about it, on the channels through which he might have come to be influenced by Saussure's ideas. Scholars have acknowledged the similarities between the two, but very little has been put forward in terms of hypotheses that could lead to a historical reconstruction of how Gramsci might have been influenced by the contents of the *Cours*. Thus the question remains open: how did the similarities between Gramsci and Saussure come about?

Gramsci sat his last university examination early in 1915, yet he continued to work more or less constantly on his thesis until 1918. The *Cours* was first published in 1916, based on the notes from the courses that Saussure taught at the University of Geneva in the last years of his life. Turin linguists showed a certain promptness in taking notice of the *Cours*, even if they did not immediately fully appreciate its novelty. Despite the constraints that the War posed to intellectual work and the transnational circulation of new ideas, Matteo Bartoli mentioned the first edition of the *Course in General Linguistics* as early as 1917, in an article which he probably wrote during the first half of the year;[79] however, his reference is to one of the relatively less innovative sections of the book, in which Saussure deals with the *causes des changements phonétiques* ['Causes of Phonetic

---

should be noted that Bréal, too, had been rather critical of universal, artificial languages (see Bréal 1901).

76. See above: section 2.2.2.

77. See Lo Piparo 1979, p. 110 note 53, and p. 249, Salamini 1981, Mansfield 1984, Helsloot 1989, Sberlati 1998, pp. 358–9, Blasco Ferrer 1999, Boothman 2004, pp. 33–45, and Schirru 2008b, p. 783 note 52.

78. See De Mauro 2010a. Cf. De Mauro 1995.

79. Bartoli 1917, p. 383 note 3.

Changes']⁸⁰ and discusses the explanations (including long-established ones) that were dominant at the time.

One of the first Italian scholars to discuss the *Cours* in its entirety was a young lecturer at the University of Turin, Benvenuto Terracini. Terracini had seen Gramsci occasionally in library reading rooms, when the young Sardinian student was in close contact with Bartoli.⁸¹ Terracini reviewed the *Cours* in a Turinese academic journal, the *Bollettino di filologia classica* ['Classical Philology Bulletin'], in 1919. His review might have been one channel through which Gramsci gained contact with Saussure's concepts.⁸² By then, however, Gramsci had become absorbed by political activities and militant journalism, so it is unclear whether he still had the time to read academic periodicals that were not directly relevant to his political commitments. He was now spending much of his time in the editorial offices of the Turin Socialist press, in the local sections of the Socialist Party, and in various factories, rather than in university libraries.

In any case, it can be assumed that Gramsci's familiarity with the works of Italian linguists, starting from his years at the University of Turin, entailed some indirect knowledge of Saussure's work. For instance, a very brief and generic reference to Saussure and the distinction between diachrony and synchrony can be found in Giulio Bertoni's *Principi generali* ['General Principles'], part of Bertoni and Bartoli's *Breviario di neolinguistica*.⁸³ Gramsci must have known Bertoni's contribution to this volume, given that both his prison notebooks and letters contain critical remarks on it. So, it might seem advisable to opt for a cautious conclusion; namely, that Bartoli's courses (including bibliographical indications) and general intellectual influence were the means by which the cultural climate of the time produced the affinities discussed above (as well as those highlighted by other commentators). Such a conclusion can be accepted, without further elaboration, as far as the earlier affinities are concerned, from 1916 to 1921.

As for later years, attention should be paid to Gramsci's lasting interest in philology and linguistics, as well as his wide-ranging curiosity for new intellectual ideas.⁸⁴ For instance, the contents of the *Course in General Linguistics* were

---

80. Cf. Saussure 1959, pp. 147–51.
81. See Zucaro 1957.
82. See Terracini 1919. This classical philology journal was edited by Luigi Valmaggi, who had been among Gramsci's university teachers (cf. Schirru 2011, pp. 963–4).
83. Bertoni and Bartoli 1928, p. 17.
84. In March 1927, Gramsci wrote to his sister-in-law, Tatiana Schucht, about his intention to carry out a methodological and theoretical study of comparative linguistics. In the same letter, he also referred to his deserting a potentially successful career in language studies: 'A major intellectual "remorse" of my life is the deep sorrow that I caused my good professor Bartoli at the University of Turin, who was convinced that I was the archangel destined to put to definitive rout the Neogrammarians' (Gramsci 1994a, I, p. 84). Shortly afterwards, in April, Amadeo Bordiga (the first secretary of the *Partito Comunista d'Italia*) wrote to Gramsci from the isle of Ustica, where he had been sent

summarised and discussed also in periodicals that did not specialise in linguistics, as part of the debate[85] that was sparked by the publication, in 1934, of Ciro Trabalza's and Ettore Allodoli's grammar of the Italian language,[86] one of the books cited by Gramsci in Notebook 29. Saussure's aforementioned comparison, involving photography and the description of a *language-state*, was applied to the theoretical and methodological debate on Italian grammar by the Latinist Giambattista Pighi, in his review of Trabalza and Allodoli's book.[87] And indeed, during the late 1920s and early '30s, editorial notes mentioning Saussure, and brief discussions of Saussurean distinctions between, for example, *synchronie* [synchrony] and *diachronie* [diachrony], or *langue* [language] and *parole* [speaking], appeared in journals that Gramsci received either regularly or occasionally while in prison.[88] These references to Saussurean notions were to be found especially in the journal *La Cultura* ['Culture']. Though not a narrowly specialised periodical, *La Cultura* published articles, reviews, and editorial notes that made accurate references to the *Cours*, including some by leading linguists such as Giacomo Devoto, Roman Jakobson, and Bruno Migliorini. In his article, Jakobson critically revisited Saussurean distinctions, especially the 'differentiation ... of "static" (i.e. synchronic) linguistics from "historical" linguistics' – that is, the 'distinction between statics and dynamics'.[89] He traced this distinction back to the ideas of nineteenth- and early-twentieth-century authors, such as Tomáš G. Masaryk (1850–1937) and Jan I. Baudouin de Courtenay (1845–1929), wondering whether its origins should not be sought in 'the Hegelian conception of the structure and dialectics of the system'.[90] While in prison, Gramsci did receive the issue of *La Cultura* containing Jakobson's article.[91]

Evidently, Italian intellectual culture was not impervious to Saussurean linguistics. In general, however, the attitude of Italian culture, including that of many linguists, was not particularly receptive to Saussure's novelties and specificities.

---

by the Fascist régime, and where Gramsci also spent a period of political confinement (December 1926–January 1927) before being transferred to a prison in Milan. 'Dearest Antonio', wrote Bordiga, 'you have been receiving printed matter, including a booklet by the Geneva philological school, which that *faculté* sent you asking for your comments' (first published in Gerratana 1975, p. 152).

85. For a survey of this debate, see Trabalza 1936, pp. 173–96.
86. Trabalza and Allodoli 1934.
87. See Pighi 1934, pp. 653–6.
88. See Gramsci 1975, pp. 3141–60, Gramsci 1996a, pp. 508–9, 818. The diffusion of Saussurean linguistics was also boosted by the International Congresses of Linguists, the third of which was held in Rome in 1933: see Terracini 1933. During these years, contacts existed between Italian linguists and the Saussurean linguists based in Geneva (where the second such International Congress had taken place, in 1931), and in 1935 Bally received affectionate messages, for his seventieth birthday, from both Bartoli and Terracini: see Bibliothèque de Genève, Ms.fr. 5006, f. 15 and f. 264.
89. Jakobson 1933, p. 637.
90. Jakobson 1933, p. 638.
91. See Fondazione Istituto Gramsci (Rome), Coll. FG Sc. 29–30.

The author of the *Cours* was often regarded as a relatively unoriginal exponent of positivist and sociological approaches to the study of language, which Italian intellectuals, under the influence of the idealist philosopher Benedetto Croce, tended to brush aside as outdated and ultimately inadequate.[92] In this respect, the mediation of non-Italian cultural experiences and sources may have helped Gramsci to absorb Saussurean notions in a more specific (though still indirect) way. The central part of Gramsci's life, during which he travelled to Russia and Austria, is thus worthy of consideration in this respect.

2.2.5. *A possible channel of transmission: the* Cours *in Russia, 1917–25*

It is likely that Gramsci heard about synchronic, structural research on language through the political and scientific discussions that were taking place in Russia, during the time he spent there; and, more generally, through his encounter with the intense research activities that accompanied the early stages of Soviet language policy. To my knowledge, only one interpreter of Gramsci, Renate Holub, has pointed in this direction, though with no explicit reference to the possible influence of the *Course in General Linguistics*. In the years from 1922 (when he left Turin for Russia) to 1926 (when he was imprisoned), Gramsci

> had a wide range of experiences. He had been one of the major leaders of the Italian working-class movement, not only organizing political struggles but, as editor of a major journal, the *Ordine Nuovo*, functioning as an organizer of the cultural and ideological struggle as well. He [was] one of the top functionaries of the international working-class movement, which accorded him the privilege to intervene personally in strategic decisions at the centre of the international revolution: in Moscow.... The period 1922–4 in Moscow means the years of cultural and theoretical tension and excitement...the Russian formalist school...and the beginnings of Russian structuralism with Roman Jakobson.[93]

Let me add some details to the picture sketched out by Holub. Gramsci lived in Russia from June 1922 up until the end of November 1923 (when he left for Vienna), and again in March to April 1925. For quite a long time, it was

---

92. While Coppola 1930 denounced Saussure and the 'French school' for their preju-dicial and outmoded insistence on the social dimension of language (p. 623), Terracini 1929 resolutely linked Saussure to the tradition of German linguistics, presenting the dis-tinction between *synchrony* and *diachrony* as one of the 'most blinkered interpretations of the thought that began with the Neogrammarians' (p. 650). Writing in 1933, Croce himself was milder on this point, conceding that the French school of linguistics had been able to innovate the 'German tradition of the Neogrammarians (through Saussure and Meillet)' (cf. Croce 1943, p. 304).

93. Holub 1992, pp. 17–18.

generally believed that Gramsci had spent most of his first, longer stay in Russia recovering from physical and mental exhaustion. Indeed, he spent some time in the Serebrianii Bor sanatorium (near Moscow), where he met Eugenia Schucht and her sister, Giulia, who was later to become his wife. But later research has provided new information, presenting Gramsci as being more active and more in contact with Soviet political and cultural life than was previously thought, and, therefore, more likely to be in touch with the debates which character-ised the politics of language during the early years of the Soviet federative state. Gramsci actively participated in the activities of the Communist International. He learnt Russian, as is confirmed by the fact that at the end of 1923 he was able to undertake an Italian translation of D.B. Riazanov's commentary to the *Communist Manifesto*.[94] He also travelled to a number of Russian cities and gave public speeches and lectures.[95]

His two periods in Russia coincided with the years when practical tasks and experiments in propaganda, cultural activities and education absorbed, in an extraordinarily intense way, the energies of Soviet intellectuals – including many linguists – as well as countless obscure militants. I shall discuss this milieu again in the following sections of this chapter. Here, suffice it to say that cultural and linguistic reforms also required the mobilisation of intellectual resources at the level of theoretical production. New approaches were devised, drawing on insights from the two dominant figures of pre-revolutionary Russian linguistics, Baudouin de Courtenay[96] and Filipp F. Fortunatov (1848–1914), founders, respec-tively, of the St. Petersburg and Moscow schools of linguistics. New methods began to circulate, always in direct connection with glottopolitical issues. Inspired

---

94. See Gramsci 1992a, p. 148ff.

95. See Kopalkidi and Leontiev 2001, Grigor'eva 1998, Bergami 1991. When Russian names are part of bibliographical references, they are reproduced as printed in the ref-erenced item. The original transliteration has also been left unmodified in quotations.

96. Baudouin's relations with Saussure, who held him in high esteem, are highlighted in Tullio De Mauro's commentary to the Italian edition of the *Cours* (see Saussure 1972, pp. 338–42), and help to explain why Russian academic institutions offered a particu-larly receptive environment for the propagation of the ideas expressed in the *Cours*. 'Baudouin is now widely recognised as one of the founders of modern linguistics, through both his revolutionising of phonetics and his methodological delineation of the language sciences. Baudouin's study of the formation of the Polish language and his studies of Slavonic dialects, along with his personal contacts with major European linguists such as Saussure, Hermann Paul and Graziadio Ascoli are increasingly recognized as having exerted a lasting and reciprocal influence on Slavonic and general European linguistic sciences...In addition to this, Baudouin, a political activist and staunch opponent of Russian imperialist policies, repeatedly stressed the need for a meeting of linguistic and social science, but he found both disciplines to be at too rudimentary a level of devel-opment to pursue this agenda himself. While teaching at St. Petersburg University..., Baudouin passed this concern on to his students Polivanov, Iakubinskii, Larin and Zhir-munskii, who also shared their teacher's radicalism' (Brandist 2003, p. 215).

by 'F.F. Fortunatov's empirical studies of synchronic language forms, and by Jan Baudouin de Courtenay's insights into structural phonology',[97] Soviet Russia's linguists came to see themselves 'as new scientists of the human word'.[98]

In the first half of the 1920s, Jakobson and Grigorii O. Vinokur, another member of the Moscow Linguistic Circle, were amongst the first linguists to define the structural study of languages as the proper terrain for language planning. Vinokur worked in the Soviet administration and diplomatic service as an interpreter, after having studied philology at the University of Moscow between 1916 and 1922, and before obtaining an academic position at the same university in the 1930s;[99] and in the meantime, he also became involved in the Futurist movement.[100] True, not everyone wished to embark on a close cooperation with the newly-established Bolshevik power. With the Revolution and the onset of the Civil War, Russia's community of linguists was shaken by the sudden political changes that were taking place. Some preferred to leave the country:

> N.S. Trubetskoi fled to Bulgaria and later Austria. Roman Jakobson eventually settled in Czechoslovakia. Baudouin de Courtenay and V.K. Porzhezinskii, a leading Moscow formalist, emigrated to Poland. For those who remained behind, life was both bleak and exhilarating.... They continued to discuss their novel approaches to language and their fascination with its power to organize human experience, to shape people's worlds and provoke them to action.[101]

Although variously interpreted and valued, Ferdinand de Saussure's theories were very much part of this extraordinarily rich and fluid intellectual environment. As early as 1917–19, 'Moscow's discussion circles' began to learn about 'the Saussurean "synchronic" method'[102] from Sergei O. Kartsevskii, who had studied under Saussure in Geneva. This 'apostle of the Saussurian school', as Jakobson calls him, 'during his shortlived return to Russia, fired the young generation of Moscow linguists with the *Cours de linguistique générale*'.[103] Both Kartsevskii and Jakobson were involved in the 'methodological controversy' on the separation between 'synchronic and diachronic linguistics'[104] which sprang up among Russian scholars at the beginning of the 1920s.

---

97. Smith 1997, p. 9.
98. Ibid.
99. See Lewiki 1996, p. 975.
100. See Hirschkop 1990 (Vinokur's interpretation of Saussurean concepts is interestingly examined in this article).
101. Smith 1997, p. 59.
102. Smith 1997, p. 60. See also Phillips 1986.
103. Jakobson 1956, p. 10.
104. Matejka 1986, p. 165.

Even though the circulation of the *Cours* was initially limited,[105] concepts which were more or less directly inspired by Saussure spread widely across different fields. In 1922, Kartsevskii 'applied the Saussurean synchronic approach to the description of the Russian verbal system', and the following year 'V.V. Vinogradov...proposed the application of a rigorous synchronic method to the analysis of style in verbal art'.[106] Vinokur summarised the contents of the *Cours* in articles published between 1923 and 1925.[107] One of his articles – aimed at a wider readership than professional linguists only – offers a programmatic description of the 'static' study of language as the most suitable approach for making linguistics a 'socially useful' discipline, and contains explicit references to Saussure's notion of *linguistique synchronique* [synchronic linguistics].[108]

Vinokur's article was not an isolated case. As has been confirmed by research into the history of Soviet linguistics, 1923 was the year that marked a turning point in the history of the penetration of the *Course in General Linguistics* into Russia. At least in St. Petersburg and Moscow, more copies became available and mentions of this book became more frequent:

> References to Saussure and to his influence appear, critically filtered, in Jakobson's book on Czech versification published in 1923. The same year, references to Saussure and his Geneva school were made repeatedly in *Russkaja rěc'* ['Russian Language'], a compendium of studies by several young Russian linguists mutually associated (as the editor of the volume, Lev Ščerba, suggests in his introductory note) by their common dependence on the linguistic teaching of Baudouin de Courtenay. Moreover, in 1923, the young syntactician, M.N. Peterson, published a lucid outline of Saussure's fundamental concepts in the journal *Pečat' i revoljucija* ['The Press and the Revolution'].[109]

Finally, during 1923 – which Gramsci spent almost entirely in Russia – there were also 'oral presentations and debates devoted to the *Cours*, which took place in diverse scientific societies and research institutes of the time'.[110] Over the next two years, the contents of the *Cours* were outlined and analysed not only in articles, but also in books. The *Cours* was explicitly referred to, either as a starting point for methodologically updated linguistic research, or as the object of radical philosophical objections and criticisms.

---

105. Only a few copies of the book were available in the early 1920s (see Vinokur 1923, note 2).

106. Matejka 1986, p. 165.

107. These articles were collected in Vinokur's book *Kul'tura iazyka* ['The Culture of Language'] which had two editions, in 1925 and 1929.

108. Vinokur 1923, pp. 104–5.

109. Matejka 1986, p. 162.

110. Depretto-Genty 1986, p. 82. See also Ageeva 2009, p. 75.

Indeed, the circulation of Saussure's ideas must soon have become fairly wide, if even a vehement critic of the *Course in General Linguistics* – Valentin N. Voloshinov – openly recognised in 1929 that 'the majority of Russian thinkers in linguistics are under the determinative influence of Saussure and his disciples, Bally and Sèchehaye'.[111] He named prominent scholars who were followers of Saussure's approach: R.O. Shor, V.V. Vinogradov, and M.N. Peterson.[112] Voloshinov also noted that, surprisingly, the *Cours* had not yet been translated into Russian (the first translation was not published until the early 1930s). In fact, by 1922 A.I. Romm, another member of the Moscow Linguistic Circle, had already translated much of the *Cours* – although his translation was to remain unpublished. Shared also by other members of the Circle, an orientation towards applied linguistics emerges, interestingly enough, from the manuscript of Romm's translation. He planned to add some notes relating Saussure's examples to the current situation in the USSR, including some on the pressing issues of spelling reforms, the alteration of the Russian language in the wake of the Revolution, and the uncontrolled proliferation of acronyms and abbreviations (especially in the jargons of politics and state administration).[113]

Similarly, other scholars and institutions contributed to the spread of synchronic linguistics as a methodological basis for language policy and planning:

> The Soviet government legitimized the role of structural principles...through N.F. Iakovlev's manifesto [published in 1922] in the journal *Life of the nationalities*...He proudly recognized that his methods were based on the linguistic theories of two innovators, Saussure and Baudouin.... The 'historical-genealogical point of view' was dead, he proclaimed; now superseded by the unity of theory and practice in synchronic linguistics. Iakovlev institutionalized the Soviet project for language reform in the Moscow Linguistic Circle, where he was chair beginning in 1923, and the Scientific Research Institute for the Study of the Ethnic and National Cultures of the Peoples of the East, which he was instrumental in creating between 1923 and 1926.[114]

Such a presence of up-to-date linguistic ideas and expertise within Soviet political institutions is further confirmed by the Bolshevik militancy of a prominent linguist such as Evgenii D. Polivanov,[115] as well as by Vinokur's involvement in

---

111. Vološinov 1986, pp. 58–9.
112. For discussion, see Slusareva 1963, and Brandist and Chown 2010.
113. See Depretto-Genty 1986, and Čudakova and Toddes 1982.
114. Smith 1997, p. 70.
115. Polivanov's life is tragically emblematic of the circumstances that many linguists experienced through the different phases of the Soviet régime. He graduated from the University of St. Petersburg in 1912. Renowned as a linguist for his specialisation in Turkic and East Asian languages, he was also committed to revolutionary politics. He supported the Bolsheviks in 1917, and was accepted as a member of the Russian Communist Party

practical work within such institutions. In the early 1920s, also a former student of Saussure's Parisian courses, F.A. Braun,[116] was active at Narkompros,[117] the Ministry of Education. And in the same period, Gramsci's future sister-in-law, Eugenia Schucht, was working at Narkompros as secretary to Lenin's wife, Nadezhda K. Krupskaya.[118] In this context, it is highly probable that Gramsci's curiosity was stimulated by the ongoing debates, and that the most innovative theories circulated through to him.

2.2.6. *Final remarks*

Even if Gramsci did not learn much about either Saussure or the *Course in General Linguistics*, his thoughts on language would seem to have been affected by ideas and debates that had been inspired, more or less directly, by the *Cours*. As we have seen above, in the late 1960s Luigi Rosiello noted that some of the reflections on language included in Gramsci's *Prison Notebooks* could be located on 'Saussurean...terrain';[119] however, Rosiello did not explore the connections between the *Quaderni* and the *Cours* further, and simply acknowledged that 'it is not known that Gramsci had direct knowledge of the *Cours de linguistique générale*'.[120] Forty years on, it is possible to broaden Rosiello's interpretation. If the question is whether Gramsci read the *Cours*, existing evidence continues to suggest a negative answer;[121] but if what is asked is whether certain similarities

---

in 1919. Between 1917 and 1921, he worked as a translator for the People's Commissariat of Foreign Affairs, and for the Communist International. His views on language were condemned in 1927, when he was the president of the linguistic section of the Russian Association of Scientific Research Institutions of the Social Sciences. This resulted in his exile to Uzbekistan. Ten years later he was arrested, and he was finally executed in January 1938 at the age of 47.

116. Braun studied at the University of St. Petersburg between 1880 and 1885, where he later worked as professor of German philology. After the October Revolution, Braun worked at Narkompros, where he joined committees dealing with school and university reform. In 1921 he also carried out research in Scandinavia and Germany, and in 1922 Narkompros sent him to Berlin to supervise the compilation of a bibliography of recent German scientific publications (see Lepschy 1969).

117. Acronym for *Narodnyi komissariat prosveshcheniia* [The People's Commissariat of Enlightenment]. It was 'the Bolshevik reinvention of the Ministry of Education' (Gorham 2003, p. 10).

118. See Fiori 1991, p. 51. See also Kolpakidi and Leontiev 2001. Gramsci's future wife, Giulia, had also spent some months working for Narkompros, in 1919, as the secretary of this institution's communist group.

119. In the original: *terreno saussuriano*.

120. Rosiello 1969, p. 355.

121. In the early '30s, Gramsci read a review article in which the recent developments in linguistics were briefly discussed, and Saussure was mentioned by name (see Coppola 1930, p. 623). 'It appears to me that much has changed', he observed, in a somewhat puzzled tone (Gramsci 1975, Q6, §71, p. 737). He would not seem to have taken any notice of the reference to Saussure.

between Gramsci's ideas on language and the contents of the *Cours* can be explained in terms of an indirect influence, then I believe the answer needs to be a positive one. In interwar Europe, the circulation of the seminal ideas expressed in the *Course in General Linguistics* was already going beyond the contours of linguistics and language philosophy. Through complex networks of cultural and personal contacts, this circulation had an impact also on intellectuals who were not professional linguists.

2.3. Language and social classes

2.3.1. *Sociological linguistics and the Marxist critique of language*

Early Soviet debates probably reinforced Gramsci's emphasis on language as a collective social phenomenon, which researchers should locate in time and space. Some of the sources with which he had become familiar, through Matteo Bartoli's university courses, were also known and appreciated by Soviet linguists. This was confirmed by one of them – Evgenii Polivanov, one of Baudouin de Courtenay's most influential students (and a Bolshevik as early as 1917). In surveying Soviet linguistics, Polivanov notes that the 'transfer of the centre of gravity to the sociological side of the study of language'[122] became well established between 1917 and 1927. He also points out, however, that the search for a 'sociological linguistics' was not, at the time, a Soviet phenomenon only: 'In the West one may name, for example, de Saussure (in his last book, published after the author's death), Vendryes, Meillet, Bally, Jespersen, Jordan, Vossler, Neumann, Wrede, Gilliéron, and others'.[123]

Gramsci's receptiveness to social variation may have been stimulated by the loosely Marxist theoretical framework of Soviet linguistics and dialectology, which typically focused on class variation.[124] This would help to explain some divergences between the *Prison Notebooks* and the linguistics Gramsci had studied at Turin University, which the Italian linguist Giancarlo Schirru has recently pointed out. Schirru focuses on the way Gramsci uses the notion of *prestigio* [prestige], to argue that his recourse to this notion goes somewhat beyond

---

122. Polivanov 1974, p. 58.
123. Polivanov 1974, p. 176.
124. According to Craig Brandist, the interests and ideas shared, in the 1920s, by many of Baudouin's former students, bear 'a striking resemblance to the Italian Communist Party leader Antonio Gramsci's attempt to restructure the work of Italian linguistic geographers according to the principles of Marxism.... Gramsci's attitude towards Bartoli was very similar to that of the Leningrad linguists towards Baudouin' (Brandist 2003, p. 216).

Bartoli's teaching. In Bartoli's geographical linguistics, the notion of 'linguistic prestige' applies first and foremost to 'horizontal relations between geographical areas (i.e. the specific research field of Neolinguistics)';[125] in other words, to contacts between languages, or varieties of a language, which are geographically defined. In contrast, Gramsci also considers socially defined varieties, and expands 'the notions used in the analysis of linguistic change' to include the 'analysis of vertical relations', too:[126] in his *Prison Notebooks*, 'when language contacts are analysed, reference is constantly made to the social structure that mediates these contacts'.[127] Schirru attributes his distance from Bartoli's teachings solely to the 'mediation of French historical linguistics',[128] and especially to some of the ideas expressed by Michel Bréal in his *Essai de sémantique*. It seems reasonable to add to this mediation also the influence of early Soviet debates.

As we saw in the previous section of this chapter, the presence of up-to-date linguistic ideas and expertise within Soviet political institutions is confirmed by the Bolshevik militancy of leading linguists, who often worked for Narkompros.[129] At the same time, an interest in language was also evident among Communist political leaders and Marxist theoreticians. In this respect, it is interesting to recall D.B. Riazanov's commentary to the *Communist Manifesto*.[130] In the letters that Gramsci wrote to his wife, Giulia Schucht, from Vienna (where he lived between December 1923 and May 1924), he expressed enthusiastic appreciation for Riazanov's commentary. In 1925, Gramsci included a (partial) translation of Riazanov's commentary (which he had probably translated with his wife) in the study guides he prepared for the students of the 'Internal Party School'[131] – a correspondence school for Italian Communist militants. In a passage which

---

125. Schirru 2008a, p. 418. On Bartoli's Neolinguistics, see Appendix: 4.2.1; and also Chapter Three: 3.1.
126. Schirru 2008a, p. 418.
127. Schirru 2008a, pp. 412–13.
128. Schirru 2008a, p. 418.
129. R.O. Shor and A.I. Romm, the author of the first (unpublished) Russian translation of the *Cours*, also agreed to collaborate with Narkompros (see Čudakova and Toddes 1982, pp. 66–7). As the New Economic Policy (1921–8) became established and 'some economic stability was achieved after the Civil War, the new approaches to language developed within institutions that were either within the orbit of Party or State control' (Brandist 2008, p. 280).
130. David B. Gol'dendakh, better known as Riazanov, 'had joined the Socialist movement before Lenin' (Ulam 1998, p. 545). He supported the Bolsheviks during the revolutionary events of 1917, but soon came into conflict with the Party, and denounced the brutal and arbitrary use of force that was being made. His appointment as director of the Marx-Lenin Institute was, to a large extent, a measure taken to relegate him to the margins of political activity. Under Stalin, he was accused of having never really stopped being a Menshevik and, on the basis of this and other allegations, removed from his post and exiled (see Bravo 1973, pp. 323–6).
131. See Gramsci 1988, pp. 61–208.

Gramsci included in his translation, Riazanov quotes a language-related comment from Friedrich Engels's 1845 *Condition of the Working Class in England*:

Ready money, the dominant factor in capitalist society, is the chief stimulus in the psychological life of the bourgeoisie. Hence arises the slogan: 'Put money in thy purse!' Engels paints a vivid picture of this in the following lines: 'The English bourgeois is quite indifferent as to whether his workers die of hunger or not, so long as while life lasts they earn him plenty of money. Everything is measured in terms of money, and everything which does not bring in money is looked upon as foolish, unpractical, and ideological nonsense. The worker is, for him, not a human being, but merely "a hand", and it is thus that the bourgeois always speaks of him, even in the worker's hearing. The bourgeois recognises that, as Carlyle puts it, "cash payment is the only nexus between man and man". Even the bonds which link man and wife together may, in ninety-nine cases out of every hundred, be expressed in terms of ready money. The pitiful condition of slavery which money imposes on the bourgeoisie has left its traces in the English language. If you wish to say that an individual possesses £10,000, you express the matter thus: "So and so is worth £10,000". He who has money is considered "respectable" and is esteemed accordingly; he takes his place among "the better sort of people", and wields much influence; everything he does sets a standard for his associates. The huckstering spirit permeates the whole language. Every relationship is expressed by words borrowed from the commercial vocabulary, and is summed up in economic categories. Supply and demand – this formula represents the whole of an Englishman's outlook on life'.[132]

Here, we have direct evidence of Gramsci's familiarity with passages that 'can be considered as belonging to a field of *Sprachkritik* [language critique]', in which Marx and Engels 'make sharp considerations on the ideological implications of certain expressions'.[133] Indeed, Gramsci himself dealt with etymology and historical semantics in his writings, from the point of view of a critical study of culture and ideology. I shall reproduce only two, particularly significant passages from his prison notes (even though many more could be chosen, as could several from his pre-prison writings). The first concerns 'materialism':

The term 'materialism', in certain periods of the history of culture, should not be understood in its narrow technical philosophical sense but in the sense it acquired in the cultural polemics of the Encyclopaedists. Every mode of

---

132. Ryazanoff 1930, p. 83. Cf. Gramsci 1988, pp. 190–1 (and Engels 1969, pp. 302–3).

133. Lepschy 1985, p. 203. In prison, Gramsci had a copy of the Italian translation of Engels's book: *La condizione della classe operaia in Inghilterra* (see Gramsci 1975, pp. 3129–30).

thinking that excluded religious transcendence was labelled materialism. This included, in effect, all of pantheism and immanentism and, closer to our time, all forms of political realism as well. Even today, in Catholic polemics, the word is often used in this sense: whatever is not 'spiritualism' in the strict sense – i.e. religious spiritualism – is materialism, and that includes Hegelianism and classical German philosophy in general, in addition to the philosophy of the Encyclopaedists and the French Enlightenment. Likewise, in social life, any tendency to locate the purpose of life on this earth rather than in paradise is labelled materialism. It is interesting that this conception of materialism, which derives from feudal culture, is now used by modern industrialists against whom it was once directed. Any form of economic activity that went beyond the bounds of medieval production was 'materialism' because it seemed to be 'an end in itself', economics for the sake of economics, activity for the sake of activity, etc. (Traces of this conception can still be found in language: *geistlich* [literally, 'spiritual'], which also means 'clerical' in German; similarly, *dukhoviez* in Russian; *direttore spirituale* in Italian – in short, spirit meant the Holy Spirit).[134]

The second note that I would like to quote concerns the 'cosmopolitan and "papal-temporal" conception of Catholicism', which in Europe, according to Gramsci, ultimately lost its role as a 'universal premiss of any mode of thought or action' only in the nineteenth century, with the consolidation of liberalism:

Catholicism has played this role, traces of which still abound in the language and modes of thought of the peasantry in particular: Christian and man are synonymous, or rather Christian and 'civilised man' are synonymous. ('I'm not a Christian!' 'Then what are you, some kind of beast?') The penal colonists still say 'Christians and colonists'. (Amazement at first when the confinees, arriving on the ferry boat at Ustica, were heard to say, 'They're all Christians', 'There's nobody but Christians', 'There's not a single Christian among them.') Those in prison, on the other hand, more normally say 'civilians and detainees', or, in joking fashion, 'soldiers and civilians', although the southerners still say 'Christians and detainees'. In this same way, it would be interesting to study the whole series of semantic-historical passages that have been gone through in French, starting at 'Christian' and ending up at *crétin* (whence the Italian *cretino* [cretin]) or even at *grédin*. This phenomenon must be similar to that whereby *villein* has, from 'countryman', ended up meaning 'boor' and even 'lout and scoundrel'. In other words the name 'Christian' used by the peasantry (the peasants of some Alpine regions, it would appear) to refer to themselves

---

134. Gramsci 1975, Q8, §211, p. 1069 (English translation from Gramsci 2007b, with minor alterations).

as 'men', has, in some cases of local pronunciation, become detached from its religious meaning and has had the same fate as *manant* [villain].[135]

2.3.2. *Bukharin*

The most important Soviet theoretician and politician that needs to be mentioned, however, is Nikolai I. Bukharin (1888–1938). A prominent Bolshevik, Bukharin was held in great esteem by Lenin, and was to serve as president of the Communist International in the second half of the 1920s. In 1920, he published *The ABC of Communism*, a book written together with Evgenii A. Preobrazhensky, in which the authors expound – amongst other things – the principles of Soviet language policy. The second part of this book, where language-policy issues are addressed, had very little circulation in Italy. However, Gramsci knew this part. Indeed, on 20 June 1921, *L'Ordine Nuovo* published 'Communism and the Problem of Nationality', a chapter from the second part of Bukharin and Preobrazhensky's book. In this chapter, linguistic oppression is discussed at length, as a form of oppression against a weaker nationality, or against colonies and economically dependent peoples. The authors contrast this oppression with class solidarity and concord, which, through internationalism, should become stronger than any divisive attachment to a particular national identity or language community. Special attention is devoted to discrimination and hatred of an anti-Semitic character:

> The tsarist government persecuted the Jews, forbade them to live in certain parts of Russia, refused to admit them into the State service, restricted their entry into the schools, organized anti-Jewish pogroms, etc. The tsarist government, moreover, would not allow the Ukrainians to have their children taught the Ukrainian language in the schools. The issue of newspapers in the Ukrainian tongue was forbidden. None of the subject nationalities in Russia were even permitted to decide whether they wished to form part of the Russian State or not. The German government closed the Polish schools. The Austrian government prohibited the use of the Czech language and forcibly imposed German upon the Czechs.... If we are to eradicate the mistrust felt by the workers of oppressed nations for the workers of oppressor nations, we must not merely proclaim national equality, but must realize it in practice. This equality must find expression in the granting of equal rights in the matter of language, education, religion, etc.[136]

---

135. Gramsci 1975, Q20, §1, p. 2082 (English translation in Gramsci 1995, pp. 28–33). See Schirru 2008a for further details (including bibliographical references) clarifying Gramsci's comments.

136. Bukharin and Preobrazhensky 1969, pp. 241–6 (cf. 'La questione nazionale e i comunisti', published in *L'Ordine Nuovo*, 20 June 1921). It is interesting to quote another

This position might have contributed to shaping Gramsci's views about language-policy issues. Indeed, many of Gramsci's writings, from early articles up to the *Prison Notebooks* express a firm condemnation of imposed linguistic unity – that is, of the attempt at enforcing unification as something 'decreed by law'.[137] I shall return to this point later in this chapter, and in Chapter Three.

Bukharin also explores linguistic themes in a section dedicated to 'Language and Thought', in his 1921 manual of Marxist sociology: *Historical Materialism: A System of Sociology*.[138] Gramsci included some parts of *Historical Materialism* in the study guides he compiled for the students of the Communist Party's correspondence school (see above). It is well known, however, that in his *Prison Notebooks* he analysed Bukharin's manual critically, and eventually came to express substantial reservations about the very theoretical basis of Bukharin's arguments: the structure-superstructure model.[139] As far as linguistic topics are concerned, Bukharin's position appears to have been characterised by a simplistic schematism very far indeed from Gramsci's approach. For instance, many of Gramsci's notes on metaphor (which I have already discussed) arose as comments to *Historical Materialism*. Gramsci's reflections about the metaphoric processes constantly operating in language were, in this sense, triggered by his critical dialogue with Bukharin's book, appearing in notes where this is discussed and criticised.[140]

---

passage, also from the second part of *The ABC of Communism*: 'Under the tsar, Russian was the only permissible language in the State service and in the school; the non-Russian subjects of the tsar were not allowed to receive instruction in their native tongue. In the new schools, all trace of national oppression disappears from the realm of instruction, for those of every nationality are entitled to receive education in their respective tongues' (Bukharin and Preobrazhensky 1969, p. 283).

137. Gramsci 1975, Q1, §73, p. 82 (cf. Q23, §40, p. 2237).

138. Bukharin's manual was first published in Russian in 1921. In prison, Gramsci had a copy of a 1927 French translation (see Gramsci 1975, p. 3040). Bukharin's excursions into linguistic theory should not be underestimated: before it became a central issue in Marxist debates on language – especially with Marr's 'New Doctrine of Language', and Stalin's condemnation of Marrism – the idea that language is part of the superstructure was already present in Bukharin's work (see Brandist 2005, Lecercle 2004, Sanga 1977 and 1982; see also Stalin 1968, Formigari 1973, Rosiello 1974, Montaldi 1978, Marcellesi and Eliman 1987).

139. See Cospito 2004a and 2004b.

140. In the *Notebooks*, Gramsci presents language as a continuous process of metaphor, 'whereby words, phrases and idioms "stand in for" or denote something else.... [He] engages in such questions in his critique of Nikolai Bukharin.... Bukharin takes up Marx and Engels' point that they are developing an "immanent" philosophy. Bukharin is concerned that it would be too easy to misinterpret this notion as an endorsement of the religious notion of "immanence" meaning that God exists within the physical or temporal world. Bukharin argues that Marx and Engels could not be accepting such a notion, even in the form described by Kant or Hegel. Clearly, according to Bukharin, this literal notion of immanence is one of Marxism's key criticisms of Idealist and bourgeois philosophy that imports mystical, religious, or metaphysical notions of God into our understanding

Gramsci was aware that 'the study of languages as a cultural phenomenon grew out of political needs', and that 'the needs of normative grammar have exerted an influence on historical grammar and on its "legislative conceptions"', reinforcing 'the application of the positivist-naturalist method to the study of the history of languages conceived as the "science of language"'.[141] This position is reminiscent of Bukharin's insistence on the fact that scientific research always grows out of practical demands and class conflicts;[142] yet, it has very little in common with Bukharin's rigid dichotomy (established in the introduction to *Historical Materialism*) between bourgeois and proletarian science, or with his ensuing conclusions about the superiority of the latter.

However, despite their different approaches, Gramsci was also able to find in Bukharin an explicit focus on class variation and on cultural and professional differentiations as important objects in the study of language:

> Some...tribes ('pure cattle breeders') have no subject of conversation but their cattle, owing to the fact that the low level of their productive forces restricts their entire life to the sphere of production, and their language therefore remains directly connected with the process of production.... The increased number of words borrowed from foreign languages is a good example of the manner in which language grows. Such borrowings result from an economy of universal dimensions and the development of a number of practically identical things in many countries, or of events having universal significance (*telephone, aeroplane, radio, Bolshevism, Comintern, Soviet*, etc.). It would lead us too far afield to point out in detail that the character, the *style* of a language also changes with the conditions of the social life; but it is worth while to mention that the division of society into classes, groups, and occupations also impresses its mark on a language; the city-dweller has not the same language as the villager; the 'literary language' is different from 'common' speech. This difference may become so great as to prevent men from understanding each other; in many countries there are popular 'dialects' that can hardly be understood by the cultured and wealthy classes; this is a striking example of the class cleavage in language. And the various occupations have their special

---

of the world. To explain Marx and Engels' use of "immanence", Bukharin contends that it was only a metaphor. Gramsci, not satisfied with the superficiality of Bukharin's position, asks why some terms remain in use "metaphorically" while others are replaced with new words' (Ives 2004a, pp. 85–6). On Gramsci's views about *immanence*, see also Thomas 2009, especially its eighth chapter, and Frosini 2010.

141. Gramsci 1975, Q29, §5, p. 2347.

142. 'The philological sciences arose in the form of "grammars" of the various languages, as a result of commercial relations and the requirements of intercourse. Statistics began with merchants' "tables", each dealing with a specific country (likewise, the first beginnings of political economy; one of the earliest economists, William Petty, calls one of his works: *"Political Arithmetic"*), etc., etc.' (Bukharin 1926, p. 163).

languages; learned philosophers, accustomed to dwell in a world of subtle distinctions, write – and sometimes even speak – a language that only their fellows can understand.[143]

This passage is partly similar to some of Gramsci's statements from the prison years. In Notebook 6, he writes that language is 'tightly linked to the life of the national multitudes, and it develops slowly and only molecularly'.[144] One might say that 'every social group has a "language" of its own'; however, Gramsci specifies that, rare exceptions aside, there is 'a continuous relationship and exchange between popular language and the language of the cultured classes'.[145] In the same notebook, he also writes that 'there is no parthenogenesis in language, there is no language producing other language'.[146] Linguistic innovation occurs through the interference of different cultures, and takes place in very different ways: it can occur 'molecularly', or it can occur 'for whole masses of linguistic elements'.[147] Then he goes on to explain that molecular 'influence and interference can take place among different strata within a nation': this is what happens, for instance, with 'professional jargons – that is, the jargons of specific groups'; whereas 'a new class that acquires a leading role innovates as a "mass"'.[148] And in Notebook 29, Gramsci adds that peasants moving to the city end up 'conforming to urban speech through the pressure of the city environment. In the country, people try to imitate urban speech; the subaltern classes try to speak like the dominant classes and the intellectuals, etc.'[149]

Other reflections on language and society also reveal partial similarities between Bukharin and Gramsci. The latter writes that the formation of a person's worldview takes place under the influence of 'the external environment' – that is, of

> one of the many social groups in which everyone is automatically involved from the moment of his entry into the conscious world (and this can be one's village or province; it can have its origins in the parish and the 'intellectual activity' of the local priest or ageing patriarch whose wisdom is law, or in the little old woman who has inherited the lore of the witches or the minor intellectual soured by his own stupidity and inability to act).[150]

---

143. Bukharin 1926, p. 205.
144. Gramsci 1975, Q6, §62, p. 730.
145. Ibid.
146. Gramsci 1975, Q6, §71, p. 739.
147. Ibid.
148. Ibid.
149. Gramsci 1975, Q29, §2, pp. 2342–3.
150. Gramsci 1975, Q11, §12, pp. 1375–6 (English translation in Gramsci 1971c, pp. 323–43).

In the same note (from Notebook 11), Gramsci connects this process with the process by which every person comes to use language in a way that is socially connoted and ideologically loaded. This connection emerges again in other notebooks – for instance in Notebook 29, where Gramsci speaks of the informal training (such as mutual correction, teasing, requests to rephrase unclear sentences, and so on) that contributes to the spontaneous expansion of 'grammatical conformism' and 'national linguistic conformism'.[151] A similar connection can be found in a passage from *Historical Materialism*, where Bukharin writes that if

> we examine each individual in his development, we shall find that at bottom he is filled with the influences of his environment, as the skin of a sausage is filled with sausage-meat. Man 'is trained' in the family, in the street, in the school. He speaks a language which is the product of social evolution; he thinks thoughts that have been devised by a whole series of preceding generations; he is surrounded by other persons with all their modes of life; he has before his eyes an entire system of life, which influences him second by second. Like a sponge he constantly absorbs new impressions. And thus he is 'formed' as an individual. Each individual at bottom is filled with a social content. The individual himself is a collection of concentrated social influences, united in a small unit.[152]

Finally, Gramsci's understanding of languages as social and historical products – similar (as has been seen above) to that of Saussure, and crucial as a theoretical foundation to Gramsci's ideas on language policy and planning – is particularly evident in his comments on the semantic evolution of words. I have already noted that these comments appear mostly in notes which Gramsci wrote with reference to Bukharin, as in the notes on the use of 'dis-aster' quoted earlier. Therefore, it may not be too surprising that a comparison between those notes[153] and the following passage from *Historical Materialism* should show affinities on this point, too:

> Many oppose the conception of causality and law in nature with the argument that... this conception is itself the result of an erroneous assumption of a celestial lawgiver. No doubt that is the origin of the idea, but the idea has left its origin far behind. Language presents many cases of such evolution. When we say, for example, 'the sun has come up', 'the sun has gone down', of course we do not believe that the sun has actually 'come', or 'gone', as a man comes or goes, on two legs, but that was probably the original conception. Similarly, in the case of the word 'law', we may say that 'a law prevails', or 'applies', which

---

151. See Gramsci 1975, pp. 2342–50.
152. Bukharin 1926, p. 98.
153. Gramsci 1975, Q11, §24, pp. 1426–8, and §28, pp. 1438–9.

by no means signifies that the two phenomena (cause and effect) involve any third invisible little god, lodged in the cause, reins in hand.[154]

2.3.3. *Sociolinguistic variation and the national question in the USSR*

During the time Gramsci was in Russia, the principles that Lenin had set out with respect to language and nationality had to be transformed into policy-making decisions in some of the most highly problematic contexts of non-Russian Soviet peripheries.[155] Towards the end of 1922, the Communist Party became directly involved in language-planning programmes for non-Russian languages. The Central Committee dealt with these projects, relying mostly on Stalin's work as Commissar of the Nationalities and Chief of the Agitation-Propaganda Department. Moscow now had the opportunity to stand by the initiatives of some local élites, thus accrediting its role as patron of the advancement of the diverse Soviet nationalities. However, it also appropriated and manipulated these initiatives for its own goals. Support for the native linguistic varieties of each community had to be politically functional, with central Soviet power applying the strategy of *divide et impera*. The Bolsheviks opposed unifying identities which they felt could represent potential threats.[156] For instance, in the Volga-Urals, after abolishing the first Tatar-inspired Idel-Ural state in 1918, they suppressed Mirsaid Kh. Sultan-Galiev's communist nationalism. The Tatar Autonomous Soviet Socialist Republic (ASSR) which they finally created in 1920, as part of the Russian Soviet Federative Socialist Republic (RSFSR), did not unify the Turkic or Finno-Ugric populations of the area. In Central Asia,

> the native course of political development (between 1914 and 1924) favoured a regional Turkestanian state: providing for internal autonomy between the Tatar, Kazakh, Kirgiz, Turkmen, Uzbek and Tajik peoples, yet also for their 'organic mixture' into a common Turkic and Muslim ethnoreligious grouping. But the Bolsheviks held that the 'compactness' of nations was more progressive than 'dispersion' of tribes and clans within larger territorial units.[157]

Most probably because they feared the threat of pan-Turkism, the Bolsheviks opted, in 1924, for a policy of national demarcation, transforming the Turkestan ASSR into the Uzbek and Turkmen Republics while also creating the Tajik, Kazakh and Kirgiz ASSRs.[158] A similar strategy was applied in Northern Caucasus,

---

154. Bukharin 1926, p. 31.
155. See Goldhagen 1968, Kirkwood 1989, Zubov 1994, Smith 1997. See also section 2.4 in this chapter.
156. See Carrère d'Encausse 1971 and 1998.
157. Smith 1997, p. 49.
158. See Bruchis 1982, pp. 27–9.

despite the fact that local leaders envisaged a broad regional state rather than separate nations.

These frictions with some local élites constituted an important political issue involving language diversity. At the centre of the new state, the Bolsheviks were embarking on a huge classificatory and legislative operation with respect to linguistic plurality. They faced the problem of how to foster cultural unification, 'of collectively attaining a single cultural "climate" ', and quickly became aware of the importance of 'the general question of language' – as Gramsci wrote some years later.[159] In these comments (from Notebook 10), Gramsci does not mention Soviet debates, but he would certainly have retained memories of what he had seen and heard. Indeed, Gramsci resided in Russia during a crucial period of Soviet nationality and language policies, which began in the last years of Lenin's leadership and continued in the early phases of Stalin's ascendancy. Furthermore, in a period when Soviet society was characterised by rapid, intense linguistic innovation and by the loosening of ties between the centre and the peripheries, the Bolsheviks, and those who decided to collaborate with them, had to examine how linguistic spread was taking place. They had to focus their attention on what Gramsci would later refer to as the 'centres of irradiation [*focolai di irradiazione*] of linguistic innovations in the tradition and of national linguistic conformism in the broad national masses'; accordingly, they had to ask 'what is the centre from which linguistic innovations are presently diffused from below', and also 'if (and where) there is a spontaneous centre of diffusion from above – that is, in a relatively organic, continuous and efficient form – and whether it can be regulated and intensified'.[160]

In his book on *language culture* in revolutionary Russia, Michael Gorham offers a reconstruction of the great variety of debates on 'public discourse', and on the 'distribution of linguistic capital' within the new Soviet society, which occupied many pages in several Russian periodicals after 1917.[161] The range of topics was extremely wide: non-Russian and minority languages; purist reactions to language contacts and innovations; verbal impoverishment; proletarian modes of speaking and writing; the journalistic styles of village and factory correspondents (*sel'kory* and *rabkory*); popular literature; and folklore. These debates, as illustrated by Gorham, became particularly intense in the first half of the 1920s. Then in 1924, 'when the existence of the Union [USSR] itself was officially ratified, the task of defining and identifying nationalities began in earnest'.[162] Linguists made their contribution to this political initiative of spatial organisation

---

159. Gramsci 1975, Q10II, §44, p. 1331.
160. Gramsci 1975, Q29, §2, pp. 2344–5.
161. See Gorham 2003.
162. Grenoble 2003, p. 39.

and ordering, by providing accurate accounts of the relevant demarcations between languages.

Most of those linguists were former students of Baudouin de Courtenay. With his insistence on linguistic and ethnic democracy, and with his opposition to the proliferation of nationalisms as a viable response to ethno-linguistic oppression, Baudouin had, in some ways, anticipated Lenin's theoretical stance on nationality and language issues. Thus, on the one hand, it is not surprising that the Bolsheviks were initially able to recruit reliable specialists particularly amongst his students. On the other hand, however, in creating territorial demarcations, they did not act in accordance with Baudouin's proposals, and sometimes created arbitrary groupings in a context of widespread dialect variation and social bilingualism. The emphasis on native languages may itself have been a way to introduce divisions which did not correspond to those perceived by the local population: 'there was a lack of clear linguistic boundaries, and the native peoples often did not identify themselves with one or another ethno-linguistic group. Instead, identities were formed along religious or geographic lines'.[163]

Especially after his 1923 report on the national question at the Twelfth Congress of the Russian Communist Party, Stalin introduced an even higher degree of formal bureaucraticism and scientific oversimplification into the Bolshevik handling of language-policy issues. Also evident in Stalin's formula defining proletarian culture as 'national in form but socialist in content', this preference for superficial simplification set a political model that would soon lead to the introduction of 'a system for ranking the various nationalities, referred to as the ABCD hierarchy'.[164] This system defined what level of official recognition and promotion should be ascribed to each language, particularly in education (from primary schools to universities). Russian occupied a privileged role in this hierarchical grid, as the shared medium of communication for all nationalities and ethnic groups. This approach, initially designed for the Russian Federation (RSFSR), was also applied, *de facto*, in the process of the formation of the USSR – a process that Stalin conceived of as having to proceed 'from multiplicity to unity', with an emphasis on unity.[165]

Giancarlo Schirru has identified some significant differences between these Soviet language policies and the positions expressed in Gramsci's *Notebooks*. For Gramsci, the language-policy task that the working-class movement had to try to accomplish was that of 'popularising the national language', and not that of 'imposing a sub-standard code or an artificial international language'.[166]

---

163. Grenoble 2003, p. 45.
164. Ibid.
165. See Smith 1997, pp. 51–2.
166. Schirru 1999, p. 56.

However, partly as a result of his assimilation of Graziadio Isaia Ascoli's legacy, Gramsci was well aware that 'the linguistic centralisation of the popular masses could only be attained through a rational reorganisation of national cultural apparatuses'.[167] Therefore, Gramsci's position differs from Soviet language policy on two, interconnected points: firstly, he emphasised the 'historically elitist character of the national language', which needs to be gradually spread among the masses and cannot be taken as a given, homogeneous linguistic background shared by all the individuals within a particular population; and, secondly, he attached greater importance to the 'nexus between language and culture'.[168] Following this interpretative line, we can see how Gramsci distanced himself from those principles of Soviet language policy which guided the work of authorities and experts under Stalin, and led them to try to make administrative demarcations correspond to ethnic and linguistic ones. Gramsci seems to have condemned mechanically-established demarcations in writing that 'socio-historical distinctions and differences...are reflected in the common language'; that language 'also means culture and philosophy (if only at the level of common sense) and therefore... "language" is in reality a multiplicity of facts more or less organically coherent and co-ordinated'; that 'every speaking being has a personal language of his own'; and, finally, that culture 'unifies in a series of strata, to the extent that they come into contact with each other, a greater or lesser number of individuals who understand each other's mode of expression in differing degrees'.[169] In these passages from Notebook 10, Gramsci's approach seems to have been at odds with Soviet policies as implemented under Stalin, with regard to the links between languages, social classes and national cultures.

According to Schirru, 'Stalin believed that popular spoken languages were so centralised as to provide a relevant feature for the identification of national communities'. In addition, in Stalin's position, 'we do not find any links between linguistic unification, culture and intellectuals'.[170] Schirru, however, does not confine his discussion to Stalin, and presents Gramsci's views as discordant with Soviet language policies on more general points:

> The Bolsheviks...intended to resolve the national question in the most mechanical form, by endorsing the principle of self-determination, and to do so they needed to identify, over the entire territory, a series of geographically contiguous nations that were easily definable on the basis of empirical criteria. It was these premises, among other things, that lay behind Soviet language policy at least up to the end of the 1920s, which promoted many local linguistic

---

167. Ibid.
168. Ibid.
169. Gramsci 1975, Q10II, §44, p. 1330.
170. Schirru 1999, p. 58.

varieties to the status of national languages. We are quite obviously far from the complexity of Gramsci's analysis which, even on the language question, reacted against the simplistic nature of official Soviet Marxism...; it is however possible that he saw in some comments of the 'last' Lenin at least an awareness of the mechanicism of the Bolshevik position, to which Stalin on the other hand seemed more tenaciously bound.[171]

I largely agree with Schirru's emphasis on the discordance between Gramsci's statements and Soviet language policies; and I shall show that during his prison years, Gramsci questioned also other aspects of the policies implemented under Stalin, when the achievement of linguistic unity came to rest primarily upon the privileged role of a pre-selected language – Russian. At the same time, it can nonetheless be argued that certain inputs received from Soviet debates, with respect to the politics of language, prompted some of the positions Gramsci was to express in his prison writings; and that those inputs resulted not only in disagreement, but also in partial similarities. This was due to two facts which are insufficiently recognised in Schirru's analysis. First, at the end of the 1920s and in the early 1930s, when Stalin consolidated his power, actual language policies changed to such an extent that one should be careful not to lose sight of the discontinuity between Leninism and Stalinism in this field. Second, at least until the late 1920s, there was no perfect equivalence between the simplistic principles stated by Bolshevik leaders and the far more nuanced approaches taken by linguists in their complex socio- and geo-linguistic enquiries; and, in general, differing positions and sensibilities circulated at the time, even within the Bolshevik leadership (for instance, Bukharin's insights into sociolinguistic variation, as discussed above).

In any case, contacts with Soviet debates must have confirmed Gramsci's belief that the popular masses should be trained to master thoroughly a language which was capable of expressing the highest and most universal achievements of world intellectual culture. Much of his discussion of grammar was also grounded on the same approach. In Notebook 29, indeed, he argued that 'the national-popular mass' should no longer be excluded 'from learning the educated language'.[172] In Russia, Gramsci found that this position was supported by representatives of Soviet cultural and political life who had already attracted his attention in the late 1910s, when he was already very receptive of foreign intellectual trends in his work as editor of Socialist periodicals (*Il Grido del Popolo* and *L'Ordine Nuovo*).[173] Anatoly Lunacharsky,

171. Schirru 1999, pp. 58–9.
172. Gramsci 1975, Q29, §6, p. 2349.
173. See, for example, Lunacharsky's articles, 'La cultura nel movimento socialista' ['Culture in the Socialist Movement'], with an introduction by Gramsci, *Il Grido*

who ultimately approved of the ABCD directives as Commissar of Education, held that the 'backward' peoples of the USSR could not hope for much
progress through nativization. 'We are obliged', said Lunacharskii, 'altogether
obliged to promote them to the Russian language', the bearer of democracy
and civilization.[174]

And Nadezhda Krupskaya, Lenin's wife, claimed that 'civilization must first come
to the small peoples through the native language, the "greatest means of revolutionary propaganda and enlightenment"; second through Russian, the "great
language" of the USSR'.[175]

2.3.4. *Grammar and language education for the popular masses*

Language-status planning and minority-language rights legislation were not the
only pressing tasks in the dynamic situation created by the Russian Revolution.
Specialists' research work was expected to support practical activities in various fields. Politicians (and politicised linguists) wished to identify some suitable means with which to improve literacy among the masses and bring them
to fully-effective participation in political communication. Philosophers and
linguists very much wanted to put their conceptualisations to practical use, in
the field of revolutionary journalism (where correspondence from workers and
peasants was deemed to be of great importance by the Soviet authorities), in
the printing industry, in agitation techniques and in propaganda. Furthermore,
in the years 1922–5, debates on language policy and planning were characterised
by a recurrent emphasis on educational issues. These discussions were directly
linked with – and were in some ways the culmination of – a long militant tradition within Russian research on language and education; a tradition which had
begun in the second half of the nineteenth century. It is worth summarising
these debates, especially those concerning topics which Gramsci, too, took up in
his comments on language, both before and after his spells in Russia.

Russian academic circles and the educated reading public were influenced,
already in tsarist Russia, by *Mysl' i iazyk* ['Thought and Language'] by Aleksandr A.
Potebnia (1835–91). Originally published in 1862, this book was republished

---

del Popolo, 1 June 1918, and 'Cultura proletaria' ['Proletarian Culture'], *L'Ordine Nuovo*,
28 August 1920. On 29 September 1921, some of Lunacharsky's views were summarised
in an article entitled 'L'istruzione nella Russia dei Soviet' ['Education in Soviet Russia'],
published in the daily *Ordine Nuovo*.
174. Smith 1997, p. 54.
175. Ibid. As to the presence of Krupskaya in Gramsci's periodicals, see *inter alia* her
own 'Istruzione popolare' ['Popular Education'], and H. Roland-Holst, 'La moglie di
Lenin' ['Lenin's Wife'], published in *L'Ordine Nuovo* on 19 June 1920 and 10 November
1921 respectively.

several times. New editions appeared between 1922 and 1926,[176] that is, in the years of Gramsci's closest contact with Russian cultural life. Potebnia and his followers looked at grammar and its categories as a framework for 'the mastery of thought and for the promotion of national literary development'.[177] Moreover, Potebnia was amongst the first linguists who criticised the way in which grammar was taught in tsarist Russia's schools.

At the beginning of the twentieth century, the Russian intelligentsia was fascinated by linguistic research, and by the latest developments in anthropology, ethnography, art, and literature. These interests were closely tied to the political views of most intellectuals and educated élites: a populism which they sought to implement through philanthropic initiatives and reformist policies. Some teachers tried to form a populist alliance with linguists, so as to lobby for reforms regarding alphabets, spelling, grammar and language teaching. Most probably, the family of Gramsci's wife, the Schuchts, were familiar with this cultural and political milieu. A rich, educated family with progressive political views,[178] the Schuchts were, in many respects, typical representatives of that cultural and political environment. Gramsci's encounter with this multilingual family, of which many members had been engaged, or were engaged, in language teaching and translation, deserves attention. In some of his letters to his wife, he wrote at length about translation. And his enduring interest in language studies must have continued throughout the period in which he frequented the Schuchts (between his arrival in Russia and his imprisonment), despite the fact that linguistic themes did not loom large in his writings at that time. These writings dealt with predominantly political issues; however, he may have shared his interests in language with his wife and, more or less directly, with her family.

That Gramsci's linguistic interests continued, while he was closest to his wife's family, can be inferred from two letters which Tatiana Schucht wrote to her sister Giulia in August 1928. In these letters, Tatiana makes revealing comments casting light on the importance that linguistics had in Gramsci's life between 1922 and 1926 (when he saw his wife for the last time). While he was in prison, only one of the Schucht sisters, Tatiana, lived in Italy. On 24 August 1928, Tatiana wrote to him that she would soon ask Giulia to send, from Russia, one of Potebnia's books. 'They suggested this textbook to me' – she added – 'when they learnt about your interest in language studies'.[179] This sentence elusively refers to those connected to the Italian and international Communist movement who were coordinating

176. See Łesiów 1996, pp. 748–9. On Potebnia, see also Seifrid 2005, Kokochkina 2000, and Leont'ev and Tseitlin 1979.
177. Smith 1997, p. 18.
178. See Gramsci Jr. 2007, 2010.
179. Gramsci and Schucht 1997, p. 248. In fact, there is no direct evidence showing that Gramsci had access to Potebnia's books while in prison.

Tatiana's assistance to the prisoner. She constantly provided Gramsci not only with practical aids, but also with cultural inputs and bibliographical updates. She knew that she was writing in a country which was ruled by a politically hostile dictatorship, and that her brother-in-law's correspondence was systematically checked by his jailers. Hence she preferred to conceal the identity of her collaborators and supervisors by using a sentence with no explicit subject.[180] Six days later, on 30 August 1928, she wrote to Giulia: 'you...know how interested Antonio is in linguistics. I was told that you could have some information about important books in this field from Lunacharsky – they say he is interested in every subject, and would be very glad to give relevant advice'.[181]

Soon after the October Revolution, linguistic matters and, in particular, the issue of illiteracy gave rise – more urgently than before – to wide and intense debates. Top leaders themselves decided to intervene, given the highly problematic situation. In Gramsci's *Notebooks* we find a reference to a collection of 'articles' and 'studies' by Trotsky,[182] which includes a brief article on the use of Russian after the Revolution: 'The Struggle for Cultured Speech'. Trotsky had originally published this article in *Pravda* in 1923,[183] when Riazanov had also joined the ongoing debate on language.[184] During the same year, the main results were published of Iakov Shafir's study *The Newspaper and the Village*, containing significant data on the linguistic skills of peasants, workers, and Red Army soldiers.[185] This research, conducted during the summer of 1923, had been commissioned by the Press Subdivision of the Communist Party Central Committee, and its results were reprinted in 1924. Most of the subjects interviewed fared poorly in vocabulary tests; they showed considerable difficulties in understanding political terminology and the language of communist publications in general. Shortly afterwards, an important study entitled *The Language of the Red Army Soldier* was conducted by the psychologist Isaak Shpil'rein (who had joined the Communist Party in 1920). His findings were unsettling. Some soldiers struggled 'just to make out the unfamiliar typescript in the surveys and often had trouble understanding the menu of definitions they were to choose among'.[186] Others admitted, with evident irritation, that the abundance of foreign words in the

---

180. I have rendered the Italian phrase *mi hanno suggerito*, used by Tania, with the English pronominal subject 'they'. This translation conveys the idea of more than one person communicating with Tania, which would not be as evident in translations such as 'it was suggested to me'.

181. Schucht 1991, p. 42.

182. Gramsci 1975, Q4, §52, p. 489, Q22, §11, p. 2164.

183. Cf. Trotsky 1973, pp. 52–6. Formigari 1973 (pp. 155–9) includes Trotsky's 1923 article in her anthology of Marxist theoretical contributions to language studies.

184. See Selishchev 1971 (originally published in 1928), p. 167.

185. See Gorham 2003, p. 29.

186. Gorham 2003, p. 28.

newspapers 'prevented them from "understanding how and toward what Socialism [was] aiming" '.[187]

In December 1924, *Pravda* published an article entitled 'Stop Spoiling the Russian Language', which Lenin had written towards the end of 1919 in order to criticise the unnecessary use of foreign words in newspapers.[188] And in an article of 1925, the eminent linguist Afanasii M. Selishchev wrote about 'revolutionary waves' of foreign words, acronyms, neologisms and phraseology created by urban socialism: innovations coming from the 'centre' which did not always spread so easily across rural peripheries.[189] These studies and debates were not concerned with purism, or language norms in general, from the perspective of *les belles lettres*; they looked at how words were understood by different speakers, and how some words spread in some socio-geographical environments while failing to spread in others. They focused on the practical implications of issues which pertain – to use today's terminology – to the sociology and politics of language use and language education. Similar issues were also addressed by Gramsci. As I mentioned previously, and as I shall note again later, they can be found in his early writings, before his visits to Russia, as well as in *Prison Notebooks*.

Lunacharsky also took part in these debates, focusing especially on the internal linguistic divisions of the Russian-speaking community. He expressed his concern about language barriers, as they could prevent the working masses from reaching high-level intellectual culture and a mastery of the literary language that such culture entailed. As early as 1918, Lunacharsky spoke at the opening session of the Institute of the Living Word in Petrograd. Institutes of the Living Word appeared in both Petrograd and Moscow, each dedicated to 'research and training in various spheres of public speaking'.[190] In the first half of the 1920s, these higher-education institutions supported the work of linguists and educators whose intention was to contribute to the linguistic empowerment of the lower social classes. If helped to overcome the limits created by their exclusive knowledge of dialects or other culturally-marginal varieties, the members of these classes could become – it was hoped – members of a new, wider and more democratic speech community. Again, this is another theme which was central to Gramsci's work, from his early years as a socialist journalist up to the theoretical reflections of Notebook 29.

Lunacharsky was at the head of Narkompros, the political body that was in charge of spelling reforms, the introduction of the Latin alphabet, and also

---

187. Ibid. It has recently been pointed out that 'Shpil'rein's methodological procedures suggest an approach to language and politics similar to that we find theorised in Gramsci's work on hegemony' (Brandist 2010, p. 163).
188. See Lenin 1965c, p. 298.
189. See Smith 1997, p. 37. Cf. Selishchev 1971, p. 11.
190. Gorham 2003, p. 13.

other projects concerning scripts and the teaching of Russian in schools. 'The school reforms of the early 1920s opened the final struggle between the proponents of logical grammar, mostly traditionalist teachers, against the formalists, representatives of the new linguistics'.[191] The formal grammar of Fortunatov's Moscow school prevailed. 'Together with Narkompros, the leading pedagogical associations in the country disseminated formal methods throughout the schools'.[192] In 1924, P.O. Afanasiev's 'popular booklet, *The Native Language in the Labour School*...defined the broader role of language study within the new curriculums of the 1920s'.[193] But debates were still taking place. They centred not only on questions of grammar and standardisation, but also the attitude that school teachers were supposed to show towards dialects and other non-standard varieties. The old school grammar posited the Russian literary language of the educated élite as the true and sole absolute, whereas now this approach was also being questioned:

> Through official Narkompros directives of 1921, the formalists requested that the language of teaching in grammar and pronunciation lessons be the local dialect spoken by pupils. Only later in their studies was bookish speech to be introduced.... Education was to begin with the lower orbits of language and culture, the simple and accessible, in order to reach the higher orbits, the complex and remote fundamentals of the literary language, with greater ease.[194]

It soon became clear that the expansion of schools and schooling also meant that teachers could no longer ignore, or take for granted, the cultural and linguistic environment of their students. They needed 'to understand the systematic rules and patterns of lower-class speech in order to correct mistakes and maintain vigilance over them'.[195] The use of this contrastive method was a pressing necessity in most schools, as far as Russian-language teaching was concerned. Even if different positions arose amongst linguists and educators, with some insisting on the need to accept local varieties and others demanding more emphasis on the correct spelling and pronunciation of the literary language, two principles came to govern language education during the years when Gramsci resided in Russia. One was that the cultivated, more prestigious varieties of the Russian language could only be acquired by students insofar as their own social or regional dialects were not abruptly stigmatised. The other was that this 'cultural pluralism' rested indeed on the 'elitist' assumption that 'the written word, literacy, was

---

191. Smith 1997, p. 111.
192. Ibid.
193. Smith 1997, p. 112.
194. Smith 1997, pp. 112–13.
195. Smith 1997, p. 114.

an efficient standardizing tool to turn all those simple rural children into more abstract and complex urban thinkers'.[196]

While he was in prison, Gramsci's reflections on educational language planning revolved around the same questions, and led to partly similar answers to those which had emerged in Russia during the early Soviet period. As a fundamental theoretical premise to his views on education, he maintained that school education does not operate in either a cultural or an intellectual void. Therefore, teachers need to be trained to be able, in their teaching, to bridge the distance between 'modern culture' and 'popular culture or folklore',[197] taking the latter into serious consideration. Yet this approach should not lead to a passive contemplation of the culture – deemed to be uncontaminated by modern thought or ways of life – dominating the environment outside the school. Nor should it give rise to a romantic idealisation of the primordial characteristics of folkloric culture and local linguistic varieties, by depicting them as the only tools that can make spontaneous and immediate forms of communication possible.

Gramsci believed in the usefulness of teaching grammar, and advocated political measures to promote and generalise this teaching as a means of speeding up national linguistic unification. He hoped, however, for a form of intervention based on scientifically rigorous observation of the existing geographical and social centres from which linguistic conformism was already spontaneously spreading. He expressed these hopes in the notes in Notebook 29 – one of which, according to Tullio De Mauro, contains another implicit criticism of the 'cultural and linguistic policies of Stalin's age'.[198] Here is the passage to which De Mauro refers:

> Since the process of formation, spread and development of a unified national language occurs through a whole complex of molecular processes, it helps to be aware of the entire process as a whole in order to be able to intervene actively in it with the best possible results. One need not consider this intervention as 'decisive' and imagine that the ends proposed will all be reached in detail, i.e. that one will obtain a *specific* unified language. One will obtain a *unified language*, if it is a necessity, and the organized intervention will speed up the already existing process. What this language will be, one cannot foresee or establish: in any case, if the intervention is 'rational', it will be organically tied to tradition, and this is of no small importance in the economy of culture.[199]

---

196. Smith 1997, pp. 114–15.
197. Gramsci 1975, Q27, §1, p. 2314.
198. De Mauro 2010a, p. 60.
199. Gramsci 1975, Q29, §3, pp. 2345–6 (English translation in Gramsci 1985, pp. 183–4).

Again, however, disagreement would seem to coexist with similarities, insofar as language-related subjects are used to assess Soviet influences on Gramsci. In fact, from his years in Turin up to his prison years, Gramsci's concern with linguistic disciplines as a resource for politically-useful applications was, broadly speaking, in line with *early* Soviet approaches (prior to the consolidation of Stalin's power), regardless of the extent to which his views were directly influenced by those approaches. For instance, already in the years before his imprisonment, Gramsci saw language questions as politically relevant issues, in that they could determine the popular masses' possibilities for intellectual progress. He realised that both grassroots activism and broader political participation by the masses depended, to quite a large extent, on language knowledge and skills. Where these were poor, passivity and superficiality were likely to prevail. Indeed, the risk of language-provoked intellectual and political passivity was taken into account by Gramsci even before he went to Russia.[200] Some of his early articles (one of which I shall summarise at the end of this section) leave few doubts on this point, and suggest that Gramsci's concerns about language-related passivity were, at least in their initial stages, independent from Soviet influences. However, his contacts with Soviet cultural institutions in the first half of the 1920s must have exerted a decisive, reinforcing influence on this aspect of his linguistic convictions.

Gramsci shared some of the Soviet expectations about the potential of applied linguistics for teaching the popular masses how to use linguistic communication, and self-expression, more accurately and effectively. Following Comintern and Proletkult recommendations, as well as the example of Soviet journals and newspapers, *L'Ordine Nuovo* published factory reports, alongside articles and literary pieces written by workers.[201] In the period which includes his residence in Russia, Gramsci was particularly concerned with agitation and political communication.[202] He came to share the attention of Soviet intellectuals, and political authorities, for the acquisition by Communist rank-and-file militants of 'the skills necessary for producing meaningful public discourse. In Soviet Russia, forums for such language training included classes on writing, journalism, public speaking, and debate'.[203] Similarly, in the mid-1920s, in the materials he prepared for the above-mentioned 'Internal Party School', Gramsci announced that students would be provided with 'conversation schemes'.[204] He even gave precise instructions on how to pronounce Friedrich Engels's surname.

---

200. See Carlucci 2008, pp. 106–7.
201. It should be added that Gramsci's letters to his wife, written while he was in Vienna, contain references to the *rabkor* movement (see Gramsci 1992a, pp. 144, 321).
202. For studies on Gramsci's involvement in the training of revolutionary cadres and militants, see Somai 1979, pp. 120–59, Morgia 1988, and Lussana 2007.
203. Gorham 2003, p. 45.
204. Gramsci 1988, p. 71.

Obviously, this type of language education had a political motive. According to Gramsci, linguistically-hesitant workers always risk considering themselves more ignorant and incompetent than they really are. He wrote, in the same period, that workers are always hesitant when they have to express their opinions, and often think they should just listen to others' opinions.[205] Later, with respect to semantic and phonological accuracy, he emphasised (in Notebook 9) the importance of basic language-training aids that he suggested might be provided by periodicals:

> 1) a column in which all the foreign names and words that might be used in the various articles should be represented in the most accurate phonetic transcription possible of the Italian language – hence the need to construct a table for the translatability of foreign phonemes into Italian phonemes, using the practical and unitary criteria that the structure of written Italian allows; 2) a column which gives the meaning of words that have a specialised nature in the different languages (philosophical, political, scientific, religious etc.) or have a specialised usage in the work of a given writer.
>
> Normally, insufficient consideration is given to the importance of these technical aids since, in remembering and especially in expressing one's opinions, one does not reflect on the obstacle constituted by not knowing the pronunciation of certain names or the meaning of certain terms. When the reader comes up against too many obscurities of pronunciation or meaning, he stops, loses confidence in his own strength and aptitude, and is unable to get out of the state of intellectual passivity into which his intelligence has sunk.[206]

Again, Gramsci had autonomously expressed similar concerns in his early writings, even before he went to Russia. In an article of March 1918, he had suggested that comrades should buy a dictionary that 'indicates the correct stress and the exact value of the words they learn from books and newspapers'.[207] In this article, Gramsci explains that many workers use clumsy turns of phrase 'even when they know the meaning of the proper word, simply because they do not know how to

---

205. See Gramsci 1988, pp, 130–1.
206. Gramsci 1975, Q9, §34, pp. 1116–17. See also this passage from Notebook 5: 'it should be possible to correct the most common mistakes made by Italians, most of whom learn language from texts (newspapers, primarily) and hence are unable to stress words correctly (for example *profùgo* [instead of *profugo*, meaning 'refugee'] during the war; I have even heard a man from Milan say *rosèo* for *roseo* [rose-coloured], etc.). Some very serious errors of meaning (specific meanings broadened, or vice versa); syntactical and morphological mistakes and confusion (the subjunctives used by Sicilians: *si accomodasse, venisse,* for *si accomodi, venga* [please come in, Sir/Madam], etc.)' (Gramsci 1975, Q5, §131, p. 664).
207. Gramsci 1982, p. 707.

stress this word, and are therefore afraid of mispronouncing it'.[208] A dictionary could help the workers in overcoming this sense of linguistic inadequacy, especially if it clearly indicates 'the value of words', and their 'correct pronunciation and spelling'.[209] Thus Gramsci recommended a dictionary (which had recently been published) by the Italian grammarian and lexicographer Giulio Cappuccini, because it fulfils these requirements, and because it collects all of the spoken language: 'This means it includes the language that has superseded dialects, even if originating from dialects other than Tuscan; it also records those specifically modern words which, though of foreign origin, have now been assimilated by the organism of our language'.[210]

2.3.5. *Final remarks*

As we have seen in this section, and as we shall see again in Chapter Three, Gramsci's writings often show a sociolinguistic sensitivity which was, in many respects, ahead of his time. Such sensitivity would seem to be less acute in the writings of contemporary Italian academics, including those of Bartoli. Gramsci, instead, went through a series of mutually reinforcing experiences that made him fully aware of the importance of combining parameters which had long been used in historical linguistics (based on the notions of *time* and *space*) with new factors concerning social stratification, and with the new challenges posed to public communication by the active participation of the popular masses in political life. These personal and political experiences included, most significantly, his encounter and affiliation with the workers in Turin, as well as his contacts with debates about communication and language education in Soviet Russia.

It is also worth reiterating that, in examining the impact of Soviet sources and debates on the development of Gramsci's views, we should not lose sight of the chronological demarcations, and substantial distinctions, between different trends and phases such as:

- the initial Bolshevik approach to the politics of language, which set the ground for the flourishing of activities and experiments of the early Soviet period, and was, in turn, largely rooted in Lenin's ideas and statements (discussed in the next section of this chapter);
- the complex and innovative activities carried out by Soviet linguists and educationalists (with their sociological perspectives often prefiguring British and

---

208. Ibid.
209. Ibid.
210. Ibid.

American sociolinguistics), as long as the political context left sufficient room for independent research;
– and finally, the period of Stalin's rise to and consolidation of power, which began to exert an oversimplifying influence on policies concerning languages and nationalities during the second half of the 1920s.

2.4. Glottopolitical aspects of Lenin's influence

'It is not possible to abstract from the large debates on the relationship between internationalism and the national question when intending to place Gramsci's comments on language issues in their exact context'.[211] This remark by Lia Formigari invites us to pay special attention to debates concerning the relationship between language and internationalism. According to Formigari (a leading expert in the history of language theories and linguistic disciplines), the links between language and nationality, on the one hand, and language and social class, on the other, are the essential language issues in Marxist political theory and practice. As Formigari notices, this is due not only to historical circumstances, such as the development of the working-class movement in multinational states (the Austro-Hungarian and Tsarist empires), but also to the necessity of dealing with national questions in such a way that would favour the emergence of working-class internationalism. Obviously, long before Lenin and Gramsci, this need was already felt by Marx and Engels.

2.4.1. Early Marxist approaches to language policies: Marx and Engels

In the first volume of *Capital*, Marx famously spoke of 'the entanglement of all peoples in the net of the world-market'[212] as one of the processes leading from capitalism to socialism. This shift towards a unified world society is brought about by the assimilation of all peoples under the capitalist régime, and will eventually create the conditions for the solution of all national conflicts.[213] To an extent, Gramsci's views, too, can be traced back to this approach, which regarded the emergence of modern capitalist societies, in the form of large economic markets and centralised states, as a progressive historical advancement.

Hierarchical distinctions originated from this approach, and also from a series of pragmatic judgements about which struggles for national independence favoured social revolution (at the time Marx and Engels were writing), and which favoured social conservatism or reaction. According to these distinc-

---

211. Editor's introduction, in Formigari 1973, p. 14.
212. Marx and Engels 1996, p. 750.
213. See Monteleone 1982.

tions, some populations (such as the 'Highland Gaels and the Welsh')[214] were presented as mere 'remnants of peoples',[215] and, as such, opposed to nations of greater historical vitality – namely, the 'historic peoples of Europe'.[216] These distinctions were repeatedly made by Friedrich Engels.[217] Despite being interested in Germanic historical dialectology, Engels showed little sympathy for 'those that are nowadays called language minorities',[218] especially towards those minorities that seemed, at the time, particularly backward and isolated, culturally and economically underdeveloped, and thereby inconceivable as independent nations. For instance, in 1866 Engels stressed the 'difference between the "principle of *nationalities*" and the old democratic and working-class tenet as to the right of the great European *nations* to separate and independent existence'.[219] The applicability of the principle of nationalities was not to be unduly extended – firstly, because 'no state boundary coincides with the natural boundary of nationality, that of language';[220] and, secondly, because an absurdly wide-ranging application of that principle would provoke

> questions as to the right to independent national existence of those numerous small relics of peoples which, after having figured for a longer or shorter period on the stage of history, were finally absorbed as integral portions into one or the other of those more powerful nations whose greater vitality enabled them to overcome greater obstacles. The European importance, the vitality of a people is as nothing in the eyes of the principle of nationalities; before it, the Romanians of Wallachia, who never had a history, nor the energy required to have one, are of equal importance to the Italians who have a history of 2,000 years, and an unimpaired national vitality, the Welsh and Manxmen, if they desired it, would have an equal right to independent political existence, absurd though it would be, with the English.[221]

Engels had been developing these views for years when he wrote the above, and had become increasingly convinced that the historical development of the main European nations would lead to the assimilation of lesser nationalities.

---

214. Engels 1985, p. 156.
215. Ibid.
216. Engels 1985, p. 157. See also Salvi 1978, and Renzi 1981, pp. 169–71.
217. On this point, Engels's categories converged with those of a coeval liberal thinker, John Stuart Mill. In his *Considerations on Representative Government*, Mill referred to 'the Welshman or the Scottish Highlander' (Mill 1991, p. 431) in similar terms to Engels.
218. Ramat 1983, p. 188.
219. Engels 1985, p. 157.
220. Engels 1985, p. 156.
221. Engels 1985, p. 157.

> Nobody will venture to say that the map of Europe is definitively established. But any changes, if they are to endure, must increasingly tend by and large to give the big and viable European nations their real natural frontiers to be determined by language and fellow-feeling, while at the same time the remnants of peoples that can still be found here and there and that are no longer capable of national existence, remain incorporated into the larger nations and either merge into them or are conserved as merely ethnographic relics with no political significance.[222]

Marx and Engels were probably also influenced by the language policies of the French Revolution. The most radical part of the French bourgeoisie, the Jacobins, tried to enact measures in favour of French – against regional languages, including Basque, Breton, Occitan and Alsatian – in the name of equality for all citizens: 'The Constituent Assembly divided up the independent provinces, and it was the iron fist of the Convention that first turned the inhabitants of Southern France into Frenchmen and, in reparation for their nationality, gave them democracy'.[223]

2.4.2. *The Second International*

This preference for unification was largely based on the idea that historical progress was already in the process of creating the conditions for unification. As Eric Hobsbawm has argued, from the late eighteenth century onwards, there seemed to be little room for small, independent states within the global development of capitalism. Small nationalities were simply seen as having 'no independent future'.[224] This attitude came to be accepted on a general scale, even by people who were 'far from hostile to national liberation in principle, or practice'.[225] According to Hobsbawm, one should not regard this attitude as necessarily implying hostility to small, isolated, or less developed peoples, or to their languages and cultures. Rather, these peoples were often fatalistically regarded as the 'collective victims of the rules of progress (as they would certainly have been called then)'.[226]

Another important Marxist, Karl Kautsky, showed a marked preference for economic, political, and cultural unification,[227] despite the fact that he was, himself, a member of a small nationality (the Czechs). Unlike Marx and Engels,

---

222. Engels 1980, p. 254.
223. Engels 1977, p. 373. On the language policies of the French Revolution, see De Certeau, Julia and Revel 1975.
224. Hobsbawm 1990, p. 35.
225. Ibid.
226. Ibid.
227. Kautsky 1887 and 1908.

Kautsky's preference for unification had specifically linguistic (or, more precisely, glottopolitical) implications. He stressed that it was necessary to know languages in order to gain better access to modern international culture. On the one hand, Kautsky was wary of palingenetic solutions based on the arbitrary introduction of a universal language – as was Gramsci some years later. On the other hand, Kautsky encouraged the rising proletariat to learn one of the world's main languages – just as Gramsci later also did.[228] Finally, both Kautsky and Gramsci contemplated the possibility that one language would acquire so much cultural prestige and practical use that it would relegate even national languages to the role of dialects. Such a supranational language would absorb elements from other languages and would show marked changes in its character as the number of its speakers gradually increased.[229]

After Kautsky, the debate on nationality and internationalism became increasingly intense and complex, with linguistic themes acquiring particular importance in the controversy between him and Otto Bauer on national language and culture. The debate involved other leading socialists, from the theoreticians of Austro-Marxism – Bauer himself, and Karl Renner – to Rosa Luxemburg. In 1913, on Lenin's request, Stalin wrote *Marxism and the National Question*. Gramsci is probably referring to the opinions expressed by Stalin in this tract when he alludes, in a page of the *Prison Notebooks*, to the 'Russian critique of Austro-Marxism on the national question'.[230]

Lenin's glottopolitical reflections should also be placed within these debates. For him too, 'the debate on the issue of language is part of the wider set of discussions about the policies of the Social-Democratic Party with respect to national autonomies'.[231] Moreover, Lenin's writings feature not only generic triggers for further thought. The frequent attention that Lenin paid to the themes of juridical linguistic equality, and the number of references he made to the links between language, education, and the organisation of political power make it possible to identify in Lenin's writings well-defined language-policy recommendations. These recommendations are part of the many pages that Lenin devoted to the question of national and cultural autonomy, and constitute the largest section of his writings on language.[232]

---

228. See Gramsci 1982, p. 593.
229. See Gramsci 1982, pp. 671–2; Gramsci 1987, p. 557.
230. Gramsci 1975, Q2, §89, p. 246 (and p. 2563).
231. Formigari 1973, p. 17.
232. Lenin 1983, pp. 94–159.

2.4.3. *Lenin*

Lenin rejected the protection of a national culture, and did not in the least fear assimilation, that is, the loss of specific national traits. Assimilation was, he said, the 'bogey'[233] raised by those who support one form or another of nationalism. Between October and December 1913, Lenin wrote *Critical Remarks on the National Question*. Here, he argued that the Marxists' national programme should advocate, firstly, the equality of all nations and languages; and, 'secondly, the principle of internationalism and uncompromising struggle against contamination of the proletariat with bourgeois nationalism'.[234] In opposition to Liebman, a representative of the *Bund* (the General Union of Jewish Workers in Lithuania, Poland and Russia), Lenin writes:

> what does our Bundist mean when he cries out to heaven against 'assimilation'? He *could not* have meant the oppression of nations, or the *privileges* enjoyed by a particular nation, because the word 'assimilation' here does not fit at all, because all Marxists, individually, and as an official, united whole, have quite definitely and unambiguously condemned the slightest violence against, and oppression and inequality of nations.... In condemning 'assimilation' Mr. Liebman had in mind, *not* violence, *not* inequality, and *not* privileges. Is there anything real left in the concept of assimilation, after all violence and all inequality have been eliminated? Yes, there undoubtedly is. What is left is capitalism's world-historical tendency to break down national barriers, obliterate national distinctions, and to *assimilate* nations – a tendency which manifests itself more and more powerfully with every passing decade, and is one of the greatest driving forces transforming capitalism into socialism.[235]

In another passage of his *Critical Remarks*, Lenin insisted:

> The proletariat... stands for the fullest freedom of capitalist intercourse and welcomes every kind of assimilation of nations, except that which is founded on force or privilege.... [I]t supports everything that helps to obliterate national distinctions and remove national barriers; it supports everything that makes the ties between nationalities closer and closer, or tends to merge nations.[236]

Clearly, Lenin firmly opposed any kind of nationalism. Far from rejecting the possibility of a cultural, and eventually also linguistic, *reductio ad unum*, Lenin hoped for this, envisaging such an outcome as proceeding from an international process of economic, social, and political growth and integration. Elsewhere he

---

233. Lenin 1964a, p. 27.
234. Ibid.
235. Lenin 1964a, p. 28.
236. Lenin 1964a, p. 35.

stated: 'Our banner does not carry the slogan "national culture" but *international* culture, which unites all the nations in a higher, socialist unity, and the way to which is already being paved by the international amalgamation of capital'.[237] And in *Critical Remarks on the National Question*, he wrote that '[n]o one unobsessed by nationalist prejudices can fail to perceive that this process of assimilation of nations by capitalism means the greatest historical progress'.[238] He or she cannot but share the Marxist hope for 'the amalgamation of all nations in the higher unity, a unity that is growing before our eyes with every mile of railway line that is built, with every international trust',[239] and with the workers' internationalist spirit. But at the same time, Lenin maintains that, precisely in order to render this process wider and deeper, every form of language privilege and imposition must be rejected, and multilingualism improved, in order to protect the multiple linguistic codes which speakers normally use. Therefore, throwing off 'the feudal yoke', and 'all privileges enjoyed by any particular nation or language, is the imperative duty of the proletariat as a democratic force, and is certainly in the interests of the proletarian class struggle, which is obscured and retarded by bickering on the national question'.[240]

Other works by Lenin clarify this position. Two particularly significant passages can be quoted from two articles published in the first months of 1914, 'Corrupting the Workers with Refined Nationalism' and 'Is a Compulsory Official Language Needed?'

> Recognition of the equality of nations and languages is important to Marxists, not only because they are the most consistent democrats. The interests of proletarian solidarity and comradely unity in the workers' class struggle call for the fullest equality of nations with a view to removing every trace of national distrust, estrangement, suspicion and enmity. And full equality implies the repudiation of all privileges for any one language and the recognition of the *right* of self-determination for all nations.[241]

> The liberals differ from the reactionaries in that they recognize the right to have instruction conducted in the native language, at least in the *elementary* schools. But they are completely at one with the reactionaries on the point that a compulsory official language is necessary. What does a compulsory official language mean? In practice, it means that the language of the Great Russians, who are a *minority* of the population of Russia, is imposed upon all the

---

237. Lenin 1968, p. 549.
238. Lenin 1964a, p. 30.
239. Lenin 1964a, p. 34.
240. Lenin 1964a, p. 35.
241. Lenin 1964a, p. 290.

rest of the population of Russia. In every school the teaching of the official language must be *obligatory*. All official correspondence must be conducted in the official language, not in the language of the local population.[242]

In the second article, Lenin specifies that he is 'in favour of every inhabitant of Russia having the opportunity to learn the great Russian language',[243] but he further explains his rejection of the 'element of *coercion*'[244] that 'a *compulsory* official language'[245] necessarily involves. He also reiterates his conviction that 'the development of capitalism in Russia, and the whole course of social life in general',[246] will gradually bring all nations closer together:

> Hundreds of thousands of people are moving from one end of Russia to another; the different national populations are intermingling; exclusiveness and national conservatism must disappear. People whose conditions of life and work make it necessary for them to know the Russian language will learn it without being forced to do so. But coercion...will have only one result: it will hinder the great and mighty Russian language from spreading to other national groups, and, most important of all, it will sharpen antagonism, cause friction in a million new forms, increase resentment, mutual misunderstanding, and so on.[247]

This article contains, in its final part, two qualifying policy directives: 'there must be *no* compulsory official language',[248] and 'the population must be provided with schools where teaching will be carried on in all the local languages'.[249] But before inserting these directives into the overall framework of Lenin's proposals in the field of language policies, I shall stress a theoretical intuition which has probably already emerged from the passages quoted so far: Lenin understood that the tensions connected to linguistic diversity are much less frequent when solutions are sought which guarantee linguistic equality and democracy for the largest possible number of speakers, regardless of the linguistic code which these speakers normally use and which they feel most comfortable using. Indeed, the ethno-linguistic conflicts within a society often tend to worsen if the institutions ignore the existing linguistic plurality, or even try to repress it and impose homogeneity. This is especially true because homogeneity is often pursued by sanctioning the linguistic privileges of one particular group, whose language

---

242. Lenin 1964a, p. 71.
243. Lenin 1964a, p. 72.
244. Ibid.
245. Ibid.
246. Lenin 1964a, pp. 72–3.
247. Lenin 1964a, p. 73.
248. Ibid.
249. Ibid.

variety is chosen as the language of state institutions. Apparently neutral, this official language thus both humiliates the cultural identity of the other linguistic communities (by devaluing and marginalising their varieties) and blocks their social mobility. These intuitions of Lenin's have been confirmed, and their object analytically described in various contexts, by later specialist research.[250]

Especially in the years preceding 1917, Lenin maintained that a strong political, administrative, and educational centralisation was necessary;[251] but within this institutional framework, his support for multilingualism was unconditional. In his *Theses on the National Question* (June 1913), he wrote:

> The sum-total of economic and political conditions in Russia therefore demands that Social-Democracy should *unite* unconditionally workers of all nationalities in *all* proletarian organisations without exception (political, trade union, co-operative, educational, etc., etc.). The Party should not be federative in structure and should not form national Social-Democratic groups but should unite the proletarians of all nations in the given locality, conduct propaganda and agitation in *all* the languages of the local proletariat, promote the common struggle of the workers of all nations against every kind of national privilege and should recognize the autonomy of local and regional Party organisations.[252]

This support for multilingualism was organised around a set of theoretical intuitions and precise policy directives.[253] From Lenin's point of view, unification and integration develop and emerge historically, and cannot be imposed by the coercive repression of diversity. Unification can only mean voluntary integration, in connection with the development of the economy and of productive forces of society. Furthermore, an unbounded access to democracy, which Lenin considered to be the key to the integration of different populations, requires the equality of all languages. On this subject, as we have seen in the passages quoted above, he included some suggestions as to the kind of linguistic education to be implemented, as well as ideas concerning the acknowledgment and official practice of multilingualism by state institutions:

– 'The right of the population to receive education in the native language, the right of each citizen to use the native language at meetings and in public and state institutions';[254]

---

250. See May 2001, pp. 152, 193, 232; Kramsch 1998, pp. 65–7, 72–7; Inglehart and Woodward 1972, pp. 366, 375–6.
251. See Carrère D'Encausse 1971.
252. Lenin 1968, p. 249.
253. See also Marcellesi and Eliman 1987, pp. 445–7.
254. Lenin 1969, p. 87.

- the right to be educated in one's first language must be guaranteed by the state, in uniform schools for all children, regardless of the numeric weight of the different linguistic groups, and, ideally, even in the extreme case of a school with only one child from an ethnic-linguistic minority;[255]
- multilingualism does not contradict the institutional unity of a state, which, according to Lenin, can instead avoid making one language compulsory in school and administration, and allow for 'speeches in different languages' to be delivered 'in the common parliament';[256]
- '[t]iny Switzerland has not lost anything, but has gained from having not *one single* official language, but three: German, French and Italian'.[257] Lenin, who had direct experience of multilingual Switzerland (having lived there for a time), frequently referred to it in order to substantiate his claim that a state can renounce all forms of imposition and privilege with respect to language. In doing this, Switzerland not only preserved its institutional unity, but also created positive conditions for the development of a spontaneous tendency towards linguistic unification; that is, a widespread, spontaneous desire to learn the majority language.[258]

Lenin came from a vast empire that was ethnically and linguistically variegated. His views formed mostly in this context. He developed a clear understanding of the decisive role played by language policies in the handling of nationality- or ethnicity-based political issues.[259] This understanding should not be seen in merely tactical, almost cynical terms. His formulation of the principles which Soviet 'nationalities policy'[260] should follow was, in many respects, 'a pragmatic

---

255. See Lenin 1968, pp. 531–3, and his *Critical Remarks on the National Question* (Lenin 1964a, pp. 17–51).
256. Lenin 1964a, p. 21. Incidentally, this is what happens today in the European Parliament.
257. Lenin 1968, p. 355. Cf. Lenin 1964a, p. 20.
258. In his *Critical Remarks*, Lenin notes that, in Switzerland, egalitarian and democratic language policies had acknowledged the right to use, in official communications, not only the most prestigious and widespread idioms: 'there are *three* official languages, but bills submitted to a referendum are printed in *five* languages, that is to say, in two Romansh dialects, in addition to the three official languages. According to the 1900 census, these two dialects are spoken by 38,651 out of the 3,315,443 inhabitants of Switzerland, i.e., by a little over *one per cent*. In the army, commissioned and non-commissioned officers "are given the fullest freedom to speak to the men in their native language". In the cantons of Graubünden and Wallis (each with a population of a little over a hundred thousand) both dialects enjoy complete equality.... Let the Semkovskys, Liebmans, and other opportunists now try to assert that this "exclusively Swiss" solution is *inapplicable* to any uyezd [administrative unit: Russian *yézd*] or even part of an uyezd in Russia, where out of a population of only 200,000 forty thousand speak *two dialects* and want to have *complete equality* of language in their area!' (Lenin 1964a, p. 42).
259. See Carrère D'Encausse 1971, p. 224.
260. Grenoble 2003, p. 42.

move, an explicit attempt to appease the many minority groups that were striving for separation from, not incorporation into, the Soviet state'.[261] From a historiographical point of view, it should be noted that, with the stabilisation of Soviet power, efforts to develop literacy, in the various languages spoken by the peoples of the Soviet federal state, also served economic purposes; and indeed, these efforts became increasingly linked to the needs of the régime, similarly to what happened in Italy with Fascism – which was, unlike the Soviet régime, intolerant of linguistic plurality, and yet still tried to eradicate illiteracy.[262] From the point of view of language-policy theory, however, the approach that Lenin expressed in his writings, where he stressed the need to protect linguistic diversity and remove any privilege for Russian, cannot be reduced to an opportunistic legitimisation of 'shallow' multilingualism, to be enacted only for the purposes of modernising the workforce and improving propaganda.

Lenin's reflections are articulate and reveal a certain theoretical organicity. Indeed, the idea that by creating the necessary conditions of equality among various languages, multilingualism can encourage emulation, and reciprocal recognition among communities, finds its way into the general programme of socialist internationalism. For Lenin, this programme must oppose linguistic nationalism and, at the same time, help to strengthen those elements in the diverse cultures (national cultures above all) which are universal, democratic, and potentially socialist. In protecting 'the equality of all nationalities against the serf-owners and the police state',[263] support should be given not to '"national culture"' but international culture, which includes only part of each national culture – only the consistently democratic and socialist content'[264] of each national culture:

> The elements of democratic and socialist culture are present, if only in rudimentary form, in every national culture . . . In advancing the slogan of 'the international culture of democracy and of the world working-class movement', we take from each national culture only its democratic and socialist elements; we take them only and absolutely in opposition to the bourgeois culture and the bourgeois nationalism of each nation. No democrat, and certainly no Marxist, denies that all languages should have equal status.[265]

---

261. Ibid.
262. On Fascist language policies, see Klein 1986.
263. Lenin 1968, p. 116.
264. Ibid.
265. Lenin 1964a, p. 24.

2.4.4. *Did Gramsci know Lenin's ideas on language?*

I would now like to examine Gramsci's familiarity with the aspect of Lenin's work concerning language legislation. Gramsci, whose father-in-law was a very close friend of Lenin's, certainly did not ignore this aspect.[266] To support this claim, we need to scrutinise Gramsci's writings, and those of his associates. It may prove almost unnecessary to recall the frequency with which Gramsci turned to Lenin's authoritative views; yet it is quite difficult to compile a comprehensive list of which of Lenin's writings (including those dealing with language-policy issues) Gramsci certainly did read and use over the years. Nonetheless, as we have seen earlier in this chapter, it is possible to explore the extent of Gramsci's knowledge of the language-policy and language-planning practices which followed the October Revolution, and of the measures which were thereby enacted in various Soviet Republics. In particular, the following texts seem to confirm his knowledge of Leninist language policies:

i) In February 1918, the Turin Socialist paper *Il Grido del Popolo*, edited by Gramsci, published a text that contained part of Lenin's proposed changes to the programme of the Russian Social-Democratic Labour Party. Lenin had prepared this draft of a revised party programme for the Seventh All-Russia Conference of the Russian Social-Democratic Labour Party (Bolsheviks), which was held in St. Petersburg at the end of April 1917. On 8 February 1918, *Avanti!* (the newspaper of the Italian Socialist Party) had already reported on Lenin's draft of a new party programme, reproducing this draft more extensively than *Il Grido del Popolo* did eight days later. Both newspapers, however, published the paragraph in which Lenin put forward the recognition of the following rights:

> The right of the population to receive instruction in their native tongue in schools to be established for the purpose at the expense of the state and local organs of self-government; the right of every citizen to use his native language at meetings; the native language to be used on a level with the official language in all local public and state institutions; obligatory official language to be abolished.[267]

---

266. Gramsci must have been aware of the importance which language questions had had in the internal quarrels of the Russian Social-Democratic Party, as part of the debates on the issue of nationalities and of their autonomy. Lenin himself, in *One Step Forward, Two Steps Back*, had reconstructed the internal divisions 'over the equality of languages question' (Lenin 1965a, p. 70), which emerged during the Second Party Congress in 1903. According to Togliatti 1979 (pp. 165–6), it can be assumed that Gramsci already knew this tract by Lenin before visiting Russia.

267. Lenin 1964b, p. 472. Cf. 'La costituzione della repubblica russa' ['The Constitution of the Russian Republic'], *Il Grido del Popolo*, 16 February 1918.

In later years, Gramsci continued to remember Lenin's views, and how he had expressed them in the Party's internal debates, in the months immediately preceding the October Revolution. In the 22 September 1926 issue of the Communist Party newspaper *L'Unità*, Gramsci recalled the project of modifying the Bolshevik programme, presented by Lenin at 'the All-Russia Conference of the Bolshevik party that was held towards the end of April 1917',[268] and mentioned, among Lenin's proposals, 'the abolition of the official language'.[269]

ii) In his speeches at the Eighth Congress of the Russian Communist Party (March 1919), Lenin took up the issue of nationalities. In May 1920, *L'Ordine Nuovo* (the weekly and later daily paper, in which Gramsci had a leading editorial role)[270] printed the passages of Lenin's speeches in which he deals with nationalities policy, including a passage in which he condemns the exclusive use of Russian in school teaching.[271]

iii) In January 1921, the daily *Ordine Nuovo* published an article dedicated to the 'measures against illiteracy',[272] including the creation of schools which were 'opened especially for illiterates'.[273] The article exemplifies the multiplicity of the linguistic codes, quite diverse in terms of prestige and socio-demographical characteristics, that were used in the work undertaken to spread literacy: 'countless schoolbooks have been printed in Russian, Polish, German, Tartar, Chuvash, Mari, Vodian, Mordvin,[274] Osetin, Latvian, Estonian, and Yiddish (a dialect spoken by the Jews)'.[275]

iv) Bukharin and Preobrazhensky discussed the principles of Soviet language policy in a chapter of their book *The ABC of Communism*, published in 1920. In Italy, the second part of this book, where language policy issues are taken up in a spirit that is essentially consistent with Lenin's principles, had very little circulation. One of its chapters was published, however, in *L'Ordine Nuovo* in June 1921. As we saw above, the chapter published in *L'Ordine Nuovo* explores

---

268. Gramsci 1971a, p. 333.
269. Ibid. (In the original: *soppressione della lingua di Stato*). In the resolutions on the national question adopted by the Seventh All-Russia Conference of the RSDLP(B), the necessity of guaranteeing complete 'equality for all nations and languages' had been affirmed, and 'the abolition of a compulsory official language' demanded (Lenin 1964b, pp. 302–3).
270. See Giardina 1965, p. 1309; Leonetti 1970; D'Orsi 2004, p. 68.
271. 'La politica delle nazionalità nel pensiero di Lenin e nella pratica soviettista' ['Nationality Policies in Lenin's Thought and in Soviet Practice'], *L'Ordine Nuovo*, 29 May 1920. Cf. Lenin 1965b, pp. 194–5.
272. 'L'istruzione pubblica nella Russia soviettista' ['Public Education in Soviet Russia'], *L'Ordine Nuovo*, 9 January 1921.
273. Ibid.
274. The Italian original has *modvinio*.
275. Ibid.

linguistic oppression as a form of oppression against a weaker nationality, or against colonies and economically dependent peoples.

v) In one of his prison notes, in Notebook 2, Gramsci recalls Lenin's views concerning the possibility that 'national questions ... be resolved peacefully even under bourgeois rule – a classic example is the peaceful secession of Norway from Sweden'.[276] This example appears in two works by Lenin containing observations on language: *The Right of Nations to Self-Determination*,[277] where one section is entitled 'The Separation of Norway from Sweden'; and *On the Question of National Policy*.[278] In the first work, Lenin's glottopolitical views can be deduced from certain remarks, but they do not constitute a central theme; whereas in the second, they are explicitly expressed: 'A democratic state is bound to grant *complete freedom* for the native languages and annul *all* privileges for any one language. ... The workers of all nations have but one educational policy: freedom for the native language, and democratic and *secular* education'.[279]

2.4.5. *Affinities*

In what ways could Lenin's opinions have influenced those of Gramsci, in the specific field of language policies? I shall try to provide an answer to this question by looking at both similarities and differences. Neither, however, should be overemphasised or taken as fully coherent sets. Lenin's and Gramsci's comments on language-policy matters cannot be mechanically set against each other, owing to a) the nature and form of Gramsci's writings (day-by-day articles on immediate issues, letters, notes needing further revision); and b) the historical differences between his mainly Italian context and the immense, multinational Russian empire to which Lenin referred in most of his writings.

Even with these preliminary caveats, it is evident that Gramsci found in Lenin a re-proposal of themes he was already familiar with. Lenin, however, looked at these themes from a political point of view, and gave an original reworking of the Marxist theoretical perspective, so as to be able to apply this perspective to the issues of nationality, imperialism, and colonialism. The teaching of the linguist Matteo Bartoli, Gramsci's professor at Turin University, had already made him aware of the ethnic and linguistic plurality of some European regions, and of the presence of various language minorities within the borders of Italy.[280] To the awareness that Bartoli had passed on to him, and to the inspirations that

---

276. Gramsci 1975, Q2, §48, p. 201.
277. See Lenin 1964a, pp. 393–454.
278. See Lenin 1964a, pp. 217–25. In prison, Gramsci did not have access to Lenin's writings (Togliatti 1979, pp. 167–8; Gerratana 1995a, p. 141).
279. Lenin 1964a, p. 224.
280. See Bartoli 1912–13, pp. 67–70, 118–21.

Gramsci found both in the works of Ascoli and in his own life experiences, Lenin's writings, and the linguistic legislation they inspired,[281] added further encouragement to direct political attention to cultural and linguistic fragmentation. In particular, the positions taken by Lenin on language education, and on the judicial equality of any language, provided Gramsci with a relevant, authoritative example. They contained an appreciation of the value – historically progressive in bourgeois societies, and unassailable also in the construction of a socialist society – of real equality for speakers of different languages, in any communicative or educational environment, and regardless of the socio-cultural status of the language in question.

Gramsci's activity was often in line with Lenin's views on language policies and practices. For instance, in March 1918, Gramsci referred to imposed linguistic uniformity as 'a violation of history and freedom' (see below). *L'Ordine Nuovo* published articles defending some of Italy's minority languages – the French-speaking community of Val d'Aosta,[282] and the Slavonic language communities in north-eastern Italy.[283] In addition, this periodical lamented the gradual fading away of Irish Gaelic;[284] it denounced the anti-Arabic approach taken by educational institutions in the French colonies of North Africa;[285] and it reported a case of intolerance against a German-speaking community in the USA.[286] In April 1924, Gramsci urged the Executive Committee of the Communist Party of Italy to clearly express a political position on the situation of the Slav and German minorities in the areas annexed to Italy at the end of the First World War.[287]

---

281. See especially the resolutions of the Tenth Congress of the Russian Communist Party (March 1921), which supported the native languages of the various non-Russian populations, thus translating Lenin's theoretical principles into concrete policy statements.

282. See Chapter One, section 1.5.2.

283. See the following articles: 'Gli sloveni del Friuli' ['The Slovenes of Friuli'], signed 'A.P.', 2 March 1924; and Matvej Orlod, 'La popolazione della Venezia Giulia' ['The Population of Venezia Giulia'], 1 March 1925. These articles were published in the third, fortnightly series of *L'Ordine Nuovo*. On the importance of this series, and on Gramsci's assiduous editorial work, see Somai 1979, pp. 132–43; Leonetti 1970, pp. 103–4. In the first article, we find an interesting passage criticising the compulsory and exclusive use of Italian in official documents, and in school teaching. According to the author of the article (most probably Gustavo Mersú, who used the pseudonym 'A. Piccini') this use led to the exclusion of Slovene children from education. On these anti-Slav policies, which became particularly harsh with the Fascists' rise to power, see Klein 1986, Sluga 2000. See also Pizzorusso 1975, pp. 20–3, 229–31.

284. See 'Un pregiudizio' ['A Prejudice'], signed 'e.b.' (probably Ezio Bartalini), *L'Ordine Nuovo*, 31 January 1921.

285. See the remarks of the French Communist writer Paul Vaillant-Couturier in *L'Ordine Nuovo*, 3 May 1922.

286. See the unsigned article 'La Legione Americana' ['The American Legion'], published in *L'Ordine Nuovo* on 16 January 1922.

287. See Gramsci 1992a, pp. 342–3.

He also reminded his comrades of the presence of Albanian-speaking communities in southern Italy.[288] Lenin's conviction that militants should 'ensure that communist propaganda is carried on in every country in a language the people understand',[289] and in 'the languages of the local proletariat',[290] was revived by Gramsci in 1925, when he insisted on the necessity for the Communist Party of Italy to spread its slogans among the local masses of each Italian region, using the means of expression which could best be understood by those masses.[291]

2.4.6. *Jewish autonomy: a case of partial divergence*

In the letters he sent from prison after his arrest, Gramsci remained faithful to Leninist glottopolitical principles when inviting his sister to let her two-year-old son grow up speaking as much Sardinian as he liked.[292] Yet he also distanced himself, albeit only implicitly, from the language policy that Soviet authorities were imposing on Jews, as shown by a passage from a letter of October 1931 where Gramsci acknowledges 'the right of Jewish communities to cultural autonomy (of language, schools etc.)'.[293] This rejection of ideologically-led interference into the language choices of a community is significant for reconstructing Gramsci's attitude to Lenin's legacy, and to Soviet Communism in general.

The actual language policies enacted by the Bolsheviks, even when Lenin was still in power, did not exactly coincide with what he had stated on the matter. When Gramsci wrote his comment about Jewish cultural autonomy, this autonomy was already limited in the USSR. It was subjected to various forms of increasingly oppressive control by Jewish Communist institutions which were linked to the central power. Those Jews who dominated these institutions (most notably, the Jewish sections of the Communist Party) were determined to reshape the identity of their people in the context of a socialist state, according to their own views and ideas.[294] In language matters, their main target was Hebrew. This they labelled as the language of bourgeois nationalism, of reactionaries, and of religious and ideological obscurantism, and therefore opposed it to Yiddish in a rather arbitrary dichotomy.[295] In 1930, a letter of protest against the persecution of Hebrew in the USSR was signed by famous European intellectuals

---

288. Ibid. Gramsci's father, Francesco, was himself 'of Albanian descent' (Gramsci 1996a, p. 480).

289. The 1919 'Address to the Second All-Russia Congress of Communist Organisations of the Peoples of the East', collected in Lenin 1965c, p. 161.

290. Lenin 1968, p. 249.

291. Cf. Chapter One, section 1.6.

292. Cf. Chapter One, section 1.2.

293. Gramsci 1996a, p. 479.

294. See Traverso 1994, pp. 155–6.

295. See Gilboa 1982.

known for being amenable to the Soviet régime, including Albert Einstein and Thomas Mann.[296]

In addition to this distance from the practices of the Soviet régime,[297] Gramsci's 1931 letter also shows that even when facing the doctrinal legacy of Lenin, the most authoritative Bolshevik leader of all, Gramsci was able to retain a certain degree of independence. A comparison between Lenin's and Gramsci's views on Jewish identity and anti-Semitism cannot be undertaken, here – and, in any case, would go well beyond the scope of my argument. Yet the passage that I quote from Gramsci's letter seems to be of some relevance. On the one hand, it is clearly in harmony (at least in principle) with Lenin's broad-minded attitude to linguistic plurality; but on the other hand, Gramsci's reference to Jewish educational and cultural autonomy seems to follow a different line than Lenin's. As can be seen in the latter's *Critical Remarks on the National Question*, as well as in his other writings, Lenin was against cultural autonomy. In connection to this, he rejected the institution of special schools for minorities, and denied that any school could be exempted from following the 'general educational programme' of the state, which, in Lenin's view, was to be uniformly followed in all schools:

> As far as Marxists are concerned, no *departure* from this general programme is anywhere or at any time permissible in a democratic state (the question of introducing any 'local' subjects, languages, and so forth into it being decided by the local inhabitants).... At all events, it is by no means impossible to meet, on the basis of equality, all the reasonable and just wishes of the national minorities, and nobody will say that advocacy of equality is harmful. On the other hand, it would certainly be harmful to advocate division of schools according to nationality, to advocate, for example, special schools for Jewish children in St. Petersburg, and it would be utterly impossible to set up national schools for *every* national minority, for one, two or three children.[298]

---

296. Central Zionist Archive (Jerusalem), Archives of Jacob Klatzkin, A40/70.

297. According to Brandist 2005 (pp. 65–6) Soviet language policy had already degenerated considerably by the end of the 1920s. Apart from minor discrepancies about when changes began to take place, scholars agree in distinguishing a relatively tolerant period, up until the late 1920s or early 1930s, from a subsequent one characterised by a restriction of the multilingualism and linguistic equality previously promoted. The most important episodes in this reversion to language-policy conservatism, and Russification of non-Russian peoples, are thoroughly discussed in Smith 1997, Chapter Seven. Chronologically, they coincided with the transformation of Lenin's dictatorship into Stalin's totalitarianism as famously described by Arendt 1966.

298. Lenin 1964a, pp. 43–5. See also Lenin 1964a, p. 291: 'It is crass ignorance to confuse instruction in the native language with "dividing educational affairs within a single state according to nationality", with "cultural-national autonomy", with "taking educational affairs out of the hands of the state"'.

2.4.7. *Final remarks*

In pulling together the various threads discussed in this section, two points are worthy of particular emphasis. These are the main findings that would seem to emerge with regard to Gramsci's Leninism, when this general topic is investigated through the micro-section of language-policy matters. This aspect of Lenin's influence on Gramsci confirms, first of all, that Gramsci developed his own views independently. Even though he looked at Lenin as a most authoritative source in this field also, he did not merely adapt to either Lenin's teachings or Soviet initiatives in general. He was receptive to Lenin's innovative views, but did not turn them into dogma. Gramsci's approach to glottopolitical issues thus acquired a peculiar position in the history of Marxism, in comparison with both earlier Marxists and contemporary Soviet Marxists.

Secondly, if evidence of Lenin's influence on Gramsci may be crucial to asserting the 'totalitarian' worldview of the latter, as many interpreters have claimed,[299] then this point needs to be carefully assessed if it is to be referred to issues pertaining to language policy and planning. Contrary to what happens in other domains (the theory of the revolutionary party and the state, most notably), here Lenin's theoretical influence does not quite fit into the sort of syllogism according to which Gramsci, as a Leninist, would necessarily have favoured the displacement of plurality. One cannot help but notice that, with regard to language-policy matters, Gramsci's Leninism reveals different features from those it has traditionally been attributed by most authors within Gramscian studies. To summarise, in a few simple words, a view which is shared by almost the entire community of Gramscian scholars, one could say that Lenin was essentially a model of hostility to plurality, spontaneity and decentralisation.[300] Yet, as I hope to have shown, Lenin's influence on Gramsci turns out to have been characterised also by elements of an opposite nature, which point to the necessity of accommodating diversity.

In his writings on glottopolitical matters, Lenin resolutely rejected the bureaucratic suppression or arbitrary negation of plurality. On this point, Lenin's legacy significantly differed from the progressive, revolutionary tradition I briefly summarised at the beginning of this section (where I recalled the precedent set by the Jacobins, and especially the views of the most influential Marxists). This did not contradict, however, the objective of developing plurality in the direction of an effective cultural rapprochement between the various populations. Lenin

---

299. See the Introduction, where I summarised the debates concerning Gramsci's stance on the relationship between unifying and standardising tendencies, on the one hand, and multiplicity and diversity, on the other.

300. This has recently been confirmed by Anna Di Biagio's comparative study of Gramsci's and Lenin's use of the notion of hegemony (Di Biagio 2008).

expected a gradual reduction of differences to take place on the basis of an increasingly unified economy and through a process which can be defined as an 'intellectual progress of the mass',[301] a 'cultural unification of the human race',[302] in the words of Gramsci. As far as language-policy issues are concerned, Lenin's teachings urged there to be a protection of heterogeneity until it was gradually, not coercively, overcome.

2.5. Rationalising and unifying linguistic communication

2.5.1. *Soviet Esperantism*

Gramsci visited Russia during the heyday of speech-rationalisation experiments and Esperantism. Both were aspects of the search for radical changes in social life that flourished in Russia in the first half of the 1920s – the relatively liberal years of post-revolutionary cultural and academic life. Specialists from diverse disciplines contributed, and many leading linguists of the day were 'involved in academic institutions, editorial boards, and policy committees'.[303] From these centres of intellectual and political activity they legitimised 'the belief that language could be "engineered" to more adequately articulate the revolutionary ideas of the emerging state and society'.[304]

Historicism produced a widespread tendency to place world languages – Russian, in particular – ahead of geographically and culturally less relevant tongues, on a sort of timeline from backwardness to progress. We have already found this in some statements by Lunacharsky and Krupskaya. Existing cultures were often perceived in hierarchical terms, in light of the grand accomplishments that a future, worldwide unification of economic and cultural production was expected to bring about. But at the same time, political voluntarism called for a rational organisation of society, production and communication. In this respect, Lenin's appreciation of Taylorism served as an illustrious precedent for those who saw Frederick Taylor's techniques as applicable to communication and language reforms. Thus some Soviet linguists 'entertained visions of fully economized human speech patterns', focusing on Esperanto and other 'fusion languages which they fantasized might even surpass Russian in the long but quickening march toward a global culture'.[305]

---

301. Gramsci 1975, Q11, §12, p. 1385.
302. Gramsci 1975, Q11, §17, p. 1416.
303. Gorham 2003, p. 39.
304. Ibid.
305. Smith 1997, p. 74.

Gramsci brought Taylorism and the question of rational techniques into his discussion of grammar and national linguistic unification, in Notebook 29.[306] This is another remarkable indication of the fact that Soviet approaches most probably affected the formation of Gramsci's views. The integration of practical issues, and theoretical models, pertaining to language education with issues and models pertaining to industrial production and labour was, indeed, typical of early Soviet cultural life,[307] but much less so of contemporary Italian cultural life.

Occasionally, Gramsci also retained something of this hierarchical outlook. To him, as to most revolutionaries of his time, history sometimes seemed to be pushing all people – and all peoples – towards a united, more advanced world culture. In his *Notebooks*, Gramsci expressed this vision especially in a note on the opportunities that only major national languages can offer,[308] and in another note on the '[h]egemony of Western culture over the whole world culture'.[309] His concept of hegemony, however, was at odds with any idea of predestined, permanent superiority; the hegemony of Western culture resulting, instead, from its historical ability to develop expansive and flexible political projects, capable of attracting active participation from other continents. Unsurprisingly, then, Gramsci showed less sympathy for fixed universal languages than Soviet linguists and politicians initially did. He disapproved of 'fanatical advocates of international languages',[310] some of whom he probably met, or heard about, when he was in Russia.

In his prison writings, this disapproval is closely linked to his reflections on languages as being intrinsically metaphoric, and on the ensuing impossibility of eliminating semantic shifts that emerge through the different historical phases of a language and across all its social and content-based varieties. Again, these reflections may be seen as a reaction to various Russian memories, including, perhaps, the Soviet contexts that the famous linguist Roman Jakobson describes as follows:

> In the first years of the Russian revolution there were fanatic visionaries who argued in Soviet periodicals for a radical revision of traditional language and particularly for the weeding out of such misleading expressions as 'sunrise' or 'sunset'. Yet we still use this Ptolemaic imagery without implying a rejection of Copernican doctrine, and we can easily transform our customary talk about the rising and setting sun into a picture of the earth's rotation simply because

---

306. See Gramsci 1975, pp. 2343–9.
307. See, *inter alia*, Vinokur 1923.
308. Gramsci 1975, Q11, §12, p. 1377. I discussed this note in section 1.7.2.
309. Gramsci 1975, Q15, §61, pp. 1825–7. See Lo Piparo 1979, pp. 184–9, for discussion.
310. Gramsci 1975, Q29, §2, p. 2344.

any sign is translatable into a sign in which it appears to us more fully developed and precise.[311]

Esperanto was by far the most famous, and successful, international language during the early Soviet period. For a time, it appeared to be a viable option for universal communication, enjoying, as such, a certain degree of support. Jakobson himself 'respected its elegance'.[312] Stalin studied it as a young man. Some linguists (Baudouin de Courtenay, Otto Jespersen, Nikolai I. Marr, Antoine Meillet) were amongst its convinced supporters, as were some leading philosophers and scientists, notably Bertrand Russell and Rudolph Carnap.[313] In the USSR, Esperantism was to become outdated by the late 1920s, but up until then it met with mostly positive reactions, and was sometimes welcomed by fanatical, visionary endorsers. 'A special government commission, in cooperation with leading Esperantists, even called for its elective teaching in the public schools'.[314] Some Communists proposed the introduction of Esperanto as the working language of the Party's Central Committee and in other Soviet institutions. They worked for the popularisation of Esperanto, and some of them even called for its compulsory teaching in secondary schools.

Some of Soviet Russia's most fervent advocates of the use of Esperanto as an auxiliary international language allowing more rational human communication were Ernst Drezen (first, and last, president of the Soviet Esperanto Union, founded in 1921) and his collaborators. They constituted a 'radical fringe of the Taylorist and Bogdanovite movement'.[315] Bogdanov accepted the successes of Esperanto quite grudgingly, remaining wary of the utopianism underlying artificial languages. However, Bogdanov and those of his followers who supported Esperanto were united by a common interest in radical social engineering. In their eyes, economic and administrative modernisation could be enhanced through a more effective use of language.

With the consolidation of Stalin's power, Esperantists 'received a new lease on life ... in the service of a vital national interest, the Second Five-Year Plan'.[316] Michael Smith describes this phase in detail in his highly informative book, *Language and Power in the Creation of the USSR*, which is based on Soviet publications and archive documents dating from the years 1917–53. The Second

---

311. Jakobson 1959, p. 234. Cf. Gramsci 1975, pp. 1065, 1438.
312. Smith 1997, p. 77.
313. See Eco 1995, p. 326.
314. Smith 1997, pp. 77–8.
315. Smith 1997, p. 79. Bogdanov was a physician, philosopher, economist, and science-fiction writer. In the first decade of the twentieth century, he was also a Bolshevik leader, until his positions came into conflict with those held by Lenin. His death was the result of medical experiments that he was conducting on himself.
316. Smith 1997, pp. 154–5.

Five-Year Plan took place from 1933 to 1937. During this period, Drezen began to work on the full unification of terms and symbols within the theoretical, techni-cal, and applied disciplines. 'He even aimed for the "fixation of terms for each mechanical component of each elemental process". His goal, to repudiate every "figurative and allegorical style" in order to avoid the "imprecision and multiple meanings of different expressions"'.[317] Gramsci criticised similar initiatives in the very same years, especially in his notes on the Italian 'pragmatists'.[318]

Towards the end of this chapter, I shall further consider Gramsci's stance on Esperanto and on other projects for international auxiliary languages. Here, I would like to stress that Gramsci had already reached some conclusions on this point before he went to Russia. He had been familiar with attempts at introduc-ing artificial languages for international communication ever since his years in Turin. I have already mentioned the projects devised there by Giuseppe Peano, and the proposals for the adoption of an artificial, international language that were discussed within the Socialist Party. The proposed language was Esperanto. In 1918, Gramsci expressed negative views on this language, at a time when the debate was not based on speculation alone: in Turin, some Socialist militants were involved in an Esperantist group, whose meetings and courses were being advertised in Socialist newspapers. And it is interesting to note that, despite Gramsci's sceptical views, *L'Ordine Nuovo* continued to advertise these meetings, even after the 1918 debate.

2.5.2. *Proletarian culture*

When Gramsci came into close contact with the Russian revolutionary move-ment and the innovative cultural trends that thrived in the aftermath of the October Revolution, he held quite firmly to his own views and remained largely immune to any fantasies of linguistic palingenesis. In Russia, linguists were joining forces with futurist writers, in a common search for more rational models for human conduct and communication; models that were expected to speed up socio-historical progress. Improvements in public and workplace communication were to be accomplished through new forms of organisation, in accordance – some linguists argued – with the principles of the scientific organi-sation of labour.[319] This was applied by engineers to the industrial production processes, and was known, in its Soviet version, by the Russian acronym 'NOT' – *Nauchnaia organizatsiia truda*. As far as language-education reforms were

---

317. Smith 1997, p. 155.
318. See above, section 2.2.2. Cf. Gramsci 1975, Q7, §36, pp. 886–7, and Q11, §24, pp. 1427–8.
319. See Smith 1997, pp. 76–77, 111.

concerned, some futurists shared Bogadanov's antipathy towards traditional methods of grammar teaching. A truly proletarian order was expected to come about, as a result of organisation and popular participation: an unprecedented combination of discipline and spontaneity, capable of producing new forms of social, artistic, and cultural life. Lunacharsky and Bogdanov organised the Proletkult movement around this platform. Their aim was to break away from bourgeois influences, thus creating something radically new: a 'cultural order... dominated by a proletarian class spirit'.[320]

Gramsci did not take all of this at face value. Certainly, he did not accept the most utopian, visionary aspects of such projects. For instance, he was quite clear in asserting, throughout his life, that mainstream culture and humanistic school curricula should not be deemed irrelevant to the cultural development of the subaltern classes. This position is quite similar to that taken by Lenin after the Revolution.[321] However, while in Russia, and in the years immediately before and after his time there, Gramsci was all but indifferent to innovative, so-called

---

320. Mally 1990, p. 254.
321. See Manacorda 1964. In his early writings, as well as in the *Prison Notebooks*, Gramsci emphasises the importance of teaching Latin and Greek at school (I shall return to this aspect of Gramsci's glottopolitical views in Chapter Three). In Notebook 12, he expresses his appreciation for the teaching of Latin, although conceding that this language might be profitably replaced with another subject (see Manacorda 1970, pp. 330–5; Broccoli 1972, pp. 184–7). Moreover, Gramsci commends 'the grammatical study of Latin and Greek' imparted by the 'old school' – that is, 'the old Italian secondary school, as organised by the Casati Act' in 1859, where the role of 'mechanical coercion' was quite central: 'the real interest was the interior development of personality, the formation of character by means of the absorption and assimilation of the whole cultural past of modern European civilisation. Pupils did not learn Latin and Greek in order to speak them, to become waiters, interpreters or commercial letter-writers. They learnt them in order to know at first hand the civilisation of Greece and of Rome – a civilisation that was a necessary precondition of our modern civilisation: in other words, they learnt them in order to be themselves and know themselves consciously. Latin and Greek were learnt through their grammar, mechanically; but the accusation of formalism and aridity is very unjust and inappropriate' (Gramsci 1975, Q12, §2, pp. 1543–4). This appraisal seems to reflect the views that Lenin expressed in 1919, after the Bolsheviks had seized power: 'it is not enough to crush capitalism. We must take the entire culture that capitalism left behind and build socialism with it' (Lenin 1965b, p. 70). Lenin also warned that rejecting the 'old school' – namely, that of pre-revolutionary Russia, where students had to learn notions by rote, where 'drill-sergeant methods' of 'ceaseless drilling and grinding' were practised – could constitute a 'grave error'. This error was that of thinking 'that one can become a Communist without assimilating the wealth of knowledge amassed by mankind', that is the culture left by 'the old society' (Lenin 1966). Lenin used these words in a text, 'The Tasks of the Youth Leagues', originally published in *Pravda* in October 1920 and then published in Italian in *L'Unità* (the newspaper founded by Gramsci in 1924), on 19 January 1926. However, Lenin's writings on school education can only in part be compared to Notebook 12. Gramsci's echoing of Lenin's warnings should be seen as an original re-elaboration, conducted as part of Gramsci's autonomous reflections. Indeed, his reflections were also stimulated by Italian debates on pedagogy and by the development of Italy's school system under Fascism. On Gramsci's close and fertile relation with

'proletarian' cultural trends; and even some of his prison notes (especially the ones he included in Notebook 22, entitled *Americanism and Fordism*) would, according to some commentators, bear resemblance to Bogdanov's views.[322] Indeed, some traces of Proletkult influence, and also direct references to this institution, can be found in *L'Ordine Nuovo* and in Gramsci's pre-prison writings, especially those from the early 1920s. For instance, in an article published in June 1920, which predates by a few months the foundation in Turin of the *Istituto di Cultura Proletaria*, the Italian section of the Proletkult, and clearly refers to the creation of this new institute, Gramsci writes:

> Do elements for an art, philosophy and morality (standards) specific to the working class already exist? The question must be raised and it must be answered. Together with the problem of gaining political and economic power, the proletariat must also face the problem of winning intellectual power. Just as it has thought to organise itself politically and economically, it must also think about organising itself culturally.... According to our Russian comrades, who have already set up an entire network of organisations for 'Proletarian Culture' (Proletkult), the mere fact that the workers raise these questions and attempt to answer them means that the elements of an original proletarian civilisation already exist, that there are already proletarian forces of production of cultural values, just as the fact that the workers create class organisations in order to carry out their cultural activity means that these values too, unlike in the bourgeois period, will be created by the working class on the basis of organisation.[323]

In the same article, he also writes:

> One can easily foresee that when the working class wins its liberty, it will bring to the light of history new complexes [*complessi*] of linguistic expressions even if it will not radically change the notion of beauty. The existence of Esperanto, although it does not demonstrate much in itself and has more to do with bourgeois cosmopolitanism than with proletarian internationalism, shows nevertheless, by the fact that the workers are strongly interested in it and manage to waste their time over it, that there is a desire for and a historical push towards the formation of verbal complexes that transcend national

---

Lenin's late theoretical statements and political choices, see also Frosini 2003, pp. 95–8, and Thomas 2009.

322. See Bermani 1979, pp. 95–6. See also Bermani 1981, 1995; Sochor 1981, p. 60; Scherrer 1998, p. 175; and Brandist 2012. According to Brandist, in October 1922 Gramsci was among the Comintern delegates who met with the Chair of Proletkult, Valerian Pletnev, to develop the cultural dimensions of the work of the Communist International.

323. Gramsci 1987, pp. 556–7. (English translation from Gramsci 1999, pp. 70–2, slightly edited).

limits and in relation to which current national languages will have the same role as dialects now have.[324]

Traces of Gramsci's sympathy for radical cultural innovation – in a spirit somewhat similar to that of Proletkult – are also particularly evident in two other texts. These are Gramsci's letter to Trotsky of 8 September 1922 (published in the Russian edition of Trotsky's book, *Literature and Revolution*) regarding Italian Futurism and its founder, Filippo Tommaso Marinetti,[325] and an article of January 1921. In this article, entitled 'Marinetti rivoluzionario?' ['Marinetti the Revolutionary?'] Gramsci wrote about the new artworks that the workers were creating, and about the 'historicity' and 'possibility of a proletarian culture created by the workers themselves'.[326] However, he once again rejected, quite unambiguously, state planning and imposition in the domains of culture and language:

It is not a material factory that produces these works. *It cannot be reorganized by a workers' power according to a plan. One cannot establish its rate of production for the satisfaction of immediate needs, to be controlled and determined statistically.* Nothing in this field is foreseeable except for this general hypothesis: there will be a proletarian culture (a civilization) totally different from the bourgeois one and in this field too class distinctions will be shattered. Bourgeois careerism will be shattered and there will be a poetry, a novel, a theatre, a moral code, a language [*una lingua*], a painting and a music peculiar to proletarian civilization, the flowering and ornament of proletarian social organization. What remains to be done? Nothing other than to destroy the present form of civilization. In this field, 'to destroy' does not mean the same as in the economic field. It does not mean to deprive humanity of the material products that it needs to subsist and to develop. It means to destroy spiritual hierarchies, prejudices, idols and ossified traditions. It means not to be afraid of innovations and audacities, not to be afraid of monsters, not to believe that the world will collapse if a worker makes grammatical mistakes, if a poem limps, if a picture resembles a hoarding or if young men sneer at academic and feeble-minded senility.[327]

---

324. Gramsci 1987, p. 558.
325. See Gramsci 1964, pp. 633–5; also included in Gramsci 1966, pp. 527–8.
326. Gramsci 1966, p. 22.
327. Gramsci 1966, pp. 20–2 (English translation in Gramsci 1985, pp. 49–51). My emphasis.

2.5.3. *Sources and periodisation*

Gramsci's interest in linguistic disciplines did not end when he abandoned his university studies. The idea of a pre-Marxist Gramsci, who acquires idealist philosophical attitudes and liberal political views before being absorbed by Marxism and communist militancy, needs to be revised. This interpretation was put forward, with special emphasis on Gramsci's study of linguistics, in Franco Lo Piparo's book, *Lingua, intellettuali, egemonia in Gramsci* ['Language, Intellectuals and Hegemony in Gramsci']. In order to support his interpretation, Lo Piparo somewhat exaggerated the idealist, anti-positivist character of Matteo Bartoli's Neolinguistics, and established a rather generic parallelism between positivist trends in linguistics and dogmatic versions of Marxist socialism.[328]

It is true that Lo Piparo specified that Gramsci, despite being a communist of a peculiar kind, could not be classified as 'liberal'.[329] All the same, Lo Piparo's views appeared to be largely consistent with the image of Gramsci that some democratic and liberal socialists had adopted, in Italy, many years earlier. This was the image of the young Gramsci as an open-minded, non-dogmatic socialist, who was later led astray by the sirens of Leninist communism, before he finally returned to democratic socialism during his years in prison.[330] Through Lo Piparo's interpretation, one can easily find justification for the admiration that many progressive liberals and Crocean intellectuals have had for Gramsci (as in the case of Tullio De Mauro, under whom Lo Piparo studied). As far as language-related topics are concerned, however, such a partition of Gramsci's intellectual biography may well have caused insufficient attention to be paid to Soviet debates as possible sources of influence.

Other factors contributed to this lack of attention. Archival documents and other pieces of historical evidence were, for many years, too scarce to allow a detailed biographical reconstruction of the periods that Gramsci spent in Russia and in Vienna between 1922 and 1925. There was little information about the role of language policies in the establishment of Bolshevik rule during the early stages of Soviet power. It would, therefore, have been difficult to make plausible suppositions about the development of Gramsci's interest in language

---

328. See Rosiello 2010 and Schirru 2008a for valid criticism of Lo Piparo's arguments; and Timpanaro 1969 for an accurate and comprehensive discussion of the links between philosophy, linguistics and politics in the nineteenth and early twentieth centuries. See also Chapter Three, especially section 3.1.

329. Lo Piparo 1979, p. 150 note 71.

330. See, for instance, Tamburrano 1963. See Liguori 1996 for discussion. I shall take up this point again in Chapter Three. In more recent works, Lo Piparo has abandoned his initial caution, fully developing the idea that during his imprisonment Gramsci severed his ties with communism and went back to the linguistics and liberalism of his youth: see especially Lo Piparo 2012.

studies during this part of his adult life. But in recent years, some previously unknown sources have been made available. In view of this, and using information which had not yet come to light when Lo Piparo wrote his book, one of my main aims in this chapter has been to show: a) that in the years between the end of Gramsci's university studies and his arrest, stimulating inputs regarding linguistic subjects were by no means lacking; b) that many of them came from the politically-loaded cultural life of post-revolutionary Russia; and c) that Gramsci was most probably receptive to those inputs.

In the *Prison Notebooks*, Gramsci is, no doubt, under the influence of mostly Italian sources. From the terminology he uses to the objections he anticipates and rejects, Gramsci's arguments about grammar (collected mostly in Notebook 29) amount to a polemical dialogue with idealist positions: Croce, Gentile, and – not explicitly mentioned by Gramsci, but clearly present in his discussion – the Sicilian educationist Giuseppe Lombardo Radice. Some passages in Gramsci's notes on grammar appear to be in reply to an essay by Lombardo Radice, 'L'ideale di una educazione linguistica. Lingua e grammatica' ['The Ideal of a Language Education: Language and Grammar'],[331] which Lo Piparo rightly includes in his list of the indirect sources of Notebook 29.[332] Both the texts by the young Gramsci and the testimonies of those who had been in contact with him at the time confirm that he had already developed a special interest in the ideas of Lombardo Radice during the First World War period.

This 'Italianness' of Gramsci's sources is probably one of the reasons that led Giulio Lepschy, a leading linguist and historian of linguistics, to assert that Gramsci's 'notes on grammar appear to suffer from the isolation which was characteristic of Italian culture in those years'.[333] It is true that many prison notes immediately reveal this Italian background; and it is appropriate to speak of isolation, if one thinks of the level of innovation to which theoretical linguistics was being brought by the exponents of American and European Structuralism. However, the formation of Gramsci's ideas on language was also influenced by some non-Italian sources. This influence emerges even when it is not explicitly acknowledged by Gramsci, though his sources did not include many of the most important linguists (such as Edward Sapir, Leonard Bloomfield, Nikolai S. Trubetskoi, Louis Hjelmslev) who were contemporary with him.

In *Lingua, intellettuali, egemonia in Gramsci*, Lo Piparo points to Italian debates as Gramsci's dominant source. Nonetheless, he shows how Gramsci was influenced by non-Italians as well, especially by Jules Gilliéron (1854–1926) and Antoine Meillet (1866–1936). Yet he unconvincingly restricts this influence to

---

331. See Lombardo Radice 1970, pp. 149–68.
332. See Lo Piparo 1979, p. 258.
333. Lepschy 1985, p. 214.

Gramsci's formation at university. Evidence exists proving that Gramsci became familiar with the ideas of various linguists when he was at university (Lo Piparo uses Bartoli's lecture notes of 1912–13, which Gramsci transcribed and edited). But, as I hope to have demonstrated, Gramsci's links with early twentieth-century language studies, including those outside Italy, can now be fruitfully examined also with regard to the later phases of his life, and with reference to other sources besides those indicated by Lo Piparo. Even for the years after Gramsci had given up his university studies, up until his imprisonment, there are now sufficient elements to enable us to move beyond a mere acknowledgment of Gramsci's assimilation of some of the linguistic ideas of the day. The wide-ranging workings of the *zeitgeist* can, to a certain extent, be tracked down; and concrete experiences can be indicated as the probable channels through which that assimilation took place.

Finally, all this calls for a rebalancing and a less dichotomic interpretation of Marxist and non-Marxist influences. We have seen why Lo Piparo focuses almost exclusively on sources that can be linked to Italian idealist philosophy and liberal political views: his identification of sources, and his periodisation of Gramsci's linguistic interests, are instrumental to establishing a contrast between linguistics and Marxism. Yet we now have enough evidence to reject this contrast and pay adequate attention to the input provided by Marxist debates, and by Soviet linguists and cultural theorists.

2.5.4. *Continuity and consistency of Gramsci's glottopolitical views*

Gramsci had direct and indirect contacts with Soviet theorisations and activities in two quintessentially glottopolitical fields – *language status planning* and *language corpus planning* (including experiments in spelling, attempted reforms of language teaching, and language-policy legislation). My survey of his views on linguistic themes that were also explored by Soviet experts has revealed something crucial about Gramsci: namely, that he developed Soviet influences without letting them dictate his own views. In particular, he refused to share certain palingenetic expectations that were present in Soviet cultural life, as is also evidenced by his disagreement with those who expected socially and politically significant benefits from artificial languages.

Gramsci seems to have been encouraged to address language policy and other language-related issues by a series of experiences – most especially, the linguistic situation in which underprivileged Italian social groups found themselves at the time. What he experienced when he went to Russia certainly increased this interest in language. He absorbed, however, mostly those elements which were compatible with his own intellectual trajectory, and with his own ideas on language. He shared some positions and rejected others. For instance, he aligned himself with the broad-minded principles enunciated by Lenin with respect to language legislation, recalling, in an article of September 1926, Lenin's call for the abolition of the official state language.[334] At the same time, he agreed with those Bolsheviks who placed special emphasis on learning languages of 'great culture',[335] as he wrote in Notebook 11. In general, however, he retained a great deal of autonomy.

He remained intellectually independent, and fundamentally consistent, clinging to his belief that language-policy interventions should not be expected to produce totally predictable results – they can speed up existing sociolinguistic trends, not arbitrarily create them. In accordance with Saussure, and drawing explicitly on Ascoli's *Proemio*, at different times during his life Gramsci maintained that languages are historical and social products which cannot be intentionally revolutionised or rationalised. They have their own intrinsic dynamics, which can only be gradually manipulated (through language policy and planning) in a context of free historical development and without imposing predetermined outcomes. As a young man, Gramsci had written (on 24 January 1918):

> Language [*la lingua*] depends, to a large extent, on the complex development of economic and social activity, and reacts back on this development, determining changes in it, only to a very small extent. If an international language is created when the International does not yet exist – before trades and political life have been stably regulated according to criteria of international usefulness, before contacts between the various parts of the world have become so deep, and so frequent, as to make language trends spread rapidly across the entire world – then this language will become the conventional jargon of restricted groups only. Moreover, such a jargon will be unstable, in the same way that the jargons spoken by small groups in individual cities are also unstable, for these groups change continuously and there is not a language source they can refer to.[336]

About a month later (16 February 1918), he wrote again about the 'anxiety for a single language', which 'appeared in various periods and various forms':

> In Italy this anxiety became a national one and was expressed in the Accademia della Crusca, purism and the ideas of Manzoni. The purists presented the ideal of a definitive language: that of certain writers of the fourteenth and sixteenth centuries which should be perpetuated because it was the only beautiful language, the only true Italian.... Manzoni posed the question: how does one create the Italian language, now that Italy has been created? And

---

334. See Gramsci 1971a, p. 333.
335. Gramsci 1975, Q11, §12, p. 1377.
336. Gramsci 1982, pp. 593–4.

he responded: all Italians will have to speak Tuscan and the Italian state will have to recruit elementary school teachers in Tuscany. Tuscan will replace the numerous dialects spoken in the various regions and, now that Italy has been created, the Italian language will be created as well. Manzoni was able to obtain government support and embark on the publication of a *Novo Dizionario* [New Dictionary] which was to have contained the true Italian language. But the *Novo Dizionario* remained half finished, and teachers were recruited from among educated people in all the regions of Italy.[337]

In this article, Ascoli is mentioned by name and commended for having argued – against the views held by Manzoni's followers – that 'not even a national language can be brought about artificially *by the imposition* of the state' (my emphasis).[338] The same anti-dirigiste approach is to be applied to the process of international linguistic unification:

If a single language, one that is also spoken in a given region and has a living source to which it can refer, cannot be *imposed* on the limited field of the nation, how then could an international language take root when it is completely artificial and mechanical, completely ahistorical, not fed by great writers, lacking the expressive richness which comes from the variety of dialects, from the variety of forms assumed in different times?... When the International is formed, it is possible that the increased contacts between peoples, the methodical and regular integration of large masses of workers, will slowly bring about a reciprocal adjustment between the Aryo-European languages and will probably extend them throughout the world, because of the influence the new civilization will exert. But this process can then happen *freely* and *spontaneously*.[339]

Still in February 1918, Gramsci expressed thus the politico-philosophical principles underlying his rejection of fixed universal languages:

Purism is a rigidified and mechanistic form of linguistics, and therefore the mentality of the purist resembles the mentality of the advocate of Esperanto. I am a revolutionary, a historicist, and I maintain that the only useful and rational forms of social (linguistic, economic, political) activity are those that

---

337. Gramsci 1982, pp. 669–70. On Manzoni's views see Appendix, 4.2.4.
338. Gramsci 1982, p. 670.
339. Gramsci 1982, pp. 670–1 (English translation from Gramsci 1985, pp. 26–31). My emphasis. Discussing this article, Peter Ives writes: 'Gramsci knew that a unified Italian language would benefit the various peoples of Italy, yet this never overshadowed his awareness that a unified language should not be foisted on a people – rather, it must be created *by* them' (Ives 2004b, p. 32).

emerge spontaneously and are realized through the free activities of the energies of society.[340]

A month later, he confirmed his appreciation of linguistic freedom as a crucial condition of the establishment of a politically progressive and socially beneficial form of linguistic and cultural unification. He did this in an article on the Sicilian theatrical tradition (and on its famous actor Angelo Musco), in terms strikingly similar to those in the above-quoted article 'Marinetti rivoluzionario?' (of January 1921). Once again, Gramsci referred to imposed linguistic uniformity as 'a violation of history and freedom', as a merely superficial, bureaucratic way to get the various 'dialects' to merge into a single 'literary language'.[341] Finally, in his *Prison Notebooks*, Gramsci largely confirmed these views. In Notebook 29, he asserted that Italian linguistic unification should be pursued through language-policy interventions; but he also specified that such interventions should be designed neither to impose a predetermined variety, nor to bring sociolinguistic developments completely under political control for an indefinite period of time. These proposals were based on the same conception of languages as sociohistorical products as Gramsci had illustrated, unsystematically, throughout his prison notes.

Gramsci's position was somewhat isolated in 1935. In the years between the two world wars, linguistic intolerance was receiving an unprecedented boost from the great political expectations and violent conflicts that were then shaking the world, with their mixed corollary of noble hopes, cruelty, xenophobia, and unrestrained fears.

Soviet language policies were also moving away from the pluralism originally supported by Lenin. In Gramsci's views, there is, undoubtedly, a great deal of similarity with Leninist language-policy principles – such as that of fighting language-based oppression, and that of granting language rights as a means of achieving stable unification through a gradual process. But there is also significant discrepancy with actual Soviet language policy, due not only to the fact that Gramsci was more faithful to Lenin's teachings in this field than were Soviet policy-makers. The difference was primarily the result of Gramsci's conception of language. His opposition to imposed forms of unification had a solid theoretical basis, and this basis remained essentially the same from 1916 to 1935 – notwithstanding the fact that some aspects of his views evolved in response to shifting practical contexts, and to various intellectual and political inputs.

Soviet language policy changed significantly during the 1930s. Russian explicitly regained an official, privileged role, until its study became compulsory in

340. Letter to Leo Galetto: Gramsci 1992a, p. 90 (English translation in Gramsci 1996b, p. 474).
341. Gramsci 1982, p. 986.

March 1938. Although multilingualism and native language education were still officially operative, in actual practice restrictions were imposed on both. Less and less attention was being paid to the multiplicity and spontaneity of real cultural processes that were underway in the various linguistic communities of the USSR. Crucial changes in this field, for instance alphabet reforms, were often introduced in the form of politically motivated impositions. Cyrillic scripts became the basis for the development of alphabets in which nearly all the languages of the USSR were to be written, replacing – in the second half of the 1930s – Latin scripts, which had begun to be widely used only a few years earlier.[342] In some republics of Central Asia, at the end of the 1930s, only a few months passed from a Latin-based alphabet being officially introduced (replacing the old Arabic scripts), to steps being taken towards the introduction of a Cyrillic alphabet. This transition corresponded to 'Moscow's one-sided decision, to which, in the terror of 1937–1938, the linguists had to submit unquestioningly'.[343]

In Hannah Arendt's words, Lenin had introduced 'distinguishing features by organizing, and sometimes inventing, as many nationalities as possible, furthering national consciousness and awareness of historical and cultural differences even among the most primitive tribes in the Soviet Union'.[344] These nationalities 'were in Stalin's way when he began to prepare the country for totalitarian government':

> In order to fabricate an atomized and structureless mass, he had first to liquidate the remnants of power in the Soviets which, as the chief organ of national representation, still played a certain role and prevented absolute rule by the party hierarchy. Therefore he first undermined the national Soviets through the introduction of Bolshevik cells from which alone the higher functionaries to the central committees were appointed. By 1930, the last traces of former communal institutions had disappeared and had been replaced by a firmly centralized party bureaucracy whose tendencies toward Russification were not too different from those of the Czarist regime, except that the new bureaucrats were no longer afraid of literacy.[345]

Gramsci's distance from the language policies of Stalin's USSR originated from his conception of languages as historical, collective products. This conception excludes forms of interventions detached from, or in outright conflict with, existing historical developments. Gramsci's constant attention to linguistic diversity appears to have been based on a conception of human language – though not

---

342. See Crisp 1989, pp. 25–31.
343. Bruchis 1982, p. 35.
344. Arendt 1966, p. 319.
345. Arendt 1966, pp. 319–20.

a systematically theorised one – that took two important factors into account. These two factors were chronological development and the collective use of a language by a socially-located community of speakers – the two factors which, also for Saussure, distinguish languages from conventional systems operating on purely logical bases.[346] According to Gramsci, the 'history of languages is the history of linguistic innovations, but these innovations are not individual'; they are 'the innovations of an entire social community that has renewed its culture and "progressed" historically'.[347]

History offers examples of linguistic homogeneity resulting from the expansion of a hegemonic culture, even across different speaking communities. Gramsci discusses this in a note (from Notebook 11) which can be linked to Saussure's assertion that *le signe* [the sign] is *arbitraire* [arbitrary] 'because it is based on tradition'.[348] Here is the note in question (the emphases are mine):

> What would North-South or East-West mean without man? They are real relationships and yet they would not exist without man and without the development of civilisation. Obviously East and West are *arbitrary* and conventional, *that is historical*, constructions, since outside of real history every point on the earth is East and West at the same time. This can be seen more clearly from the fact that these terms have crystallised not from the point of view of a hypothetical melancholic man in general but from the point of view of the European cultured classes who, as a result of their world-wide hegemony, have caused them to be accepted everywhere. Japan is the Far East not only for Europe but also perhaps for the American from California and even for the Japanese himself, who, through English political culture, may then call Egypt the Near East. So because of the historical content that has become attached to the geographical terms, the expressions East and West have finished up indicating specific relations between different cultural complexes. Thus Italians often, when speaking of Morocco, call it an 'Eastern' country, to refer to its Moslem and Arab civilisation.[349]

If a hegemonic process of cultural expansion is necessary for language to become unified, this also poses certain limitations to the possibility of planning the linguistic habits of speaking communities. Unification cannot be achieved through merely coercive interventions. Nor can a language be chosen as a universal medium of communication in the expectation that its current structure and

---

346. Cf. Saussure's emphasis on the action of *temps* [time] and *masse parlante* [community of speakers].
347. Gramsci 1975, Q6, §71, p. 738.
348. Saussure 1959, p. 74.
349. Gramsci 1975, Q11, §20, pp. 1419–20 (English translation in Gramsci 1971c, pp. 446–8).

lexicon will remain unchanged, and that speaking communities will accept it without introducing uncontrollable modifications. This, however, does not equate to saying that language policy and planning should be regarded as futile, or impossible to implement, and should therefore be rejected. Quite the contrary, their contribution may well be vital, if a process of cultural-linguistic unification is to win the active consent and participation of speakers. This is why language policies should be taken seriously by all those who are interested in facilitating the spread, and the taking root, of new values and attitudes.

Although Gramsci sees cultural unification mainly as a cause, rather than a result, of linguistic unification,[350] a dialectical relationship between the two emerges from his writings, especially his late prison writings – which I shall consider again in Chapter Three. In Notebook 10, he uses the following arguments to explain why the 'question of language' is politically relevant:

> We have established that philosophy is a conception of the world and that philosophical activity is not to be conceived solely as the 'individual' elaboration of systematically coherent concepts, but also and above all as a cultural battle to transform the popular 'mentality' and to diffuse the philosophical innovations which will demonstrate themselves to be 'historically true' to the extent that they become concretely – i.e. historically and socially – universal. Given all this, the question of language in general and of languages in the technical sense must be put in the forefront of our enquiry.... Culture, at its various levels, unifies in a series of strata, to the extent that they come into contact with each other, a greater or lesser number of individuals who understand each other's mode of expression in differing degrees, etc. It is these historico-social distinctions and differences which are reflected in common language and produce those 'obstacles' and 'sources of error' which the pragmatists have talked about.
>
> From this one can deduce the importance of the 'cultural aspect', even in practical (collective) activity. An historical act can only be performed by the 'collective man', and this presupposes the attainment of a 'cultural-social' unity through which a multiplicity of dispersed wills, with heterogeneous aims, are welded together with a single aim, on the basis of an equal and common conception of the world, both general and particular, operating in transitory bursts (in emotional ways) or permanently (where the intellectual base is so well rooted, assimilated and experienced that it becomes passion).[351]

---

350. On linguistic unification being 'an effect not a cause' of the 'moral unity of the nation and the state', see also Gramsci 1975, Q3, §63, p. 344, and Q21, §5, p. 2118.
351. Gramsci 1975, Q10II, §44, pp. 1330–1.

2.5.5. *Final remarks: Soviet inputs and the development of Gramsci's views*

In the Soviet Union, language policies were part of a massive experiment, the construction of socialism after a successful revolution. The Bolsheviks were enormously influential among large parts of the international working-class movement. Communists all over the world were expected to direct their attention to the innovations in Russian political and cultural life. And most of them did so, with unshakable hope, enthusiastic curiosity, and almost unconditioned admiration.

Gramsci's reflections on the possibility of putting language planning and policy into practice – and on the usefulness of doing so, which he acknowledges more than ever in Notebook 29 – help us to grasp two salient features of his contacts with Soviet debates:

i) through these contacts, he had the opportunity to experience a particular type of practice-oriented, applicative use of linguistic research. This opportunity reinforced his opinion that debates on language need not necessarily lead to rather futile discussions about irrelevant components – purely aesthetic, formalistic aspects of arts and literature – of what orthodox Marxist trends usually indicate as superstructure.

ii) Gramsci's reflections on language policy and planning highlight his far from passive response to Soviet inputs, and provide a constant point of reference to trace the development, and assess the autonomy, of his ideas on language.

In this chapter, I have shown that the influence of Soviet contexts and initiatives can be inferred from several of Gramsci's ideas concerning language. In so doing, I hope to have cast light on the significance that the Russian period had for the formation of Gramsci's ideas on language – a page in his intellectual biography which has, to date, attracted very little scholarly interest. At the same time, I have shown that, on the whole, Gramsci used his sources, and developed his own views, autonomously; he did not merely adapt to Soviet initiatives. Gramsci's selective affinity for Soviet approaches indicates that he was familiar with – and receptive to – some of these approaches; it does not suggest that his work depended upon inputs, or replicated trends, of Soviet origin.

Chapter Three
Political Implications

The aim of this third chapter is to show how Gramsci's positive relationship with cultural and linguistic heterogeneity contributed to shaping his political and intellectual profile. I shall begin with a recapitulation of some particularly significant elements, most of which have been discussed in the previous chapters.

Gramsci was born in a small town on the island of Sardinia. His first encounters with intellectuals interested in the island's language, Sardinian, as well as its local varieties and literary products, took place during his childhood and early youth. In the village of Ghilarza, where he spent most of his childhood, Gramsci met a priest – Michele Licheri – who was also an amateur scholar of local history and dialects. One of Gramsci's secondary school teachers, at the *liceo* where he studied in Cagliari, was the linguist Francesco Ribezzo; and another was Raffa Garzia – an important journalist, writer and philologist, who later taught Sardinian linguistics at Cagliari University. Traces of these encounters can be found in Gramsci's letters and journalistic production. However, the most important linguist who directly contributed to Gramsci's intellectual formation was Matteo Bartoli.

Bartoli was a prominent figure in early-twentieth-century linguistics.[1] In 1911, Gramsci went to Turin to study at the university. Soon, Bartoli began to think that this young Sardinian student was destined to become a linguist himself, and encouraged him to collaborate

---

1. See Appendix, section 4.2.1.

in the preparation of teaching and research materials. Significantly, Bartoli, like Gramsci, came from an area on the margins of the Italian linguistic domain, Istria, and he was well aware of the cultural and political issues which went hand-in-hand with the linguistic fragmentation of this area. Istria and the surrounding areas on the northern coast of the Adriatic Sea were (and still are) characterised by a high degree of multilingualism, with contacts between several varieties of both Romance and Slavonic languages. As early as 1915, at the beginning of his career as a journalist, Gramsci referred to Bartoli's research on the linguistic areas of Dalmatia.[2] It is probable that Gramsci's own attention to the Slav populations originated from Bartoli's work, although Gramsci especially developed the historical and political aspects of this.[3]

Throughout his life Gramsci used Sardinian. He did so not only to converse with family and friends about traditional, regional matters and everyday life, but also – at least on some occasions – to talk about politics and contemporary non-Sardinian affairs. He repeatedly praised the virtues of dialects for theatrical dialogues. He never indulged, though, in overpraise, thus differing from those authors whom Tullio De Mauro would later call *dialettomani*, that is, extreme supporters of the preservation and promotion of dialects.[4] The unification of language at the national and, over a longer period of time, also at the international level was, for Gramsci, a potentially progressive development from a political point of view, and thus worthy of being speeded up through purposeful interventions.

Both in Sardinia and at Turin, Gramsci was involved in various forms of translation, which I discussed in Chapter One. This practical activity constituted an early source for Gramsci's interest in translation and translatability, which is

---

2. See Gramsci 1980, pp. 43–6.
3. See Martinelli 1972, pp. 156–7. See also Boothman 2008b, pp. 34–5.
4. Cf. De Mauro 1991a, p. 307ff. and pp. 357–62. Gramsci never came to share a static conception of the counterposition between dialects, as the languages of spontaneous and nature-inspired art, and national languages, as the linguistic codes most suitable to expressing modern, rational worldviews. On the contrary, in the years 1930–3, some of his prison notes further problematised the distinction between *lingua* and *dialetto*. The history of languages, which are understood by Gramsci as socio-cultural collective products, shows that neither educated languages nor dialects are necessarily linked, by a sort of constitutive bond, to a certain worldview. On this point, he observes that in the sixteenth century, a 'truly national-popular' culture developed which was expressed 'in the dialects, but in Latin as well' (Gramsci 1975, Q5, §104, pp. 632–3); and that in Rome, from 1847 to 1849, 'the liberals make use of dialect as a weapon; after 1870 the clericals do' (Q3, §79, p. 359). Nor should the relationship between *dialetto* and *cultura folclorica* [folkloric culture] be understood in mechanical, absolute terms (see Q9, §132, pp. 1192–4; Q14, §15, pp. 1670–4). No immediate, necessary correspondences persist through history; in fact, when looking at the historical mutations undergone by both dialects and folklore, the latter turns out to be 'more unstable and fluctuating than language [*la lingua*] and dialects' (Q9, §15, p. 1105).

currently attracting considerable scholarly attention internationally.[5] In particular, in 1919, when Sardinian troops were sent to Turin to repress popular demonstrations, Gramsci turned to his native knowledge of Sardinian to conduct a campaign aimed at creating solidarity between the local working-class and the Sardinian soldiers – the latter usually from peasant backgrounds. Gramsci did not look at regional languages as symbols of identity by which boundaries might be erected, leading to the exclusion of those who do not share that particular identity. On the contrary, he emphasised the common demands of the Southern peasants and Northern working-class population and used Sardinian words in a manner that was functional to the achievement of this inclusive goal.

Early in 1922, Gramsci's collaborators organised musical events in Turin, which also included folk songs in regional languages (*dialetti*, as Italians usually call those Romance varieties spoken in the peninsula that do not have the status of national languages). Working along the same lines, *L'Ordine Nuovo* – the weekly and later daily paper directed by Gramsci – published articles defending some of Italy's minority languages: the French-speaking community of Val d'Aosta and the Slavonic language communities in north-eastern Italy. This periodical also lamented the fading away of Irish Gaelic, denounced the anti-Arabic approach of French educational institutions in North Africa, and reported a case of intolerance against a German-speaking community in the United States. Of course, *L'Ordine Nuovo* also stressed the merits of early Soviet multilingual policies which promoted national and minority languages.[6]

The periods that Gramsci spent in Russia between 1922 and 1925 offered him further opportunities and new sources with which to develop his linguistic interests. At this time, he came into contact not only with practical issues concerning translation, but also with debates about the 'translatability'[7] of political philosophies and strategies then taking place in the Third International, and he was particularly engaged by Lenin's recommendation that Russian political strategies should be translated 'into the European languages'[8] with greater accuracy. Gramsci also came into close contact with a multilingual family – that of his Russian, Swiss-born wife – for many of whose members translation and language teaching were sources of occupation. As shown in Chapter Two, he may have met – or read about – radical innovators not unlike those he would later dismiss as fanatical advocates of international languages. As recounted by Roman Jakobson, in the first years of the Russian Revolution there were visionaries who argued for a revision of traditional language and particularly for the abandonment of such

---

5. See Ives and Lacorte 2010.
6. See Chapter Two, section 2.4.4.
7. Gramsci 1975, Q11, p. 1468.
8. Ibid. For discussion, see Paggi 1984, pp. 3–24, and Thomas 2009, pp. 238–40.

'misleading expressions as "sunrise" or "sunset" ',[9] on the basis of the Ptolemaic views which they were held to perpetuate. Jakobson observes that the use of these expressions does not imply 'a rejection of Copernican doctrine'.[10] Similarly, Gramsci writes in his *Prison Notebooks*: 'When I use the word "disaster" no one can accuse me of believing in astrology, and when I say "by Jove!" no one can assume that I am a worshipper of pagan divinities'.[11] Today, nobody 'thinks that the word "dis-aster" is connected with astrology or can claim to be misled about the opinions of someone who uses the word'; likewise, 'even an atheist can speak of "dis-grace" without being thought to be a believer in predestination'.[12]

What consequences, if any, did the above activities have on the development of Gramsci's political views? Did Gramsci's reflections on language leave any significant trace on his approach to politics? If so, how was his approach influenced by language-related reflections? And when did this influence become apparent in Gramsci's writings? These are the questions that I shall seek to answer in this final chapter. Before I begin to develop my argument, however, I shall devote the next section to the essential task of clarifying and stressing those points about Gramsci's ideas on language which, in the course of this chapter, will lead me to express reservations about the works of the major experts in the field – Peter Ives, Franco Lo Piparo and Tullio De Mauro. I shall start especially from Ives's interpretation, while taking up those of De Mauro and Lo Piparo also in later sections of this chapter.

3.1. Gramsci and the linguistics of his time

Past attempts at exploring the connections between Gramsci's interest in linguistics and his political views have produced some extremely controversial interpretations. Gramsci's views on language have been presented as almost an alternative to the theories of language that historical-comparative, Structuralist, and Generativist linguists have used in their work.[13] At the same time, these trends in the history of linguistics have been conflated with trends and movements in the history of political thought. For instance, Lo Piparo establishes an 'epistemological continuity between the theories of the neo-grammarians and the positivist Marxism of the Second International',[14] which other interpreters have come to question on the basis of various elements, including Gramsci's

---

9. Jakobson 1959, p. 234.
10. Ibid.
11. Gramsci 1975, Q11, §28, p. 1438.
12. Gramsci 1975, Q11, §24, p. 1428.
13. De Mauro 1979b provides a particularly significant example of an anti-Chomskyian use of Gramsci's ideas on language.
14. Rosiello 2010, p. 48.

interest 'in a typical product of German anthropo-linguistic positivism', namely, in the book by Franz Nikolaus Finck (1867–1910), *Die Sprachstämme des Erdkreises* ['The Linguistic Stocks of the World'].[15] More recently, Peter Ives has extended this aspect of Lo Piparo's thesis to include also Saussurean and Chomskyian linguistics, stressing the similarities and continuity between the Neogrammarians',[16] Structuralist and Chomskyian approaches to language.[17]

It remains largely unquestionable that research on the internal functioning of verbal signs advanced, during the twentieth century, thanks mostly to the notions elaborated by various currents within Structuralism and, later, by Generativism. These notions are still hard to replace in descriptive, analytical work. However, the historical links between Generativism and linguistic Structuralism appear to be complex, problematic and open to debate. Going further back in time, the same can be said of the links between these two trends and their nineteenth-century predecessors. For instance, if one looks at the judgments that contemporary linguists expressed about Saussure, it is easy to see that some did emphasise his continuity with the Neogrammarians,[18] but others focused on his novelty and found his work to be more akin to that of the 'French school'[19] of Antoine Meillet and Joseph Vendryes, than to what Gramsci called the 'German philological method'.[20] More recently, many philosophers, linguists, social scientists, and discourse analysts have convincingly identified theoretical flaws in Saussure- and Chomsky-inspired language studies, and also the political implications of some of these flaws. Detractors of Saussurean and Chomskyian linguistics are especially critical of the idea that the specific nature of linguistic systems should be studied as an ideally homogeneous, static, and politically neutral object. Yet it is generally accepted that the idea that language should be studied in this way did not have the same effects on Saussure and Chomsky, leading the former to highlight the social and collective nature of language, whereas the latter has focused on the essentially individual nature of language (native speakers' competence).[21]

---

15. Ibid. On Finck's book, see Appendix, section 4.2.2.

16. On this group of German scholars – who resolutely theorised sound-change laws and analogy as privileged forms of explanation in the field of historical linguistics, and who had enthusiastic followers in Italy around the late nineteenth and early twentieth centuries – see Timpanaro 1969, p. 317ff. See also Tagliavini 1982, Chapter One; Lehmann 1992, pp. 31–3, and Morpurgo Davies 1998, pp. 229–69. Cf. Appendix, section 4.2.1.

17. See Ives 2004a, 2004b. See also the introduction to Ives and Lacorte 2010, as well as the chapter by Marcus Green and Peter Ives (especially p. 294).

18. See Terracini 1929, p. 650.

19. See Sechehaye 1927, p. 240. On the French school, see also Terracini 1925, and Iordan and Orr 1937.

20. Gramsci 1982, p. 525.

21. In order not to overestimate the affinities and continuities between Saussure-inspired Structuralist linguistics and Chomskyian linguistics, it is perhaps useful to

Moreover, as is convincingly argued in a paper by Giancarlo Schirru,[22] Gramsci's own critique of positivist scientific objectivism, which Ives treats as an *ante litteram* rejection of Saussurean and Chomskyian linguistics, did not lead him to underplay how important it is that specialists in a particular discipline rigorously use those technical conceptualisations which have proved most useful for methodologically accurate and verifiable explanations of facts. And this is particularly true, Gramsci argued in his prison notes, for a discipline like linguistics. In this respect, it is important to bear in mind that Gramsci was primarily concerned with – and directly involved in – political struggles, not academic debates. As far as the latter are concerned, Gramsci did not ignore them, and he certainly did not ignore academic debates in the field of linguistics. However, Gramsci's writings do not provide any significant evidence to justify presenting him as a linguist or a philosopher of language in the narrow sense of the terms; that is, a specialist who fully developed and/or used, in his work, a somewhat systematic theory of language. His writings do not contain new theories for studying the internal elements of language – namely, for studying how languages work and change with regard to the intrinsic functioning of verbal signs (*internal linguistics*, in Saussure's terminology). Quite the contrary: in his writings, Gramsci praised historical-comparative linguistics for its rigorous study of phonological and semantic change. Although he expressed some views remarkably similar to Saussure's synchronic linguistics, on the whole Gramsci remained cautious about theoretical innovations in the field of linguistics proper.[23] In this field, he took notions and data from the writings of traditional scholars – both famous linguists from the past, such as Ascoli and Bréal, and young Italian linguists like Giacomo Devoto and Vittore Pisani.

---

mention the strong opposition with which the latter was met by some exponents of European linguistic Structuralism, such as André Martinet and Tullio De Mauro.

22. Schirru 2008a.

23. Under Croce's influence, the young Gramsci wrote that 'language is not just a means of communication – it is first of all a work of art, it is beauty' (Gramsci 1982, p. 593); and that 'language should not be confused with vocabulary: a vocabulary is a museum of embalmed corpses' (Gramsci 1980, p. 683), a statement almost identical to the following passage from Croce's *Aesthetics*: 'Language is not an arsenal of arms, and it is not a vocabulary, a collection of abstractions, or a cemetery of corpses more or less well embalmed' (Croce 1990, p. 189). In the *Prison Notebooks*, however, we find no trace of Croce's philosophical reduction of linguistics to aesthetics; in fact, Gramsci writes that linguists 'study languages precisely insofar as they are not art but the "material" of art, a social product, a cultural expression of a given people' (Gramsci 1975, Q6, §71, p. 738). Similarly, in Notebook 29 Croce's views on the absurdity of a sentence such as 'this round table is square' are rejected (Q29, §1, pp. 2341–2; cf. Croce 1966, pp. 172–6), and although Gramsci does not cite the *Essai de sémantique* here, he does essentially confirm Bréal's view that verbal language has its own 'special logic', which 'even allows us to say, if we wish, that a circle is square' (Bréal 1900, p. 219).

Even the influence that Gramsci received from Bartoli was only apparently based on radical methodological innovations, namely Bartoli's opposition to the methods of the Neogrammarians. In actual fact, there was mostly continuity between the work of Matteo Bartoli (who even attempted to introduce a new phonetic law in Indo-European linguistics) and that of traditional historical linguists.[24] For instance, one of Bartoli's most influential contributions to the history of the Italian language was his attempt to make sense of the capricious coexistence of voiced and unvoiced intervocalic consonants in Italian, where we have, for example, *ago* [needle] from Latin *acum*, but *amico* [friend] from Latin *amīcum*. He moved beyond previous explanations based on phonetic rules and suggested, instead, that words with voiced consonants entered into Tuscan (on which modern Italian is based) from northern Italo-Romance dialects, where voicing applies regularly between two vowels.[25] In this case, the geographical methods theorised and applied by Bartoli were ultimately based on a well-known factor, namely, linguistic borrowing. But as many have argued (most notably Bloomfield), this factor does not really undermine the epistemological validity of phonetic 'laws'; in fact, insofar as it helps to explain the exceptions to regular change, borrowing essentially confirms the utility of assuming that phonetic changes are, in principle, regular, that they occur 'across the board' and not just in some words.[26]

Unsurprisingly, Gramsci always called for great care in assessing the validity of new methods, and the tenability of innovative discoveries such as those on Etruscan by the linguist Alfredo Trombetti. 'Trombetti's thesis...is this: Etruscan, like pre-Hellenic languages and the languages of Asia Minor, is an intermediate language between the Caucasian group and the Aryo-European group, with stronger affinities to the latter'.[27] Gramsci identified various flaws in the arguments used to support this claim, and noted that:

---

24. See Devoto 1947; Benincà 1994, pp. 599ff.; Grassi *et al.* 2004, Chapter Three. See also Appendix, section 4.2.1.

25. See Meyer-Lübke 1927 (abridged and recast by Bartoli), p. 101. Cf. Rohlfs 1966–9, I, pp. 286–9. On Bartoli's early formulation of this view, already in the *Dispense di glottologia* edited by Gramsci, see Schirru 2011, p. 951.

26. See Bloomfield 1976 (first published in 1933). By *borrowing*, linguists mean the adoption of a word from a different (variety of the) language. While this can easily be reconciled with the premise of regular sound change, things become more complex in cases of *imitation* (a notion also present in Bartoli, and later renewed through the study of *languages in contact*) of certain sounds, or of certain morphological or syntactical structures, by some – but not all – speakers, in some – but not all – words, and only in certain contexts or registers.

27. Gramsci 1975, Q3, §86, p. 365.

The lexical forms and their meanings must be compared throughout the homogeneous historical phases of the respective languages, and therefore one must not only 'produce' the phonological history but also the semantic history of each form and compare the oldest meanings. Trombetti does not adhere to any of these rudimentary criteria: *a*) in his comparisons he is satisfied with the most generic kindred, and not so kindred, meanings...; *b*) it is enough for him that words being compared contain a succession of consonant sounds that resemble one another, such as *t, th, d, dh, s*, etc., or else *p, ph, f, b, bh, v, w*, etc.; he gets rid of the other consonants by designating them as prefixes, suffixes or infixes.[28]

Gramsci also added that the 'kinship of two languages cannot be proven through the comparison, however well grounded, of a number (even a very large number) of words, unless one has proofs of a phonetic, morphological (and, to a lesser extent, syntactical) character'.[29] These comments were based on the objections that numerous linguists had raised about Trombetti's work.[30] Gramsci was, indeed, interested in this debate, and had accumulated sufficient specialist knowledge as to be able to appreciate and discuss this and other debates. In his discussion, however, he followed the dominant methodological and theoretical models of historical linguistics. Not only in his notes on Trombetti, but also in the pages where he sarcastically dismissed Achille Loria's pseudo-positivist explanation of the different phonological characteristics of various Italian dialects,[31] as well as the prison notes where he criticised Giulio Bertoni's idealist linguistics,[32]

28. Gramsci 1975, Q3, §156, pp. 408–9.
29. Gramsci 1975, p. 409.
30. See, in particular, Pisani 1929.
31. Gramsci 1975, Q28, §1, p. 2323. See also Gramsci 1982, pp. 575–6. Loria was among those who tried to explain sound-change in language by reference to the effects on speakers of topography, climate and health conditions.
32. 'Bartoli was wrong to collaborate with Bertoni on the compilation of the *Manualetto* [Bertoni and Bartoli 1928]; it was definitely a mistake, and he bears scientific responsibility. Bartoli is valued for his concrete studies. By leaving it to Bertoni to write the theoretical section he misleads students and sets them on an erroneous course: in this case, modesty and unselfishness become a fault. Furthermore, not only has Bertoni failed to understand Bartoli, he has also failed to understand Croce's aesthetics in the sense that he has been unable to derive from Crocean aesthetics rules for the research and construction of the science of language. He has done nothing but paraphrase, exalt, and wax eloquent about certain impressions; he is essentially a positivist who swoons at the sight of idealism because it is more fashionable and provides the occasion for flights of rhetoric. It is amazing that Croce has praised the *Manualetto* without noticing or pointing out Bertoni's incongruities; it seems to me that, more than anything else, Croce wanted to give favourable notice to the fact that in this branch of studies, where positivism reigns, there was an attempt to pursue a new idealist approach' (Gramsci 1975, Q3, §74, pp. 351–2. English translation from Gramsci 1996b). 'In certain respects, Bertoni's research is partly a return to certain etymological systems: "sol quia solus est" implicitly contains in itself the image of "solitude" in the immense sky and so on; "how

Gramsci was far from introducing theoretical innovations or new analytical data regarding the study of the internal elements of language. In this respect, it thus seems quite misleading to present his reflections as almost an alternative to the theories of historical-comparative, Structuralist, and Generativist linguistics.[33]

On the other hand, Gramsci developed interesting ideas about the external relations of language with cultural, social and political life. His views on these relations are important in themselves and, since an accurate understanding of Gramsci's views could also help to expand and renovate the contribution of 'Marxism...to the study of the function of language in society',[34] his views are worthy of an accurate examination against the background of the historical context in which they originated. Gramsci's writings remain relevant to the current scholarly context, and can inspire new research into what Ferdinand de Saussure called *external linguistics* – especially research into the role that language, languages, and also linguistic research play in social life and political conflicts. At the same time, Gramsci's ideas on language are interesting in that they allow us to reconstruct his intellectual biography more thoroughly and to understand some specific aspects of his political theory and practice. In other words, his ideas on language can only be correctly understood if one does not forget that they were the ideas of a political leader who helped to found the Communist Party of Italy (in 1921) and played a significant role in the Italian and international working-class movement during the years preceding the advent of Fascism in Italy and of Stalinism in Soviet Russia. Gramsci was not a professional linguist, a historian or sociologist of languages, or an expert of language-policy issues; however, as I shall argue in this chapter, his constant attention to linguistic themes

---

beautiful it is that in Apulia the dragonfly with its wings in the form of a cross is called *la morte* [death]" and so on' (Gramsci 1975, Q6, §20, p. 701; cf. §71, pp. 737–8). 'The "idealist" current has found its most complete expression in Bertoni: it involves a return to old rhetorical conceptions, to words which are "beautiful" and "ugly" in and by themselves, conceptions which have been glossed over with a new pseudo-scientific language' (Q29, §5, pp. 2347–8).

33. According to Luigi Rosiello, Gramsci 'demonstrates that he knows how to correctly posit the problem about the relationship that must exist between linguistic science and the way Marxist theory is to be applied and specified. Gramsci posits the problem mentioned above in the same way as Friedrich Engels does in his essay on *The Franconian Dialect* (1881–1882). In this work, Engels showed how it is possible to correctly integrate the methods elaborated and the results achieved by linguistics in his times in a global materialistic theory of history and society. In other words, Gramsci – and before him Engels – starts forging not so much an illusory pretense for grounding a Marxist theory of language [*linguaggio*], but rather an epistemologically correct proposal aimed at utilising linguistic science within the framework of a more powerful theory, which should be capable of instituting the nexuses necessary for explaining interactive relationships between linguistic systems and the historically determined structure of social relationships' (Rosiello 2010, p. 33).

34. Lepschy 1985, p. 222.

left important traces in the approach that he took to revolutionary politics and cultural unification programmes.

3.2. Language and politics in Gramsci's writings

In newspaper articles and theatre reviews from the years immediately following the First World War, Gramsci started to speak out against attempts to *impose* cultural and linguistic unity. He endorsed the views of Italy's most important linguist of the nineteenth century, Graziadio Isaia Ascoli, arguing that not only international linguistic unification, but even *national* unification could not be implemented without a gradual process of cultural, social, and economic growth.[35] Although politically desirable (as a means to promote intellectual improvement, progressive political struggles, and mutual understanding among all men) unification could only be achieved by guiding the development of existing historical processes. It should not be sought by ignoring, or utterly suppressing, the cultural heritage of the past and those continuations of the past which were still dynamic in the present.

As shown in Chapter Two, Gramsci echoed Ferdinand de Saussure's scepticism about the possibility of intervening intentionally on the development and autonomous functioning of semiotic systems. In 1916, Gramsci exemplified this with the symbols on playing cards, recalling the failure of past revolutionaries to replace kings and queens with bourgeois icons, such as republican fasces or the symbolic figures of Freedom and Equality.[36] Even at the beginning of the 1920s, when he was most sensitive to the influence of vanguard movements, such as the Italian futurists and the Russian Proletkult, Gramsci maintained that cultural and linguistic renewal should not be an arbitrary imposition inspired by the enlightened plans and well-intentioned pragmatism of intellectual or political élites. In an article of June 1920, he asserted that the working class, once it had won its liberty, would bring to the light of history new conditions for the general development of linguistic self-expression and communication. Among the workers – he explained – there was a desire for, and a historical tendency towards, the formation of languages that would transcend national limits, and in relation to which national languages would have the same role dialects had at the time.[37] Especially in this period (1919–21), Gramsci shared the hope, then widespread across Europe, in the advent of a revitalising, proletarian civilisation characterised by new ways of thinking and new forms of culture, art, and language. Yet in an article on Marinetti's futurism, published in *L'Ordine Nuovo*

---

35. See Gramsci 1982, pp. 668–74.
36. See Gramsci 1980, pp. 283–4.
37. See Gramsci 1987, p. 557.

on 5 January 1921, Gramsci stated quite unambiguously that this new civilisation should be the result of free historical development, and could not be planned by a working-class power.[38]

The links between language and politics, however, were only partly explored by Gramsci at this stage. The theoretical implications of his attitude to linguistic plurality had not yet reached their full potential, in that they remained far from fully influencing his overall attitude to political action and theory. In the articles that he wrote between 1916 and 1922, his sympathetic attention to diversity, and his wariness of rigidly planned unification, seem to be confined to cultural and linguistic subjects; whereas his political views would seem to reveal something of a mechanical and messianic approach to revolution, which he still tended to see as the event that would rapidly bring about a completely new social, economic, and political situation. For instance, in the article on Marinetti of January 1921,[39] Gramsci separated the political and economic domains from those of culture and language:

> It is relatively easy to outline right from this moment the shape of the new state and the new economic structure. In this absolutely practical field, we are convinced that for a certain time the only possible thing to do will be to exercise an iron-like power over the existing organization, over that constructed by the bourgeoisie. From this conviction comes the stimulus to struggle for the conquest of power and from it comes the formula by which Lenin has characterized the workers' state: 'For a certain time the workers' state cannot be other than a bourgeois state without the bourgeoisie'.
>
> The battlefield for the creation of a new civilization is, *on the other hand*, absolutely mysterious, absolutely characterized by the unforeseeable and the unexpected. Having passed from capitalist power to workers' power, the factory will continue to produce the same material things that it produces today. But in what way and under what forms will poetry, drama, the novel, music, painting and moral and linguistic works be born? It is not a material factory that produces these works. It cannot be reorganized by a workers' power according to a plan. One cannot establish its rate of production for the satisfaction of immediate needs, to be controlled and determined statistically. Nothing *in this field* is foreseeable except for this general hypothesis: there will be a proletarian culture (a civilization) totally different from the bourgeois one and in this field too class distinctions will be shattered. Bourgeois careerism will be shattered and there will be a poetry, a novel, a theatre, a moral code, a

---

38. See Gramsci 1966, p. 20.
39. I quoted several passages from this article also in Chapter Two, section 2.5.2.

language, a painting and a music peculiar to proletarian civilization, the flowering and ornament of proletarian social organization.[40]

As time went by, and dreams of a new society began to look much more unrealistic than they had between 1916 and 1922 (the year that the Fascists seized power in Italy), Gramsci continued to explore the links between language and politics. Eventually, a much closer interconnection between the processes of political, cultural, and linguistic unification would emerge in his thought. However, this only happened later in Gramsci's life, despite the fact that he had already integrated his thoughts on language with his economic and political views in a letter of 1918.[41] The influence that Gramsci's political thought received from his familiarity with the theme of diversity and unification in language reached its full potential only with his mature reflections, during his prison years. Initially, the boundaries between linguistic and political issues were only crossed with respect to specific topics (such as ethnic minorities in Italy and Esperanto), and with limited theoretical awareness.

In September 1923, Gramsci suggested that the Communist slogan 'workers' and peasants' government' should be changed, in order to adapt it to the Italian situation, to 'workers' and peasants' *federal* republic'.[42] In February 1924, in a letter to the newly-founded newspaper *L'Unità*, published under a pseudonym (and convincingly attributed to Gramsci only sixty years later),[43] he imagined the communist overthrow of capitalism as a move towards the creation of a system in which 'popular culture can develop autonomously'.[44] Interestingly, this statement is made with specific reference to a people with a very particular cultural identity – the Sardinian people; a people, moreover, whom Gramsci realistically describes in this letter as demographically and politically weak. In April 1924, Gramsci urged the Executive Committee of the Communist Party to clearly express a political position on the situation of the Slav and German minorities in the areas annexed to Italy at the end of the First World War. He also reminded his comrades that 'in southern Italy, especially in Apulia, Calabria and Sicily, there are many Albanians (approximately 300,000) and many contacts exist between Apulia and Albania; so many, that Apulia's regional newspaper used to publish (I am not sure if it still does) a page in Albanian'.[45] Here, Gramsci is clearly thinking back to the teachings of Matteo Bartoli:

---

40. Gramsci 1966, pp. 20–2 (my emphases). Cf. Lenin 1964c, p. 471.
41. See Gramsci 1992a, p. 90 (quoted in translation in Chapter Two, section 2.5.4).
42. Gramsci 1992a, p. 130. My emphasis.
43. See Chapter One: 1.5.1.
44. 'I sardi e il blocco proletario', published in *L'Unità* on 26 February 1924.
45. Gramsci 1992a, p. 342.

Where is Albanian spoken today?... It is also spoken outside of Albania... in Italy, where there are approximately 300,000 Albanians, scattered virtually everywhere in the South of the country; in some places they are believed to be Greek, yet Greeks only live in a couple of villages in the extreme parts of Apulia. Albanian colonies in Italy bear great historical significance, because they have contributed to keeping national feelings alive in Albania, and because they gave Albania a literature.[46]

In 1925, Gramsci asked the instructors of the Communist Party's internal school to translate 'party watchwords' into a language that the local masses could understand.[47] In doing so, he probably intended to follow Lenin's directives, especially that the language of the local proletariat should be used and that great care should be taken when choosing the language used in conducting propaganda among the masses and for working within Party organisations.[48] While Gramsci was in Russia, a similar position with respect to language was also advocated in Iakov Shafir's study of how the peasants understood the Bolshevik press.[49] Finally, in an article of 1926, Gramsci insisted that the large groups of Slav peasants living in Istria and Friuli could be politically organised only if careful consideration were given to the question of nationality that existed in these areas.[50]

Later in 1926, Gramsci was arrested. In a letter of May 1927, he expressed his positive intention to study various languages (another aspect of his personality which, perhaps, does not quite fit into any portrayal of Gramsci as a 'totalitarian' pursuer of unification):

> I have definitely decided to make the study of languages my main occupation; after German and Russian, I want to systematically take up again English, Spanish and Portuguese, which I had studied rather superficially in recent years; and also Rumanian, which I had studied at the university only in its Romance aspect and that I think I can now study completely, that is, also in the Slavic part of its lexicon (which in fact is more than 50 percent of the Rumanian vocabulary).[51]

---

46. Bartoli 1912–13, p. 121.
47. Gramsci 1988, p. 133.
48. See Chapter Two, sections 2.4.3 and 2.4.5.
49. The study, *The Newspaper and the Village*, was carried out by Shafir during the summer of 1923, and its results were discussed at the First Conference of Worker Correspondents in November 1923. See Gorham 2003, p. 34ff. See also Chapter Two, section 2.3.4.
50. See Gramsci 1971a, p. 106.
51. Gramsci 1994a, I, p. 112. Whilst in prison, Gramsci translated widely from German and Russian, and also translated some passages from English for practice (see Gramsci 2007a).

In other letters he sent from prison, Gramsci not only urged his sister to let her two-year-old son grow up speaking as much Sardinian as he liked, he also distanced himself – although only implicitly – from the language policy that Soviet authorities were imposing on Jews, as shown by a passage from a letter of October 1931 where Gramsci acknowledges the right of Jewish communities to cultural and linguistic autonomy. As we have seen in Chapter Two, when Gramsci wrote this letter Jewish cultural autonomy was already limited in the USSR. Gramsci could have ascribed to Latin features similar to those which Soviet authorities ascribed to Hebrew, from a rigidly classist and dogmatically progressive point of view. Latin, too, had been the language of educated groups, these groups usually belonging to the upper strata of the population.[52] Although it was mostly studied in connection with the culture of ancient Rome, Latin also lent itself to associations with clericalism. Like Hebrew, Latin was a dead language, having lacked native speakers for centuries. This analogy between Hebrew and Latin was put forward by the Soviet Jewish intelligentsia in its battle in favour of Yiddish and against the supporters of Hebrew.[53] Latin and Hebrew were also presented as dead, educated languages of a similar kind in works that Gramsci certainly, or almost certainly, knew: for instance, in Antoine Meillet's *Les langues dans l'Europe nouvelle* ['Languages in the New Europe'];[54] and in the above-mentioned book by the German linguist F.N. Finck, *Die Sprachstämme des Erdkreises*, which Gramsci translated while in prison. Finally, until at least the First World War, a sense of diffidence prevailed within the Italian working-class movement with respect to classical, humanistic education. This was often deemed irrelevant, if not pernicious, to working-class children, for whom improved vocational schools were, instead, advocated. In actual fact, various leaders of the working class ended up sharing the views of conservative educationalists, agreeing that the function of *licei* (humanistic upper-secondary schools), and of Latin as part of the curriculum of these prestigious schools, should be that of separating the young generations of the bourgeoisie from those of the proletariat.[55] Despite all this, Gramsci stressed the value of teaching Latin at school. He had already expressed this position in some of his early writings. During the prison years, while conceding that an eventual replacement of Latin with other subjects could possibly be acceptable, he again displayed no hostility to this language, and re-asserted the largely positive effects of its teaching in schools for all children (Notebook 12).

---

52. On this use of Latin, see Waquet 1988.
53. See the documents collected and discussed by Shneer 2004, pp. 51–2, and Gilboa 1982, pp. 56–7.
54. Meillet 1928.
55. See Borghi 1951, and Bertoni Jovine 1975.

In Gramsci (as in many other authors) language and education are partly overlapping areas. How unification should be achieved is, indeed, a crucial issue in both areas. Unification is not only a matter of overcoming the cleavages existing amongst groups which are defined mainly geographically; it is also a matter of 'ideological unity between the bottom and the top',[56] between intellectuals and popular masses. In other words, a political programme aimed at achieving cultural renovation and unification needs to take socio-cultural stratifications into account. Pedagogically 'conservative' as it may have seemed to some commentators,[57] Gramsci's attitude towards Latin is, therefore, noteworthy from the point of view of cultural and linguistic policies. This attitude helps to clarify Gramsci's overall approach, and confirms that he did not expect the new unitary culture to be the product of a mere dismantling of mainstream highbrow culture.

To wind up this section of the present chapter, it is useful to link its subject matter to the analysis of the role of Sardinian in Gramsci's life, which I conducted in Chapter One. It has often been claimed that Gramsci was just one of the many modernist intellectuals, involved in progressive political movements, who advocated the benefits of cultural and linguistic unification, showing antipathy to local or traditional forms of cultural and linguistic identity. Examples of this attitude are easy to find, from the French Jacobins onwards. Such an attitude would be clearly expected of a communist leader like Gramsci, since he has been repeatedly accused of having merely re-elaborated the supposedly 'totalitarian' plans of the ideologues of the Russian Soviet régime. This interpretation is, in fact, questionable with respect to the early history of the Soviet multinational state, which despite ferocious political repression nonetheless allowed the implementation of generally tolerant national and linguistic policies (the case of Hebrew being rather exceptional). In Gramsci's case, to be sure, similar interpretations are absolutely inaccurate. They are oversimplifying and largely untenable. Gramsci's Marxist belief in the prominence of class relations did not marginalise his attention to issues which are today often associated with the notions of ethnic, cultural and sociolinguistic identity.

3.3. The role of linguistic themes in shaping Gramsci's politics

Some recent archival findings reveal the same kind of awareness that emerges from Gramsci's writings on cultural and linguistic subjects: diversity cannot

---

56. Gramsci 1975, Q8, §213, p. 1070.
57. Here, I am especially referring to the interpretation that sociologist of education Harold Entwistle put forward in his book, *Antonio Gramsci: Conservative Schooling for Radical Politics* (on the teaching of classical languages, see Entwistle 1979, pp. 170–5).

simply be denied, bureaucratically deleted or violently removed. One document that is particularly worth mentioning is the transcript, produced by Gramsci's wife, of one of the speeches he gave in Russia in the early 1920s. This is the most salient passage:

> Young, mature and old [in terms of political views, not of their age] elements live in society at the same time. In accordance with this coexistence, we see that radical, liberal, conservative and absolutist parties also coexist. The parties which prevail are those which are closest to the people's personality and temperament. The existence of all these different political parties is inevitable. In its life, the state should adjust to the balance of forces created by these parties. Sensible politicians, even when fighting against them, should not try completely to annihilate any of these parties, because such a goal is impenetrable and its accomplishment would only push the disease back inside the system.[58]

Gramsci probably gave this speech in 1922. At the time, he felt the need to set limits to the scope of his statements. That is, he confined their pertinence to the life and workings of the bourgeois state, before the working class made its revolution. In this phase of his life, Gramsci was still firmly convinced that the transfer of the means of economic production and distribution from the hands of Russian capitalists to those of the Russian proletariat had created the conditions for the disappearance of class conflicts, and, therefore, of different political parties. Nonetheless, in this speech he expressed a concept which would appear again in his prison notes, and which is remarkably consistent with his views about linguistic unification: namely, that imposed unification is only an exterior form of integration, and does not bring about the progressive political potential of real unification; and that, instead, real unification will only be achieved once historical developments have created the necessary conditions for its achievement. As we shall see in the following pages, when this concept appeared again in Gramsci's *Prison Notebooks*, it was given a much more universal significance, and was used to criticise the results of the Russian Revolution itself, as they materialised during the 1920s.

Research on Gramsci's correspondence with Italian and international Communist cadres has also shown that he refused to overcome political disagreements by pitilessly repressing opponents. In the mid-1920s, he had the courage to warn Italian and international comrades about the risks of Stalin's attempt to impose a unified political line through the complete annihilation of any opposition.[59] On 14 October 1926, Gramsci wrote to the Central Committee of the Communist Party of the Soviet Union, where the conflict between the opposition,

---

58. Published (in Italian) in Gramsci Jr. 2010, pp. 59–60.
59. See Chapter One of Fiori 1991, and Daniele 1999.

headed by Trotsky, Zinoviev and Kamenev, and the majority, headed by Stalin and Bukharin, was becoming increasingly harsh. Gramsci wrote on behalf of the Political Bureau of the Communist Party of Italy (hence the plural 'we' used in this and the next letter quoted below):

> Comrades, in these past nine years of world history you have been the organizing and propulsive element of the revolutionary forces in all countries. The function which you have fulfilled has no precedent to equal it in breadth and depth, in the entire history of humanity. But today you are destroying your work. You are degrading, and run the risk of annihilating, the leading function which the CPSU won through Lenin's contribution. It seems to us that the violent passion of Russian affairs is causing you to lose sight of the international aspects of Russian affairs themselves; is causing you to forget that your duties as Russian militants can and must be carried out only within the framework of the interests of the international proletariat.[60]

Gramsci regarded the proposals of the opposition as expressing a narrow-minded approach concerning solely the interests of the urban working classes. He accused the leaders of the opposition of re-proposing a trade-unionist, corporatist mentality, in that their proposals advocated immediate benefits for the industrial proletariat in such a way which would alienate the support of the rural masses, and would thus make an alliance between peasants and urban working classes impossible. Consequently, Gramsci stated that the Communist Party of Italy rejected the position of the minority, and instead agreed with the 'right wing' of the Communist Party of the USSR; that is, with Stalin and Bukharin. 'We now declare that we consider basically correct the political line of the majority of the Central Committee of the CPSU, and that the majority of the Italian Party will certainly take the same position, if it becomes necessary to debate the whole question'.[61] Yet he qualified this endorsement of the political line of the majority by adding that:

> Only a firm unity and a firm discipline in the party which governs the workers' State can ensure proletarian hegemony... But unity and discipline in this case cannot be mechanical and enforced; they must be loyal and due to conviction, and not those of an enemy unit imprisoned or besieged, whose only thought is of escape or an unexpected sortie.
>
> This, dearest comrades, is what we wished to say to you, in the spirit of brothers and friends, even if younger brothers. Comrades Zinoviev, Trotsky, Kamenev have contributed powerfully to educating us for the revolution; they have at times corrected us with great energy and rigour; they have been our

---

60. Gramsci 1992a, pp. 458–9 (English translation from Gramsci 1978, pp. 426–32).
61. Gramsci 1992a, p. 460.

masters. To them especially we address ourselves, as those principally responsible for the present situation, because we like to feel certain that the majority
of the Central Committee of the USSR does not intend to win a crushing victory in the struggle, and is disposed to avoid excessive measures.[62]

On 26 October, Gramsci once again expressed his concerns, in a letter to Togliatti,
who at the time represented the Communist Party of Italy at the Moscow-based
Communist International:

> We started off from the point of view, which seems to me correct, that in our
> countries [outside the USSR] there do not exist just parties, in the sense of
> technical organizations, but also the great working masses, which are politi-
> cally stratified in a contradictory fashion, but which as a whole tend towards
> unity. One of the most forceful elements in this unitary process is the exis-
> tence of the USSR, linked to the real activity of the CPSU and to the wide-
> spread conviction that the USSR is moving along the road to socialism. Insofar
> as our parties represent the entire active complex of the USSR, they have a
> specific influence on all political layers of the broad masses; they represent
> the unitary tendency; they operate on a historical terrain which is basically
> favourable, despite the contradictory superstructures.
>
> But it should not be thought that this factor, which makes the CPSU the
> most powerful mass organizer that has ever appeared throughout history,
> has now been acquired in a stable and decisive form: quite the contrary....
> [O]ur aim is to contribute to the maintenance and creation of a unitary plan,
> in which the various tendencies and personalities can draw closer and merge,
> even ideologically.[63]

A few months later, after being arrested, Gramsci showed that he still had a good
personal relationship with Amadeo Bordiga, the first Secretary of the Communist
Party of Italy, despite the fact that Bordiga was by then regarded as a deviation-
ist and, as such, had been ostracised by the Party's leadership. The testimony
of a Socialist, Sandro Pertini (who would later become president of the Italian
Republic), regarding the period he spent with Gramsci in the same Fascist prison
(Turi di Bari), is also worth quoting: 'Gramsci was always loyal and a true friend
to me. In order to understand the significance of our friendship, it should be
stressed that, at the time, Socialists and Communists ... were tearing each other
to pieces – they would bitterly oppose each other'.[64]

Whilst in prison, Gramsci criticised *An Outline of Political Economy* by
I.A. Lapidus and K.V. Ostrovitianov, which was at the time the 'standard Soviet

---

62. Gramsci 1992a, pp. 461–2.
63. Gramsci 1992a, pp. 470–1 (English translation in Gramsci 1978, pp. 437–40).
64. From Paulesu Quercioli 1977, p. 275.

textbook of economics'.[65] Gramsci found this book dogmatic because of its presentation of Marxist economics as a historical reality, as if Marx's critical theories had already been put into practice. In contrast, he held that those theories needed to be adapted open-mindedly to the existing circumstances and ongoing historical processes; and that, even in the USSR, real historical processes were still far from corresponding to Marxist theoretical principles.[66] Still on economic issues, he rejected the dominant communist interpretation of the 1929 Wall Street crash, and the ensuing Great Depression, as events announcing the imminent collapse of capitalism; rather, he interpreted such events as typical of post-First-World-War capitalism, and defined this phase of capitalism as a complex process of crises and recoveries:

> Whoever wants to give one sole definition of these events or, what is the same thing, find a single cause or origin, must be rebutted. We are dealing with a process that shows itself in many ways, and in which causes and effects become intertwined and mutually entangled. To simplify means to misrepresent and falsify. Thus, a complex process, as in many other phenomena, and not a unique 'fact' repeated in various forms through a cause having one single origin.[67]

In general, the essential differences between Gramsci's early political writings and his *Prison Notebooks* (written between 1929 and 1935) derived from a reconsideration of the strategies best suited to establishing socialism in advanced capitalist societies. In the *Notebooks*, with respect to the life of the party, this reconsideration takes the form of a recurrent emphasis on the benefits of 'democratic centralism',[68] as opposed to the setbacks caused by the imposition of a superficial political unity through bureaucratic centralism.[69]

---

65. Carr and Davies 1969, p. 924.
66. See Gramsci 1975, Q10II, §37, pp. 1285–7.
67. Gramsci 1975, Q15, §5, p. 1755. Among the 'other phenomena' one should certainly include language – itself a complex 'multiplicity of facts' and not, as we shall see in section 3.3.4, a 'single thing'.
68. The notion of democratic centralism occurs in Lenin's writings. However, when a Democratic-Centralist tendency emerged in 1919–20, formed of Bolsheviks demanding more democracy and less central control in the internal life of the Party, Lenin condemned this group (see Ulam 1998, pp. 468–9). It is worth recalling that, in the following years, many Democratic Centralists gravitated around the left-wing, Trotskyist groups and, generally speaking, formed part of the opposition to the leadership of the Communist Party of the Soviet Union, and to Stalin's increasing domination of this party – until they were expelled in 1927. In any case, Gramsci took up, re-contextualised and developed the formula *democratic centralism* in an original way (see Paggi 1984, pp. 190–7, 212, and Femia 1987, pp. 151ff.).
69. This does not, of course, mean that Gramsci's *Notebooks* contain no residues of an approach to the material and cultural emancipation of the underprivileged social strata which will probably strike most of today's readers as belonging 'to a past we can no longer share' (Bellamy and Schecter 1993, p. 166). See, for instance, the oft-quoted

3.3.1. Necessary conditions

Only at this stage of his work did Gramsci's awareness of the difficulty of achieving cultural and linguistic unity have a full impact on the development of his political views. As we saw in Chapter Two, during his prison years Gramsci's glottopolitical views remained fundamentally consistent with the anti-dirigiste stance he had professed in his articles and theatre reviews in the years immediately following the First World War. On the one hand, during the prison years he continued to see linguistic unification as an aim to be pursued if a unified language is a necessity, in which case 'the organized intervention will speed up the already existing process'.[70] On the other hand, he also continued to warn against those forms of linguistic universalism which are not 'the historical expression of adequate and necessary conditions'.[71] Language-policy interventions could not be expected to produce totally predictable outcomes. They could speed up existing social and cultural processes; but they could not arbitrarily create these processes. Even when organised interventions were successful in obtaining a unified language, it could not be foreseen what this language would be: 'in any case, if the intervention is "rational", [the new language] will be organically tied to tradition, and this is of no small importance in the economy of culture'.[72]

In striking concordance with these statements on language policy, and applying a pattern of argumentation similar to that of these and other passages on language, he wrote, on a quintessentially political matter: 'destroying parliamentarism is not as easy as it seems'.[73] Even though dictatorships might abolish parliamentary democracy, within their newly created one-party states they would witness the resurgence of a certain degree of latent social conflict and concealed political debate. Gramsci saw parliamentary democracy as a formal arrangement which, in itself, did not guarantee the effective passage of citizens 'from the led groups to the leading group'.[74] As a communist, he was willing to move beyond

---

note on Machiavelli and the rise of modern political parties, where Gramsci claims that the modern party, 'as it develops, overturns the whole system of intellectual and moral relations, in that its development means precisely that any given act is seen as useful or harmful, as virtuous or as wicked, only in so far as it has as its point of reference the modern Prince itself [the party], and helps to strengthen, or to oppose, the power of the modern Prince' (Gramsci 1975, Q13, §1, p. 1561). On the other hand, it could be claimed that notes like this simply describe the way in which modern political parties operate in civil society (cf. Gramsci 1975, Q2, §75, pp. 230–9 – especially the following comment: 'To acquire democracy within the state it may be necessary – indeed, it is almost always necessary – to have a strongly centralised party').

70. Gramsci 1975, Q29, §3, p. 2345.
71. Gramsci 1975, Q5, §23, p. 557.
72. Gramsci 1975, Q29, §3, pp. 2345–6.
73. Gramsci 1975, Q14, §74, p. 1742.
74. Gramsci 1975, Q8, §191, p. 1056.

bourgeois parliamentarism and create a new society (including new forms of political representation) with which to replace capitalist societies. He seems to have alluded to this ultimate goal, for instance, in a famous letter to his wife, in which he described the ideal '[m]odern man' as 'a modern type of Leonardo da Vinci who has become a mass-man or collective man while nevertheless maintaining his strong personality and originality as an individual'.[75] Yet, on a more practical level, Gramsci was now well aware that *in the absence of the necessary and adequate conditions* unity could be as counterproductive in political life as it was in language. In other words, he was – more than he had been during the early 1920s – utterly concerned about the shortcomings of *imposing* new social and political arrangements.

Accordingly, he wrote that 'it is impossible to abolish...parliamentarism, without radically abolishing its content, individualism, and this in its precise meaning of "individual appropriation" of profit and of economic initiative for capitalist and individual profit'.[76] Evidently, Stalin's régime was far from accomplishing this radical, epoch-making goal. Rather than sanctioning the composition of conflicts and ultimate unification of society, an event such as the exclusion of Trotsky from power was in fact a 'symptom (or prediction) of the intensification of struggles'.[77] Again, freely developing social forces could not – and should not – be repressed. Gramsci made the vivid conclusion that it is impossible to make bad weather go away 'by abolishing the barometer'.[78]

3.3.2. *Centres of irradiation*

The concordance of Gramsci's political views with his views on language and language-policy issues is neither sporadic nor, as it were, fortuitous (I shall illustrate this point in more depth in my Conclusions). Quite the contrary, during the prison years, similarities and interconnections often emerge between Gramsci's reflections on political behaviours and on linguistic behaviours. Sometimes, the same terminology is used to describe the spread of a prestigious worldview, in the political life of a community, and the spread of prestigious linguistic forms in a community of speakers. For instance, in Notebook 29 Gramsci offers a list of the 'centres [*focolai*] of irradiation of linguistic innovations in the tradition and of national linguistic conformism in the broad national masses'. These are: '1) The education system; 2) newspapers; 3) artistic writers and popular writers; 4) the theatre and sound films; 5) radio; 6) public meetings of all kinds, including

---

75. Gramsci 1994a, II, pp. 194–5.
76. Gramsci 1975, Q14, §74, p. 1742.
77. Gramsci 1975, Q14, §76, p. 1744.
78. Ibid.

religious ones; 7) the relations of "conversation" between the more educated and less educated strata of the population . . . ; 8) local dialects'.[79] This note from Notebook 29, and other notes on language included in the *Quaderni del carcere*, can fruitfully be compared with a note from Notebook 13, entitled 'Number and Quality in Representative Systems of Government', which Gramsci had originally drafted in Notebook 9 (in August 1932).[80] Here, again, the topic is quintessentially political: the 'critique . . . of the parliamentary system of government', and, in general, of 'all representative systems' based on 'numbers'.[81] However, when the discussion moves from how electoral support is generated to the formation of ideas, and to how a common core of opinions, cultural values, and political attitudes comes to be shared by large numbers of individuals, Gramsci's terminology and arguments become remarkably similar to the terminology and arguments he often uses with regard to language. There is no parthenogenesis in language.[82] Similarly, ideas and opinions 'are not spontaneously "born" in each individual brain: they have had a *centre* of formation, *of irradiation*, of dissemination, of persuasion – a group of men, or a single individual even, which has developed them and presented them in the political form of current reality'.[83] Once again, we find the phrase *centro di irradiazione*, which is often used by Gramsci with regard to language (either *centri di irradiazione* or *focolai di irradiazione*).

In one of his annotations on his copy of Alfredo Panzini's grammar of the Italian language,[84] Gramsci observes that in societies 'where there exists "hero worship" *in grammar, as in politics* and so on, there exists no directive organic *centre*'.[85] And in another note from his *Quaderni*, he lists the centres through which the dominant social group spreads its own worldview, when this group is able to get the rest of society to accept its worldview on the basis of consent, without having to use coercion:

> publishing houses (which either explicitly or implicitly have a programme and are linked to a given tendency); political newspapers; reviews of every kind – scientific, literary, philological, popular and so on; various periodicals, including even parish bulletins. . . . The press is the most dynamic part of this ideological structure, but not the only one. Everything that directly or indirectly influences or may influence public opinion belongs to it: libraries,

---

79. Gramsci 1975, Q29, §3, p. 2345.
80. See Francioni 1984, p. 143.
81. Gramsci 1975, Q13, §30, pp. 1624–6.
82. Cf. Gramsci 1975, Q6, §71, p. 739.
83. Gramsci 1975, p. 1625 (my emphasis).
84. See Appendix: section 4.2.3.
85. Quoted in Martinelli 1989b, p. 685 (my emphasis).

schools, associations and clubs of different kinds, right up to architecture, street layout and street names.[86]

Interestingly, some of these centres coincide with those which Gramsci lists in the above-quoted note on the spread of linguistic innovations. The notion of centres from which linguistic forms spread was typical of the geographical approach to historical linguistics which Gramsci had studied under Bartoli.[87] However, as we also saw in Chapter Two, Soviet linguists used similar notions. For instance, they discussed the themes of 'sociolinguistic differentiation' and 'unification around a single centre' [*Ob"edinenie vokrug odnogo tsentra*], and they also emphasised the analogies between specifically linguistic norms and social norms in general.[88] Moreover, a similar concern with language spread, from the highly innovative centres of modern urban life to conservative rural peripheries, was typical of the debates involving Soviet politicians, language-policy officials, and agitators in the 1920s. Indeed, ever since the events of 1917, and before the heavy restrictions that Stalinism imposed on cultural life and academic debates, linguistic divides had attracted priority attention, and had given rise to a wide range of reflections and proposals. These were aimed at improving a practical situation which, in the aftermath of the February Revolution of 1917, had turned out to be quite desperate, especially among the peasants:

> the peasants and their spokesmen in 1917 were painfully aware of the linguistic gulf that separated them from the Revolution in the towns. 'We can't understand many of your words', complained one peasant to the S[ocialist]-R[evolutionary] leaders of the Kurgan' peasant congress during a debate on the structure of the state – 'you have to speak in Russian'. Imported words ('republic', 'constitution', 'federation', 'democracy', 'regime', 'annexation', and even 'revolution') were misunderstood and mispronounced by peasants. Thus the word 'republic' (*respublika*) appeared as *despublika* and *razbublika* in various peasant letters; 'regime' (*rezhim*) became *prizhim*; 'constituent' (*uchreditel'noe*) was transformed into *chereditel'noe* (on the basis that the Constituent Assembly would decide everything 'in its turn', or *cheredom*); 'revolution' (*revoliutsiia*)

---

86. Gramsci 1975, Q3, §49, pp. 332–3.
87. See Bertoni and Bartoli 1928, Part 2, Chapter Two; Grassi *et al.* 2004, Chapter Three. See also Boothman 2012.
88. See Selishchev 1971. My quotations are taken from the titles of two sections in the first chapter of Selishchev's classic study of the changes that Russian underwent during the years from 1917 to 1926 – *Iazyk revoliutsionnoi epokhi* ['Language in a Revolutionary Period']. See also Selishchev's 1925 article, *Des traits linguistiques communs aux langues balkaniques* ['On the Common Linguistic Features of Balkan Languages'], published in Antoine Meillet's *Revue des études slaves* ['Slavonic Studies Review'] – especially Selishchev's description of the disappearance of 'levelling centres [*centres niveleurs*] based on Roman civilisation' from the Balkans around the third century A.D. (Seliščev 1925, pp. 42–43).

was pronounced and written as *revutsia, levoliutsiia,* and *levorutsia;* the 'Bolshe-viks' (*bol'sheviki*) were confused with a party of *bol'shaki* (peasant elders) and of *bol'shie* (big people); while 'annexation' (*anneksiia*) was thought by many peasant soldiers to be a small Balkan kingdom neighbouring *kontributsiia* (the Russian word for 'indemnity') and at least on one occasion was confused with a woman called 'Aksinia'. 'Who is this Aksinia?' one peasant asked another who had heard about her from an 'oratater' (*oratel'* instead of *orator*). 'God knows who she is. They say that because of her there will be a great harm, and that if there is Aksinia there will be another war against us after we have made peace with the Germans'. 'Ooh she must be bad: over one woman there is war again!' (*Ish' ved' kakaia vrednaia: ot odnoi baby i opiat' voina!*).[89]

This situation had immediate, far-reaching political implications. Sometimes it also had paradoxical, and yet tragic consequences. These are described in a report commissioned by the Duma in 1917, from which the historian Orlando Figes quotes the following passage:

> There are occasions when a deputy returning from Petrograd, where he has been deluged by noisy rhetoric and the storm of party arguments and debates, replies to the question about what he had heard there: 'I have forgotten! I've forgotten everything I heard. I heard so much that in the end I could remember nothing'. He has become confused and forgotten all. And his fellow-villagers put him into jail because they have paid him to travel to the city and he has told them nothing.[90]

3.3.3. *The Jacobins*

Gramsci, too, in his prison notes, addressed the practical links between language and politics. These links are based not only on similar conceptual models – and thus on similar terminological usages, with which to describe the spread of language and the spread of worldviews (as in the above-mentioned case of *centri di irradiazione*) – but also on intrinsic, historical connections. As in his early (pre-prison) writings about dialects, and about Albanians and other ethno-linguistic minorities living in Italy, linguistic diversity is seen as a factor which those aiming at political and cultural unification need to consider carefully. In the first set of notebooks that Gramsci used while in prison (namely, Notebooks 1–4, in which he wrote mainly between 1929 and 1931), we can find remarks on the

---

89. Figes 1997, pp. 324–5. See also Mazon 1920.
90. Figes 1997, p. 326.

emergence of writers using the Roman dialect (*romanesco*) at the time of the 1527 Sack of Rome 'and especially the French Revolution',[91] and on the fact that

> every political movement creates a language of its own, that is, it participates in the general development of a distinct language, introducing new terms, enriching existing terms with a new content, creating metaphors, using historical names to facilitate the comprehension and the assessment of particular contemporary political situations.[92]

In other prison notes, historical instances of the practical interconnections between politics, culture and language are again taken from the period of the French Revolution. By generating widespread political consent, the French Jacobins were largely – yet not entirely – successful in overcoming fragmentation, and in bridging the cultural gap between the cities and the surrounding countryside, as well as between Paris, the revolutionary centre, and the rest of the country. Coercive measures, according to Gramsci, were relatively marginal and were used only in particularly difficult cases. In this way, the Jacobins offered a positive example – which Gramsci uses in his prison writings, often setting it against the negative example of the Italian *Risorgimento* – of how hegemony works in societies where the dominant groups look beyond their own immediate interests and manage to include the demands of large sections of the population into their own political programmes:

> the internal contradictions in the French social structure that took shape after 1789 were resolved, relatively speaking, only with the Third Republic, and France now has sixty years of stable political life after eighty years of progressively longer waves of upheavals: 1789–94, 1794–1815, 1815–30, 1830–48, 1848–70.... [I]deologies come into contact and confrontation with one another, until only one of them – or, at least, a single combination of them – tends to prevail, to dominate, to spread across the entire field, bringing about, in addition to economic and political unity, intellectual and moral unity, not on a corporate but on a universal level: the hegemony of a fundamental social group over the subordinate groups. The state-government is seen as a group's own organism for creating the favourable terrain for the maximum expansion of the group itself. But this development and this expansion are also viewed concretely as universal; that is, they are viewed as being tied to the interests of the subordinate groups, as a development of unstable equilibriums between the interests of the fundamental group and the interests of the subordinate groups in which the interests of the dominant group prevail – but only up

---

91. Gramsci 1975, Q3, §79, p. 359.
92. Gramsci 1975, Q1, §43, pp. 31–2.

to a certain point; that is, without going quite as far as corporate economic selfishness.[93]

'In real history' this process of cultural and political unification takes place 'horizontally and vertically; that is, through economic activity (horizontally) and territory (vertically) combining and diverging in various ways':[94]

each of these combinations may be represented by its own organized economic and political expression. It is also necessary to bear in mind that international relations become intertwined with these internal relations of a nation-state, and this, in turn, creates peculiar and historically concrete combinations. An ideology born in a highly developed country is disseminated in a less developed country and has an effect on the local interplay of combinations.... This relation between international and national forces is further complicated by the fact that frequently within each nation[95] there are a number of national territorial sectors, with different structures and diverse relations of force at all levels (thus, in France, the Vendée was allied with international reactionary forces and represented them in the heart of French territorial unity; similarly, Lyons represented a node of particular relations, etc.).[96]

Finally, in another note (from Notebook 19) concerning the anti-revolutionary guerrilla in the Vendée region (in western France), Gramsci writes:

Without the agrarian policy of the Jacobins, Paris would have had the Vendée at its very doors. The resistance of the Vendée properly speaking is linked to the national question, which had become envenomed among the peoples of Brittany and in general among those alien to the slogan of the 'single and indivisible republic' and to the policy of bureaucratic-military centralisation – a slogan and a policy which the Jacobins could not renounce without committing suicide. The Girondins tried to exploit federalism in order to crush Jacobin Paris, but the provincial troops brought to Paris went over to the revolutionaries. Except for certain marginal areas, where the national (and linguistic) differentiation was very great, the agrarian question proved stronger than aspirations to local autonomy. Rural France accepted the hegemony of Paris; in other words, it understood that in order definitively to destroy the old regime it had to make a bloc with the most advanced elements of the Third Estate, and not with the Girondin moderates. If it is true that the Jacobins 'forced'

---

93. Gramsci 1975, Q4, §38, pp. 456–8 (English translation in Gramsci 1996b – slightly modified).
94. Gramsci 1975, p. 458.
95. The second draft (Notebook 13) has 'state' [*Stato*] instead of 'nation': Gramsci 1975, Q13, §17, p. 1585.
96. Gramsci 1975, p. 458.

its hand, it is also true that this always occurred in the direction of real historical development. For not only did they organise a bourgeois government, i.e. make the bourgeoisie the dominant class – they did more. They created the bourgeois State, made the bourgeoisie into the leading, hegemonic class of the nation, in other words gave the new State a permanent basis and created the compact modern French nation.[97]

3.3.4. *Language and hegemony*

In essence, academic and political debates about language spread and unification gave Gramsci the opportunity to appreciate the complexity of immanent historical processes and socio-political conflicts, as opposed to theoretical abstractions and crude revolutionary strategising. Along with other sources, debates on the socio-geographical dimension of language led him to consider the difficulty of spreading new worldviews, and the importance of cultural differences between social classes, as well as among various geographical groups within each of these classes. Almost certainly, those debates were one of the sources of inspiration for his own attention to diversity in political life, and for his rejection of simplistic Marxist revolutionary programmes based on the structure-superstructure model (whereby innovations in the former mechanically trigger innovations in the latter),[98] or on the expected palingenetic effects of one homogeneous class (the proletariat) ousting another equally homogeneous class (the bourgeoisie) from power.

---

97. Gramsci 1975, Q19, §24, p. 2029 (English translation in Gramsci 1971c, pp. 55–84). These issues have been studied by Michel de Certeau, Dominique Julia and Jacques Revel in their famous book on the language policies of the French Revolution (De Certeau, Julia and Revel 1975).

98. In his prison notes, Gramsci appears increasingly dissatisfied with the naturalistic metaphor which Marxists used when stating that 'the "anatomy" of a society is constituted by its "economy"' (Gramsci 1975, Q11, §50, p. 1473). In contrast, Gramsci's revised version of Marxism (to which he refers as 'the philosophy of praxis') is based on his awareness of the level of complexity that the relationships between economy and politics had reached in advanced capitalist societies; and it thus involves 'asserting the moment of hegemony as essential' and 'attaching "full weight" to the cultural factor, to cultural activity, to the necessity for a cultural front alongside the merely economic and merely political ones' (Gramsci 1975, Q10I, §7, p. 1224). Gramsci puts forward these arguments in a series of notes where he criticises Benedetto Croce's dismissal of Marxism. He criticises Croce for failing to acknowledge that Marxists had abandoned dogmatic versions of the structure-superstructure model. In doing so, Gramsci probably has in mind, above all, 'the "last" Lenin's theoretical statements and . . . concrete acts' (Thomas 2009, p. 234 note 97). On the whole, however, one has the impression that he is extending to contemporary Marxism in general what is, in fact, largely specific to his own Marxism, as theorised in his prison writings.

This attention to cultural and political diversity was to be a crucial factor in securing a considerably high degree of intellectual appeal and political credibility for Gramsci's legacy during the second half of the twentieth century:

> It is from Gramsci that we learned to understand – and practise – the discipline imposed by an unswerving attention to the 'peculiarities' and unevenness of national-cultural development. It is Gramsci's example which cautions us against the too-easy transfer of historical generalisations from one society or epoch to another, in the name of 'Theory'.[99]

This praise for Gramsci's Marxism 'as a living, developing, constantly renewable stream of ideas', and not 'as a quasi-religious body of dogma', is expressed by Stuart Hall in a succinct essay in which he stresses Gramsci's 'boldness and independence of mind',[100] and singles out the most distinctive points in Gramsci's work. These, Hall believes, are also relevant for present-oriented research. Amongst these points, he includes Gramsci's 'writing on cultural questions, on language and popular literature and, of course, his work on ideology'.[101]

> His work on the necessarily contradictory nature of the subjects of ideology, their fragmentary, pluri-centered character, has been extraordinarily generative.... Nothing is so calculated to destroy the simple minded notion of ideology as 'correct thoughts' parachuted into the empty heads of waiting proto-revolutionary subjects as Gramsci's stubborn attendance to the real, living textures of popular life, thought, and culture which circumscribe the historical effectivity of even the most coherent and persuasive of 'philosophies'.[102]

I shall return to this aspect of the reception of Gramsci's work in my Conclusions. I am now going to round off this section by quoting extensively from a note where the transition from linguistic and cultural themes to more strictly political ones is particularly evident. This note was written (towards the end of 1932) in Notebook 10, that is, in one of the two notebooks – the other being Notebook 11 – that are not only chronologically, but also theoretically, central in Gramsci's prison writings. In this note, Gramsci makes it quite clear that cultural unification is a politically desirable achievement; but, at the same time, he expresses some of the most positive judgements on liberal-democratic rights that can be read in any of his writings, stressing that liberal democracy had been able to produce an

---

99. Hall 1991, p. 7. Eric Hobsbawm made similar remarks concerning the originality of Gramsci's Marxism: 'One of the reasons why historians, Marxist and even non-Marxist, have found him so rewarding is precisely his refusal to leave the terrain of concrete historical, social and cultural realities for abstraction and reductionist theoretical models' (Hobsbawm 2011, p. 338).
100. Hall 1991, p. 8.
101. Hall 1991, p. 9.
102. Ibid.

appealing (though ultimately insufficient) answer to the question of how unification can be achieved without imposition. Quite significantly, Gramsci comes to express these positive judgements through a series of interrelated reflections in which language and other cultural issues have a prominent position, if not a catalysing role. Unlike the articles from his pre-prison years, this note shows full theoretical awareness of the similarities and connections between socio-political and cultural-linguistic unification.[103] Here, the attention that Gramsci had long been paying to the themes of linguistic variation and cultural diversity seems to achieve its full potential in influencing his general political views:

> It seems that one can say that 'language' is essentially a collective term which does not presuppose any single thing existing in time and space. Language also means culture and philosophy (if only at the level of common sense) and therefore the fact of 'language' is in reality a multiplicity of facts more or less organically coherent and co-ordinated. At the limit it could be said that every speaking being has a personal language of his (or her) own, that is his own particular way of thinking and feeling. Culture, at its various levels, unifies in a series of strata, to the extent that they come into contact with each other, a greater or lesser number of individuals who understand each other's mode of expression in differing degrees, etc. It is these historico-social distinctions and differences which are reflected in common language... From this one can deduce the importance of the 'cultural aspect', even in practical (collective) activity. An historical act can only be performed by the 'collective man', and this presupposes the attainment of a 'cultural-social' unity through which a multiplicity of dispersed wills, with heterogeneous aims, are welded together with a single aim... Since this is the way things happen, great importance is assumed by the general question of language, that is, the question of collectively attaining a single cultural 'climate'.[104]

Gramsci goes on to relate linguistic and cultural unification to the educational relationships whereby teachers and pupils actively influence each other. The gradual process of cultural development that results from these educational relationships constitutes a 'relationship of "hegemony"'.[105] As such, hegemony exists throughout society. It exists between generations, between intellectual and

---

103. According to Giancarlo Schirru, this note marks a turning point also in the development of Gramsci's prison notes, from an early phase of his prison work, when politics and language had remained separate in his reflections, to a phase in which his 'theory seems capable of using the same tools in political and linguistic analysis' (Schirru 2008a, p. 420).

104. Gramsci 1975, Q10II, §44, pp. 1330–1 (English translation in Gramsci 1971c, pp. 348–51).

105. Gramsci 1975, p. 1331.

non-intellectual sections of the population, between the rulers and the ruled. Furthermore, a relationship of hegemony occurs not only within a nation, or between the social forces that form a nation, but also internationally, between 'complexes of national and continental civilisations'.[106]

> One could say therefore that the historical personality of an individual philosopher is also given by the active relationship which exists between him and the cultural environment he is proposing to modify. The environment reacts back on the philosopher...This is why one of the most important demands that the modern intelligentsias have made in the political field has been that of the so-called 'freedom of thought and of the expression of thought' ('freedom of the press', 'freedom of association'). For the relationship between master and disciple in the general sense referred to above is only realised where this political condition exists, and only then do we get the 'historical' realisation of a new type of philosopher, whom we could call a 'democratic philosopher' in the sense that he is a philosopher convinced that his personality is not limited to himself as a physical individual but is an active social relationship of modification of the cultural environment.[107]

3.4. Gramsci's specificity

3.4.1. A man 'in flesh and blood'

For the interpretation I have so far put forward, I owe much to Franco Lo Piparo's 1979 book, *Lingua, intellettuali, egemonia in Gramsci*. My work may be seen as an update, in the light of subsequently published material, and a reappraisal of Lo Piparo's work. A great deal of the material that I have examined, including primary sources, was not used by Lo Piparo (some of it was unknown in 1979). To a large extent, my findings confirm the general claim of Lo Piparo's groundbreaking book, and of Tullio De Mauro's preface to it – namely, that linguistics played an important part in shaping Gramsci's political thought. However, in addition to disagreeing with some specific aspects of Lo Piparo's interpretation

---

106. Ibid. Again, this is also true of linguistic change: 'the linguistic fact...cannot have strictly defined national boundaries', and 'the national language cannot be imagined outside the frame of other languages that exert an influence on it through innumerable channels which are often difficult to control' (Gramsci 1975, Q29, §2, pp. 2343–4). Moreover, the plural noun *complessi* is often used by Gramsci in passages concerning language (see Gramsci 1975, Q7, §25, p. 874, Q11, §20, p. 1420, Q29, §3, p. 2345; see also Gramsci 1987, pp. 556–8, quoted extensively in Chapter Two, section 2.5.2).

107. Gramsci 1975, Q10II, §44, pp. 1331–2.

(as I did in Chapters One and Two),[108] I do not wholly agree with the way in which Lo Piparo and De Mauro presented their arguments. At times, in my view, they have failed to avoid exaggeration: for instance when De Mauro writes, in his preface, that Gramsci produced no less than a 'linguistic theory';[109] and especially when Lo Piparo states, in a later article, that Gramsci was not a Marxist and that the 'primitive matrix of his philosophy should not be searched for in Marx or in Lenin or in any other Marxist, but in the science of language'.[110] De Mauro himself has come to realise that similar statements may well be misinterpreted, and ironically summarised the most extreme conclusions that could be drawn from them as follows: 'A Marxist? Gramsci was not a Marxist at all. Gramsci was not a politician at all. Gramsci was a linguist. Gramsci was an Ascolian. Only by chance did he become the Secretary of the Communist Party'.[111] Contradicting Lo Piparo's previous assertions,[112] conclusions of this kind would diminish Gramsci's distinctiveness, in a similar way to the conclusions of others who (from largely incompatible political standpoints) also refused to appreciate that distinctiveness: from those Communists who, while in prison with Gramsci, accused him of being no longer a revolutionary, but rather 'a social democrat' and a follower of the liberal philosopher Benedetto Croce;[113] to anti-communist interpreters who, instead, saw Gramsci as a dogmatic and 'totalitarian' Leninist.

Generalisations are important for interpreting authors; but they should not lead us to overlook either the differences between various authors, or the internal complexity of each individual author. In the past (as I recalled in my Introduction), many interpreters became involved in heated debates on Gramsci's alleged totalitarianism. These debates focused on pluralism,[114] and centred on Gramsci's evaluation of political democracy – that is, his stance on the plurality of political programmes and initiatives as guaranteed by liberal-democratic institutions, and on the relationship between leaders and masses within the state as well as within political parties. Gramsci's views on these matters are part of a wider dialectical relationship (whose problematic existence characterises many of his writings) between the value, on the one hand, of unity and homogeneity,

---

108. See especially section 2.5.3.

109. A similar exaggeration is also expressed by Salamini, in a passage which is otherwise acceptable and no doubt insightful: 'Gramsci is one of the few Western Marxist theorists to take an active interest in language and arrive at *a general theory of language,* not dissimilar from contemporary structural linguistics' (Salamini 1981a, p. 182; my emphasis). Cf. Appendix, 4.5.1.

110. Lo Piparo 2010b, first published in 1987, p. 21.

111. De Mauro 2010b, first published in 1991, p. 258.

112. Originally, Lo Piparo's emphasis was on linguistic disciplines as *one* of the sources (and not *the* source) for the development of Gramsci's thought; and on Gramsci as a communist of a peculiar kind who could not, nonetheless, be presented as a liberal.

113. See the testimonies collected by Paulesu Quercioli 1977 and Bermani 2007.

114. See Mouffe 1979, Femia 1995, Liguori 1996, Vacca 1999a.

and, on the other, of multiplicity and diversity. To seek a synthesis to this dialectic, for the sake of an unequivocal and persuasive interpretation of Gramsci, would be an extremely difficult task. Moreover, such an attempt would be inappropriate, and probably destined to fail from the outset, given the complexity of Gramsci's thought and the evolution that his thought underwent through the various phases of his life and political work. This is probably true of all great figures, and certainly of an author who never edited his pre-prison writings and prison notes for publication.

Excessive generalisations can lead not only to oversimplifying Gramsci's views, but also to judging these views according to criteria that are dominant today, but were not so in his time. In other words, when discussing Gramsci's work, we should be careful not to apply our contemporary mindset in an anachronistic manner. Gramsci operated in an intricate, dramatically unstable material and ideological context. He lived at a time when traditionally elitist versions of liberal parliamentary rule were giving way to new democracies in which larger and larger masses of the population became organised through weighty political parties. Needless to say, this was not a smooth process. Unsurprisingly, many intellectuals predicted radical forms of cultural renovation and social rebirth, and were influenced by politico-philosophical approaches that harshly criticised democracy 'from the outside' – that is, emphasising the need to discard democracy as a whole, rather than to improve or modify certain aspects of it. Gramsci was also exposed to this influence, especially during his youth.[115] The difficulties of liberal-democratic institutions were seen as incorrigible degenerations. These institutions were rejected in the name of utopian, often ambiguous alternatives – which were, nonetheless, expected to grant political power a new, more authentic legitimacy. Towards the end of the First World War, the news of the Russian Revolution was received by large sectors of the Italian working class with enthusiasm and insistent calls for the Italian labour movement to follow the Bolsheviks' example. But the instability of those years, in fact, soon led to Mussolini's dictatorship; and Gramsci's later reflections took place in one of the prisons where this one-party régime locked up its opponents. Hence the great distance between his historical period and our own, with respect to the meaning and value normally attached to such terms as *democracy, pluralism,* and *totalitarianism.*[116]

One of the best-known and most authoritative Italian intellectuals of the twentieth century, Norberto Bobbio (1909–2004), repeatedly suggested that Gramsci's intellectual biography be studied as the variable evolution of a man

---

115. See Cafagna 1988.
116. See Bobbio 1991, Benvenuti and Pons 1999, Ausilio 2009, Caputo 2009, and Liguori 2009.

'in flesh and blood',[117] and not as a perfect example of some pure political category (communism, Marxism, Leninism, and so on). Bobbio also noted that the *Prison Notebooks* contain some stimulating observations on the relationship between hegemony and democracy, which have remained worthy of scholarly and political consideration through more recent historical phases.[118] They reveal Gramsci's distance from messianic and millenarian versions of communism, as well as his growing reluctance to envisage revolution as a resolutive event after which all divergences will vanish – the once-and-for-all imposition of a new order. While this distance certainly makes Gramsci a Marxist of a special type, it does not necessarily make him a social-democratic reformist. Furthermore, Bobbio insisted that *reform* and *revolution* are themselves historical concepts whose meaning, viability, and desirability change according to different historical phases. There are circumstances that favour revolutionary programmes. From the time when the Communist Party of Italy was founded, to the years that Gramsci spent in prison (1927–33), until the end of the Second World War, the crisis in society was so wide and deep as to produce, on the political Right, fears of an imminent decline of the West, and, on the Left, widespread expectations of the advent of a new world. Those who opposed Fascism, even from moderate political positions, suffered various forms of violence, and then themselves turned to violence in the struggle that led to the victory over Fascism and Nazism. When violence appears to be the only means to renovate political life, Bobbio concludes, the fascination of drastic renovation (*renovatio ab imis*) is hard to escape.[119]

Thus, a communist like Gramsci cannot be reproached for 'failing to face up to a problem such as the relative validity of liberal-democratic institutions',[120] nor to the problem of what institutions would be created by the working class once in power: these problems were 'foreign to the tradition of Marxist political thought with which he identified, if without dogmatic rigidity'.[121] Incidentally, these comments of Bobbio's are of particular note, as it is well-known that his reading of Gramsci was never an apologetic one. For Gramsci – a thinker who was also a man of action, and whose thought and praxis are inseparable – the fundamental theoretical problem necessarily derived from his activities as a revolutionary, thus essentially consisting in the search for the best strategy for seizing power. Gramsci, who was, not without reason, a severe critic of the decomposing Italian state, above all else saw the negative aspects of the old institutions. Their safeguarding was not and could not be amongst his primary concerns. Nor could he

---

117. See Bobbio 1990, p. 18.
118. See Bobbio 1991. See also Morera 1990.
119. Bobbio 1977, pp. 57–8.
120. Bobbio 1978, p. 595.
121. Bobbio 1978, pp. 595–6 (English translation in Martin 2002, I, p. 88).

be primarily concerned with the institutions of the proletarian state, as this new state was yet to come about.[122]

3.4.2. *Gramsci's Marxism*

There is, perhaps, some exaggeration in Bobbio's interpretation, too, especially in his comment about Gramsci's limited attention to 'the problem of the validity of liberal-democratic institutions'. However, I find Bobbio's recommendations pertinent to my discussion, and would like to broaden them by adding that communism itself should not be regarded as an absolute category, nor all its exponents as a perfectly homogeneous group. In response to Bobbio's call to study Gramsci without trying to reduce him to a mere reflection of some 'Platonic form' – be that of Marxism or Leninism, or communism in general – historical research should aim at reconstructing in what way Gramsci was a communist in the social and geopolitical circumstances of his own historical period. This has been my aim in this chapter, which, in highlighting Gramsci's attention to linguistic, cultural and also political diversity, has by no means sought to prove that Gramsci ultimately became a social democrat or a liberal.

For example, Gramsci never embraced general ideas of rational choice or purely spontaneous formation of consent; nor did he accept the idea of ideologically-neutral state institutions as merely reflecting, and thus effectively representing, the political divisions and cultural developments existing in society. Most of Gramsci's prison work was aimed at confuting the philosophical premises of both positivist Marxism and Croce's liberal idealism – with the former including, for Gramsci, not only simplistic Soviet formulations as exemplified by Bukharin's popular manual, but also the reformist gradualism typical of the Second International.[123] For Gramsci, historical renewal in different social strata and geographical areas is neither a mechanical nor a simultaneous process.[124] In other words, human history should not be conceived of as a single,

---

122. See Bobbio 1978, p. 596.
123. See Gramsci 1975, Q9, §6, pp. 1099–1100, and Q16, §26, pp. 1898–9.
124. 'A negro just arrived from Africa can become one of Ford's employees, while still staying a fetishist for a long time and while still remaining convinced that cannibalism is a normal, justified way of gaining nourishment' (Gramsci 1975, Q11, §66, p. 1501). '[E]ven today many people are Ptolemaic and not Copernican. There are many "conformisms", many struggles for new "conformisms" and various combinations of that which already exists (variously expressed) and that which one is working to bring about (and there are many people who are working in this direction). It is a serious error to posit a "single" progressive line, along which every new gain accumulates and becomes the premise of further gains. Not only are the lines multiple, but even in the "most progressive" ones there are retrogressive moments' (Q15, §58, p. 1821; see also Q10II, §48, pp. 1335–6; and the comments on Antonio Labriola's 'pseudo-historicism' – 'a mechanism that is rather empirical and very close to the most vulgar evolutionism' – in Q11, §1, on pp. 1366–8).

purely spontaneous process that, without the active intervention of political actors or institutions, is ultimately bound to produce the necessary conditions for the emergence of socialism. In fact, Gramsci's continuous concern with diversity and unification proves precisely how he conceived of the unity of humankind as a possible outcome, which had to be fought for – not as a pre-existing feature, whose complete unfolding could be seen as inevitable and therefore taken for granted.[125]

In addition, as Peter Ives usefully underlines in his work on language and hegemony in Gramsci, his understanding of languages as socio-historical products reinforced his critical stance on the state and the formation of consent. Gramsci's reflections on spontaneity in language are consistent with his reflections on spontaneity in collective political history, and both contribute to characterising his definition of *hegemony*, in which he denies the possibility that consent can be entirely spontaneous – the parthenogenesis of an absolutely free, uncontaminated will. Given that previous models of correct linguistic usage have exerted influences and left traces on how speakers use language, and that later generations of speakers have internalised those models to the point of following them instinctively in their linguistic practice, spontaneous grammars cannot not be seen as 'the opposite of normative grammars, they are not the individual or internal expression that is totally consented to as opposed to external imposition'.[126] Likewise, the supposedly spontaneous formation and spread of collective orientations and political views, far from being the result of 'free will made with no influence or pressure from history, nor limited by external structures',[127] in fact consists of a process whereby the influence of previous political leaderships, state institutions, cultural hierarchies, social stratifications, unequal power relations, and even coercion, has been forgotten, or has simply remained undocumented.[128]

In this perspective, the hegemony of the leading social class is never entirely separate from coercion, and once this class has seized power, the expansion of its hegemony is always, to a degree, backed by state institutions and coercion. Accordingly, state and civil society should be seen as intertwined and essentially related elements. Normally, hegemony manifests itself in civil society, in that a fully working ethical-cultural leadership only requires the use of state coercion in exceptional circumstances, against marginal 'groups who do not "consent" either actively or passively';[129] this is not enough, however, to claim that

---

125. See Gramsci 1975, Q11, §17, p. 1416.
126. Ives 2004a, p. 97.
127. Ibid.
128. Cf. Gramsci 1975, Q3, §48, pp. 328–32.
129. Gramsci 1975, Q12, §1, p. 1519.

state institutions are neutral, autonomous political institutions. Famously, in the *Prison Notebooks* the state is equated with 'political society + civil society, that is, hegemony protected by the armour of coercion'.[130] In other words, the state is 'the entire complex of practical and theoretical activities with which the ruling class not only justifies and maintains its dominance, but manages to win the active consent of those over whom it rules'.[131] Consent does not simply emerge from civil society through the competition of divergent views, with the most rational views spontaneously prevailing over less persuasive ones. As long as economic, social and cultural power is unjustly and ineffectively distributed, the liberal assumption that civil society is the site of consent, and that the functions of democratic states are limited to those of a 'gendarme' or 'night watchman',[132] is an empty, abstract idea. It will only cease to be such when, with 'the beginning of an era of organic freedom', 'conspicuous elements of regulated society make their appearance'[133] – that is to say, with the transition towards communism. And even then, the advent of regulated society will not take place at once, but through a process 'that will probably last for centuries'.[134]

Therefore, it seems safe to conclude by saying that Gramsci remained a Marxist revolutionary socialist and did not lean towards social democracy or liberalism; that he was, indeed, a communist, though in an outstandingly personal way:

> [A]nyone who has acquired a certain familiarity with Gramsci's work knows that his thought has original and personal features which do not allow easy schematisations – almost entirely inspired by polemical political motives – such as 'Gramsci is Marxist-Leninist', or 'he is more of a Leninist than a Marxist', or 'he is more of a Marxist than a Leninist', or 'he is neither Marxist nor Leninist'; as if 'Marxism', 'Leninism', 'Marxism-Leninism' were clear and distinct concepts where one can sum up this or that theory or group of theories without leaving any uncertainty whatsoever, and one could use them like a ruler to measure out the length of a wall.[135]

3.4.3. *Final remarks*

To be sure, Gramsci's approach differed from the approach that Soviet Communists took to cultural and political diversity under Stalin. As we have seen in the present and previous chapters, this can be proved with a reasonable degree of accuracy by following the evolution of Gramsci's theoretical and

---

130. Gramsci 1975, Q6, §88, pp. 763–4.
131. Gramsci 1975, Q15, §10, p. 1765.
132. Gramsci 1975, p. 763.
133. Gramsci 1975, p. 764.
134. Gramsci 1975, Q7, §33, p. 882.
135. Bobbio 1969, pp. 78–9 (English translation in Mouffe 1979, p. 24).

practical work. I believe it is only by focusing on these specific, historically identifiable differences, that we can throw into relief the original and distinctive features of Gramsci's work. In contrast, the use of merely theoretical, static definitions would entail the problematic task of having to make explicit which historical realities fall under which definition. As Bobbio suggests, only after grouping the various strands of revolutionary socialism into non-overlapping sets, would it be possible to compare each set to Gramsci's theory and practice in a way that is both objective and capable of being disproved.

At any rate, in this chapter I have cast light not only on the existence, but also on the causes of the distinctive features of Gramsci's work. Although there is no reason for singling out the influence of linguistics as the sole, decisive factor, I hope to have shown that his lifelong interest in linguistic subjects played a key role in causing these distinctive features to emerge.

Conclusions: Gramscian Links between Language and Politics

Gramsci in linguistics...

In the specific context of a recently-unified country such as Italy, which was experiencing all the difficulties of a slow, uneven process of social and political integration, a large part of Gramsci's glottopolitical views can be traced back to the approaches that saw the emergence of large, modern and centralised states as a progressive historical advancement. To a certain extent, Gramsci inherited both the strengths and the weaknesses of these approaches; thus entailing some degree of disregard, or devaluation, of the rights of localised groups with distinctive cultural and linguistic traditions. In Chapter Two, I recalled that Marx's writings, and those of Engels, show a certain degree of hostility towards smaller-sized national states and small economic markets. Engels made repeated distinctions between vitally alive and politically decayed nationalities, or between great historic peoples and mere remnants of peoples. But this was not confined to Marxists. The liberal thinker John Stuart Mill, in his 1861 *Considerations on Representative Government*, distinguished between nationalities that were 'inferior' or 'superior in civilization', and stated that '[w]hatever really tends to the admixture of nationalities, and the blending of their attributes and peculiarities in a common union, is a benefit to the human race', especially in the case of nationalities which were 'small' and had 'no hope of reasserting [their] independence'.[1]

---

1. Mill 1991, pp. 431–2. Mazzini, the father of Italian republicanism, held similar views.

Mill believed that modern nation-states were a mark of progress in human history, and maintained that 'smaller nationalities – the equivalent of "ethnic minorities" in modern political parlance – should be assimilated into the nation-state via its "national" culture and language'.[2]

Later Marxists embraced the idea that there could eventually be a supra-national language, which would probably absorb elements from other languages, and whose character would change as the number of its speakers gradually increased. This possibility of a worldwide spread of a single language was accepted, in a way which some of today's advocates of linguistic rights and equality might find naïve (perhaps even hypocritical), by Kautsky, Lenin, and also Gramsci,[3] on condition that such a spread should be the result of historical development, not of imposition.

If various threads of late nineteenth-century political thought perceived small states as being destined to give way to larger ones, and tacitly expected individuals to abandon their sense of belonging to an ethnic minority or local linguistic identity, then it is not surprising that the preservation of small-scale ethnic affiliations was also discouraged in practical terms. Three intellectual and juridical tendencies helped to shape political life in most Western countries. Firstly, there was the tendency to understand unification and fragmentation in hierarchical terms; that is, to see growing levels of unification as an improvement over fragmentation, especially micro-fragmentation. The second tendency was to associate growing unification with modernity and with material and intellectual progress, while the permanence of local culture was associated with backwardness and with the past. Thirdly, nation-states, usually with a largely dominant language for public communication, tended to accommodate internal plurality (of religious faiths, ethnic origin, cultural background, and so on) through individual citizenship rights, rather than through collective rights aimed at protecting the specific features of a minority.

Antoine Meillet, one of the linguists of the time most sensitive to glottopolitical matters (such as the spread of common languages, and the links between language and nationality), was resolute in asserting that Western-European states should accord privileges to national languages.[4] In his book *Les langues dans l'Europe nouvelle*, Meillet repeatedly referred to the 'general progress of civilisation', and often based his argument on the distinction between 'great

---

2. May 2001, p. 21.

3. See also the following remarks on the possibility of 'a European union': 'It is fair to say that the course of history is heading toward this union and that there are many material forces that will only be able to develop within this union. If this union were to come into existence in *x* years, the word "nationalism" will have the same archaeological value as "municipalism" has today' (Gramsci 1975, Q6, §78, p. 748. English translation from Gramsci 2007b).

4. See especially Meillet 1928, p. 185.

languages of culture' on the one hand and, on the other, lesser languages and local varieties with limited literary traditions.

In Italy, during Gramsci's lifetime, there was neither a completely negative perception of dialectophony nor a systematic persecution of tongues different from the national language. A relatively positive perception of dialects can be found in the works of a number of historians and philologists of the time (such as Pasquale Villari, Giovanni Crocioni, and Ernesto Monaci).[5] In the first decades of the twentieth century, this positive appreciation was expressed in many ways and in diverse fields, from literary and theatrical production to a more or less extemporary promotion of some aspects of folklore and traditional regional cultures.[6] Dialects were the subject of some excellent linguistic research, most notably in the work of Clemente Merlo, in the articles published in the *Archivio Glottologico Italiano* (founded by Graziadio Isaia Ascoli in 1873), and – to mention a work that can be seen as somewhat emblematic – in the entry *Dialetto*, written by Bertoni and Trabalza for the *Enciclopedia Italiana* ['Italian Encyclopaedia'].[7] The educationalist Giuseppe Lombardo Radice advocated the pedagogical value of highlighting differences and similarities between the dialects and the national language, in the primary-school curriculum that he drew up as part of Giovanni Gentile's 1923 reform of the Italian school system.[8]

Historical research has shown, however, that even those who did a great deal to defend the dignity of dialects in education, such as Ascoli and Lombardo Radice, tended to believe in the cultural superiority of national languages. They assumed, as the latter put it, that a 'unified language…, though adhering to the spirit of all the localised languages from which it has emanated, supersedes and subordinates all of them'.[9] Furthermore, despite all the attention paid to dialects by linguists and folklorists, attempts were made to reduce the vitality of dialects and to limit the presence of minority languages within the Italian borders.[10] These attempts began in the late nineteenth century, and took place especially in schools,[11] where an extreme, anti-dialect interpretation of Manzoni's views on language had become dominant. A further shift towards the imposition of linguistic uniformity by central political institutions occurred at the end of the

---

5. See Gensini 2005. See also Cirese 1998, pp. 115–88.
6. In Notebook 8, Gramsci makes incidental comments on the proliferation of 'the many Meneghino, Turinese, Bolognese, etc., "families"' (in the light of 'some interesting notes' by the Romance philologist and literary critic Cesare De Lollis): Gramsci 1975, Q8, §100, pp. 999–1000. Gramsci refers to these initiatives, aimed at the promotion of local traditions, in somewhat negative terms, seeing them as politically regressive attempts to rigidify and ossify cultural differences between social classes.
7. See Foresti 2005, pp. 33–5.
8. See Coveri 1981–2, Gensini 2005.
9. Quoted in Klein 1986, pp. 48–51. See also De Mauro 1979c and 1980a.
10. See De Mauro 1991, pp. 88–9, 307, 357. See also Raffaelli 1984, Foresti 2005.
11. See Gensini 2005, pp. 19–23, 28–30.

First World War.[12] Fascism then increased the level of imposed unification still further, by discarding the more tolerant instructions that Lombardo Radice had included in his school curricula, and by introducing, in the early 1930s, a campaign against dialects.[13]

The specificity of Gramsci's views can only be accurately assessed against the background I have sketched out in the previous paragraphs. Gramsci believed that diversity, including linguistic diversity, could not simply be denied, bureaucratically abolished or violently removed. Yet he also believed that modernity offered great opportunities for overcoming cultural and linguistic cleavages, in that modern economic and cultural trends would promote universal unification at a national level, and, ultimately, also at an international level.[14] The characteristics of the unified language that was eventually to emerge through this process of unification were not entirely predictable, and could not be determined from the outset. In this respect, Gramsci combined the legacy of Ascoli's glottology with the approach to language policy taken by those Marxist authors (Lenin in particular) who believed that the fight against language-based privileges and oppression was not necessarily incompatible with the perspective of gradually overcoming linguistic diversity. Gramsci set out to promote 'the *autonomous* birth of the need for literacy',[15] as well as favourable conditions for future linguistic unification. While large sectors 'of the eighteenth-century Italian bourgeoisie' had fought against dialects, 'hoping that these would disappear and be replaced by a

---

12. 'Essentially, this anti-dialect attitude served the interests of the postwar ruling classes, and it is no coincidence that Fascist language policies eventually came to take the same approach' (Carannante 1978, p. 626).

13. See Cortelazzo 1984, p. 110, Coveri 1984, Mengaldo 1994, pp. 13–16, and Sluga 2000, especially pp. 169–70.

14. Once again, it is worthwhile recalling the letters that Gramsci wrote to his sister-in-law, Tatiana Schucht, on Jewish identity. He recognised the right of Jewish communities to cultural and linguistic autonomy. At the same time, however, he denied the relevance of the concepts of race, and of cultural difference (which he saw as the result of specific and often accidental historical contingencies) as an absolute, essential form of difference. In this context, Gramsci wrote: 'How many societies does each individual belong to? And doesn't each of us make continuous efforts to unify his conception of the world in which there continues to subsist heterogeneous fragments of fossilized cultural worlds? And does there not exist a general historical process that tends to unify all of humanity continually? Don't the two of us, by writing to each other, continually discover reasons for discord and at the same time manage to come to agreement on certain questions? And doesn't each group or party or sect or religion tend to create its own "conformism" (not understood in a herd-like or passive sense)? What matters in the problem at hand is that the Jews were freed from the ghetto only after 1848 and had remained in the ghetto or in any event segregated from European society for almost two thousand years and not of their own accord but due to outside imposition. From 1848 on the process of assimilation in the Western countries has been so rapid and thoroughgoing that one is entitled to think that only imposed segregation prevented their complete assimilation in the various countries...' (Gramsci 1994a, II, p. 82).

15. Carannante 1973, p. 550.

previously defined and codified language', Gramsci argued for the *'autonomous formation of a national language'*.[16] He never took a hostile position towards the acquisition of dialects or minority languages. Even though he wanted the national language, together with the knowledge of foreign languages, to spread throughout Italian society, he never implied that other languages which were still used locally in Italy should necessarily be abandoned.[17]

Arguably, Gramsci placed those minority languages that enjoyed considerable social status and rich cultural traditions on a somewhat higher level than varieties with merely local currency and little socio-cultural prestige. One might also argue that he relegated the fate of dialects, viewed as local varieties with less prestige, to the private sphere of individual rights and choices. In doing so, he was following a well-established tradition. Indeed, this form of recognition of linguistic diversity, which involves neither the protection nor (obviously) the promotion of dialects, characterises much of the history of liberal political thought.[18] In contrast to this, in the case of varieties that are more widely used and are culturally prestigious, Gramsci and his associates at *L'Ordine Nuovo* seem to have been prepared to go beyond purely individual and negative forms of linguistic freedom, and to argue for some degree of active protection – as can be seen especially in the 1921 article 'Un pregiudizio', where Ireland's loss of its 'national tongue' is lamented; and in 'Il Comunismo e la Val d'Aosta' (from 1919), where only French is considered, and no mention is made of the less prestigious Franco-Provençal patois.

Gramsci and his collaborators seem to have been open-minded about public forms of recognition of the right to use widespread, culturally prestigious tongues in schools and in public administration – especially when these tongues were spoken by the members of an oppressed nationality who, though a minority within one country, constituted a majority in another, usually bordering, country. However, it is interesting to note that Gramsci, as shown in Chapter Two, recognised that the Jews, too, had the right to use their language in schools; that is, he recognised this right with respect to a group whose status as a nation was repeatedly debated by Marxists. Gramsci himself seems, at times, to question the status of the Jews as a nation,[19] though not to deny this status in principle.[20]

With his creative, independent, and open-minded way of adopting and re-elaborating dominant political and scholarly trends, Gramsci was able to resist abstract – and, in actual fact, coercive – drives towards linguistic unification. These drives are seen at work even in approaches originally based not on ideological

---

16. Carrannante 1973, pp. 553–4. Emphases in the original.
17. See also Rosiello 2010, p. 40, and Ives 2004a, p. 34.
18. For an overview, see May 2001.
19. See Gramsci 1996a, p. 476.
20. See Gramsci 1996a, p. 479.

hostility to diversity, but simply on pragmatism. Many such pragmatic approaches still led to a lack of attention to linguistic diversity, and sometimes also to deliberate oppression of diversity. Against the background of his historical period, Gramsci's awareness of linguistic diversity and his rejection of imposed unification highlight the specific and farsighted aspects of his approach to glottopolitical issues. He lived in a time when both Marxist and liberal politics were realised through policies which attacked linguistic and cultural diversity. These attempts at suppressing diversity occurred in several socially advanced countries and in different historical contexts: for instance, with Manzonianism in Italian schools (long before the Fascists extended attempts to suppress linguistic diversity to the entire Italian society); with US language policies during the 1920s;[21] and later also in the USSR, when Lenin's language-policy principles came to be applied in ways which did not fully correspond to his proposals.

Today, Gramsci's views still deserve the attention of scholars. Practitioners of critical linguistics, language policy, and sociolinguistics do not seem to have fully appreciated all of Gramsci's ideas on the relationship between unification and

---

21. The two cases of German and Chamorro speakers are particularly significant. During the nineteenth century, German migrants brought their language to North America and used it widely in cultural life (such as in newspapers) and education, both in Pennsylvania (where German-speaking groups had long been present) and elsewhere: 'in 1839, a number of states passed laws allowing German as the language of instruction in public schools, where numbers warranted... The growing acceptance of German-language education might have continued well into the twentieth century had it not been for two events. From the 1880s, state legislation was passed in several states mandating English as the only language of public (and even private) education.... Although many of these laws were subsequently rescinded by the courts, the deleterious effects on German bilingual schooling were reinforced by the subsequent anti-German hysteria surrounding the First World War. The most (in)famous case of language restrictionism at this time occurred in Nebraska. A 1913 state law required public schools to provide instruction in any European language if 50 or more parents requested it; German was the only language ever requested. In 1918 the law was repealed on the basis that it was pro-German and thus un-American. The legislation that replaced it went so far as to prohibit any public- or private-school teacher from teaching a subject in a foreign language or, indeed, from teaching a foreign language *as a subject*... The new law was overturned in the Supreme Court in 1923... However, by then, the damage was done. By the 1930s, bilingual instruction of any type in German had all but disappeared in the United States, while the study of German as a foreign language had fallen from 24 per cent of secondary-school students nationally in 1915 to less than one per cent in 1922' (May 2001, pp. 211–12). 'The formerly Spanish island of Guam [one of the Mariana Islands], whose indigenous language is Chamorro, was annexed by the United States in 1898. Under Spanish rule Chamorro had been a language of education in Guam, though Spanish was spoken by the local elite. Along with compulsory education, a previously unfamiliar language – English – was now imposed. In 1922 the speaking of Chamorro was forbidden in school precincts.... Chamorro dictionaries were collected and burnt... The thinking behind early United States language policy in Guam was set out, as coherently as it deserved, in the *Guam Recorder* for February 1925: "This is American territory. It is American to have public schools where only English is taught. Americans have an obligation and such they have never shirked" ' (Dalby 2002, pp. 141–2).

diversity, although this topic is crucial to their disciplines.[22] Gramsci is known as the theorist of hegemony, but insufficient attention has been paid to his writings and his life as a source of interesting observations and concrete examples regarding language issues. That language planners should look at language in society first, in order to select prestigious models and identify emergent trends to which language policy and standardisation could be connected, is indeed a recommendation that remains relevant today. So, too, is Gramsci's insistence on the risks of linguistically reinforced passivity and exclusion (though these risks were, in part, specific to a country like early-twentieth-century Italy, characterised as it was by poor schooling and high illiteracy rates, and by the historical presence of a prestigious literary language that members of the dominant groups could actively use with varying degrees of confidence and accuracy, while large sections of the population had only passive competence in it). Moreover, as shown in Chapter Two, Gramsci's comments on linguistic subjects should not be seen as the inconsistent observations of a politician with only a superficial, intermittent interest in language. Most of his comments reflected a conception of language which he developed gradually, in the course of many years, though he did not systematise it through specialist (theoretical or case-specific) contributions to linguistic disciplines.

Let me clarify this point about Gramsci's relevance by briefly comparing a few passages from the *Prison Notebooks* with recent historical and linguistic research. In Notebook 29, Gramsci problematised the distinction between normative and descriptive grammars, qualifying the extent to which this distinction actually existed in history. Because of the kind of training he had received in linguistics, and the period in which he had received it (under the dominant influence of diachronic linguistics), Gramsci regarded 'historical grammars' [*grammatiche storiche*] as typical examples of scientific descriptions of languages. Having asked whether the purpose of these descriptions is 'to record the history of an aspect of civilisation' or, instead, 'to modify an aspect of civilisation',[23] Gramsci went on to express the following views on the relationship between 'historical grammar' and 'normative grammar':

> We are dealing with two distinct and in part different things, like history and politics, but they cannot be considered independently, any more than politics and history. Besides, since the study of languages as a cultural phenomenon grew out of political needs (more or less conscious and consciously expressed), the needs of normative grammar have exerted an influence on historical grammar and on its 'legislative conceptions' (or at least this traditional element has

---

22. See Appendix, especially sections 4.5.3 and 4.5.4.
23. Gramsci 1975, Q29, §1, p. 2342.

> reinforced, during the last century, the application of the positivist-naturalist method to the study of the history of languages conceived as the 'science of language').[24]

In the same notebook, Gramsci also defined the political significance that debates on language often have. He stated that when these debates arise, various problems are in the process of coming to the fore: the formation and enlargement of the ruling class, and the need to establish more intimate and secure relationships between those in government and the 'national-popular mass' [*massa popolare-nazionale*] – that is, the need to extend 'cultural hegemony'.[25]

Today, most historians are well aware that 'even apparently disinterested knowledge',[26] including linguistic knowledge, can be mobilised for political purposes (as was the case, for instance, in India under British colonial rule).[27] And, as far as linguists are concerned, they, too, have acknowledged that: a) 'grammar studies were traditionally linked to the description, codification and interpretation (for religious, ritual, literary, or cultural purposes) of a corpus of texts, and of a language variety, not easily accessible to part of the population'; b) 'familiarity with these texts, and with the grammar studies necessary to approach them, was a condition for membership in the dominant group'; and c) 'modern scientific grammar (as developed by both historical linguistics and contemporary theoretical linguistics) has escaped these preconceptions, but it has failed to remove all the effects of these preconceptions'.[28] Therefore, Gramsci's writings remain relevant to the present scholarly context, and can inspire new research on the role that language, language education, and also linguistic research play in social life and political conflicts.

On this point, I shall conclude by quoting the words of a scholar of political science, Ronald Schmidt, who has discussed the links between language policy and political theory. He has found that the latter disciplinary field contains 'a treasure-trove of materials that can be usefully "mined"' by language scholars, especially those 'interested in language policy'.[29] Gramsci's political life and thought are, indeed, part of this treasure-trove, even though a fully-fledged or systematic theory of language cannot be found in his writings.

---

24. Gramsci 1975, Q29, §5, p. 2347 (English translation in Gramsci 1985, pp. 184–5).
25. Gramsci 1975, Q29, §3, p. 2346.
26. Burke 2008, p. 133.
27. See Cohn 1996, especially Chapter Two, and obviously Said 2003.
28. Lepschy and Lepschy 1999, pp. 40–3.
29. Schmidt Sr. 2006, p. 97.

... and linguistics in Gramsci

In the previous section, I drew some conclusions regarding the place that should be assigned to Gramsci in the history of language studies, especially in those fields which are known today as the sociology of language and the study of language planning and language policy (including educational language policies). Let me now draw some conclusions on the role to be given to linguistic themes in a reconstruction of Gramsci's intellectual and political biography, and in explaining Gramsci's current worldwide influence.

The path that I followed in Chapters One, Two and Three began with Gramsci's life, and then led me to discuss the origins of Gramsci's ideas on language and language-related subjects. Finally, it brought me to an examination of the effects that the development of these ideas had on the general development of Gramsci's political theory and practice. I shall now follow the same path in drawing my further conclusions. At the same time, I shall also outline the ultimate Gramscian connections between language and politics, by bringing to the fore Gramsci's implicit awareness and understanding of these fundamental connections – that is, by making explicit something that is not immediately discernible in his writings, but would seem to lie at the heart of his reasoning.

From the point of view of linguistics, Tullio De Mauro has established a parallel between Gramsci and such theorists as Wittgenstein and Vygotsky, drawing attention to the significance of contextual, practical experiences for the development of their ideas on language.[30] In Gramsci's case, his Sardinian-Italian bilingualism operated in the complex socio-cultural and sociolinguistic context of early-twentieth-century Italy. Other significant experiences were Gramsci's university studies in linguistics, and his appreciation of the nineteenth-century Italian debates between Ascoli and the followers of Manzoni. Later, Gramsci's interest in language was rekindled by his encounter with Soviet applied linguistics and language policies.

We have also seen that, from the point of view of political philosophy, Norberto Bobbio identified a high degree of specificity in Gramsci's Marxism. Far from constituting a limitation, Gramsci's specificity (his irreducibility to 'easy schematisations', in Bobbio's words) is the source of the fecundity, and enduring relevance, of his work.[31] Although sometimes met with suspicion or open criticism, this idea of Gramsci as a Marxist of a 'different' kind, as an open Marxist, has been put forward by diverse authors in various historical periods – for instance, by Stuart Hall.[32] To be sure, few other Marxists have retained their

---

30. See De Mauro 1979b. Cf. Introduction.
31. See Chapter Three, section 3.4.2.
32. See 3.3.4. With regard to Gramsci, Hall has spoken of 'a genuinely "open" Marxism' (Hall 1986, p. 6), and Hobsbawm of 'a rather surprising Marxist' (Hobsbawm 2011, p. 316). See also Appendix, section 4.3.

worldwide influence – let alone increased it, as Gramsci has – following the economic, political and intellectual transformations of the 1980s and 1990s. A question thus arises: while the specificity of Gramsci's Marxism may account for his current worldwide influence among political and social theorists and analysts, what accounts for this specificity?

I shall answer this question by expanding on what I said in Chapter Three.[33] As further confirmation of the deep-level cross-fertilisation between politics and language that took place in Gramsci's thought during his prison years, it is important to note that the expression 'adequate and necessary conditions', used by Gramsci in his comments on the limits of linguistic universalism,[34] closely resembles the expression he used in the same period (October to November 1930) to define one of the two premises on which historical materialism rests – that 'no society sets itself tasks for the accomplishment of which the *necessary and sufficient conditions* do not already exist', and that 'no society perishes until it has first developed all the forms of life implicit in its internal relations'.[35]

On the one hand, Gramsci explicitly derives these two premises from Marx,[36] and reiterates them in other prison notes.[37] On the other hand, in the *Notebooks* Gramsci also mentions Michel Bréal's *Essai de sémantique*. In the fifth chapter of this book, Bréal explains that the difference of vowel between 'man' and 'men' is by no means primitive, in that the 'softening' of *a* into *e* is due to the influence of a final syllable (*flectional apparatus*) originally present but later eroded 'by the wear and tear of ages'.[38] He thus concludes:

> Though not significative in its origin, this change of vowel has ended by becoming significative. Perhaps there may even be a more intimate connection between this advent of meaning and the downfall of the flectional apparatus, for it may be suspected that the people [*le peuple*] does not abandon what is useful to it, until it feels that it already possesses a substitute.[39]

These lines are strikingly consistent with the premises of Gramsci's Marxism, and show, once more, how his readings in linguistics could activate a positive relationship between Marxism and language studies, rather than the conflictual

---

33. See especially sections 3.3 and 3.4.
34. '[I]nsofar as the so-called universal conventional languages are not the historical expression of adequate and necessary conditions, they become an element of social stratification and of the fossilization of certain strata' (Gramsci 1975, Q5, §23, p. 557. English translation in Gramsci 1996b).
35. Gramsci 1975, Q4, §38, p. 455. My emphasis.
36. See Marx 1987, p. 263.
37. See Gramsci 1975, Q7, §20, p. 869; Q10II, §6, p. 1244; Q11, §22, p. 1422; Q13, §17, pp. 1579–83; Q15, §17, p. 1774.
38. Bréal 1900, p. 58.
39. Bréal 1900, p. 59.

relationship that takes centre stage in Lo Piparo's interpretation, as well as in other, similar interpretations.

Another fundamental premise of Gramsci's political thought is that every individual is a philosopher.[40] Ultimately, this is one of the main reasons why Marxism should not be, according to Gramsci, an external body consisting of scientific knowledge that experts impose from above or, to use Hall's terms, 'parachute' into the lives of subaltern groups, into the complexity of really existing political struggles. Interestingly, in the 1930s the Romanian Romance philologist and left-wing politician Iorgu Iordan, together with John Orr (professor of French at the University of Edinburgh), used the difference between *feeling* and *knowing* in a manner not too far from Gramsci's own use of these two terms. They did so in order to explain Saussure's distinction between *subjective analysis*, as 'applied by men when they speak', and the *objective analysis* of the linguist. The latter is

> based on special historical knowledge, not on a feeling for the language like the former. In a word like *amabas* [Latin for 'you used to love', 'you were loving'], he [Saussure] says, a Roman would see three elements (*ama-ba-s*), or possibly only two (*ama-bas*), whereas a linguist picks out four (*am-a-ba-s*). Similarly, a Parisian feels the word *enfant* [child] as a single unit, while the linguist breaks it down into two constituents, *en-* and *-fant*, Latin *in-fans, in-fantem*, 'not talking'. In the life of language it is of course only the subjective analysis that matters, because it alone is productive of new, analogical, formations. But objective analysis is not to be disdained, because, for one reason, it springs from the same source as its counterpart.[41]

This distinction between subjective and objective analysis, as two different levels on which the same underlying faculty manifests itself, is similar to Gramsci's views on the quantitative – but not qualitative – difference between popular philosophies and the philosophies of professional intellectuals. According to Gramsci, the 'popular element "feels" but does not understand or know'; while the 'intellectual element "knows" but does not understand and, above all, does not feel. The two extremes, therefore, are pedantry and philistinism on the one hand and blind passion and sectarianism on the other'.[42]

Evidently, though Gramsci was neither a professional linguist nor a philosopher of language, theoretical reflections and practical experiences involving languages did play a considerable role in creating the specific features of his politics. But in order to back up this claim, a crucial question needs to be asked: going beyond factual information and methodological examples, is there one deep-level message that those concerned with politics could learn from the work of

---

40. Cf. Chapter One, section 1.7.1.
41. Iordan and Orr 1937, p. 288.
42. Gramsci 1975, Q4, §33, pp. 451–2.

language scholars? In other words, what is the most politically relevant lesson that modern (nineteenth- and twentieth-century) linguistics could teach?

At least in Gramsci's case, I believe that there is such a lesson, and that it has to do with the relationship between historically changing collective practices and theory-based prescriptive abstractions. In recent years, various aspects of this relationship have been explored through the study of what is often referred to as *authority* (sometimes also *ownership*) *in language*, especially the question of who has authority over one language and can therefore decide how this language should be used, what is correct and what is not.[43] In his book *Language and Politics*, the sociolinguist and historian of linguistics John Joseph states that this question 'is an eternal one' and is largely 'unanswerable':

> a language is not a thing, but a practice always characterised by diversity, into which attempts at imposing unity are introduced. These attempts are what we normally mean by linguistic authority, but they inevitably bump up against the sort of authority represented by *usage*, the earlier practice, which has behind it the force of custom and a certain social authenticity.... Ever since being institutionalised as the 'scientific' study of language in the nineteenth century, linguistics has taken the position that any imposed authority in language is ultimately impotent in the face of the one authority that matters, namely, usage – what the people as a whole implicitly decides will be the course of their language.[44]

This point is already quite relevant to my discussion of Gramsci, and it becomes even more significant if another question is asked: how do people *as a whole* make decisions about the course of their language? This question refers not so much to the ultimate causes of linguistic change, as to the way in which language works and the particular direction linguistic changes take – that is, to the reasons why certain linguistic forms are dominant (for example, 'you aren't' or 'you are not', in English), while other forms are perceived as less correct (in

---

43. Books were published with such titles as *I padroni della lingua* ['The Owners of Language'] (Sobrero 1978), *Authority in Language* (Milroy and Milroy 1985), and *Who Owns English?* (Hayhoe and Parker 1994) – the latter including a chapter by David Crystal, the leading expert on the worldwide spread of the English language, entitled 'Which English or English Which?'. With striking sociolinguistic sensitivity, which foreshadows the debates of these past three decades, and an underlying awareness of the political implications of sociolinguistic matters, Gramsci notes in his copy of Panzini's Italian grammar: '*Who is it who writes* grammar? In other words, does the writer express a real historical movement or an "arbitrary individuality"? Who gives him "authority"? Does it come from an educated stratum of the population which has already been formed, unified and which really does speak and write according to that grammar, or does it come solely from an arbitrary claim to represent an abstract model deduced from writers and their usage? But then one must ask: which writers and what usage and by whom?' (In Martinelli 1989b, p. 686. Gramsci's emphasis).

44. Joseph 2006, p. 9.

this example, 'you ain't') or antiquated ('thou art not'). Those speakers who happen to be professional or amateur linguists certainly know and can relate those reasons, and may perhaps even call upon rationality, precision, or logic, to explain the dominance of 'you are not' over 'you ain't' (less so to explain the falling out of use of 'thou art not'). But what about all the other speakers? In Chapter Two, I showed that Gramsci's view of language takes two important factors into account – chronological development, and collective use by a socially-located community of speakers – which, according to Saussure, too, distinguish verbal language from conventional systems operating on purely logical bases. Now, it is worth stressing that Gramsci does not discuss the role of logical and competent reasoning with reference to language only. In Notebook 11, he focuses on the process of diffusion of a new conception of the world, and of new collective practices. His conclusion is that within the population at large this process does not have a 'rational and logically coherent form':

> the exhaustive reasoning which neglects no argument, positive or negative, of any significance, has a certain importance, but is far from being decisive. It can be decisive, but in a secondary way, when the person in question is already in a state of intellectual crisis, wavering between the old and the new, when he has lost his faith in the old and has not yet come down in favour of the new.[45]

Still in the same note, a few lines ahead of this passage, another argument further substantiates Gramsci's rejection of explanations based on purely rational choices, which he sees as dominant only among professional philosophers – not among ordinary people. In the existing society, professional intellectuals – though often lacking an intimate adherence to concrete reality (they 'know', but fail to 'feel') – are the only ones to have enough time as well as adequate material and intellectual resources for making entirely rational, 'scientific' choices:

> Imagine the intellectual position of the man of the people: he has formed his own opinions, convictions, criteria of discrimination, standards of conduct. Anyone with a superior intellectual formation, with a point of view opposed to his, can put forward arguments better than he and really tear him to pieces logically and so on. But should the man of the people change his opinions just because of this? Just because he cannot impose himself in a bout of argument? In that case he might find himself having to change every day, or every time he meets an ideological adversary who is intellectually superior. On what elements, therefore, can his philosophy be founded? and in particular his philosophy in the form which has the greatest importance for his standards of conduct? The most important element is undoubtedly one whose character

---

45. Gramsci 1975, Q11, §12, p. 1390.

is determined not by reason but by faith. But faith in whom, or in what? In particular in the social group to which he belongs, in so far as in a diffuse way it thinks as he does. The man of the people thinks that so many like-thinking people can't be wrong, not so radically, as the man he is arguing against would like him to believe...[46]

Something similar happens with language as a collective activity. Take, for example, *il pane* [bread] (from Latin *illum panem*, literally 'that bread'), which has become the standard form in Italian, driving out other forms (such as *lo pane, el pan, 'l pan, i'(p)pane, 'o ppanə*) that are still used today in some parts of the peninsula, and in some contexts or types of text. The fact that speakers in a certain social group, within a certain geographical area and at a given moment in time, perceive *il pane* as 'proper' Italian, as more correct than forms from other language varieties or earlier periods, has little to do with accurate etymological considerations or the pronouncements of grammarians.[47] As in the case of the 'man of the people' in the above-quoted passage, who 'has no concrete memory' of the reasons behind his 'standards of conduct', and 'could not repeat' those reasons persuasively,[48] most people ignore the historical origins of a given form, or experts' arguments in favour of its adoption (in those cases where such arguments were explicitly formulated). Indeed, in his (or her) everyday use of language, the layperson pays little attention to these origins and arguments.

This kind of collective behaviour, based mainly on 'faith' (or 'custom', as Joseph calls it), can be seen at work also in diachrony, and applies not only to conservation, but to innovation, too. Even in the case of peasants moving to the city, who end up 'conforming to urban speech', or, to use another Gramscian example, in the case of 'subaltern classes' who 'try to speak like the dominant classes',[49] linguistic changes are very rarely the result of rationally motivated innovations, knowingly adopted by single individuals – at any rate, the changes that become widely accepted and established are 'the innovations of an entire social community that has renewed its culture and "progressed" historically'.[50]

---

46. Gramsci 1975, Q11, §12, p. 1391.
47. The same could be said of the predominance of the *passato prossimo* [perfect] tense in present-day Italian, with the *passato remoto* [past historic] tense used only in formal registers and to refer to actions that took place long ago (cf. French *je suis allé* vs. *j'allai*). This use differs not just from the use of *passato remoto* only, or *passato prossimo* only, in southern (especially Sicilian) and northern varieties respectively; it also differs from the way in which the two tenses were used in Tuscany, at least until a few decades ago, and, therefore, from the specific conceptualisation of time formerly operating in Tuscan (from which, broadly speaking, modern Italian derives). One hardly need add that none of these ways of expressing time is more logical than the others.
48. Gramsci 1975, p. 1391.
49. Gramsci 1975, Q29, §2, pp. 2342–3.
50. Gramsci 1975, Q6, §71, p. 738. Cf. Bloomfield 1976, p. 157: a 'speaker is free to invent' new linguistic forms, but 'any form he invents is a nonsense-form', unless he succeeds in 'getting fellow-speakers to accept it as a signal for some meaning'.

Languages may change in a certain direction because of various internal and external factors – including reduced articulatory effort, analogy, avoidance of homophones, increased structural symmetry (as when a language comes to have, say, the same number of front and back vowels), 'imperfect' first-language acquisition, language contact, imitation of varieties used by particularly prestigious groups, identity and group formation (that is, people's desire to mark sameness and otherness through language). All these factors can contribute to the failure or (usually partial) success of a certain language policy. But despite the fact that different strands of modern linguistics have presented these (and other) factors as relatively more or less important, it is generally agreed that logical coherence, exhaustive reasoning and metalinguistic awareness are not decisive factors – until now, they have been far from decisive in determining the course of linguistic change.

It thus becomes clear why the influence of language studies on Gramsci's political views was not the result of some occasional, superficial parallelism between political and linguistic habits. This influence was based on the fact that the Gramsci of the *Prison Notebooks* was able to sense the deep analogies between languages and political ideologies, with regard to the processes of consensus formation and collective action.

Obviously, Gramsci did not go as far as Saussure did in drawing, from these analogies, conclusions about the 'impossibility of revolution';[51] nor did he underestimate the potential efficacy of political mobilisation and organisation. These two points would seem to pose major limitations to the influence of language studies on Gramsci's political views. But this is the case only if we understand this influence as a source for a rather naïve emphasis on the 'spontaneity' of historical processes: either in the form of binding continuity and limited freedom (first point); or in the form of absolute freedom and unlimited individual creativity (second point). In fact, Gramsci's understanding of freedom as necessarily linked to organisation and discipline – not as pure, unrestrained spontaneity – can itself be seen as having been influenced by the implicit political implications of modern language studies. He repeatedly stressed, in his writings, that the more a group, or an individual person, becomes aware of the origins of their models of conduct – and, therefore, able to choose to which models they really wish to conform – the freer they become. So freedom exists as a relative property and, from this Gramscian point of view, it consists in the ability 'to work out consciously and critically one's own conception of the world'.[52] Again,

---

51. Saussure 1959, p. 74. Cf. Chapter Two, section 2.2.3. Although Gramsci tends to exclude a sudden rationalisation of social life and a radical demolition of past culture, his revolutionary politics (including, especially in Notebook 29, his politics of language and culture) does not diminish the potential impact of disciplined and centrally co-ordinated state agencies, political parties, academic and educational institutions, and so on.

52. Gramsci 1975, Q11, §12, p. 1376.

this is consistent with what happens in language, where freedom, *also at the individual level*, can consist of a highly personal selection, or consciously innovative actualisations, of pre-existing models, but almost never of absolutely spontaneous creativity: if a speaker (or a writer) 'started using a personally arbitrary language (if he became a "neologist" in the pathological sense of the word) and if others were to imitate him (each with an arbitrary language), the situation would be described as Babel'.[53]

After decades in which language-sensitive research, and linguistically informed theories, have flourished in many different disciplinary fields, these points about language may sound relatively obvious to many of today's readers. Their implications for political philosophy were, however, of great import to an early-twentieth-century Marxist. As a result of the influence of language studies, Gramsci's thought acquired, firstly, a multifaceted complexity, largely unaffected by simplistic versions of either liberal-leaning rationalism or economic determinism. Unsurprisingly, his philosophy of praxis remained relevant throughout the second half of the century, when the epistemological foundations of various disciplines, including political theory, were greatly influenced by linguistic theory and language philosophy, in what has come to be known as the 'linguistic turn';[54] and when, moreover, essentialist (or reductionist) versions of Marxism, which presented the hard facts of economic production as the determinant factors in shaping conflicting worldviews and in activating historical processes, appeared to lose much of their philosophical and political value.[55]

Secondly, and more specifically, Gramsci's experiences and reflections concerning linguistic diversity helped to make him aware of the importance of working towards unification through a careful consideration of diversity – not through its denigration or coercive elimination. In the course of his life, this constant attention to cultural and linguistic themes contributed to shaping his political thought and actions, and would seem to have functioned as some sort of antidote, as it were, to extreme, abstract expectations of social and cultural palingenesis, and to theoretical simplifications and dogmatism.

---

53. Gramsci 1975, Q23, §7, p. 2193. Even particularly creative ways of using a language, including the use of new linguistic forms (neologisms), need to follow, to a lesser or greater degree, an analogical pattern that links them up to existing grammar and lexical bases (within the same language, or from other languages), and need to conform – again, to some degree – to formal properties such as stress, pitch, phonological and syllabic structure, or morpho-syntactic order: consider, for instance, 'quixotic', 'the use of *radars* and satellites', '*glocal* economy', 'I went online and *googled* his name', or the famous 'Fut! I should have been that I am, had the maidenliest star in the firmament twinkled on my bastardising' (*King Lear*, I, ii, 138–40).

54. Rorty 1967. Cf. Ives 2004a, Chapter One.

55. See Callinicos 1982, and Laclau and Mouffe 1985.

Appendix
Gramsci's Legacy, 1937–2007

In the sections below, I shall discuss Gramsci's influence in Italy and in the English-speaking world, emphasising aspects that are especially relevant to scholars in linguistic disciplines. While reviewing some of the most significant secondary literature, I will discuss the shift that has occurred, from an early period with only a very small number of works by Italian linguists, to the recent flourishing of publications by cultural and social theorists, philosophers of language, and linguists of various persuasions.

This Appendix deals mainly with material published in Italian and English before 2007 – the year that marked the seventieth anniversary of Gramsci's death, and which saw the emergence of significantly new developments in Gramscian studies, especially in Italy.[1] Eventually, this year may prove to have a periodicising value, the post-2007 period witnessing the consolidation of a new and different phase in Gramscian studies, though it is perhaps too early to express conclusive views on this point.

---

1. The major innovations were the publication of a digital version of the *Quaderni del carcere* edited by D. Ragazzini (published as a supplement to *L'Unità* on 27 April 2007), and of the first volume of the *Edizione nazionale degli scritti di Antonio Gramsci: Quaderni di traduzioni* (Gramsci 2007a), edited by G. Cospito and G. Francioni.

4.1. The reception of Gramsci's writings: the letters

Gramsci's correspondence is normally divided into two parts. One includes the letters that he wrote before being arrested and jailed, namely from the time he was a student in Cagliari, in his native Sardinia, up to 1926. The other consists of the letters that he wrote from prison. The first group of letters is far more heterogeneous in terms of contents and addressees. It has taken decades to find these letters, which are preserved in institutional and personal archives. A substantial collection of letters written between 1908 and 1926 (edited by A.A. Santucci) appeared in 1992, as part of the critical edition of Gramsci's works by the Italian publishing house Einaudi.[2] While an improved edition (providing a larger collection of letters) has recently appeared in Italian,[3] an equivalent collection in English has not been published as yet.[4]

Gramsci's letters from prison are different in character. The process by which they came to be published, and widely appreciated, was also different. They were written by Gramsci to a small number of people within his family, as prescribed by the rules to which his prison life was subject. The number of topics Gramsci felt comfortable writing about was also quite limited, as a result of the constant censorship that his jailers operated. These letters were published for the first time as early as 1947. When this first edition appeared, Gramsci's noble resistance to the hardship of his political imprisonment made a very favourable impression on the Italian public, especially on intellectuals and political activists. The country had just come out of a Fascist dictatorship and had not yet been plunged into the fierce anti-communism of the Cold War. The 1947 edition, however, was far from complete. The editorial note at the beginning of the book reads:

> The volume we are presenting to the public does not include all the letters written by Gramsci during his ten years of imprisonment. Some disappeared during Fascism and the War, and it has not yet been possible to recover them; others concern family matters, and it seemed inappropriate to publish them here. For the same reason, some passages have been removed from the letters published in this edition. This is, therefore, a selection – though a large one, sufficient to give a full picture of the hardship experienced by the author, of

---

2. Gramsci 1992a. Here, I use the phrase 'critical edition' in a broad sense to refer to the series of volumes published by Einaudi between 1965 and 1992 (Gramsci 1965, 1975, 1980, 1982, 1984, 1987, 1992a). In a more specific sense, the definition 'critical edition' should probably be used to refer only to Valentino Gerratana's edition of the *Quaderni del carcere* (Gramsci 1975), to the American edition of the *Prison Notebooks*, currently in course of publication (Gramsci 1992b, 1996b, 2007b), and now especially to the *Edizione nazionale degli scritti di Antonio Gramsci* (see previous note).

3. Gramsci 2010.

4. Boothman 2008b, p. 48, explains that this English-language edition is 'now nearing conclusion'.

his strength as a man and revolutionary militant, of his individual and spiritual interests, and of his vast and deep humanity.[5]

This was the first instance of what would become a long tradition of selecting Gramsci's writings. This selective approach had significant consequences on the way in which Gramsci's thought has been transmitted and assessed. Both in Italy and in the English-speaking world, these consequences still affect the knowledge that many scholars have of Gramsci's ideas – especially those scholars, including most practitioners in linguistic disciplines, who are not directly involved in Gramscian studies. As a result of this and other factors, not all of what Gramsci wrote has been read, studied, or written about to the same degree.

Selections of Gramsci's prison letters were published in English starting from the late 1950s.[6] A translation of the 1947 Italian edition, carried out by the Scottish poet Hamish Henderson in the years 1948–59, was published in 1974, while a selection of only 94 letters, translated and edited by Lynne Lawner, was published in 1973.[7]

The first critical edition of the *Lettere dal carcere* ['Letters from Prison'] was published in 1965, edited by the Gramscian scholars Elsa Fubini and Sergio Caprioglio.[8] As time went by, this edition, which included 428 texts, became outdated, since, during the following decades, more letters were found and published, making a new edition necessary. A collection of all the letters available at the time was eventually published (in English) by the Columbia University Press in 1994, edited by Frank Rosengarten and translated by Raymond Rosenthal. This led to a slightly paradoxical situation, albeit one which reveals how much interest Gramsci's legacy had come to attract, in the USA, by the mid-1990s. Italian readers would need to turn to an English translation of Gramsci's letters, if they wished to read the most comprehensive collection.

This paradoxical situation was only partially overcome in 1996, with the publication of a new Italian edition of the prison letters,[9] consisting of 506 texts (494 by Gramsci, and 12 by his correspondents). However, the legal actions over questions of copyright that followed its publication compromised the circulation of the new edition, and this two-volume edition was ultimately withdrawn from Italian bookshops. Hence the only edition still in print, and widely circulating, remained Paolo Spriano's *Lettere dal carcere*,[10] which contained only

---

5. Gramsci 1947, p. 5.
6. Cf. issues 9 and 10 of the journal *New Reasoner* (summer and autumn 1959).
7. For the history of the publication and circulation of Gramsci's letters in the Anglophone world, we can now refer to the critical outlines provided by Eley 1984, Forgacs 1989 and 1995a, Buttigieg 1995a, Lussana 2000, pp. 97–8, and Boothman 2005.
8. Gramsci 1965.
9. Gramsci 1996a.
10. Gramsci 1971b.

156 letters. The tendency to select Gramsci's writings on the basis of different criteria depending on the circumstances, from political convenience to the search for better readability through thematic partitions or anthologies, from technical considerations by editors and publishers to copyright matters, has not ended yet. Different degrees of availability continue to characterise the letters and – to a much greater extent, as I shall point out – Gramsci's other writings.

4.2. Lost, unpublished and recently published material

4.2.1. *Matteo Bartoli's glottology course of 1912–13*

Gramsci had his first contacts with intellectuals who were interested in linguistics, and in the study of dialects and folklore, when still living in Sardinia. However, the main influence on the young Gramsci in the fields of dialectology and historical linguistics came from Matteo Bartoli. With Bartoli, at Turin University, Gramsci studied *glottologia* [glottology] – a discipline better known in the English-speaking world as comparative philology. Bartoli soon became aware of the outstanding qualities of his Sardinian student and, in the academic year 1912–13, asked Gramsci to transcribe and edit the lecture notes of his course.

In the history of linguistics in Italy, Bartoli is amongst the most prominent figures of the first half of the twentieth century. He became professor at Turin University after studying and conducting research at various different Italian and European universities, including Vienna, Florence, Strasbourg, and Paris.[11] The main lines of Bartoli's contribution to linguistics can be sketched out as follows: he took part in the reaction against positivist historical linguistics, especially the Neogrammarians, and stressed the importance of studying linguistic phenomena against the background of specific geographical and cultural environments. In this attempt to provide an alternative to the Neogrammarians' modes of inquiry, his work – under the changing denomination of *neolinguistica* [Neolinguistics], *linguistica areale* [Areal Linguistics] and, finally, *linguistica spaziale* [Space Linguistics] – led to two major achievements: 'the definition of "areal norms"'[12] for historical-linguistic investigation, whereby changes in language could be dated based on their geographical disposition; and the project of an Italian linguistic atlas, the *Atlante Linguistico Italiano*. Research into the history of linguistics has shown, however, that Bartoli's Neolinguistics was ultimately meant to complete and perfect diachronic reconstruction, without 'destroying the

---

11. On Bartoli, see De Mauro 1964 and 1996a, Devoto 1947 and 1973, Terracini 1948, and Vidossi 1948.
12. De Mauro 1996a, p. 69. Cf. Bartoli 1925 and 1945.

conclusions reached by the Neogrammarians, which were in fact taken as a starting point'.[13]

On a more general theoretical level, Bartoli's geographically oriented version of linguistic research acquainted Gramsci with crucial questions concerning diversity, as they had been addressed by scholars of historical linguistics, especially since the 1870s. Historical linguistics built its reputation on the success of the comparative method. This method emerged at the beginning of the nineteenth century, and reached scientific prominence thanks to its ability to reconstruct the history of the Indo-European linguistic family on the basis of systematic, formal correspondences between member languages; yet this method increasingly faced problems and objections, which eventually came to challenge the family-tree theory of linguistic relationship. This theoretical model rested on the assumption that languages split in a clear-cut way and then change independently; that is, that the branches of a linguistic family arose by the sudden breaking up of a parent language which contained no internal varieties. 'This is the same thing as assuming, firstly, that the parent community was completely uniform as to language, and secondly, that this parent community split suddenly and sharply into two or more daughter communities, which lost all contact with each other'.[14] Innovative comparative philologists, and scholars who pioneered dialect geography (most notably Jules Gilliéron),[15] showed that linguistic change often took place in a much more complex way, and highlighted the presence of cleavages, as well as contacts and mutual influences, between and within linguistic communities. In the last analysis, Bartoli's geographical method was yet another attempt to assess these controversies and seek innovative solutions to them, while retaining an attitude to linguistic change, as the epistemological centre of gravity of language studies, typical of nineteenth-century linguists.

Bartoli's lecture notes, edited by Gramsci, have not yet been published.[16] Even though there is little reason to doubt that Gramsci had a merely practical role in the production of these notes, it seems advisable that Bartoli's lecture notes be made available in the form of a philologically accurate edition, with an introduction and a comment. The new *Edizione nazionale degli scritti di Antonio*

---

13. Benincà 1994, p. 601. On the fundamental similarities between Neolinguists and Neogrammarians, which can be identified behind disagreements on specific points, see also Iordan and Orr 1937, pp. 273–8.

14. Bloomfield 1976, p. 310.

15. In the notes that Gramsci transcribed for Bartoli's 1912–13 course, Gilliéron and Edmont's linguistic atlas of France is praised for the methodological innovations it had introduced (see Lo Piparo 1979, p. 101).

16. The notes (Bartoli 1912–13) were aimed at those attending Bartoli's glottology course. These notes were retrieved and succinctly described by Renzo De Felice (see De Felice 1964). A copy, lithographically printed (in Turin) and reproducing Gramsci's handwriting, is currently held in the archives of the Fondazione Istituto Gramsci in Rome.

Gramsci ['National Edition of Antonio Gramsci's Writings'] is expected to fulfil this task. Even though their author is Bartoli, and not Gramsci, these lecture notes are indeed useful as a document of the latter's familiarity with specific trends in linguistics at the time of his university studies.

4.2.2. *Gramsci's translation of Finck's work*

Trained as an Indo-Europeanist, Franz Nikolaus Finck was primarily concerned with general linguistics and language typology. He was among the few linguists of his time who pursued a systematic exploration of linguistic diversity across the whole of mankind, and did not limit their work to major Indo-European languages. Finck was influenced by a 'tradition that counted W. v[on] Humboldt among its pillars',[17] and that he himself continued. In 1909, he published a compendium of the 'linguistic universe as then known',[18] *Die Sprachstämme des Erdkreises*. In this book, he provided a description of the languages of the world according to linguistic characteristics, as well as geographical, ethnic, and historical factors. In prison, Gramsci had a copy of both this book and another one by Finck, *Die Haupttypen des Sprachbaus* ['The Main Types of Language Structure'].[19] In 1929 Gramsci translated *Die Sprachstämme des Erdkreises* in its entirety, rendering its title in Italian as *Le famiglie linguistiche del mondo* ['The Linguistic Families of the World']. Unfortunately, this work did not escape the fate of most of the other translations that Gramsci carried out in prison, being excluded from both the thematic edition and the critical chronological edition of Gramsci's prison notebooks (see below). Researchers who had access to Gramsci's manuscripts had the opportunity to analyse his translations. But only the publication of the *Quaderni di traduzioni* ['Translation Notebooks'], part of the new *Edizione nazionale* of Gramsci's writings, has made his translation of Finck's book available to the general public.

4.2.3. *Gramsci's comments on Panzini's Italian grammar*

Alfredo Panzini (1863–1939) was an Italian novelist and essayist, and was also interested in lexicography. In his early writings, Gramsci mentioned Panzini's *Dizionario moderno. Supplemento ai dizionari italiani* ['Modern Dictionary: Supplement to Italian Dictionaries'],[20] seemingly regarding this dictionary as a

---

17. Plank 1996, p. 296.
18. Ibid.
19. See Gramsci 1996a, pp. 124–5, 132, 296–7.
20. Today, Panzini's work as a lexicographer is received with great interest and generally positive appreciation (see Mengaldo 1994, p. 29; Serianni 2006; Tosi 2007).

useful work of reference.[21] Whilst in prison, however, he expressed vehement criticisms of Panzini's intellectual profile. One of these later criticisms was directed at Panzini's *Guida alla grammatica italiana* ['Guide to Italian Grammar'], a brief, popularising grammar book, first published in 1932. Gramsci read the enlarged 1933 edition[22] and jotted down extensive comments on his copy. The most substantial of these annotations seem to have subsequently been incorporated into the observations included in Notebook 29.[23] Due to a series of rather bizarre circumstances, Gramsci's copy of Panzini's grammar disappeared for a long time and was almost forgotten, despite the existence of Gramsci's annotations being mentioned in two newspaper articles dating from 1950 and 1977.[24] On the whole, it could probably be argued that most of these annotations do not have much to add to the reflections on grammar that Gramsci expressed in Notebook 29; however, certain comments that he wrote directly on his copy of Panzini's book deserve careful consideration. The most extensive and significant ones can be read in articles by the historian Renzo Martinelli,[25] and it is now hoped that all of Gramsci's comments will be included in the new national edition of his writings.

4.2.4. *Early work on Manzoni*

In order to complete this survey of Gramsci's unpublished materials, I shall now introduce a piece of writing, perhaps a group of writings, whose fate remains, to date, shrouded in mystery. We know that Gramsci continued to work on linguistic subjects after he stopped attending university. Although he never graduated, early in 1918 he was still working on what should have been his thesis.[26] As part of this work, Gramsci probably set out to write a contribution on the Italian novelist Alessandro Manzoni.

For much of his life, Manzoni had been concerned with the 'lack of a "standard" language' in unified Italy, especially 'in comparison to the powerful nation-states of France and England, if not Germany'.[27] In 1868, he was appointed to head a government commission on linguistic unification. 'Having rewritten his classic novel, *I Promessi Sposi* [The Betrothed], in an Italian closely modelled on spoken, bourgeois Florentine "Italian", Manzoni's solution was to take Florentine

---

21. Gramsci 1982, p. 670.
22. For a recent reprint, see Panzini 1999.
23. See Martinelli 1989b.
24. Chiaretti 1950 and 1977.
25. Martinelli 1989a and 1989b.
26. See Gramsci 1982, p. 612.
27. Green and Ives 2010, p. 295.

as the "standard" Italian'.[28] On the whole, Manzoni's views on language were relatively more complex,[29] but especially on this occasion his proposals reflected his preference for pragmatic solutions: arguing that all the regions of Italy should adopt contemporary Tuscan – or, more precisely, the 'living' language of educated Florentines – as a national language, he suggested that dictionaries and grammar books based on Florentine should be subsidised; that school teachers for all of Italy should be recruited amongst candidates who either came from, or had been educated in, Tuscany (the region around Florence); and that scholarships should be made available to students and teachers wishing to spend a period of residence in Florence.

Gramsci refers to his own work on Manzoni in a letter of 17 November 1930: 'ten years ago I wrote an essay on the language question according to Manzoni'.[30] This essay should date from approximately 1918–19, but at present all traces of it seem to have been lost, and it remains doubtful whether this essay ever came into existence at all. Interestingly, promotional material by the Turin-based publishing house Utet from the years 1918–20 mentions a collection of Manzoni's writings on language, edited by Antonio Gramsci, as due to be published shortly.[31] It is difficult to tell whether the essay recalled in the letter of November 1930, the work for Gramsci's thesis, and work on an edition of Manzoni's writings, were one and the same, or three separate pieces of work. At any rate, only further archival research could tell us if any of these materials, whose potential relevance to a language-oriented understanding of Gramsci would probably be considerable, still exist and need to be added to the list of currently unpublished works. To date, however, there is no new evidence indicating that such a discovery might soon occur. Therefore, there is no substantial reason to reject the opinions of those scholars who believe that some of these early writings have been lost,[32] and that others simply remained projects.[33]

4.3. Pre-prison writings and prison notes

In a book that was published only a few years ago, the Italian linguist Tullio De Mauro (whose central role in interpreting and popularising Gramsci's ideas on language I have already mentioned in previous chapters) criticises Giuseppe

---

28. Ibid. See also Serianni 1990, Marazzini 1999, Chapter Nineteen.
29. Cf. Manzoni 2000a, 2000b, 2000c, 2005.
30. Gramsci 1994a, I, p. 360.
31. See, for example, the list of recent and forthcoming publications by Utet that was printed in the periodical *Conferenze e prolusioni* on 16 April (p. 161), 1 August (back cover), and 16 August 1920 (p. 301). See also Bergami 1975, p. 557.
32. See Rosiello 1976, p. 21.
33. See Bergami 1977, p. 70.

Vacca, the president of the Fondazione Istituto Gramsci, for focusing too narrowly on Gramsci as 'the leader of the Communist Party, the founder of the Communist Party',[34] whose interests lay solely in the fields of 'politics and political history'.[35] According to De Mauro, this image of Gramsci, which originated in the editions of Gramsci's writings 'that Palmiro Togliatti cut out during the postwar period',[36] plays down Gramsci's interest in language and amounts to a fragment – incomprehensible in itself – of what would later emerge from the new 'edition of the *Notebooks* edited by Valentino Gerratana'.[37]

Which are the editions that De Mauro speaks of as having been 'cut out' (*ritagliate*, in the original) by Togliatti? They are the six volumes of the thematically organised edition of Gramsci's *Prison Notebooks*, devised and edited by Togliatti together with Felice Platone, and published by Einaudi between 1948 and 1951; and, presumably, also the five volumes of the first edition of Gramsci's pre-prison writings,[38] published between 1954 and 1971. Togliatti, who was then the secretary of the Italian Communist Party, has ever since been held responsible for the choice of collecting Gramsci's prison notes into thematically homogeneous volumes.[39] Although De Mauro's critical judgment is perhaps excessive, it is true that the complex and, broadly speaking, unfinished state of Gramsci's prison work, not to mention its diachronic development, did not fully emerge from these volumes. Furthermore, as well as the flaws of the first edition of Gramsci's prison notes, we must add the suppression of some politically unwelcome passages – a quantitatively marginal, but nonetheless disruptive censorship which had also been operated on the first edition of Gramsci's *Letters from Prison* mentioned above.[40] On the other hand, the readability of these six volumes, and the solid intellectual image of Gramsci that their thematic organisation conveyed, allowed the *Prison Notebooks* to exert an enormous influence on Italian culture in the second half of the twentieth century. This influence reached well beyond the borders of Communist Party membership, and had a great impact on various

---

34. De Mauro 2004, p. 98.
35. Ibid.
36. De Mauro 2004, p. 99.
37. Ibid. The first edition of Gramsci's *Prison Notebooks* conditioned the fate that his notes on language were to have before the critical edition was published, as convincingly shown by Franceschini 1988, pp. 230–1.
38. The publication of a new edition of Gramsci's pre-prison writings began in 1980, but stopped after the forth volume (see Gramsci 1980, 1982, 1984 and 1987), leaving the period 1921–26 uncovered and, therefore, failing to replace the previous edition with regard to this period.
39. At a closer look, the choice of a thematic partition appears to have been the result of numerous, complex factors. Togliatti's role needs to be considered alongside that of others, above all that of the economist Piero Sraffa, who had been close to Gramsci before and during his imprisonment (see Gerratana 1995b, Vacca 2005, pp. 25–7).
40. See Liguori 1996, pp. 49 and 57, Fiori 1991, pp. 101–2, Gerratana 1987, pp. 152–4.

sectors and strands of Italian cultural life. A differently conceived edition may not have had the same impact.[41]

The later edition of Gramsci's notebooks – the one which, from De Mauro's point of view, finally remedied the defects of the first edition – is the 'critical edition of the Istituto Gramsci edited by Valentino Gerratana',[42] first published in 1975. The appearance of this edition marked a turning point in the history of Gramscian studies. Consisting of four volumes, it reproduced 29 notebooks, and left out only the notebooks that Gramsci had used for translations. It made possible a fuller understanding of Gramsci's work, in terms of both the content of the prison notes and the process through which they had been written. The complexity and openness of this process clearly appeared from the presence, in many cases, of two different versions of the same note – one that was written first, and one that Gramsci copied later, often with variations, into a different notebook. Many influential contributions to the literature on Gramsci, published after 1975, owe much to the excellent quality of this new edition, whose fourth and last volume entirely consists of philological and critical-historical aids, including a description of the manuscripts, indexes, explanatory notes, and a list of the books that Gramsci had in prison. Gerratana's edition led to new awareness as to the importance of studying the development of Gramsci's concepts and of the terminology used to express them. This awareness has greatly enhanced the interpretation of the *Quaderni*.[43] Attention has also been paid to philological questions that Gerratana left unresolved (for instance, by not including Gramsci's translation notebooks in his edition) or treated in a way that other scholars soon came to question.[44]

The publication of Gramsci's prison notes in English began with two small volumes in 1957. Both these books were the product of a communist background, their editors being members of the Communist Party of the USA and of the Communist Party of Great Britain respectively.[45] One of the two volumes is now hardly remembered: *The Open Marxism of Antonio Gramsci*, edited by Carl Marzani. However, in the light of what I said in Chapters Two and Three, it is worth noting that in the wake of 1956 (when idealised images of the Soviet-led realisation of socialism tragically collapsed) Marzani presented Gramsci as a different kind of Marxist, who had largely avoided the dogmatism of other Marxists.[46]

---

41. On Togliatti's editorial work, see also Daniele 2005.
42. Gramsci 1975.
43. See Frosini and Liguori 2004, Thomas 2009.
44. For instance, Francioni 1977 and 1984.
45. See Buttigieg 1995a, Forgacs 1995a, 1995b, and Boothman 2005 for discussion and historical contextualisation.
46. In my Introduction, as well as in the following chapters, I looked at various ways in which this picture of Gramsci has been understood in different periods and can be understood today, while also looking – of course – at the opposite position, which presents

The other collection published in 1957, *The Modern Prince and Other Writings*, edited and translated by Louis Marks, was made available to the Anglo-American readership by two Communist publishing houses, Lawrence and Wishart (in London) and International Publishers (in New York). *The Modern Prince* was to remain the main source of the spread of Gramsci's ideas in the Anglophone world throughout the 1960s, until new editions appeared in the early 1970s, boosting – as well as responding to – an increased attention to Gramsci in the English-speaking world. The greater interest in Gramsci, and the increase in the circulation of his prison writings, culminated in an ambitious project that the Columbia University Press undertook in 1992, with the publication of the first volume of a complete edition: Antonio Gramsci, *Prison Notebooks*, edited and translated by Joseph Buttigieg.

For the purposes of my discussion, it is sufficient to list the essential bibliographical details of each existing edition:

Selections from the Prison Notebooks (*SPN*), edited and translated by Quintin Hoare and Geoffrey Nowell-Smith, London, 1971;
Selections from Political Writings 1910–20 (*SPW*, I), edited by Quintin Hoare and translated by John Mathews, London, 1977;
Selections from Political Writings 1921–26 (*SPW*, II), edited and translated by Quintin Hoare, London, 1978;
Selections from Cultural Writings (*SCW*), edited by Geoffrey Nowell-Smith and David Forgacs, and translated by William Boelhower, London, 1985;
A Gramsci Reader (*GR*), edited by David Forgacs, London, 1988;[47]
Pre-Prison Writings (*PPW*), edited by Richard Bellamy and translated by Virginia Cox, Cambridge, 1994;
Further Selections from the Prison Notebooks (*FSPN*), edited and translated by Derek Boothman, London, 1995.

In most disciplines, certainly in linguistic disciplines, Hoare and Nowell-Smith's edition (*SPN*) has been the most referenced one to date, functioning as the canonical gateway to Gramsci's thought for those who did not use Italian editions. For researchers in linguistic subjects, a useful addition to *SPN* was provided by the publication of *SCW*. Here, however, I wish to outline the evident imbalance that characterises English-language editions, when compared to the Italian ones. The coverage of Gramsci's prison writings is almost as complete in English as it is in

---

Gramsci as an orthodox Communist, fundamentally aligned with Soviet policies and re-proposing the 'totalitarian' core of Lenin's programme.

47. Also published in the USA, with a slightly different title: *An Antonio Gramsci Reader*, New York, 1988.

Italian, whereas such equivalence does not exist for the pre-prison writings. This is true, in spite of the fact that some of the volumes listed above do include early writings (even though this may seem to be belied by their titles).

It is probable that the circulation of Gramsci's works will assume new characteristics within the next few years. This transformation would seem to have started from Italy, but changes will probably take place, and are perhaps already taking place, also in countries where English is either a native language, or is widely used in academic and cultural life. The initiatives of 2007 already represented a first step towards a new phase, while a powerful boost is expected to come from the new Italian edition of all of Gramsci's writings – the *Edizione nazionale*. This project is expected to provide far more exhaustive coverage than did previous editions.

As for English translations, the complete edition of the *Prison Notebooks*, which the Columbia University Press is in the process of publishing (three volumes have appeared so far), is moving in a similar direction; that is, towards a greater circulation of Gramsci's works in their entirety, and in the form of accurate, philologically reliable, commentated editions. However, it is unlikely that this edition will enjoy the same diffusion as the one-volume *Selections from the Prison Notebooks*. In the present historical phase, those who turn to Gramsci, in the Anglophone world, are mostly academics and theorists in search of tools to use in their analyses of power, ideology, politics, society, language, and cultural identity. Their interest in Gramsci differs from the more directly political interest that British intellectuals and politicians on the Left had thirty or fourty years ago.[48] It also differs from the dedicated attention to Gramsci's life and writings that the representatives of strictly-defined Gramscian studies display in their works – especially those operating within specialised institutions, such as the Fondazione Istituto Gramsci and the International Gramsci Society. In the English-speaking world, Gramsci seems to be appealing to a readership that is sufficiently well-qualified to offer original elaborations of his categories, but that is not always interested in taking a close look at either his biography or the philological and interpretative debates that surround his works. In this context, a complex multi-volume edition has the merit of providing a sound foundation to the study of Gramsci, filling the gaps that selections necessarily leave; but it also runs the risk of attracting little attention from scholars in disciplines where Gramsci has never been particularly influential.

Furthermore, other texts are still poorly known (and are sometimes simply unavailable in English) even to those who are nonetheless showing a growing interest in Gramsci and becoming actively involved in new fields of

---

48. See Hobsbawm *et al.* 1995, Boothman 1999.

research inspired by his legacy. This is the case of many of the passages in his writings – from the pre-prison writings to the letters – that contribute to defining his approach to the *politics, sociology* and *history* of languages.[49]

Finally, a similar pattern also characterises the circulation of biographical studies,[50] as well as the circulation of texts that were not authored by Gramsci – from Bartoli's lecture notes (see above), to the articles written by the editorial staff of *L'Ordine Nuovo*, the weekly, and later daily, paper of which Gramsci was the editor in chief. These texts are nearly unknown in the Anglophone world. Therefore, notwithstanding the far-reaching presence of Gramsci's legacy in many English-speaking countries, what Joseph Buttigieg wrote more than twenty years ago is, in many respects, still valid today: 'the non-specialist anglophone reader has direct access only to a partial and somewhat disjointed version of Gramsci's "literary" legacy'.[51]

4.4. Gramsci's writings on language

While substantial collections, with extensive introductions and accurate commentaries, exist of Gramsci's writings on subjects in which he did not receive a specialist training, such as pedagogy and education,[52] none of the existing

---

49. The *sociology of languages* (according to the definition proposed by Berruto 2003, Chapter Six) has only emerged, as an autonomous disciplinary field, in recent decades. *Politics of language* is a definition that has not been generally accepted yet to indicate a well-defined, autonomous discipline; nonetheless, research is currently being conducted in a field that has, in recent decades, come to be widely identified as *language policy and planning* (see Kaplan and Baldauf Jr. 1997; Ricento 2006), and a major concern with the political aspects of language also characterises recent research on language and power (see Fairclough 2001), language and ideology (see Hodge and Kress 1993), as well as critical approaches to the study of language and discourse (see Fairclough 1995). In contrast, the historical study of languages, often as a comparative study of different languages and literatures belonging to the same language family, already existed, as an established and autonomous discipline, in Gramsci's time. Therefore, only the definition *history of languages* can be used, with reference to Gramsci, without incurring anachronisms. However, even if the other disciplines are fairly recent, attention to both the sociological and political implications of language has been paid throughout the history of modern and pre-modern linguistics. Moreover, in Gramsci's own time, sociolinguistic and glottopolitical approaches were being developed – albeit with little or no terminological emphasis placed on their novelty – by various linguists, especially Antoine Meillet (see Meillet 1928; for discussion, see Berruto 1974, pp. 8–13, and Lehmann 1992, pp. 35–6).

50. Excellent biographical insights can be found in Davidson 1977, and Germino 1990. Great importance is still to be ascribed to Fiori's *Antonio Gramsci: Life of a Revolutionary*, translated into English by Tom Nairn (original Italian edition: Fiori 1966). At present, an up-to-date, comprehensive biography of Gramsci, based on the most recent interpretations and archival findings, does not exist in either Italian or English.

51. Buttigieg 1986, p. 10.

52. See, for instance, Gramsci 1974.

publications can be said to do justice to Gramsci's linguistic reflections. I shall now briefly review the anthologies of Gramsci's writings on linguistic subjects that have been published thus far.

The first publication that is worth mentioning is 'Scritti sulla lingua' ['Writings on Language'], in Antonio Gramsci, *Marxismo e letteratura* ['Marxism and Literature'], edited by Giuliano Manacorda and published in 1975.[53] This collection of Gramsci's writings on language is quite rich, and also well-commentated through footnotes. It is based on the thematic edition of Gramsci's *Prison Notebooks* (see above), though the order of some of the notes was modified by Manacorda. All of Notebook 29 is included, with the only exception of the last, very short note. In this note, Gramsci indicates a possible title, 'Lingua nazionale e grammatica' ['National Language and Grammar'],[54] for the study for which he might have eventually used the preparatory notes included in Notebook 29. Manacorda's volume also reproduces the theatre reviews that Gramsci wrote for the Socialist newspaper *Avanti!* between 1916 and 1920, some of which contain interesting observations on linguistic topics. Unfortunately, Manacorda neither included the comments on language that can be found in Gramsci's letters, nor provided a comprehensive collection of the ones that appear in his pre-prison writings.

History, Philosophy and Culture in the Young Gramsci was edited by Pedro Cavalcanti and by the founder and long-time editor of the journal *Telos*, Paul Piccone, in 1975. This slim volume gathers some fifty pieces from Gramsci's journalistic production, defined by the editors as 'short essays written for mass circulation newspapers'.[55] Part I, entitled *Culture*, provides an English translation of two important articles, 'Analfabetismo' ['Illiteracy'] and 'La lingua unica e l'esperanto' ['A Single Language and Esperanto']. Part III also includes an interesting article of March 1916, on Armenia. Here, Gramsci expresses the wish that a book series could be published on the 'language, the history, the culture and the poetry of the Armenian people'.[56] This passage is symptomatic of the importance that Gramsci accorded to language-related aspects in defining what would nowadays be called the 'identity' of a people. On the whole, Cavalcanti and Piccone's anthology is noteworthy as an early attempt to provide the English-language readership with a glimpse of Gramsci's treatment of linguistic subjects in the years before his imprisonment. Questions can be raised, however, as to the real circulation of this English translation. In order to evaluate the influence of this rarely referenced publication, it should be noted that the number of copies currently circulating is quite small. The limited presence of this book in public

53. Manacorda 1975.
54. Gramsci 1975, Q29, §9, p. 2351.
55. Cavalcanti and Piccone 1975, p. 5.
56. Gramsci 1980, p. 185.

and university libraries in Italy, the UK, and the USA casts doubts over its availability, both today and in the past.

The next publication that needs to be mentioned is the anthological appendix that one of Tullio De Mauro's associates, Emilia Passaponti, prepared for *Linguaggio e vita sociale* ['Language and Social Life'], published in 1978. This publication was based on a lecture that De Mauro had given at the Istituto Togliatti in Frattocchie, near Rome, and was only printed and circulated in the form of 'proofs for the tutors and students' of the courses organised by the Italian Communist Party (as one can read on the frontispiece). In other words, *Linguaggio e vita sociale* was designed only for Communist activist circles, and, not surprisingly, it is today almost a bibliographical rarity. In her appendix, Passaponti collects early articles, as well as passages from Gramsci's letters and prison notes (with almost all of Notebook 29). Regrettably, this selection of Gramsci's writings lacks the necessary explanatory notes.

Three relevant publications appeared in English during the 1980s. A selection entitled 'Notes on Language' was published by the journal *Telos*, in the spring issue of 1984.[57] Translated into English by Steven Mansfield and Livio Alchini, and including a clear and accurate introduction by the former,[58] this publication consists of notes from Gramsci's *Prison Notebooks*. It not only fails to include the many comments on language that can be found in Gramsci's letters and pre-prison writings, but it also omits other notes of equivalent, if not greater, value from the prison notebooks themselves. A year later, another selection appeared, under the title of 'Language, Linguistics and Folklore', in *SCW*. Introduced by an expert of Italian literature and cultural studies, David Forgacs, and thoroughly footnoted, this section of *SCW* includes texts from Gramsci's *Prison Notebooks*, with a prevalence of notes from Notebook 29.[59] As revealed also by the concordance table at the end of the volume, this section quite closely follows the first Italian edition of the *Prison Notebooks* – that is, Togliatti's thematically organised edition. In a different section of *SCW*, the editors also provide a new English translation of 'A Single Language and Esperanto', one of the articles that Gramsci wrote as a 'contribution to a brief altercation with his editors on *Avanti!* in 1918 over the desirability of... promoting the study and use of Esperanto, the international language invented by L.L. Zamenhof in 1887'.[60] Towards

---

57. Now also included in the third volume of *Language and Politics: Mayor Themes in English Studies*, edited by John Joseph and published by Routledge in 2009.

58. Mansfield 1984.

59. Some of these notes were then republished in the 2000 *Routledge Language and Cultural Theory Reader*, edited by L. Burke, T. Crowley and A. Girvin, in the section on 'Unity and Diversity in Language'.

60. Editors' note, in Gramsci 1985, p. 26. On the Esperantist leanings of anarchists and other libertarian socialists in Gramsci's years, see Levy 1999, 2012.

the end of the 1980s, Forgacs also edited 'Philosophy, Common Sense, Language and Folklore', in *GR*. This section consists of prison notes only, including four notes on grammar (out of the nine notes constituting Notebook 29). Perhaps, it is not so much this section that is worthy of attention, but the fact that Forgacs's *Antonio Gramsci Reader* provided the first, widely circulating English translation of 'Analfabetismo'.[61] First published in 1917, this article offers an early formulation of some aspects of Gramsci's stance on national linguistic unification (which I discussed in Chapter One).

In the early 1990s a new selection was published, entitled *Grammatica e linguistica* ['Grammar and Linguistics'].[62] This extremely short book (fewer than fifty pages) has an introduction of just a few lines, no explanatory notes or other forms of commentary to the anthologised texts, and a completely inadequate bibliography. It gathers early articles as well as notes from the prison years, and contains letters from both before and after Gramsci's arrest; however, a whole series of relevant texts is not included. Finally, a brief mention should be made of the section 'Appunti sulla linguistica e la grammatica' ['Notes on Linguistics and Grammar'], in Antonio Gramsci, *Critica letteraria e linguistica* ['Literary and Linguistic Criticism'], edited by Rocco Paternostro and published in 1998.[63] In fact, this section is mainly a reproduction of the one that had appeared twenty-three years earlier in *Marxismo e letteratura* (see above). The order and partition of the texts are the same. Changes have been made with respect to the footnotes (which in Paternostro's edition have been suppressed altogether) and the length of some of the texts (with passages being cut out more frequently and more extensively).

4.5. Gramsci and linguistic disciplines

4.5.1. *Early research*

In addition to Gramsci's own writings, the above-mentioned volume *Critica letteraria e linguistica* collects the most important contributions from secondary literature (in some cases only in the form of extracts). As we have seen, the selection of Gramsci's writings included in this volume was not a great advance over other existing collections; however, the part of the book devoted to secondary

---

61. For the sake of precision, it must be observed that the editor's inclusion of this article on illiteracy in the group of previously untranslated texts (see Gramsci 1999, pp. 14, 68) is incorrect, a translation having appeared – as we have seen – in Piccone and Cavalcanti's 1975 selection.
62. Gramsci 1993.
63. Gramsci 1998.

literature also includes two rich bibliographical sections (one providing summaries of important studies, the other listing only the essential data of other relevant publications), and it is now an indispensable tool for those who wish to widen their knowledge of language-oriented Gramscian studies. What is immediately evident is that most of the collected contributions from the 1950s and '60s were the work of a single scholar, Luigi Rosiello. Apart from minor, not particularly relevant exceptions, there are only two substantial contributions by other authors – Luciano Amodio and the well-known historian Renzo De Felice. The latter is included as the author of an article presenting the above-mentioned lecture notes from Bartoli's course in glottology.[64]

Paternostro's collection offers a good picture of these early years, when Gramscian scholarship was only very marginally concerned with linguistic themes. Rosiello was quite isolated in his attention to such themes. A distinguished linguist, he emphasised the theoretical insights that can be drawn from Gramsci's writings, and compared them to the dominant trends in twentieth-century linguistics, in particular to Saussurean Structuralism.[65] Besides Rosiello's, only a few significant contributions were published before 1979, including an article by Antonio Carrannante, in which Gramsci's views on dialects, language education, and national linguistic unification were considered,[66] and the sections on language from two books, one by Mario Alighiero Manacorda and the other by Angelo Broccoli, that dealt mainly with Gramsci's views on education and schooling.[67]

It was only at the end of 1970s that a major, book-length contribution to the study of Gramsci's linguistic interests appeared, with the publication of Franco Lo Piparo's *Lingua, intellettuali, egemonia in Gramsci*. Lo Piparo's book was, and remains, a scholarly cornerstone. It cast light on the role that linguistics played in the formation of Gramsci's thought, especially in his innovative conception of hegemony. Even though my views differ in some respects from Lo Piparo's, as emerged especially in Chapters Two and Three, I would like to stress that his research prepared the ground for most subsequent contributions. In Rosiello's latest interventions and in the recent contributions by Peter Ives, Derek Boothman, and Giancarlo Schirru, Lo Piparo's arguments continue to function as explicit counterparts, which are sometimes rejected but can never be ignored.[68]

---

64. Gramsci 1998, pp. 304–5. Cf. De Felice 1964.
65. See Rosiello, 1959, 1969 and 1976.
66. See Carrannante 1973.
67. See Manacorda 1970, Broccoli 1972. Other works on language and Marxism published in the same period contain comments on Gramsci – such as Formigari 1973, Propat 1974, Coluccia 1977.
68. See Rosiello 2010 (originally published in 1986), Schirru 2008a, and most of the contributions included in Ives and Lacorte 2010.

In his preface to Lo Piparo's book, De Mauro overtly spoke of a 'Gramscian linguistic theory',[69] and of the precious help that Gramsci's ideas could provide to many scholars, not only linguists, who were then starting to pay more attention to 'the pragmatic and social dimension of linguistic facts': 'today, and in the forthcoming future, Gramsci will have a lot to teach to all of us linguists, anthropologists, and sociologists'.[70] De Mauro underlined the value and current relevance of Gramsci's reflections on language, regretting that these reflections had long been underestimated, and encouraging scholars, including historians, to pay more attention to this aspect of Gramsci's legacy.[71]

Between the end of the 1970s and the beginning of the 1980s, De Mauro's endorsement of Gramsci's views on language, along with other supportive contributions by some of De Mauro's students,[72] marked a turning point in attitudes to Gramsci.[73] It seems appropriate to speak of a general turning point in that the Italian trend coincided, broadly speaking, with the beginning of an increment in the production of language-oriented studies outside Italy. We could perhaps go so far as to say that the 1980s saw the discovery by non-Italians of Gramsci's linguistic interests.

4.5.2. *Exploring Gramsci's ideas on language*

We have seen that De Mauro has repeatedly insisted that there is a general neglect of Gramsci's interest in language. On this point, the reception of Gramsci was, for a long time, inadequate in a number of ways, and is still partly inadequate today. Therefore, De Mauro is probably right in deploring a persistent tendency to overlook Gramsci's exploration of linguistic themes, as is Niels Helsloot, when he writes that for many years Gramsci's name was rarely mentioned in linguistics, 'even in work that explicitly dealt with the social character of language'.[74] However, it would be very hard to deny that the scenario has changed over the last thirty years. On the one hand, Gramscian scholars have become more systematically aware of Gramsci's wide range of interests – from his linguistic interests, to those pertaining to anthropology and educational theory. On the other hand, sociologists of language and education, anthropologists, and linguists worldwide are now paying more attention to the Sardinian thinker.

---

69. In Lo Piparo 1979, p. xv.
70. In Lo Piparo 1979, pp. xv–xvi.
71. See also De Mauro and Giarrizzo 1980.
72. Gensini 1980a, 1980b, pp. 59–63, Passaponti 1981, Lo Piparo 2010b (originally published in 1987).
73. See also Sgroi 1982, Vignuzzi 1982, pp. 717–23.
74. Helsloot 2005, p. 236.

From the early 1980s, valuable interpretations of aspects of Gramsci's ideas on language began to appear in the form of articles in important periodicals, including the *International Journal of the Sociology of Language, Telos*, and the *Journal of Pragmatics*.[75] This secondary literature grew during the 1990s, with the addition of contributions comparing Gramsci's views on language with those of other thinkers both inside and outside Marxism.[76] This research gave rise to the publication of new books in which Gramsci's views on language were among the topics considered,[77] and of Derek Boothman's book *Traducibilità e processi traduttivi. Un caso: Antonio Gramsci linguista* ['Translatability and the Processes of Translation: The Case of Antonio Gramsci, the Linguist'],[78] which is specifically and entirely devoted to Gramsci's reflections on language and translation.

Special attention ought to be paid to Peter Ives's work, which consists of a series of articles and books. In terms of disciplinary training and current academic position, Ives's background is not in language studies, as in the cases of both De Mauro and Lo Piparo, but in political and social theory. The central aim of most of Ives's research is that of re-evaluating Gramsci's thought by giving reflections on language a more substantial place in the general interpretation of Gramsci's political thought. This approach owes much to previous research by Lo Piparo, who placed the origins of Gramsci's notion of hegemony within a non-Marxist intellectual network of Italian and French linguists from the nineteenth and early twentieth centuries. In applying this internal linguistic turn to the study of Gramsci, Ives compares him to classic authors in social theory[79] and in the philosophy of language,[80] and to post-Marxist political theorists – including Ernesto Laclau and Chantal Mouffe.[81] The conceptualisation of language and politically relevant linguistic issues is central to these comparisons.

Ives's views, however, differ from those of Lo Piparo. Concerning the significance of Gramsci's linguistic reflections for the development of his political thought, the two authors have reached contrasting conclusions. Lo Piparo claims a) that 'gramscian hegemony has its original matrix'[82] in the works of linguists and philosophers such as 'Ascoli, Bartoli, Gilliéron, Meillet, Croce',[83] and b) that the influence of these works pushed Gramsci towards liberalism by making him aware of the importance of spontaneous consent and the inefficacy of state

---

75. See Salamini 1981b, Mansfield 1984, Helsloot 1989, Mueller 1990.
76. See Brandist 1996a, 1996b, McNally 1997, Sberlati 1998, Schirru 1999, Boothman 2004b.
77. See, for example, Salamini 1981a, Holub 1992.
78. Boothman 2004a. Cf. the editors' introduction in Ives and Lacorte 2010.
79. Ives 2004b.
80. Ives 1997.
81. Ives 2004a.
82. Lo Piparo 2010a, p. 136.
83. Ibid.

imposition. In general, those who share Lo Piparo's interpretation tend to under-play Gramsci's Marxist perspective, and to perceive his legacy as ultimately external to Marxism. In contrast, Ives highlights that Gramsci's reflections on the history of languages reinforced his critical stance on consensus formation. Given that official models have influenced the way we speak (and write), our spontane-ous grammars cannot be seen as the opposite of normative grammars. Sponta-neous grammar is not a matter of purely personal choice or internal expression, which is totally consented to as opposed to external imposition and institutional influences.[84] Accordingly, those whose interpretation is in line with Ives's tend to see linguistics as a source that did not contradict, but rather supported a Marxist critique of liberal views – especially the view that the state is formed of ideologically neutral institutions, separate from the processes of consensus for-mation that take place in civil society. I dealt with this crucial point in Chapter Three. There, not only did I distance myself from Lo Piparo's conclusions, but I also went beyond Ives's interpretation by showing how the influence of linguis-tics introduced highly original, idiosyncratic features into Gramsci's Marxism.

Going back to the development of language-oriented Gramscian scholarship, it is interesting to recall more data from recent years. Gramsci's name is men-tioned in recent prestigious reference works, such as the *International Encyclo-pedia of Linguistics*[85] and the *Handbook of Pragmatics*,[86] and it appears as the heading of a specific entry in the *Lexicon Grammaticorum*,[87] the *Concise Ency-clopedia of Pragmatics*,[88] and the *Concise Encyclopedia of Sociolinguistics*.[89] In 2005, at the international symposium *Gramsci, Materialism and Culture* held in Toronto, Ives presented a paper entitled 'Global English and Gramsci's Material-ist Approach to Language', later published as an article.[90] His paper was not iso-lated. This conference had quite a high proportion of papers whose titles showed an explicit concern with Gramsci's ideas on language: 'Gramsci's Theory of Lan-guage and Political Hegemony', by Massimo Verdicchio; ' "Language" and "Trans-lations", "Praxis" and "Culture" in Gramsci's Prison Notebooks', by Rocco Lacorte; and 'Aspetti teorici intorno all'idea di grammatica e storia di Antonio Gramsci' ['Theoretical Aspects of Antonio Gramsci's Ideas on Grammar and History'], by Stefano Selenu. Some forty years earlier, in similar conferences on Gramsci, Rosiello's paper would probably have been the only one about language and

84. See Ives 2004a, pp. 83 and 97.
85. Fairclough 1992a.
86. Helsloot 1995.
87. De Mauro 1996b.
88. Helsloot 1998.
89. Helsloot 2001.
90. Ives 2006.

linguistics. An irreversible change would seem to have taken place,[91] though we shall see (in the following sections of this Appendix) that some questions remain open as to the real scope of this change.

4.5.3. *Using Gramsci's ideas on language*

Having looked at how Gramsci's reflections on language and other related topics have been studied, I shall now consider how his thought has been drawn upon and originally developed within language studies. Gramsci's best-known concepts (*hegemony*, above all; but also *passive revolution, historical bloc, folklore, consent and coercion, state and civil society*, and *subaltern groups*), and, in a minority of cases, also his views on language, have been referred to and adopted in various disciplines. They are often used also in the work of scholars whose research is not primarily *on* Gramsci. Some of these scholars have as thorough a knowledge of Gramsci's life and writings as scholars operating within Gramscian studies, and may often be working in direct connection with Gramsci experts. Others, however, are intellectuals and academics who are less familiar with Gramsci's work. The latter are not always 'philologically cautious interpreters';[92] nonetheless, they form an extremely important group, in so far as they 'ingeniously *use* Gramsci to understand the contradictions of the present'.[93]

In Italy, as well as in the Anglophone world, Gramsci's contribution to the theorisation of the connections between culture and political power has influenced many disciplinary fields. Some fall within a broad definition of language studies, while others stand on the border between the study of language and the study of other social, cultural, or historical phenomena.[94] One could start by recalling Gramsci's presence amongst the sources of one philosopher who tried to bring Marxism and language studies together, Ferruccio Rossi-Landi,[95] who was active and fairly influential in both Italian and Anglo-American philosophy of language. An attempt at working out a Marxist theoretical framework, to support a form of research in which dialectology, linguistic history, and anthropology would converge, was also undertaken by the Italian dialectologist Glauco Sanga, with abundant references to Gramsci's *Prison Notebooks*.[96]

---

91. The seventieth anniversary of Gramsci's death confirmed this trend. Both the international conference organised by the International Gramsci Society in May 2007, and the one organised by the Istituto Gramsci Toscano in November of that year, had sessions devoted to linguistic subjects.
92. Liguori and Meta 2005, p. 30.
93. Ibid.
94. See, for example, Crehan 2002, and also Campani and Lapov 2005.
95. Rossi-Landi 2003 (first published in 1968), 1975, 1978, and 1985.
96. Sanga 1977, 1982.

In the field of linguistic history, it is worth stressing that Gramsci's views have been mentioned in the following, influential books: *Dal latino all'italiano moderno* ['From Latin to Modern Italian'] by the Italian linguist Marcello Durante,[97] and *The Social History of Language* edited by the historians Peter Burke and Roy Porter.[98] Gramsci's comments on the role of linguistic differences in fostering localist resistance to the French Revolution were mentioned by the Italian linguist Lorenzo Renzi in his study of the origins of 'linguistic Jacobinism'.[99] In addition, one should not forget either the discussion of Gramsci's views in Pier Vincenzo Mengaldo's authoritative volume on the history of the Italian language in the twentieth century,[100] or the remarks on Gramsci in a prestigious publication sponsored by the Società Dante Alighieri, *La lingua nella storia d'Italia* ['Language in the History of Italy'].[101] Finally, Gramsci's ideas also appear in seminal books by the Italian linguist Claudio Marazzini, which provide an accurate history of the debates that accompanied the various stages of Italy's linguistic unification.[102] Marazzini highlights Gramsci's posthumous influence on language studies, and does not turn to the latter for merely historical, documentary purposes. Rather than limiting himself to either quoting or summarising Gramsci's views, Marazzini adopts some of Gramsci's reflections as far-reaching explanatory tools;[103] as does Riccardo Tesi in his recent history of the Italian language.[104]

In Great Britain, Gramsci's influence has been particularly intense on cultural studies in general, and especially on two eminent intellectuals – Stuart Hall, and Raymond Williams, who was involved in the publication of the English translation of Rossi-Landi's 1978 book, *Marxism and Ideology*.[105] Even when presented as studies of Gramsci's concepts, many works produced in the Anglophone world have taken a present-oriented, applicative approach. This is the case of various works concerned with language and education, from the books of the educational sociologist Harold Entwistle[106] to the contributions collected in the 2002

---

97. Durante 1981.
98. Burke and Porter 1987.
99. Renzi 1981.
100. Mengaldo 1994.
101. Serianni 2002.
102. Marazzini 1977, 1993.
103. See especially Marazzini 1999.
104. Tesi 2005.
105. 'Raymond Williams had a special regard for the work of Ferruccio Rossi-Landi' (publisher's note, in Rossi-Landi 1990, p. xii). On the connections between critical research on language and the work of British cultural studies, Fairclough and Wodak write: 'Critical discourse analysis applies to language types of critical analysis which have developed within "Western Marxism" ... Gramsci and Althusser have inspired a great deal of work in critical analysis, some of which has influenced critical discourse analysis, including the work of Stuart Hall and the Centre for Contemporary Cultural Studies at Birmingham in the UK' (Fairclough and Wodak 1997, pp. 260–1).
106. Entwistle 1978 and 1979.

volume *Gramsci and Education*;[107] and we should include here also the influential articles, books, and interviews by two distinguished representatives of North-American academia, Stanley Aronowitz and Edward Said.[108]

Noam Chomsky, too, has shown some familiarity with Gramsci's life and thought. Chomsky has given a somewhat emblematic critique of Gramsci. This is based on his dissatisfaction with Gramsci's understanding of human nature as the 'totality of historically determined social relations'.[109] This dissatisfaction comes from Chomsky's rationalist philosophical outlook, and from his consequent attack on the 'empiricist ideology'[110] that, he says, has appealed to many trends in Marxist thought and, as a scientific hypothesis, to 'radical behaviourism'[111] and functionalist linguistics. Currently, many linguists and language philosophers tend to attach considerable importance to innate factors – also as a result of the wide and enduring influence of Chomsky's own work. In their view, these factors determine human nature, and the predisposition to use languages that is part of human nature, prior to specific socio-historical conditions and influences. However, the fact that Chomsky discusses Gramsci is a top-level confirmation of the importance that the latter has assumed in the eyes of leading intellectuals in the Anglophone world.

Noteworthy data can also be observed in the works of other exponents of contemporary language studies. For instance, many authors concerned with the political economy of languages, and with the recent debates on multilingualism, linguistic rights, and the international spread of English, are not indifferent to Gramsci.[112] It has been pointed out that a Gramscian notion of hegemony is currently used 'in virtually every discussion of language policy and power',[113] and it 'is often employed by those critical of the potential imperialistic aspects of "global English"'.[114] Regarding the field which is usually referred to as sociolinguistics,[115]

---

107. Borg, Buttigieg and Mayo 2002. Even though I am only reviewing literature written in English or Italian, the international impact of Pierre Bourdieu's ideas makes it necessary to mention here *Language and Symbolic Power* – a collection of Bourdieu's writings on language, education, and politics (translated from French, and published by Polity in 1991) which contains several references to Gramsci.

108. See Aronowitz 2002; Aronowitz and Giroux 1986; Said 2003, 2004, 2005.

109. Quoted in Chomsky 1976, p. 128 (from *The Modern Prince*); cf. Gramsci 1975, Q13, §20, p. 1599.

110. Chomsky 1976, p. 128.

111. Chomsky 2003, p. 114. See also Chomsky 1979, Chapter Four, and 1988, pp. 593–5.

112. See Phillipson 1992, Edwards 1995, Skutnabb-Kangas 2000, Sonntag 2003, Ndhlovu 2006, and Mazzaferro 2008.

113. Friedman 1996. See also the entries under the heading 'Gramsci, Antonio' in Trask 1997, and in Swann *et al.* 2004.

114. Ives 2006, p. 125.

115. This broad definition includes, alongside sociolinguistics proper, also the studies in the ethnography of speaking and in the sociology of language use and language education (see Berruto 2003, Chapter One).

at least two very influential authors have mentioned Gramsci in their works, namely Basil Bernstein and Dell Hymes.[116] In Italy, Gramsci's views on education, dialects and national linguistic unification have been discussed by Arturo Tosi.[117] This sociolinguist, who also operates in British academia, has given well-balanced summaries of Gramsci's position. It would be wrong, however, to over-emphasise Gramsci's influence. As with Chomsky's, most of these accounts and applications of Gramsci's views seem to be based on a highly selective knowledge of his life and work. Unsurprisingly, in his passionate critique of the negative consequences that the dominance of a Chomskyian outlook has brought about in language studies, Dell Hymes observes: 'That Gramsci studied philology has been noticed, but not turned to account.... [T]he challenge of thinking about language as problematic from a thoroughgoing sociohistorical standpoint has hardly been taken up'.[118] These comments originally referred to the USA, but they could be applied to other countries.

Largely overlapping with the sociolinguistic and glottopolitical studies mentioned in the previous paragraphs, another sector where Gramsci has exerted a considerable influence is that of critical approaches to linguistics. This is a wide definition: this sector includes *critical linguistics* proper[119] and other forms of critical discourse analysis (initially practised mostly in English universities), as well as much of the research on the interfaces between language, culture, power, and ideology. Here, too, Gramsci's name is almost always associated with the concept of hegemony. Many proponents of critical approaches to linguistics have introduced this concept into their work, explicitly taking it from Gramsci. In some cases, they have directly used the existing translations of his writings (normally *SPN* and/or *SCW*); in other cases, they have relied on secondary sources. However, Gramsci's ideas on language have been paid little (if any) attention. For example, Norman Fairclough, one of the most influential exponents of this branch of language studies, acknowledges that hegemony 'also includes...the relationships set up between different language varieties (different languages, different dialects), and the emergence of a dominant standard variety'.[120] He notes that Gramsci himself considered this discursive dimension of cultural hegemony, and refers readers (through *GR*) to Notebook 29. Generally, however, Fairclough's major contributions make no specific use of Gramsci's comments on the history, the sociology and the politics of language, in spite of the fact that

116. See Bernstein 1990, p. 134, Hymes 1996, 2001.
117. See Tosi 1995, pp. 153–4, Tosi 2001, pp. 63–7, Tosi 2004.
118. Hymes 1996, pp. 97–8.
119. See Fairclough 1992a.
120. Fairclough 1995, p. 95.

Gramsci and his concept of hegemony are a fully assimilated theoretical component of Fairclough's work.[121]

4.5.4. *Gramsci's influence and its limits: some examples*

Gramsci's language-sensitive version of Marxism is at the centre of many theoretical frameworks for the study of language-related discrimination and social subordination. A somewhat canonical concept of hegemony has been produced by assembling and summarising Gramsci's reflections on the mainly consent-based leadership that a social group comes to exert on other groups during a particular historical period; and this aspect of Gramsci's legacy has appealed to many of those conducting research on the connections that language has with society, power, and ideology. For instance, in 2003 this use of Gramsci was advocated by the authors of *The Hegemony of English*. Interestingly, the introduction to this volume reacts against the conception of linguistic enquiry that was prospering in many academic institutions in the USA. This conception is accused of hampering the application of critical approaches, such as Gramsci's, to educational language planning:

> Because most language educators and sociolinguists do not really conduct research in the 'hard sciences', they disingenuously attempt to adopt the 'neutrality' posture in their work in the social sciences, leaving out the necessary built-in self-criticism, skepticism... However, a discourse of critique based, for instance, on the ideological understanding of the asymmetrical power relation between dominant and subordinate (euphemistically called uncommon or minority) languages is often viewed as contaminating 'objectivity' in language studies and language education. For example, by pretending to treat sociolinguistics as hard science, the sociolinguist 'scientist' is often forced to either dismiss factors tied to ideology or to make *the inherently political nature of language analysis and language education* invisible. In fact, even when sociolinguists, particularly in the United States, describe the relationship between language functions and class (see, for example, the work of William Labov), their analyses never go beyond a mere description of class position and its correlate linguistic functions. In their view, doing a rigorous class analysis that would call for a Marxist framework would be to exit science.[122]

Many other authors advocate and practise a present-oriented use of hegemony.[123] Instead of listing all the books and articles that may represent significant

---

121. See Fairclough 1992b and 2001.
122. Macedo *et al.* 2003, p. 3.
123. For instance, Lippi-Green 1997, Suarez 2002, and Tollefson 1991 and 2006. James Tollefson's 1991 book, *Planning Language, Planning Inequality*, exemplifies quite well

examples of Gramsci's influence, and of its limitations, I shall now focus on two books in particular. They document the influence that Gramsci often exerts on authors approaching language from a socially and politically critical point of view. Yet these books also reveal those limits of Gramsci's influence that Dell Hymes's words, quoted above, hint at. The first book, by Marnie Holborow, was published in 1999 and has on the front cover the title *The Politics of English*, while the frontispiece adds a subtitle that is particularly noteworthy for the purposes of my work: *A Marxist View of Language*. The second book is *Language and Minority Rights: Ethnicity, Nationalism and the Politics of Language* by Stephen May, first published in 2001.

Holborow mentions Gramsci quite a few times. In most cases, she does so in rather generic terms, as when she refers to Gramsci's definition of *folklore*.[124] Her confutation of John Honey's arguments in favour of the superiority of standard English[125] places dialectophony at the centre of Holborow's reflections. As I showed in Chapter One, Gramsci had specific views on this matter – that is, on the alleged superiority of standard national languages over dialects. But Holborow does not relate much of her discussion to Gramsci's position, inserting only a partly pertinent quotation from Notebook 29, via *SCW*.[126] Perhaps, a more thorough consideration of Gramsci's comments on language would have been appropriate, in a work that is explicitly located within a Marxist theoretical perspective; a book, furthermore, which focuses on the worldwide dominance of English, a politically-relevant issue that could indeed have been fruitfully addressed by applying Gramsci's ideas on cultural and linguistic unification to the present.

Especially the fifth chapter of Holborow's book strengthens the impression that, within language studies, the presence of Gramsci's ideas continues to be weakened by the limited number of writings that are in circulation, and that are given due consideration. Holborow's insistence on the inherent multiplicity of and within languages, and on the *continuum*-like situation in which standard and non-standard varieties coexist and influence each other, could have drawn on Gramsci's reflections.[127] Gramsci's writings provide numerous insightful points for a critical study of the politics of language. And as became apparent

---

the indirect use of Gramsci that is sometimes made in language studies. In this book, Tollefson gives a definition of *hegemony* which is clearly Gramscian in its fundamental features; but he does not turn directly to Gramsci's texts, nor does he mention Gramsci's name, referencing, instead, a sociological work on language and membership by L.D. Harman (Harman 1988, pp. 160–3) where the term *hegemony* is, however, explicitly taken from Gramsci.

124. See Holborow 1999, pp. 149–51, 157.
125. Honey 1997 (pp. 69, 111), too, quotes from Gramsci's prison notes.
126. See Holborow 1999, p. 178.
127. See especially Holborow 1999, pp. 182–5.

from my discussion (especially in Chapter One), some of these points regard precisely the *continuum* connecting highly prestigious varieties to lowly, less prestigious ones.

What is most striking about Stephen May's book, *Language and Minority Rights*, is the small number of explicit references to the views that Gramsci expressed on language and cultural identities. The author seems familiar only with Gramsci's best-known concepts, most notably his concept of hegemony. He applies these concepts to historical contexts quite different from the contexts which Gramsci wrote about.[128] May is interested in Gramsci as an influential interpreter of political power, and especially as a theorist of cultural and ideological leadership. Little attention is paid to a whole series of significant elements, in Gramsci's life and writings, which could have been relevant to May's critical discussion of the role of language in society, education, and politics. Gramsci's comments on language policy and planning, and on the rights of speakers of minority or non-standard languages, are almost completely neglected. So, too, is Gramsci's position regarding the role of language in creating and maintaining a sense of membership and identity. This position could have usefully been considered in May's discussion of linguistic nationalism; in particular, in his remarks on 'nationhood' as a 'conscious choice and a particular construction of history',[129] not directly equatable with 'pre-existing ethnic, cultural and/or linguistic communities'.[130]

Elsewhere in May's book, Gramsci's reflections seem to be echoed, perhaps through the mediation of secondary literature or other indirect sources. May

---

128. See, for instance, May 2001, p. 92.

129. May 2001, pp. 60–1.

130. May 2001, p. 60. Cf. Gramsci's attack on the idea that 'the origin of a "new Italian culture" is to be sought and found in the thirteenth century. Research along such lines is purely rhetorical and is guided by modern political interests. The new culture was not a "national" but a class culture; both "politically" and "culturally", it would assume a "communal" and local form, not a unitary form. As a result, it was born in "dialect" and would have to wait until the great [Tuscan] florescence of the fourteenth century before it could meld linguistically, and even then only up to a certain point. Before that, cultural unity did not exist – quite the opposite. What existed was a cultural "Euro-Catholic universality", and the new culture reacted against this universality (which was based in Italy) by means of the local dialects and by bringing to the fore the practical interests of municipal bourgeois groups.... In reality, the nascent bourgeoisie imposed its own dialects, but it failed to create a national language. If a national language did indeed come into existence, it was limited to the litterati, and they were assimilated by the reactionary classes, by the courts; they were aulic rather than "bourgeois litterati"' (Gramsci 1975, Q6, §116 and §118, pp. 787–9. English trans. in Gramsci 2007b). In any case, the 'question of... language... reflects [the] problem... of the moral and intellectual unity of the nation and the state, sought in the unity of the language'. For Gramsci, the 'unity of the language... is one of the external means, and not an exclusively necessary one, of national unity. Anyway, it is an effect and not a cause' (Gramsci 1975, Q21, §5, p. 2118. English translation in Gramsci 1985, pp. 206–12).

writes that 'the establishment of a state-endowed or "national" language must be regarded as an inherently deliberate (and deliberative) political act; an act, moreover, that advantages some individuals and groups at the expense of others'.[131] These words are reminiscent of Gramsci's often-quoted statements (from Notebook 29) that '[w]ritten normative grammar . . . always presupposes a "choice" . . . and is thus always an act of national-cultural politics',[132] and that every time the question of language 'surfaces, in one way or another, it means that a series of other problems are coming to the fore: the formation and enlargement of the governing class, the need to establish more intimate and secure relationships between the governing groups and the national-popular mass, in other words to reorganise cultural hegemony'.[133]

Other exceptions can be found to May's limited recourse to Gramsci's ideas on the history, sociology, and politics of languages. For example, *SPN* is indicated as one of the sources supporting the view that 'boundaries between languages, and the classification of dialects, have invariably followed the politics of state-making rather than the other way around'.[134] In another section of the book, Gramsci is referred to as a classic author in political and social theory, and specific reference is made to his views on language education.[135] However, this reference is not directly to Gramsci's texts, but to a secondary source: a work by Donaldo Macedo,[136] one of the authors of *The Hegemony of English* (see above).

4.5.5. *Final remarks*

Let me now summarise what I have said so far on the use of Gramsci's ideas within language studies, and, more generally, on the contacts between research on language and research on Gramsci. Most of the comments he specifically made on language have been overlooked, and this is particularly evident in the works that Gramsci has inspired outside Italy. One should not conclude, however, that Gramsci's presence in language studies has been superficial or insignificant. To be precise, his influence seems to have been *partial*. It has been hampered by an overly selective knowledge of his writings and by a lack of direct appreciation of the context (both historical and biographical) in which Gramsci's reflections originated. In this sense, the fact that Gramsci was not a mere theoretician but also a man of action, and that he did not regard his writings as self-sufficient,

---

131. May 2001, p. 152.
132. Gramsci 1975, Q29, §2, p. 2344.
133. Gramsci 1975, Q29, §3, p. 2346.
134. May 2001, p. 151.
135. May 2001, p. 215.
136. Macedo 1994. A new edition of Stephen May's book appeared in 2012, with no significant changes from the previous edition as far as his use of Gramsci is concerned.

scholarly publications, has been largely overlooked. At the same time, Gramsci's presence within linguistic disciplines has only very rarely led to a thorough consideration of the role that languages played in his life. It is these deficiencies regarding Gramsci's presence within language-related research that my work has aimed to set right. Having said this, it is by no means my intention to deny that Gramsci's influence left recognisable traces on at least some sectors of language studies.

On the international scene, Gramsci has been appreciated for his thoughts on the dynamics supporting dominant ideologies within societies where power, wealth, and cultural resources are unequally distributed. In this respect, there seems to be common features in all the sectors of language studies that were more significantly affected by Gramsci's influence. These sectors are mostly made up of the works of authors whose viewpoints may vary, but who all regard the role that language plays in societies (and in the history of societies) as being loaded with political implications. A degree of social criticism is present in almost all of these approaches. Not surprisingly, Gramsci's influence is wider amongst authors who study the manifold connections between social change and the use of languages. Social change is usually understood by these authors as resulting from conflicts between classes or other politically relevant, collective entities. Unlike Chomskyan approaches, the primary focus here is on those elements in language that are cultural, rather than natural – historical products, rather than genetically-conditioned innate properties.

However accurate and direct the attention to Gramsci's texts may or may not be, one central aspect of his attitude to the study of language seems to have been inherited by most of the approaches that I have discussed or mentioned in this Appendix – from Phillipson's influential book on *Linguistic Imperialism*, to Fairclough's version of discourse analysis. Gramsci believed that the study of language grew out of political needs and conflicts and exerted, in turn, an active influence on such needs and conflicts.[137] Therefore, he rejected the idea – which was instead reinforced by positivist-naturalist research on language, and later by many Structuralist approaches – that describing linguistic structures is a neutral, objective act free of political implications.[138] We saw a similar rejection in the above-quoted passages from the introduction to *The Hegemony of English*, and from Stephen May's book. A similar attitude appears in Tony Crowley's introduction to his book, *Language in History*,[139] where reference to

---

137. See especially Gramsci 1975, Q29, §4 and §5, pp. 2346–7.
138. See Ives 2004a, pp. 95–7.
139. '[T]here is a view which holds that in the nineteenth century the study of language became scientific, principally by means of dropping its prejudices and adopting instead the scientific methodology of positivism.... [Even today] it might be thought that the "language question", as it has been known at least since Dante, could be dealt

Gramsci is repeatedly made, and it also emerges, most notably, from Norman Fairclough's description of the inadequacies of mainstream sociolinguistics:

> When one focuses on the simple existence of facts without attending to the social conditions which made them so and the social conditions for their potential change, the notion that the sociolinguist herself might somehow affect the facts hardly seems to arise. But... if the facts of the existing sociolinguistic order are seen as lines of tension, as a temporary configuration representing the current balance of class forces, then the effect of sociolinguistic research might either be to legitimize these facts and so indirectly the power relations which underlie them, or to show the contingency of these facts despite their apparent solidity, and so indirectly point to ways of changing them. For instance, sociolinguistics has often described sociolinguistic conventions in terms of what are the 'appropriate' linguistic forms for a given social situation; whatever the intention, this terminology is likely to lend legitimacy to 'the facts' and their underlying power relations.[140]

---

with objectively or neutrally. However,... the significance of language in history transcends any scientific approach to language' (Crowley 1996, pp. 4–5).

140. Fairclough 2001, p. 7.

References

Abbruzzese, Antonio 1987 [1911], *Voci e modi errati dell'uso sardo*, Bologna: Arnaldo Forni.

Ageeva, Inna 2009, 'La critique de F. de Saussure dans *Marxisme et philosophie du langage* de V.N. Vološinov et le contexte de la réception des idées saussuriennes dans les années 1920–1930 en Russie', *Cahiers de l'ILSL*, 26: 73–84.

Angioni, Giulio 1987, 'Quella originale riflessione sulla cultura popolare', *Nuova Rinascita Sarda*, 2, 4 (special issue on *Gramsci e la Sardegna*): 21–4.

Arendt, Hannah 1966, *The Origins of Totalitarianism*, New York: Harcourt Brace.

Aronowitz, Stanley 2002, 'Gramsci's Theory of Education: Schooling and Beyond', in Borg *et al.* 2002.

Aronowitz, Stanley and Henry Giroux 1986, *Education under Siege: The Conservative, Liberal and Radical Debate over Schooling*, London: Routledge & Kegan Paul.

Ascoli, Graziadio Isaia 1975, *Scritti sulla questione della lingua*, ed. by C. Grassi, Turin: Einaudi.

Atkinson, Dorothy 1983, *The End of the Russian Land Commune 1905–1930*, Stanford, CA: Stanford University Press.

Ausilio, Manuela, 'Intransigenza-tolleranza', in Liguori and Voza 2009.

Baratta, Giorgio 2003, 'Gramsci tra noi: Hall, Said, Balibar, Coutinho', in *Le rose e i quaderni. Il pensiero dialogico di Antonio Gramsci*, Rome: Carocci.

Baratta, Giorgio and Andrea Catone (eds.) 1995, *Antonio Gramsci e il 'progresso intellettuale di massa'*, Milan: Unicopli.

Bartoli, Matteo 1912–13, 'Etnografia balcanica', in *Appunti di Glottologia* (lithographically printed lecture notes, currently held in the archives of the Fondazione Istituto Gramsci, Rome).

—— 1917, review of *Aree e limiti linguistici nella dialettologia italiana moderna* by A. Trauzzi, *Giornale Storico della Letteratura Italiana*, 69: 376–94.

—— 1925, *Introduzione alla neolinguistica*, Geneva: Olschki.

—— 1945, *Saggi di linguistica spaziale*, Turin: Rosenberg & Sellier.

Battaglia, Salvatore 1970, *Grande Dizionario della Lingua Italiana*, Volume VI, Turin: Utet.

Bellamy, Richard and Darrow Schecter 1993, *Gramsci and the Italian State*, Manchester: Manchester University Press.

Benincà, Paola 1994, 'Linguistica e dialettologia italiana', in *Storia della linguistica*, edited by G. Lepschy, Volume III, Bologna: Il Mulino.

Benvenuti, Francesco and Silvio Pons 1999, 'L'Unione Sovietica nei *Quaderni del carcere*', in Vacca 1999b, Volume I.

Bergami, Giancarlo 1975, 'Gustavo Balsamo Crivelli', *Belfagor*, 30, 5: 537–68.

—— 1977, *Il giovane Gramsci e il marxismo. 1911–1918*, Milan: Feltrinelli.

—— 1991, 'L'esperienza di Gramsci nel Comintern', *Nuova Antologia*, 126, 2179: 114–59.

—— 1993, 'Radici sarde e studentato torinese di Gramsci', *Nuova Antologia*, 128, 2185: 135–62.

Berlinguer, Mario 1967, 'La sua fede non fu mai umiliata', *La Nuova Sardegna*, 27 April.

Bermani, Cesare 1979, 'Letteratura e vita nazionale. Le osservazioni sul folclore', in *Gramsci: un'eredità contrastata. La nuova sinistra rilegge Gramsci*, Milan: Ottaviano.

—— 1981, 'Breve storia del Proletkul't italiano', *Primo Maggio*, 16: 27–40.

—— 1987, *Gramsci raccontato*, Rome: Istituto Ernesto De Martino-Edizioni Associate.

—— 1995, *'L'Ordine Nuovo* e il canto sociale', in Baratta and Catone 1995.

—— 2007, *Gramsci, gli intellettuali e la cultura proletaria*, Milan: Cooperativa Colibrì.

Bernstein, Basil 1990, 'Education, symbolic control, and social practices', in *Class, Codes and Control*, Volume IV: *The Structuring of Pedagogic Discourse*, London: Routledge.

Berruto, Gaetano 1974, *La sociolinguistica*, Bologna: Zanichelli.

—— 2003, *Fondamenti di sociolinguistica*, Bari: Laterza.

Bertoni, Giulio and Matteo Bartoli 1928 [1925], *Breviario di neolinguistica*, Modena: Società tipografica modenese-Antica tipografia Soliani.

Bertoni Jovine, Dina 1975, *La scuola italiana dal 1870 ai giorni nostri*, Rome: Editori Riuniti.

Bettoni, Camilla 2008, 'Migrazioni e competenze linguistiche', in *Lingua, cultura e cittadinanza in contesti migratori. Europa e area mediterranea*, edited by G. Berruto *et al.*, Perugia: Guerra.

—— 2010, 'Tra lingua, dialetto e inglese: mezzo secolo di emigrazione italiana in Australia', in *Into Italy and Out of Italy: Lingua e cultura della migrazione italiana*, edited by A. Ledgeway and L. Lepschy, Perugia: Guerra.

Blasco Ferrer, Eduardo 1999, 'Il pensiero linguistico di Gramsci nei *Quaderni del Carcere*', in Orrù and Rudas 1999.

Bloomfield, Leonard 1976 [1933], *Language*, London: Allen & Unwin.

Bobbio, Norberto 1969, 'Gramsci e la concezione della società civile', in Rossi 1969, Volume I.

—— 1976, *Quale socialismo? Discussione di un'alternativa*, Turin: Einaudi.

—— 1977, 'Gramsci e il PCI', in Coen 1977.

—— 1978, 'Gramsci e la cultura politica italiana', *Belfagor*, 33, 5: 593–9.

—— 1990, *Saggi su Gramsci*, Milan: Feltrinelli.

—— 1991, 'La democrazia nei Quaderni', in *Antonio Gramsci dopo la caduta di tutti i muri*, supplement to *L'Unità*, 15 January.

Boninelli, Giovanni M. 2007, *Frammenti indigesti. Temi folclorici negli scritti di Antonio Gramsci*, Rome: Carocci.

Boothman, Derek 1999, 'Gramsci e la Gran Bretagna', in *Liberalismi e Socialismi. Gramsci e Gobetti: eresie a confronto*, edited by G. Vagnarelli and F.M. Moriconi, San Benedetto del Tronto: Assessorato alla Cultura-Biblioteca G. Lesca.

—— 2004a, *Traducibilità e processi traduttivi. Un caso: A. Gramsci linguista*, Perugia: Guerra.

—— 2004b, 'Traduzione e traducibilità', in Frosini and Liguori 2004.

—— 2005, 'Le traduzioni di Gramsci in inglese e la loro ricezione nel mondo anglofono', *inTRAlinea*, 7, available at <http://www.intralinea.it/volumes/boothman2005.pdf>.

—— 2008a, 'The Sources for Gramsci's Concept of Hegemony', *Rethinking Marxism*, 20, 2: 201–15.

—— 2008b, 'Political and Linguistic Sources for Gramsci's Concept of Hegemony', in *Hegemony: Studies in Consensus and Coercion*, edited by R. Howson and K. Smith, New York: Routledge.

—— 2012, 'Gramsci's Interest in Language: The Influence of Bartoli's *Dispense di glottologia* (1912–13) on the *Prison Notebooks*', in Carlucci 2012.

Borg, Carmel, Joseph Buttigieg and Peter Mayo (eds.) 2002, *Gramsci and Education*, Oxford: Rowman & Littlefield.

Borghese, Lucia 1981, 'Tia Alene in bicicletta. Gramsci traduttore dal tedesco e teorico della traduzione', *Belfagor*, 36, 6: 635–65.

Borghi, Lamberto 1951, *Educazione e autorità nell'Italia moderna*, Florence: La Nuova Italia.

Borsellino, Nino 1983, 'Gramsci, Pirandello e il dialetto', in *Pirandello dialettale*, edited by S. Zappulla, Palermo: Palumbo.

Bourdieu, Pierre 1991, *Language and Symbolic Power*, Cambridge: Polity.

Brandist, Craig 1996a, 'Gramsci, Bakhtin and the Semiotics of Hegemony', *New Left Review*, 216: 94–109.

—— 1996b, 'The Official and the Popular in Gramsci and Bakhtin', *Theory, Culture and Society*, 13, 2: 59–74.

—— 2003, 'The Origins of Soviet Socio-linguistics', *Journal of Sociolinguistics*, 7, 2: 213–31.

—— 2005, 'Marxism and the Philosophy of Language in Russia in the 1920s and 1930s', *Historical Materialism*, 13, 1: 63–84.

—— 2008, 'Language and its Social Functions in Early Soviet Thought', *Studies in East European Thought*, 60, 4: 279–83.

—— 2010, 'Psychology, Linguistics and the Rise of Applied Social Science in the USSR: Isaak Shpil'rein's *Language of the Red Army Soldier*', in Brandist and Chown 2010.

—— 2012, 'The Cultural and Linguistic Dimensions of Hegemony: Aspects of Gramsci's Debt to Early Soviet Cultural Policy', in Carlucci 2012.

Brandist, Craig and Katya Chown (eds.) 2010, *Politics and the Theory of Language in the USSR 1917–1938: The Birth of Sociological Linguistics*, London: Anthem Press.

Bravo, Gian Mario 1973, 'D. Rjazanov', in *Il Manifesto e i suoi interpreti*, Rome: Editori Riuniti.

Bréal, Michel 1900 [1897], *Semantics: Studies in the Science of Meaning*, London: William Heinemann.

—— 1901, 'Sur le choix d'une langue internationale', *Revue de Paris*, 8, 4: 229–46.

Broccoli, Angelo 1972, *Antonio Gramsci e l'educazione come egemonia*, Florence: La Nuova Italia.

Bruchis, Michael 1982, *One Step Back, Two Steps Forward: On the Language Policy of the Communist Party of the Soviet Union in the National Republics*, Boulder, CO: East European Monographs.

Bukharin, Nikolai 1926 [1921], *Historical Materialism: A System of Sociology*, London: Allen & Unwin.

Bukharin, Nikolai and Evgenii Preobrazhensky 1969 [1920], *The ABC of Communism*, Harmondsworth: Penguin.

Burke, Peter 2008, *What is Cultural History?*, Cambridge: Polity.

Burke, Peter and Roy Porter (eds.) 1987, *The Social History of Language*, Cambridge: Cambridge University Press.

Buttigieg, Joseph 1986, 'The Legacy of Antonio Gramsci', *Boundary 2*, 14, 3: 1–17.

—— 1995a, 'Negli Stati Uniti. 1', in Hobsbawm *et al.* 1995.

—— 1995b, 'La circolazione delle categorie gramsciane negli Stati Uniti', in Righi 1995.

Cafagna, Luciano 1988, '"Figlio di quei movimenti". Il giovane Gramsci e la critica della democrazia', in Sbarberi 1988.

Callinicos, Alex 1982, *Is There a Future for Marxism?*, London: Macmillan.

Cammett, John M. 1967, *Antonio Gramsci and the Origins of Italian Communism*, Stanford, CA: Stanford University Press.

Campani, Giovanna and Zoran Lapov 2005, 'Nation-State and Cultural Diversity in Italy', in *Nation-State Building Processes and Cultural Diversity*, ed. by J. Blaschke, Berlin: Parabolis.

Caprioglio, Sergio 1982, 'Quei mesi a Torino tra i sardi della brigata', *L'unione Sarda*, 27 April.

—— 1987, 'Gramsci, si può sapere di più', *L'Unità*, 23 February.

—— 1988, 'Per l'edizione critica degli scritti di Gramsci. Un volo per Mosca', in Sbarberi 1988.

Caputo, Renato 2009, 'Totalitario', in Liguori and Voza 2009.

Carcano, Giancarlo 1977, *Cronaca di una rivolta. I moti torinesi del '17*, Turin: Stampatori.

Carlucci, Alessandro 2008, 'Grammatica, educazione linguistica, passività', in Lussana and Pissarello 2008.

—— (ed.) 2012, *New Approaches to Gramsci: Language, Philosophy and Politics*, monographic issue of the *Journal of Romance Studies*, 12, 3.

Carr, Edward H. and Robert W. Davies 1969, *Foundations of a Planned Economy 1926–1929*, London: MacMillan.

Carrannante, Antonio 1973, 'Antonio Gramsci e i problemi della lingua italiana', *Belfagor*, 28, 5: 544–56.

—— 1978, 'Le discussioni sulla lingua italiana nella prima metà del Novecento', *Belfagor*, 33, 6: 621–31.

Carrère D'Encausse, Hélène 1971, 'Unité prolétarienne et diversité nationale. Lénine et la théorie de l'autodétermination', *Revue française de science politique*, 21, 2: 221–55.

—— 1998, *Lénine*, Paris: Fayard.

Carsano, Giovanni 1952, 'Come la Brigata Sassari fraternizzò con i lavoratori', *L'Unità* (Piedmont edition), 27 April.

Cavalcanti, Pedro and Paul Piccone 1975, introduction to *History, Philosophy and Culture in the Young Gramsci*, Saint Louis: Telos Press.

Chiaretti, Tommaso 1950, 'Sono arrivati i libri che Gramsci lesse in carcere', *L'Unità*, 19 March.

—— 1977, 'Perché Gramsci leggeva Panzini', *La Repubblica*, 26 May.

Chironi, Agostino 1967, 'Una riunione in osteria', *Rinascita Sarda*, 5 May.

—— 1988, 'I miei incontri con Gramsci. La riunione in osteria', *PCI Regione Informazioni*, 18, 1–2: 35.

Chomsky, Noam 1976, *Reflections on Language*, London: Temple Smith.

—— 1979, *Language and Responsibility*, Hassocks: Harvester Press.

—— 1988, *Language and Politics*, Montreal: Black Rose Books.

—— 2003, *Chomsky on Democracy and Education*, ed. by C.P. Otero, London: Routledge.

Cirese, Alberto Mario 1998 [1971], *Cultura egemonica e culture subalterne*, Palermo: Palumbo.

Coen, Federico (ed.) 1977, *Egemonia e democrazia, Quaderni di Mondoperaio*, 7.

Cohn, Bernard S. 1996, *Colonialism and its Forms of Knowledge*, Princeton: Princeton University Press.

Coluccia, Rosario 1977, 'La prospettiva marxista nell'analisi del rapporto lingua-società', in *Messaggi e ambiente*, edited by G.R. Cardona and F. Ferrara, Rome: Officina.

Coppola, Goffredo 1930, review of *Sommario di linguistica arioeuropea* by A. Pagliaro, *Pegaso*, 2, 11: 622–6.

Cortelazzo, Manlio 1984, 'Il dialetto sotto il Fascismo', *Movimento operaio e socialista*, 7, 1: 107–116.

Cospito, Giuseppe 2004a, 'Egemonia', in Frosini and Liguori 2004.

—— 2004b, 'Struttura-superstruttura', in Frosini and Liguori 2004.

Coveri, Lorenzo 1981–2, 'Dialetto e scuola nell'Italia unita', *Rivista Italiana di Dialettologia*, 5: 77–97.

—— 1984, 'Mussolini e il dialetto. Notizie sulla campagna antidialettale del fascismo (1932)', *Movimento operaio e socialista*, 7, 1: 117–32.

Crehan, Kate 2002, *Gramsci, Culture and Anthropology*, London: Pluto Press.

Crisp, Simon 1989, 'Soviet Language Planning 1917–1953', in *Language Planning in the Soviet Union*, edited by M. Kirkwood, London: Macmillan.

Croce, Benedetto 1933, review of *Silloge linguistica dedicata alla memoria di Graziadio Isaia Ascoli nel primo centenario della nascita*, *La Critica*, 31: 52.

—— 1943, *Pagine sparse*, Volume III, Naples: Ricciardi.

—— 1966, *Problemi di estetica e contributi alla storia dell'estetica italiana*, Bari: Laterza.

—— 1990 [1902], *Estetica come scienza dell'espressione e linguistica generale. Teoria e storia*, edited by G. Galasso, Milan: Adelphi.

Crowley, Tony 1996, *Language in History: Theories and Texts*, London: Routledge.

Čudakova, Mariètta O. and Evgenii A. Toddes 1982, 'La première traduction russe du *Cours de linguistique générale* de F. de Saussure et l'activité du Cercle linguistique de Moscou', *Cahiers Ferdinand de Saussure*, 36: 63–91.

Cutrì, Maria 1949, 'Mangiavamo l'erba con Anto' su gobeddu', *Vie Nuove*, 37: 15.

D'Agostino, Mari 2007, *Sociolinguistica dell'Italia contemporanea*, Bologna: Il Mulino.

Dalby, Andrew 2002, *Language in Danger*, London: Penguin.

Daniele, Chiara (ed.) 1999, *Gramsci a Roma, Togliatti a Mosca. Il carteggio del 1926*, Turin: Einaudi.

—— 2005, *Togliatti editore di Gramsci*, Rome: Carocci.

Davico Bonino, Guido 1972, *Gramsci e il teatro*, Turin: Einaudi.

Davidson, Alastair 1977, *Antonio Gramsci: Towards an Intellectual Biography*, London: Merlin Press.

—— 2008, 'The Uses and Abuses of Gramsci', *Thesis Eleven*, 95: 68–94.

De Certeau, Michel, Dominique Julia and Jacques Revel 1975, *Une politique de la langue: la Révolution française et les patois*, Paris: Gallimard.

De Felice, Renzo 1964, 'Un corso di glottologia di Matteo Bartoli negli appunti di Antonio Gramsci', *Rivista storica del socialismo*, 21: 219–21.

Deias, Antonio 1997, 'Ghilarza: inizia il cammino', *Società sarda*, 5: 56–70.

Delitala, Enrica 1973–74, 'Materiali per lo studio degli esseri fantastici del mondo tradizionale sardo', *Studi sardi*, 23: 306–54.

De Mauro, Tullio 1964, 'Bartoli, Matteo Giulio', in *Dizionario biografico degli italiani*, Volume 6, Rome: Enciclopedia Italiana Treccani.

—— 1979a, 'Gramsci e le vicende linguistiche del teatro del Novecento', in *L'Italia delle Italie*, Rome: Editori Riuniti.

—— 1979b, preface to Lo Piparo 1979.

—— 1979c, 'Graziadio Isaia Ascoli di fronte ai problemi linguistici dell'Italia unita', in De Mauro 1980b.

—— 1980a, 'Giuseppe Lombardo Radice e l'educazione linguistica', in De Mauro 1980b.

—— 1980b, *Idee e ricerche linguistiche nella cultura italiana*, Bologna: Il Mulino.

—— 1991a [1963], *Storia linguistica dell'Italia unita*, Bari: Laterza.

—— 1991b, 'Ancora Saussure e la semantica', *Cahiers Ferdinand de Saussure*, 45: 101–9.

—— 1995, 'Gramsci e la linguistica', *Il cannocchiale*, 3: 61–71.

—— 1996a, 'Bartoli, Matteo Giulio', in Stammerjohann 1996.

—— 1996b, 'Gramsci, Antonio', in Stammerjohann 1996.

—— 1996c, 'Peano, Giuseppe', in Stammerjohann 1996.

—— 1998, *Prima persona singolare passato prossimo indicativo*, Rome: Bulzoni.

—— 2004, *La cultura degli italiani*, edited by F. Erbani, Bari: Laterza.

—— 2010a [1999], 'Language from Nature to History: More on Gramsci the Linguist', in Ives and Lacorte 2010.

—— 2010b [1991], 'Some Notes on Gramsci the Linguist', in Ives and Lacorte 2010.

De Mauro, Tullio and Giuseppe Giarrizzo 1980, 'Gramsci e la linguistica', *Le Forme e la Storia*, 1, 3: 381–98.

De Murtas, Angelo 1982, 'A Roma con Gramsci sotto la pioggia. Gli ottanta anni di Agostino Chironi', *La Nuova Sardegna*, 18 March.

Depretto-Genty, Catherine 1986, 'Diffusion et réception du Cours de linguistique générale de F. de Saussure dans l'URSS des années 1920', in *IVe Colloque de linguistique russe*, Toulouse: Université de Toulouse Le Mirail.

Devoto, Giacomo 1947, 'Matteo Bartoli', *Word*, 3, 3: 208–16.

—— 1951, *I fondamenti della storia linguistica*, Florence: Sansoni.

—— 1973, 'Matteo Bartoli', in *Civiltà di persone*, Florence: Vallecchi.

Devoto, Giacomo and Gabriella Giacomelli 2002 [1971], *I dialetti delle regioni d'Italia*, Milan: Bompiani.

Di Biagio, Anna 2008, 'Egemonia leninista, egemonia gramsciana', in Giasi 2008, Volume I.

D'Orsi, Angelo 1999, 'Lo studente che non divenne "dottore". Gramsci all'Università di Torino', *Studi Storici*, 40, 1: 39–75.

—— 2002, 'Lo studente che non divenne "dottore". Antonio Gramsci nella Facoltà di Lettere', in *Allievi e maestri. L'Università di Torino nell'Otto-Novecento*, Turin: Celid.

—— 2004, introduction to A. Gramsci, *La nostra città futura. Scritti torinesi 1911–1922*, Rome: Carocci.

Durante, Marcello 1981, *Dal latino all'italiano moderno. Saggio di storia linguistica e culturale*, Bologna: Zanichelli.

Eco, Umberto 1995, *The Search for the Perfect Language*, Oxford: Blackwell.

Edwards, John 1995, *Multilingualism*, London: Penguin.

Edwards, Stewart (ed.) 1973, *The Communards of Paris, 1871*, London: Thames and Hudson.

Eley, Geoff 1984, 'Reading Gramsci in English: Observations on the Reception of Antonio Gramsci in the English-Speaking World 1957–1982', *European History Quarterly*, 14, 4: 441–78.

Engels, Friedrich 1969 [1845], *The Condition of the Working Class in England*, London: Granada.

—— 1977 [1848], 'The Frankfurt Assembly Debates the Polish Question', in *Marx and Engels Collected Works*, Volume 7, London: Lawrence and Wishart.

—— 1980 [1859], 'Po and Rhine', in *Marx and Engels Collected Works*, Volume 16, London: Lawrence and Wishart.

—— 1985 [1866], 'What Have the Working Classes to Do with Poland?', in *Marx and Engels Collected Works*, Volume 20, London: Lawrence and Wishart.

Entwistle, Harold 1978, *Class, Culture and Education*, London: Methuen.

—— 1979, *Antonio Gramsci: Conservative Schooling for Radical Politics*, London: Routledge & Kegan Paul.

Espa, Enzo 1999, *Dizionario sardo-italiano dei parlanti la lingua logudorese*, Sassari: Carlo Delfino.

Fairclough, Norman 1992a, 'Critical Linguistics', in *International Encyclopedia of Linguistics*, Volume 1, Oxford: Oxford University Press.

—— 1992b, *Discourse and Social Change*, Cambridge: Polity.

—— 1995, *Critical Discourse Analysis: The Critical Study of Language*, Harlow: Longman.

—— 2001, *Language and Power*, Harlow: Longman.

Fairclough, Norman and Ruth Wodak 1997, 'Critical Discourse Analysis', in *Discourse as Social Interaction*, edited by T.A. Van Dijk, London: Sage.

Femia, Joseph V. 1987, *Gramsci's Political Thought*, Oxford: Clarendon Press.

—— 1995, 'Gramsci e il problema del totalitarismo', in Righi 1995.

Ferri, Franco 1987, 'Centralismo', in Ricchini *et al.* 1987.

Figes, Orlando 1997, 'The Russian Revolution of 1917 and its Language in the Village', *Russian Review*, 56, 3: 323–45.

Finck, Franz Nikolaus 1910, *Haupttypen des Sprachbaus*, Leipzig: Teubner.

—— 1923, *Die Sprachstämme des Erdkreises*, Leipzig: Teubner.

Finocchiaro, Maurice A. 1984, 'Gramsci: An Alternative Communism?', *Studies in Soviet Thought*, 27, 2: 123–46.

Fiori, Giuseppe 1966, *Vita di Antonio Gramsci*, Bari: Laterza.

—— 1970, *Antonio Gramsci: Life of a Revolutionary*, translation by T. Nairn, London: NLB.

—— 1977, preface to Paulesu Quercioli 1977.

—— 1991, *Gramsci Togliatti Stalin*, Bari: Laterza.

Foresti, Fabio 2005, 'La "Società Dialettologica Italiana" del 1873 e la politica linguistica del primo sessantennio uni-

tario (1861–1921)', *Rivista Italiana di Dialettologia*, 29: 29–58.

Forgacs, David 1989, 'Gramsci and Marxism in Britain', in Martin 2002, Volume IV.

—— 1995a, 'In Gran Bretagna', in Hobsbawm *et al.* 1995.

—— 1995b, 'Le edizioni inglesi di Gramsci', in Righi 1995.

Formigari, Lia (ed.) 1973, *Marxismo e teorie della lingua*, Messina: La Libra.

Francescato, Giuseppe 1993, 'Sociolinguistica delle minoranze', in *Introduzione all'italiano contemporaneo. La variazione e gli usi*, edited by A.A. Sobrero, Bari: Laterza.

Franceschini, Fabrizio 1988, 'Fortuna delle note linguistiche e demologiche di Gramsci', *Beiträge zur Romanischen Philologie*, 27, 2: 229–238.

Francioni, Gianni 1977, 'Per la storia dei "Quaderni del carcere"', in *Politica e storia in Gramsci. Atti del convegno internazionale di studi gramsciani. Firenze, 9–11 dicembre 1977*, Volume II: *Relazioni, interventi, comunicazioni*, edited by F. Ferri, Rome: Editori Riuniti-Istituto Gramsci.

—— 1984, *L'officina gramsciana*, Naples: Bibliopolis.

—— 1992, 'Proposte per una nuova edizione dei Quaderni del carcere', *IG Informazioni*, 4, 2: 8–186.

Frassati, Luciana 1979, *Un uomo, un giornale. Alfredo Frassati*, Volume 2, Rome: Edizioni di Storia e Letteratura.

Friedman, Kerim K. 1996, 'Habitus, Hegemony and Historical Blocs: Locating Language Policy in Gramsci's Theory of the State', paper presented at the American Anthropological Association Panel *Gramsci, Hegemony and the Critique of Anthropology*, San Francisco, 23 November.

Frosini, Fabio 1999, 'Riforma e Rinascimento: il problema della "unità ideologica tra il basso e l'alto"', in *Scuola intellettuali e identità nazionale nel pensiero di Antonio Gramsci*, edited by L. Capitani and R. Villa, Rome: Gamberetti.

—— 2003, *Gramsci e la filosofia*, Rome: Carocci.

—— 2010, *La religione dell'uomo moderno. Politica e verità nei Quaderni del carcere di Antonio Gramsci*, Rome: Carocci.

Frosini, Fabio and Guido Liguori (eds.) 2004, *Le parole di Gramsci*, Rome: Carocci.

Garin, Eugenio 1997 [1958], 'Gramsci nella cultura italiana', in *Con Gramsci*, Rome: Editori Riuniti.

Gensini, Stefano 1980a, 'Linguistica e questione politica della lingua', *Critica marxista*, 18, 1: 151–65.

—— 1980b, 'Questioni linguistiche nella storia della cultura italiana: da Dante ai contemporanei', in *Lingua e dialetti nella cultura italiana da Dante a Gramsci*, edited by T. De Mauro *et al.*, Messina: D'Anna.

—— 2005, *Breve storia dell'educazione linguistica dall'Unità a oggi. Con un'appendice di documenti d'epoca*, Rome: Carocci.

Gentile, Emilio 2002, 'Fascism in Power: The Totalitarian Experiment', in *Liberal and Fascist Italy 1900–1945*, edited by A. Lyttelton, Oxford: Oxford University Press.

Germino, Dante 1986, 'Antonio Gramsci: From the Margins to the Center, the Journey of a Hunchback', *Boundary 2*, 14, 3: 19–30.

—— 1990, *Antonio Gramsci: Architect of a New Politics*, Baton Rouge: Louisiana State University Press.

Gerratana, Valentino 1975, 'Note di filologia gramsciana', *Studi Storici*, 16, 1: 126–54.

—— 1987, 'I Quaderni, un cantiere che continua a produrre', in Ricchini *et al.* 1987.

—— 1995a, 'Il concetto di egemonia nell'opera di Gramsci', in Baratta and Catone 1995.

—— 1995b, 'La prima edizione dei "Quaderni del carcere"', in Righi 1995.

—— 1997, 'Il cantiere dei "Quaderni"', *L'Unità*, 20 January.

Giardina, Giovanni 1965, 'Ricordi dell'Ordine Nuovo', *Il Ponte*, 10: 1303–10.

Giasi, Francesco (ed.) 2008, *Gramsci nel suo tempo* (2 volumes), Rome: Carocci.

Gilboa, Yehoshua 1982, *A Language Silenced: The Suppression of Hebrew Literature and Culture in the Soviet Union*, New York: Herzl Press.

Goldhagen, Erich (ed.) 1968, *Ethnic Minorities in the Soviet Union*, London: F.A. Praeger.

Gorham, Michael S. 2003, *Speaking in Soviet Tongues: Language Culture and the Politics of Voice in Revolutionary Russia*, De Kalb, IL: Northern Illinois University Press.

Gramsci, Antonio 1947, *Lettere dal carcere*, Turin: Einaudi.

—— 1964, *2000 pagine di Gramsci* (2 volumes), edited by G. Ferrata and N. Gallo, Milan: Il Saggiatore.

—— 1965, *Lettere dal carcere*, edited by S. Caprioglio and E. Fubini, Turin: Einaudi.

—— 1966, *Socialismo e fascismo. L'Ordine Nuovo 1921–1922*, Turin: Einaudi.

—— 1971a, *La costruzione del Partito comunista*, Turin: Einaudi.

—— 1971b, *Lettere dal carcere*, selected and edited by P. Spriano, Turin: Einaudi.

—— 1971c, *Selections from the Prison Notebooks*, edited and translated by Q. Hoare and G. Nowell-Smith, London: Lawrence and Wishart.

—— 1974, *La formazione dell'uomo. Scritti di pedagogia*, edited by G. Urbani, Rome: Editori Riuniti.

—— 1975, *Quaderni del carcere* (4 volumes), edited by V. Gerratana, Turin: Einaudi.

—— 1976, *Scritti 1915–1921*, edited by S. Caprioglio, Milan: Moizzi.

—— 1977, *Selections from Political Writings 1910–20*, edited by Q. Hoare and translated by J. Mathews, London: Lawrence and Wishart.

—— 1978, *Selections from Political Writings 1921–26*, edited and translated by Q. Hoare, London: Lawrence and Wishart.

—— 1980, *Cronache torinesi 1913–1917*, edited by S. Caprioglio, Turin: Einaudi.

—— 1982, *La città futura 1917–1918*, edited by S. Caprioglio, Turin: Einaudi.

—— 1984, *Il nostro Marx 1918–1919*, edited by S. Caprioglio, Turin: Einaudi.

—— 1985, *Selections from Cultural Writings*, edited by D. Forgacs and G. Nowell-Smith, translated by W. Boelhower, London: Lawrence and Wishart.

—— 1987, *L'Ordine Nuovo 1919–1920*, ed. by V. Gerratana and A.A. Santucci, Turin: Einaudi.

—— 1988, *Il rivoluzionario qualificato. Scritti 1916–1925*, edited by C. Morgia, Rome: Delotti.

—— 1992a, *Lettere 1908–1926*, edited by A.A. Santucci, Turin: Einaudi.

—— 1992b, *Prison Notebooks*, Volume I, edited and translated by J.A. Buttigieg, New York: Columbia University Press.

—— 1993, *Grammatica e linguistica*, Rome: Editori Riuniti.

—— 1994a, *Letters from Prison* (2 volumes), edited by F. Rosengarten, translated by R. Rosenthal, New York: Columbia University Press.

—— 1994b, *Vita attraverso le lettere*, ed. by G. Fiori, Turin: Einaudi.

—— 1994c, *Pre-Prison Writings*, edited by R. Bellamy and translated by V. Cox, Cambridge: Cambridge University Press.

—— 1995, *Further Selections from the Prison Notebooks*, edited and translated by D. Boothman, London: Lawrence and Wishart.

—— 1996a, *Lettere dal carcere* (2 volumes), edited by A.A. Santucci, Palermo: Sellerio.

—— 1996b, *Prison Notebooks*, Volume II, edited and translated by J.A. Buttigieg, New York: Columbia University Press.

—— 1998, *Critica letteraria e linguistica*, edited by R. Paternostro, Rome: Lithos.

—— 1999 [1988], *The Antonio Gramsci Reader: Selected Writings 1916–1935*, edited by D. Forgacs, London: Lawrence and Wishart.

—— 2007a, *Quaderni del carcere*, Volume 1: *Quaderni di traduzioni (1929–1932)*, edited by G. Cospito and G. Francioni, Rome: Istituto della Enciclopedia Italiana.

—— 2007b, *Prison Notebooks*, Volume III, edited and translated by J.A. Buttigieg, New York: Columbia University Press.

—— 2010, *Epistolario*, Volume 1: *gennaio 1906–dicembre 1922*, edited by D. Bidussa *et al.*, Rome: Istituto della Enciclopedia Italiana.

Gramsci, Antonio and Tatiana Schucht 1997, *Lettere (1926–1935)*, Turin: Einaudi.

Gramsci, Antonio Jr. 2007, 'La famiglia Schucht', *Italianieuropei*, 7, 2: 200–12.

—— 2010, *I miei nonni nella rivoluzione*, Rome: Edizioni Riformiste.

Grassi, Corrado, Alberto A. Sobrero and Tullio Telmon 2004, *Introduzione alla dialettologia italiana*, Bari: Laterza.

Green, Marcus and Peter Ives 2010, 'Subalternity and Language: Overcoming the Fragmentation of Common Sense', in Ives and Lacorte 2010.

Grenoble, Lenore A. 2003, *Language Policy in the Soviet Union*, Dordrecht: Kluwer Academic Publishers.

Grigor'eva, Irina V. 1998, 'Rossiiskie stranitsy biografii Antonio Gramshi (1922–1926 gg.) po dokumentam arkhiva Kominterna', *Rossiia i Italiia*, 3 (XX vek): 96–123.

Hall, Stuart 1986, 'Gramsci's Relevance for the Study of Race and Ethnicity', *Journal of Communication Inquiry*, 10, 2: 5–27.

—— 1991, 'Reading Gramsci', introduction to Roger Simon, *Gramsci's Political Thought: An Introduction*, London: Lawrence and Wishart.

Harman, Lesley D. 1988, *The Modern Stranger: On Language and Membership*, Amsterdam: Mouton de Gruyter.

Hayhoe, Mike and Stephen Parker (eds.) 1994, *Who Owns English?*, Buckingham: Open University Press.

Helsloot, Niels 1989, 'Linguists of All Countries…!' On Gramsci's Premise of Coherence', *Journal of Pragmatics*, 13: 547–66.

—— 1995, 'Marxist linguistics', in *Handbook of Pragmatics*, edited by J. Blommaert, J.-O. Östman and J. Verschueren, Amsterdam: John Benjamins.

—— 1998, 'Gramsci, Antonio (1891–1937)', in *Concise Encyclopedia of Pragmatics*, edited by J.L. Mey, Amsterdam: Elsevier.

—— 2001, 'Gramsci, Antonio (1891–1937)', in *Concise Encyclopedia of Sociolinguistics*, edited by R. Mesthrie, Amsterdam: Elsevier.

—— 2005, review of *Language and Hegemony in Gramsci* by Peter Ives, *Historiographia Linguistica*, 32, 1–2: 235–42.

Hirschkop, Ken 1990, 'Short Cuts through the Long Revolution: The Russian Avant-Garde and the Modernization of Language', *Textual Practice*, 4, 3: 428–41.

Hobsbawm, Eric J. 1974, 'The Great Gramsci', *The New York Review of Books*, 29, 5: 39–44.

—— 1990, *Nations and Nationalism since 1780*, Cambridge: Cambridge University Press.

—— 2011, *How to Change the World: Marx and Marxism 1840–2011*, London: Little, Brown.

Hobsbawm, Eric J. *et al.* (eds.) 1995, *Gramsci in Europa e in America*, Bari: Laterza.

Hodge, Robert and Gunther Kress 1993, *Language as Ideology*, London: Routledge.

Holborow, Marnie 1999, *The Politics of English: A Marxist View of Language*, London: Sage.

Holub, Renate 1992, *Antonio Gramsci: Beyond Marxism and Postmodernism*, London: Routledge.

Honey, John 1997, *Language is Power: The Story of Standard English and its Enemies*, London: Faber and Faber.

Hymes, Dell 1996, *Ethnography, Linguistics, Narrative Inequality: Toward an Understanding of Voice*, London: Taylor and Francis.

—— 2001, preface to *'Languaging' in and across Human Groups: Perspectives on Difference and Asymmetry*, monographic issue of *Textus*, 14, 2.

Inglehart, Ronald F. and Margaret Woodward 1972, 'Language Conflicts and Political Community', in *Language and Social Context*, edited by P.P. Giglioli, Harmondsworth: Penguin.

Iordan, Iorgu and John Orr 1937, *An Introduction to Romance Linguistics: Its Scholars and Schools*, London: Methuen.

Iorio, Pino 1997, *L'italiano parlato dai sardi*, Oristano: S'Alvure.

Ives, Peter 1997, 'The Grammar of Hegemony', *Left History*, 5, 1: 85–103.

—— 2004a, *Language and Hegemony in Gramsci*, London: Pluto Press.

—— 2004b, *Gramsci's Politics of Language: Engaging the Bakhtin Circle and the Frankfurt School*, Toronto: University of Toronto Press.

—— 2006, '"Global English": Linguistic Imperialism or Practical Lingua Franca?', *Studies in Language & Capitalism*, 1: 121–42, available at <http://www.languageandcapitalism.info/>.

—— 2010, 'Global English, Hegemony and Education: Lessons from Gramsci', in *Gramsci and Educational Thought*, edited by P. Mayo, Chichester: Wiley-Blackwell.

Ives, Peter and Rocco Lacorte (eds.) 2010, *Gramsci, Language and Translation*, Lanham, MA: Lexington Books.

Jakobson, Roman 1933, 'La scuola linguistica di Praga', *La Cultura*, 12, 3: 633–41.

—— 1956, 'Serge Karcevski', *Cahiers Ferdinand de Saussure*, 14: 9–16.

—— 1959, 'On Linguistic Aspects of Translation', in *On Translation*, edited by R. Brower, Cambridge, MA: Harvard University Press.

Jay, Martin 1984, *Marxism and Totality: The Adventures of a Concept from Lukács to Habermas*, Berkeley, CA: University of California Press.

Joseph, John E. 2004, 'The Linguistic Sign', in *The Cambridge Companion to Saussure*, edited by C. Sanders, Cambridge: Cambridge University Press.

—— 2006, *Language and Politics*, Edinburgh: Edinburgh University Press.

Kaplan, Robert B. and Richard Baldauf Jr. 1997, *Language Planning from Practice to Theory*, Clevedon: Multilingual Matters.

Kautsky, Karl 1887, 'Die moderne Nationalität', *Die Neue Zeit*, 5: 392–405, 442–451.

—— 1908, *Nationalität und Internationalität*, Stuttgart: Paul Singer.

Kaye, Harvey J. 1981, 'Antonio Gramsci: An Annotated Bibliography of Studies in English', *Politics & Society*, 10, 3: 335–53.

Klein, Gabriella 1986, *La politica linguistica del Fascismo*, Bologna: Il Mulino.

Kokochkina, Elena 2000, 'De Humboldt à Potebnja: évolution de la notion d'"innere Sprachform"', *Cahiers Ferdinand de Saussure*, 53: 101–22.

Kolpakidi, Aleksander and Jaroslav Leontiev 2001, 'Il peccato originale. Antonio Gramsci e la formazione del PCd'I', in *P.C.I. La storia dimenticata*, edited by S. Bertelli and F. Bigazzi, Milan: Arnoldo Mondadori.

Kramsch, Claire 1998, *Language and Culture*, Oxford: Oxford University Press.

Labande-Jeanroy, Thérèse 1925a, *La Question de la langue en Italie de Baretti à Manzoni. L'unité linguistique dans les théories et les faits*, Paris: Champion.

—— 1925b, *La Question de la langue en Italie*, Paris: Istra.

Laclau, Ernesto and Chantal Mouffe 1985, *Hegemony and Socialist Strategy: Towards a Radical Democratic Politics*, London: Verso.

Lecercle, Jean-Jacques 2004, *Une philosophie Marxiste du langage*, Paris: Presses Universitaires de France.

Lehmann, Winfred P. 1992, *Historical Linguistics*, London: Routledge.

Lenin, Vladimir 1964a, *Collected Works*, Volume 20, Moscow: Progress Publishers.

—— 1964b, *Collected Works*, Volume 24, Moscow: Progress Publishers.

—— 1964c [1917], *The State and Revolution*, in *Collected Works*, Volume 25, Moscow: Progress Publishers.

—— 1965a, *Collected Works*, Volume 7, Moscow: Progress Publishers.

—— 1965b, *Collected Works*, Volume 29, Moscow: Progress Publishers.

—— 1965c, *Collected Works*, Volume 30, Moscow: Progress Publishers.

—— 1966 [1920], 'The Tasks of the Youth Leagues', in *Collected Works*, Volume 31, Moscow: Progress Publishers.

—— 1968, *Collected Works*, Volume 19, Moscow: Progress Publishers.

—— 1969, *Collected Works*, Volume 41, Moscow: Progress Publishers.

—— 1983, *Lenin on Language*, Moscow: Raduga.

Leonetti, Alfonso 1970, *Note su Gramsci*, Urbino: Argalìa.

Leont'ev, A.A. and R.M. Tseitlin 1979, 'Potebnia, Aleksandr Afanas'evich', in *Great Soviet Encyclopedia*, Volume 20, London: Macmillan.

Lepre, Aurelio 1998, *Il prigioniero. Vita di Antonio Gramsci*, Bari: Laterza.

Lepschy, Anna Laura and Giulio Lepschy 1999, *L'amanuense analfabeta e altri saggi*, Florence: Olschki.

Lepschy, Giulio 1969, 'Contributo all'identificazione degli ascoltatori di Saussure a Parigi: Fedor-Friedrich Braun', *Studi e Saggi Linguistici*, 9: 206–10.

—— 1985, 'Linguistics', in *Developing Contemporary Marxism*, edited by Z.G. Barański and J.R. Short, London: Macmillan.

Łesiów, Michał 1996, 'Potebnja, Oleksandr Opanasovyč', in Stammerjohann 1996.

Levy, Carl 1999, *Gramsci and the Anarchists*, Oxford: Berg.

—— 2012, 'Gramsci's Cultural and Political Sources: Anarchism in the Prison Writings', in Carlucci 2012.

Lewiki, Andrzej M. 1996, 'Vinokur, Grigorij Osipovič', in Stammerjohann 1996.

Leydi, Roberto 1963, *Canti sociali italiani*, Volume 1: *Canti giacobini, repubblicani,*

antirisorgimentali, di protesta postunitaria, contro la guerra e il servizio militare, Milan: Edizioni Avanti.

Liguori, Guido 1996, *Gramsci conteso. Storia di un dibattito 1922–1996*, Rome: Editori Riuniti.

—— 2004, 'Ideologia', in Frosini and Liguori 2004.

—— 2009, 'Democrazia', in Liguori and Voza 2009.

Liguori, Guido and Chiara Meta 2005, *Gramsci. Guida alla lettura*, Milan: Unicopli.

Liguori, Guido and Pasquale Voza (eds.) 2009, *Dizionario gramsciano. 1926–1937*, Rome: Carocci.

Lih, Lars T. 2011, *Lenin*, London: Reaktion Books.

Lilliu, Giovanni 1999, 'Gramsci e la lingua sarda', in Orrù and Rudas 1999.

Lippi-Green, Rosina 1997, *English with an Accent: Language, Ideology, and Discrimination in the United States*, London: Routledge.

Loi Corvetto, Ines 1993, 'La Sardegna', in I. Loi Corvetto and A. Nesi, *L'italiano nelle regioni. La Sardegna e la Corsica*, Turin: Utet.

Lombardi Satriani, Luigi M. 1980, *Antropologia culturale e analisi della cultura subalterna*, Milan: Rizzoli.

Lombardo Radice, Giuseppe 1970 [1913], 'L'ideale di una educazione linguistica. Lingua e grammatica', in *Lezioni di didattica e ricordi di esperienza magistrale*, Florence: Sandron.

Longiave, Ignazio 1910, *Vocabolario sardo-italiano*, Sassari: Gallizzi.

Lo Piparo, Franco 1979, *Lingua, intellettuali, egemonia in Gramsci*, Bari: Laterza.

—— 2004, *Filosofia, lingua, politica. Saggi sulla tradizione linguistica italiana*, Rome: Bonanno

—— 2010a, 'Le radici linguistiche del liberalismo gramsciano', in *Tornare a Gramsci. Una cultura per l'Italia*, edited by G. Polizzi, Rome: Avverbi.

—— 2010b [1987], 'The Linguistic Roots of Gramsci's Non-Marxism', in Ives and Lacorte 2010.

—— 2012, *I due carceri di Gramsci. La prigione fascista e il labirinto comunista*, Rome: Donzelli.

Luperini, Romano 1999, 'Gramsci e la letteratura: verso un'ermeneutica materialistica', in *Controtempo. Critica e letteratura fra moderno e postmoderno: proposte, polemiche e bilanci di fine secolo*, Naples: Liguori.

Lussana, Fiamma (ed.) 2000, *La Fondazione Istituto Gramsci. Cinquant'anni di cultura, politica e storia*, Florence: Pineider.

—— 2007, *In Russia prima del Gulag. Emigrati italiani a scuola di comunismo*, Rome: Carocci.

Lussana, Fiamma and Giulia Pissarello (eds.) 2008, *La lingua/le lingue di Gramsci e delle sue opere*, Soveria Mannelli: Rubbettino.

Macedo, Donaldo 1994, *Literacies of Power: What Americans Are Not Allowed to Know*, Boulder, CO: Westview Press.

Macedo, Donaldo, Bessie Dendrinos and Panayota Gounari 2003, *The Hegemony of English*, Boulder, CO: Paradigm Publishers.

Mally, Lynn 1990, *Culture of the Future: The Proletkult Movement in Revolutionary Russia*, Berkeley, CA: University of California Press.

Manacorda, Giuliano 1975, introduction to Antonio Gramsci, *Marxismo e letteratura*, Rome: Editori Riuniti.

Manacorda, Mario A. 1964, *Il marxismo e l'educazione*, Volume 1: *I classici: Marx, Engels, Lenin*, Rome: Armando.

—— 1970, *Il principio educativo in Gramsci*, Rome: Armando.

Mannu, Francesco I. 2002, *Su patriota sardu a sos feudatarios*, edited by L. Carta, Cagliari: Cuec.

Mansfield, Steven R. 1984, introduction to A. Gramsci, 'Notes on Language', *Telos*, 59: 119–26.

Manzoni, Alessandro 2000a, *Scritti linguistici inediti I*, edited by A. Stella and M. Vitale, in *Edizione Nazionale ed Europea delle Opere di Alessandro Manzoni*, Volume 17, Milan: Centro Nazionale Studi Manzoniani.

—— 2000b, *Scritti linguistici inediti II*, edited by A. Stella and M. Vitale, in *Edizione Nazionale ed Europea delle Opere*, Volume 18, Milan: Centro Nazionale Studi Manzoniani.

—— 2000c, *Scritti linguistici editi*, edited by A. Stella and M. Vitale, in *Edizione Nazionale ed Europea delle Opere*, Volume 19, Milan: Centro Nazionale Studi Manzoniani.

—— 2005, *Postille al Vocabolario della Crusca nell'edizione veronese*, edited by D. Isella, in *Edizione Nazionale ed Europea delle Opere*, Volume 24, Milan: Centro Nazionale Studi Manzoniani.

Marazzini, Claudio 1977, *La lingua come strumento sociale. Il dibattito linguistico in Italia dal Manzoni al neocapitalismo*, Turin: Marietti.

—— 1993, 'Le teorie', in *Storia della lingua italiana*, Volume I: *I luoghi della codificazione*, edited by L. Serianni and P. Trifone, Turin: Einaudi.

—— 1999, *Da Dante alla lingua selvaggia. Sette secoli di dibattiti sull'italiano*, Rome: Carocci.

Marcellesi, Jean Baptiste and Abdou Eliman 1987, 'Language and Society from a Marxist Point of View' in *Sociolinguistics: An International Handbook of the Science of Language and Society*, edited by U. Ammon, N. Dittmar and K.J. Mattheier, New York: Walter de Gruyter.

Martin, James (ed.) 2002, *Antonio Gramsci: Critical Assessments of Leading Political Philosophers* (4 volumes), London: Routledge.

Martinelli, Renzo 1972, 'Una polemica del 1921 e l'esordio di Gramsci sull'*Avanti!* torinese', *Critica marxista*, 10, 5: 148–57.

—— 1989a, 'Gramsci il grammatico', *L'Unità*, 27 June.

—— 1989b, 'Un dialogo fra grammatici. Panzini e Gramsci', *Belfagor*, 44, 6: 681–8.

Marx, Karl 1987 [1859], *A Contribution to the Critique of Political Economy*, in *Marx and Engels Collected Works*, Volume 29, London: Lawrence and Wishart.

Marx, Karl and Frederick Engels 1976, *Collected Works*, Volume 5, London: Lawrence and Wishart.

—— 1996, *Collected Works*, Volume 35, London: Lawrence and Wishart.

Matejka, Ladislav 1986, 'On the First Russian Prolegomena to Semiotics', appendix to Vološinov 1986.

Matt, Luigi 2008, 'La conquista dell'italiano nel giovane Gramsci', in Lussana and Pissarello 2008.

May, Stephen 2001, *Language and Minority Rights: Ethnicity, Nationalism and the Politics of Language*, Harlow: Longman.

Mazon, André 1920, *Lexique de la guerre et de la révolution en Russie, 1914–1918*, Paris: Champion.

Mazzaferro, Gerardo 2008, *The Sociolinguistics of English as a Global Language*, Rome: Carocci.

McNally, David 1997, 'Language, History, and Class Struggle', in *In Defense of History: Marxism and the Postmodern Agenda*, edited by E.M. Wood and J.B. Foster, New York: Monthly Review Press.

Meillet, Antoine 1928 [1918], *Les langues dans l'Europe nouvelle*, Paris: Payot.

Melis, Guido (ed.) 1975, *Antonio Gramsci e la questione sarda*, Cagliari: Della Torre.

Mengaldo, Pier Vincenzo 1994, *Storia della lingua italiana. Il Novecento*, Bologna: Il Mulino.

Meyer-Lübke, Wilhelm 1927, *Grammatica storica della lingua italiana e dei dialetti toscani*, edited by M. Bartoli, Turin: Chiantore.

—— 1935, *Romanisches Etymologisches Wörterbuch*, Heidelberg: Carl Winters Universitätsbuchhandlung.

Migliorini, Bruno 2000 [1960], *Storia della lingua italiana*, Milan: Bompiani.

Mill, John Stuart 1991, *On Liberty and Other Essays*, edited by J. Gray, Oxford: Oxford University Press.

Milroy, James and Lesley Milroy 1985, *Authority in Language: Investigating Language Prescription and Standardisation*, London: Routledge & Kegan Paul.

Miselli, Bianca (ed.) 1988, *Noi e Gramsci*, Cagliari: Castello.

Mondolfo, Rodolfo 1962, *Da Ardigò a Gramsci*, Milan: Nuova Accademia.

—— 1968, *Umanismo di Marx. Studi filosofici 1908–1966*, Turin: Einaudi.

Montagnana, Mario 1949, *Ricordi di un operaio torinese*, Volume I: *Sotto la guida di Gramsci*, Rome: Rinascita.

Montaldi, Danilo 1978 [1953], 'La linguistica, le classi e il teorico della sconfitta', *Rivista Italiana di Dialettologia*, 2: 59–68.

Monteleone, Renato 1982, *Marxismo, internazionalismo e questione nazionale*, Turin: Loescher.

Monticone, Alberto 1958, 'Il socialismo torinese e i fatti dell'agosto 1917', *Rassegna storica del Risorgimento*, 45, 1: 57–96.

Morera, Esteve 1990, 'Gramsci and Democracy', *Canadian Journal of Political Science*, 23, 1: 23–37.

Morgia, Corrado 1988, introduction to Gramsci 1988.

Morpurgo Davies, Anna 1998, *Nineteenth-Century Linguistics*, London: Longman.

Mouffe, Chantal (ed.) 1979, *Gramsci and Marxist Theory*, London: Routledge & Kegan Paul.

Mueller, Janel 1990, editor's foreword, *Modern Philology*, 87, 3: 219–24.

Murru Corriga, Giannetta (ed.) 1977, *Etnia, lingua, cultura. Un dibattito aperto in Sardegna*, Cagliari: Edes.

Nairn, Tom 1982, 'Antonu su gobbu', in *Approaches to Gramsci*, edited by A. Showstack Sassoon, London: Writers and Readers.

Ndhlovu, Finex 2006, 'Gramsci, Doke and the Marginalisation of the Ndebele Language in Zimbabwe', *Journal of Multilingual and Multicultural Development*, 27, 4: 305–18.

Nicholson, Jenifer 2000, 'Biography and Language: A Neglected Aspect of the Life and Work of Antonio Gramsci', *Auto/Biography*, 8, 1–2: 63–70.

Noce, Teresa 1975, *Rivoluzionaria professionale*, Milan: La Pietra.

Omezzoli, Tullio 1995, 'Lingue e identità valdostana', in Woolf 1995.

Orrù, Eugenio and Nereide Rudas (eds.) 1999, *Il Pensiero permanente. Gramsci oltre il suo tempo*, Cagliari: Tema.

Paggi, Leonardo 1984, *Le strategie del potere in Gramsci*, Rome: Editori Riuniti.

Paladini Musitelli, Marina 1996, *Introduzione a Gramsci*, Bari: Laterza.

Palumbo, Piero 1977, 'Ero in clinica con Gramsci: mi regalò l'"Imitazione di Cristo"', *Gente*, 12 May.

Panzini, Alfredo 1999, *Grammatica italiana*, Palermo: Sellerio.

Pareto, Vilfredo 1935 [1916], *The Mind and Society: A Treaty on General Sociology*, Volume I, edited by A. Livingston, New York: Dover.

Pasolini, Pier Paolo 1972, 'Dal Laboratorio (Appunti *en poète* per una linguistica marxista)', in *Empirismo eretico*, Milan: Garzanti.

—— 1987, *Volgar'eloquio*, edited by G.C. Ferretti, Rome: Editori Riuniti.

Passaponti, Emilia 1981, 'Gramsci e le Questioni linguistiche', in *Lingua, linguaggi e società*, edited by S. Gensini and M. Vedovelli, Florence: Linari.

Paulesu Quercioli, Mimma (ed.) 1977, *Gramsci vivo nelle testimonianze dei suoi contemporanei*, Milan: Feltrinelli.

—— 1991, 'A undici anni già lavorava', in *Antonio Gramsci dopo la caduta di tutti i muri*, supplement to *L'Unità*, 15 January.

—— 1999, 'Le donne di Gramsci', in Orrù and Rudas 1999.

—— 2003, *Le donne di casa Gramsci*, Ghilarza: Iskra.

Pellicani, Luciano 1976, *Gramsci e la questione comunista*, Florence: Vallecchi.

—— 1977, 'Gramsci e il messianesimo comunista', in Coen 1977.

Phillips, Katharine H. 1986, *Language Theories of the Early Soviet Period*, Exeter: University of Exeter Press.

Phillipson, Robert 1992, *Linguistic Imperialism*, Oxford: Oxford University Press.

Piccone, Paul 1974, 'Gramsci's Hegelian Marxism', *Political Theory*, 2, 1: 32–45.

—— 1976, 'Gramsci's Marxism: Beyond Lenin and Togliatti', *Theory and Society*, 3, 4: 485–512.

—— 1991–2, 'Gramsci's *Prison Notebooks*— The Remake', *Telos*, 90: 177–83.

Pighi, Giambattista 1934, 'Grammatica e grammatiche', *Vita e pensiero*, 25, 10: 652–7.

Pira, Michelangelo 1966, 'Non considerava la Sardegna come l'ombelico del mondo ma non rinnegava neppure la validità delle sue esperienze isolane', *La Nuova Sardegna*, 24 July.

—— 1978, *La rivolta dell'oggetto. Antropologia della Sardegna*, Milan: Giuffrè.

Pisani, Vittore 1929, 'Divagazioni etrusche', *Nuova Antologia*, 64, 1367: 123–7.

Pittau, Massimo 2000, *Dizionario della lingua sarda*, Volume I: *Sardo-Italiano*, Cagliari: Ettore Gasperini.

Pizzorusso, Alessandro 1975, *Il pluralismo linguistico in Italia fra Stato nazionale e autonomie regionali*, Pisa: Pacini.

Plank, Frans 1996, 'Finck, Franz Nikolaus', in Stammerjohann 1996.

Podda, Giuseppe 1977, appendix to S. Cardia Marci, *Il giovane Gramsci*, Cagliari: In.E.S.

—— 1999, 'Alle radici del nazional-popolare', in Vacca 1999b, Volume II.

Poddu, Mario 2000, *Ditzionàriu de sa limba e de sa cultura sarda*, Cagliari: Condaghes.

Poggi Salani, Teresa 1986, *Per lo studio dell'italiano. Avviamento storico-descrittivo*, Novara: Liviana-De Agostini.

Polivanov, Evgenii D. 1974, *Selected Writings: Articles on General Linguistics*, edited by A.A. Leont'ev, Paris: Mouton.

Portantiero, Juan Carlos 1977, 'Los usos de Gramsci', introduction to Antonio Gramsci, *Escritos políticos, 1917–1933*, Mexico City: Ediciones Pasado y Presente.

Prezzolini, Giuseppe 1904, *Il linguaggio come causa d'errore. H. Bergson*, Florence: Spinelli.

Propat, Maria Teresa 1974, 'Linguistica e grammatica', *I problemi della pedagogia*, 20, 2–3: 201–11.

Raffaelli, Sergio 1984, 'Prodromi del purismo xenofobo fascista', *Movimento operaio e socialista*, 7, 1: 79–86.

Raicich, Marino 1981, *Scuola, cultura e politica da De Sanctis a Gentile*, Pisa: Nistri-Lischi.

Ramat, Paolo 1983, 'Grammatica storica', in *Dizionario Marx-Engels*, edited by F. Papi, Bologna: Zanichelli.

Rapone, Leonardo 2011, *Cinque anni che paiono secoli. Antonio Gramsci dal socialismo al comunismo (1914–1919)*, Rome: Carocci.

Renzi, Lorenzo 1981, *La politica linguistica della Rivoluzione francese. Studio sulle origini e la natura del Giacobinismo linguistico*, Naples: Liguori.

Restaino, Franco 1963, 'Con Gramsci a Is Arenas. Domenica 26 ottobre 1924: il primo convegno dei comunisti sardi a Cagliari', *Rinascita sarda*, 25 April.

Ricchini, Carlo, Eugenio Manca and Luisa Melograni (eds.) 1987, *Gramsci. Le sue idee nel nostro tempo*, Rome: L'Unità.

Ricento, Thomas (ed.) 2006, *An Introduction to Language Policy: Theory and Method*, Oxford: Blackwell.

Richet, Denis 1988, 'Journées révolutionnaires', in *Dictionnaire critique de la Révolution Française*, edited by F. Furet and M. Ozouf, Paris: Flammarion.

Righi, Maria Luisa (ed.) 1995, *Gramsci nel mondo. Atti del convegno internazionale di studi gramsciani. Formia, 25–28 ottobre 1989*, Rome: Fondazione Istituto Gramsci.

Rohlfs, Gerhard 1966–9, *Grammatica storica della lingua italiana e dei suoi dialetti* (3 volumes), Turin: Einaudi.

Romagnino, Antonio 2005, 'Garzia Raffa 1877–1938', in *I 2000 sardi più illustri*, Volume 8, Cagliari: L'Unione Sarda.

Romano, Salvatore Francesco 1965, *Antonio Gramsci*, Turin: Utet.

Rorty, Richard (ed.) 1967, *The Linguistic Turn: Recent Essays in Philosophical Method*, Chicago: Chicago University Press.

Rosiello, Luigi 1959, 'La componente linguistica dello storicismo gramsciano', in *La città futura. Saggi sulla figura e il pensiero di Antonio Gramsci*, edited by A. Caracciolo and G. Scalia, Milan: Feltrinelli.

—— 1969, 'Problemi linguistici negli scritti di Gramsci', in Rossi 1969, Volume II.

—— 1974, *Linguistica e marxismo. Interventi e polemiche*, Rome: Editori Riuniti.

—— 1976, 'Lingua, nazione, egemonia', *Il Contemporaneo*, supplement to *Rinascita*, 24 December.

—— 2010 [1986], 'Linguistics and Marxism in the Thought of Antonio Gramsci', in Ives and Lacorte 2010.

Rossi, Angelo and Giuseppe Vacca 2007, *Gramsci tra Mussolini e Stalin*, Rome: Fazi.

Rossi, Pietro (ed.) 1969, *Gramsci e la cultura contemporanea* (2 volumes), Rome: Editori Riuniti-Istituto Gramsci.

Rossi-Landi, Ferruccio 1975, *Linguistics and Economics*, Paris: Mouton.

—— 1978, *Ideologia*, Milan: ISEDI.

—— 1985, *Metodica filosofica e scienza dei segni*, Milan: Bompiani.

—— 1990, *Marxism and Ideology*, trans. by R. Griffin, Oxford: Clarendon Press.

—— 2003 [1968], 'Capitale e proprietà privata nel linguaggio', in *Il linguaggio come lavoro e come mercato*, Milan: Bompiani.

Russo, Luigi 1947, 'Antonio Gramsci e l'educazione democratica in Italia', *Belfagor*, 2, 4: 395–411.

Ryazanoff, David 1930, *The Communist Manifesto of Karl Marx and Friedrich Engels*, London: Martin Lawrence.

Said, Edward W. 2003 [1978], *Orientalism*, London: Penguin.

—— 2004, *Power, Politics and Culture*, edited by G. Viswanathan, London: Bloomsbury.

—— 2005, 'Gramsci in Palestina', *L'Unità*, 22 February.

Salamini, Leonardo 1981a, *The Sociology of Political Praxis: An Introduction to Gramsci's Theory*, London: Routledge.

—— 1981b, 'Gramsci and Marxist Sociology of Language', *International Journal of the Sociology of Language*, 32: 27–44.

Salvetti, Patrizia 1975, *La stampa comunista da Gramsci a Togliatti*, Parma: Guanda.

Salvi, Sergio 1978, *Patria e matria*, Florence: Vallecchi.

Sanga, Glauco 1977, 'Il dialetto. Note di linguistica materialista', *Rivista Italiana di Dialettologia*, 1: 13–44.

—— 1982, 'Principii di linguistica materialista', in *Ideologia, filosofia, linguistica*, edited by D. Gambarara and A. D'Atri, Rome: Bulzoni.

Santucci, Antonio A. 1995, editor's note, in Hobsbawm *et al.* 1995.

—— 2005, *Antonio Gramsci. 1891–1937*, edited by L. La Porta, Palermo: Sellerio.

Saussure, Ferdinand de 1959, *Course in General Linguistics*, edited by C. Bally and A. Sechehaye in collaboration with A. Reidlinger, translation by W. Baskin, New York: Philosophical Library.

—— 1967–74, *Cours de linguistique générale* (3 volumes), edited by R. Engler, Wiesbaden: Otto Harrassowitz.

—— 1972, *Cours de linguistique générale*, edited by T. De Mauro, Paris: Payot.

Savoia, Leonardo M. 2001, 'La legge 482 sulle minoranze linguistiche storiche. Le lingue di minoranza e le varietà non standard in Italia', *Rivista Italiana di Dialettologia*, 25: 7–50.

Sbarberi, Franco (ed.) 1988, *Teoria politica e società industriale*, Turin: Bollati Boringhieri.

Sberlati, Francesco 1998, 'L'arcangelo e i grammatici. Antonio Gramsci storico della lingua', *Annali di Italianistica*, 16: 339–63.

Scalambrino, Francesco 1998, *Un uomo sotto la mole. Biografia di Antonio Gramsci*, Turin: Il Punto.

Scherrer, Jutta 1998, 'The Relationship between the Intelligentsia and Workers: The Case of the Party Schools in Capri and Bologna', in *Workers and Intelligentsia in Late Imperial Russia: Realities, Representations, Reflections*, edited by R.E. Zelnik, Berkeley, CA: International and Area Studies.

Schirru, Giancarlo 1999, 'I *Quaderni del carcere* e il dibattito su lingua e nazionalità nel socialismo internazionale', in Vacca 1999b, Volume II.

—— 2008a, 'La categoria di egemonia e il pensiero linguistico di Antonio Gramsci', in *Egemonie*, edited by A. d'Orsi, Naples: Dante & Descartes.

—— 2008b, 'Filosofia del linguaggio e filosofia della prassi', in Giasi 2008, Volume II.

—— 2011, 'Antonio Gramsci studente di linguistica', *Studi Storici*, 52, 4: 925–73.

Schmidt Sr., Ronald 2006, 'Political Theory and Language Policy', in Ricento 2006.

Schucht, Tatiana 1991, *Lettere ai familiari*, Rome: Editori Riuniti.

Scolè, Pierluigi 2007, 'Esperienze di reclutamento territoriale. Le truppe alpine italiane dalle origini alla Grande Guerra (1872–1918)', in *Fare il soldato. Storie del reclutamento militare in Italia*, edited by N. Labanca, Milan: Unicopli.

Sechehaye, Albert 1927, 'L'école genevoise de linguistique générale', *Indogermanische Forschungen*, 44: 217–41.

Sechi, Salvatore 1967, 'La Sardegna tra guerra e dopoguerra', *Il movimento di liberazione in Italia*, 88: 3–32.

—— 1969, *Dopoguerra e fascismo in Sardegna*, Turin: Einaudi.

Seifrid, Thomas 2005, *The Word Made Self: Russian Writings on Language 1860–1930*, Ithaca, NY: Cornell University Press.

Selenu, Stefano 2005, 'Alcuni aspetti della questione della lingua sarda attraverso la diade storia-grammatica: un'impostazione di tipo gramsciano', in *Antologia Premio Gramsci. IX Edizione*, edited by G. Serra, Sassari: Edes.

Seliščev, Afanasij M. 1925, 'Des traits linguistiques communs aux langues balkaniques', *Revue des études slaves*, 5: 38–57.

Selishchev, Afanasii M. 1971 [1928], *Iazyk revoliutsionnoi epokhi: iz nabliudenii nad russkim iazykom poslednikh let (1917–1926)*, Letchworth: Herts Prideaux Press.

Serianni, Luca 1990, 'Manzoni, manzoniani e antimanzoniani', in *Storia della lingua italiana. Il secondo Ottocento*, Bologna: Il Mulino.

—— (ed.) 2002, *La lingua nella storia d'Italia*, Florence: Società Dante Alighieri-Libri Scheiwiller.

—— 2006, 'Panzini lessicografo tra parole e cose', in *Che fine fanno i neologismi? A cento anni dalla pubblicazione del Dizionario moderno di Alfredo Panzini*, edited by G. Adamo and V. Della Valle, Florence: Olschki.

Sgroi, Salvatore C. 1982, 'Pirandello, Gramsci e il teatro: il rapporto tra lingua e dialetto nella lettura gramsciana del Pirandello "siciliano" e nei *Quaderni del carcere*', *Le Forme e la Storia*, 3, 1–3: 285–348.

Shneer, David 2004, *Yiddish and the Creation of Soviet Jewish Culture 1918–1930*, Cambridge: Cambridge University Press.

Skutnabb-Kangas, Tove 2000, *Linguistic Genocide in Education – or Worldwide Diversity and Human Rights?*, London: Lawrence Erlbaum Associates.

Sluga, Glenda 2000, 'Italian National Identity and Fascism', in *The Politics of Italian National Identity*, edited by G. Bedani and B. Haddock, Cardiff: University of Wales Press.

Slusareva, Nataliia 1963, 'Quelques considérations des linguistes soviétiques à propos des idées de F. de Saussure', *Cahiers Ferdinand de Saussure*, 20: 23–46.

Smith, Michael 1997, *Language and Power in the Creation of the USSR 1917–1953*, New York: Mouton de Gruyter.

Soave, Sergio 1995, 'Fascismo, Resistenza, Regione', in Woolf 1995.

Sobrero, Alberto A. 1978, *I padroni della lingua*, Naples: Guida.

Sochor, Zenovia A. 1981, 'Was Bogdanov Russia's Answer to Gramsci?', *Studies in Soviet Thought*, 22, 1: 59–81.

Sole, Leonardo 1999, 'La sintassi modulare del giovane Gramsci', in Orrù and Rudas 1999.

Somai, Giovanni 1979, *Gramsci a Vienna. Ricerche e documenti 1922–1924*, Urbino: Argalìa.

Sonntag, Selma K. 2003, *The Local Politics of Global English*, Lanham, MA: Lexington Books.

Spano, Giovanni 2004 [1851], *Vocabolariu Sardu-Italianu*, edited by G. Paulis, Nuoro: Ilisso.

Spriano, Paolo 1960, 'La sommossa dell'agosto 1917', in *Torino operaia nella grande guerra (1914–1918)*, Turin: Einaudi.

—— 1963, introduction to *La cultura italiana del '900 attraverso le riviste: 'L'Ordine Nuovo' (1919–1920)*, Turin: Einaudi.

Stalin, Giuseppe 1968, *Il marxismo e la linguistica*, Milan: Feltrinelli.

Stammerjohann, Harro (ed.) 1996, *Lexicon Grammaticorum*, Tübingen: Max Niemeyer.

Suarez, Debra 2002, 'The Paradox of Linguistic Hegemony and the Maintenance of Spanish as a Heritage Language in the United States', *Journal of Multilingual and Multicultural Development*, 23, 6: 512–30.

Swann, Joan, Ana Deumert, Theresa Lillis and Rajend Mesthrie 2004, *A Dictionary of Sociolinguistics*, Edinburgh: Edinburgh University Press.

Tagliavini, Carlo 1982 [1949], *Le origini delle lingue neolatine*, Bologna: Pàtron.

Tamburrano, Giuseppe 1963, *Antonio Gramsci. La vita, il pensiero, l'azione*, Manduria: Lacaita.

Telmon, Tullio 2001, *Piemonte e Valle d'Aosta*, Bari: Laterza.

Terracini, Benvenuto 1919, review of *Cours de linguistique générale* by Ferdinand de Saussure, *Bollettino di filologia classica*, 25, 7–8: 73–9.

—— 1925, 'Influssi della Linguistica generale sulla Linguistica storica del latino', *Rivista di filologia e di istruzione classica*, 3, 1: 21–62.

—— 1929, 'Paleontologia ascoliana e linguistica storica', in *Silloge linguistica dedicata alla memoria di Graziadio Isaia Ascoli nel primo centenario della nascita*, Turin: Chiantore.

—— 1933, 'Il III Congresso internazionale dei linguisti in Roma', *Nuova Antologia*, 68, 1482: 626–31.

—— 1948, 'Matteo Bartoli', *Belfagor*, 3, 3: 315–25.

Tesi, Riccardo 2005, *Storia dell'italiano. La lingua moderna e contemporanea*, Bologna: Zanichelli.

Thomas, Peter D. 2009, *The Gramscian Moment: Philosophy, Hegemony and Marxism*, Leiden: Brill.

Timpanaro, Sebastiano 1969, 'Carlo Cattaneo e Graziadio Ascoli', in *Classicismo e illuminismo nell'Ottocento italiano*, Pisa: Nistri-Lischi.

Togliatti, Palmiro *et al.* 1945 [1938], *Gramsci*, Rome: Società editrice l'Unità.

—— 1979, *On Gramsci and Other Writings*, edited by D. Sassoon, London: Lawrence and Wishart.

Tollefson, James W. 1991, *Planning Language, Planning Inequality*, London: Longman.

—— 2006, 'Critical Theory in Language Policy', in Ricento 2006.

Tosi, Arturo 1995, *Dalla madrelingua all'italiano. Lingue ed educazione linguistica nell'Italia multietnica*, Florence: La Nuova Italia.

—— 2001, *Language and Society in a Changing Italy*, Clevedon: Multilingual Matters.

—— 2004, 'The Language Situation in Italy', *Current Issues in Language Planning*, 5, 3: 247–335.

—— 2007, 'Dictionaries of Neologisms and the History of Society', in *Languages of Italy: Histories and Dictionaries*, edited by A. Tosi and A.L. Lepschy, Ravenna: Longo.

Trabalza, Ciro 1908, *Storia della grammatica italiana*, Milan: Hoepli.

—— 1936, *Nazione e letteratura. Profili, saggi, discorsi*, Turin: Paravia.

Trabalza, Ciro and Ettore Allodoli 1934, *La grammatica degl'italiani*, Florence: Le Monnier.

Trask, Robert L. 1997, *A Student's Dictionary of Language and Linguistics*, London: Arnold.

Traverso, Enzo 1994, *The Marxists and the Jewish Question: The History of a Debate (1843–1943)*, Atlantic Highlands, NJ: Humanities Press.

Tripodi, Giuseppe 1989, 'Rileggendo le Lettere dal carcere. Luoghi e cose del cosmo sardo nella memoria di Gramsci detenuto', *Liceo Classico A. di Savoia. Tivoli*, 2: 7–25.

Trotsky, Leon 1973, *Problems of Everyday Life and Other Writings on Culture and Science*, New York: Monad Press.

Tyndale, John W. 1849, *The Island of Sardinia*, London: Bentley.

Ulam, Adam 1998, *The Bolsheviks*, Cambridge, MA: Harvard University Press.

Vacca, Giuseppe 1999a, *Appuntamenti con Gramsci*, Rome: Carocci.

—— (ed.) 1999b, *Gramsci e il Novecento* (2 volumes), Rome: Carocci.

—— 2005, introduction to Daniele 2005.

—— 2012, *Vita e pensieri di Antonio Gramsci. 1926–1937*, Turin: Einaudi.

Vailati, Giovanni 1911, *Scritti (1863–1909)*, Leipzig: Barth.

Vercillo, Federica 2004, 'Le *latino sine flexione* de Giuseppe Peano', *Cahiers Ferdinand de Saussure*, 57: 73–85.

Vico, Giambattista 2008, *La scienza nuova*, edited by P. Rossi, Milan: Rizzoli.

Vidossi, Giuseppe 1948, 'Pro e contro le teorie di M. Bartoli', *Annali della Scuola Normale Superiore di Pisa*, 17: 204–19.

Viglongo, Andrea 1967, 'Amò Torino come la nativa Sardegna', *Torino. Rivista bimestrale del comune*, 3: 31–6.

Vignuzzi, Ugo 1982, 'Discussioni e polemiche novecentesche sulla lingua italiana', in *Letteratura italiana contemporanea*, Volume III, edited by C. Mariani and M. Petrucciani, Rome: Lucarini.

Vinokur, Grigorii O. 1923, 'Kul'tura iazyka (Zadachi sovremennogo iazykoznaniia)', *Pechat' i revoliutsiia*, 5: 100–11.

Virdis, Maurizio 1988, 'Areallinguistik', in *Lexikon der Romanistischen Linguistik*, edited by G. Holtus *et al.*, Tübingen: Niemeyer.

Vološinov, Valentin N. 1986 [1929], *Marxism and the Philosophy of Language*, translated by L. Matejka and I.R. Titunik, Cambridge, MA: Harvard University Press.

Vossler, Karl 1908, *Positivismo e idealismo nella scienza del linguaggio*, Bari: Laterza.

Wagner, Max Leopold 1989 [1957–63], *Dizionario etimologico sardo*, Cagliari: Gianni Trois.

—— 1993 [1951], *La lingua sarda. Storia, spirito e forma*, Tübingen: Francke.

—— 1996 [1921], *La vita rustica della Sardegna riflessa nella lingua*, edited by G. Paulis, Nuoro: Ilisso.

Walzer, Michael 1989, 'Antonio Gramsci's Commitment', in *The Company of Critics: Social Criticism and Political Commitment in the Twentieth Century*, London: Peter Halban.

Waquet, Françoise 1988, *Le latin ou l'empire d'un signe*, Paris: Albin Michel.

Woolf, Stuart J. (ed.) 1995, *La Valle d'Aosta*, Turin: Einaudi.

Zubov, Andrej 1994, 'Minoranze nazionali e nazionalità dominate nello Stato sovietico (1918–1939)', in *Le minoranze tra le due guerre*, edited by U. Corsini and D. Zaffi, Bologna: Il Mulino.

Zucaro, Domenico 1957, 'Antonio Gramsci all'Università di Torino 1911–1915', *Società*, 13, 6: 1091–1111.

Index of Names

Index of Subjects